D1580137

# SPANISH RAGGLE-TAGGLE

*By the same author*

RAGGLE-TAGGLE. Adventures
with a fiddle in Hungary and
Roumania in 1933.

"AGUA - A - A!"

# SPANISH
# RAGGLE–TAGGLE

Adventures with a Fiddle in North Spain

by WALTER STARKIE, Litt.D.

PROFESSOR OF SPANISH IN DUBLIN UNIVERSITY
CORRESPONDING MEMBER OF THE SPANISH ACADEMY
Author of "Raggle-Taggle"

Frontispiece and title-page design by
ARTHUR RACKHAM

LONDON
JOHN MURRAY, ALBEMARLE STREET, W.

*First Edition 1934*

TO

# HIS GRACE THE DUKE

OF

BERWICK AND ALBA

———

*La luna para salir*
*Le pide licencia al cielo*
*Y para cantar yo aquí*
*Licencia pido primero.*

# PREFACE

IN the following pages I have endeavoured to describe a summer journey I made alone on foot in Spain, earning my living as a wandering minstrel.

In Spain the wandering minstrel has had a long and honoured tradition ever since the Middle Ages when the *juglar* wandered from castle to castle reciting the epic poems. A *juglar* may be defined as one who performs before the public whether as rhapsodist, fiddler, ballad-singer, story-teller, juggler or buffoon. His duty was to amuse and entertain the people : for this reason he was as welcome in the baronial castle as in the public square.

A modern *juglar* has to wear a tighter belt and a more ragged coat than in the golden days long ago, but he may still get his eye full as well as his ear full, and as he saunters through the countryside his mind becomes enriched with many a golden sentence and tune.

" You're only a scavenger of tunes with that fiddle of yours," says one cynical friend. " Half angel, half devil," says another, slightly more sympathetically.

" Have it your own way," I replied. " My fiddle will win me hospitality in Spain."

" You can always tell them over there the story of the Lynch stone," said a black-haired man from the West of Ireland, gravely. " That will open the doors quicker than a tune on your fiddle."

" A word to the wise," I replied. No Irishman wandering to Spain forgets that story which is written over Lynch's castle in Galway in one of the streets, where the skull and crossbones tell the fate of the young son of the house, who, for killing a Spaniard, was executed by his own father, the mayor of the town.

The rights of the guest will be as sacred in Spain as in my country, and I shall leave my home like the picaresque knave, Guzmán de Alfarache, " to see the world and travel from place to place, commending myself to God and well-disposed persons." All will be well if I can preserve myself as the Gypsies say—" Fat, ragged and saucy."

In preparing this book I wish to express my deep indebtedness to my friend, Professor Ramón Menéndez Pidal, whose book, *Poesía Juglaresca y Juglares*, inspired me to live the life of a modern *juglar*. To his inspiration also I owe many happy days of wandering through the land of the Cid and the Seven Infantes of Salas. I wish also to thank Miss D. E. Yates, the secretary of the Gypsy Lore Society, and Professor W. A. Goligher, of Dublin University, for kind advice.

W. S.

*August* 1934.

# CONTENTS

# CONTENTS

# PART I

What care I for my house and land?
    What care I for my treasure, O?
What care I for my new-wedded lord,
    I'm off with the raggle-taggle Gypsies, O!

Last night you slept on a goose-feather bed,
    with the sheet turned down so bravely, O!
And to-night you'll sleep in a cold, open field,
    along with the raggle-taggle Gypsies, O!

What care I for a goose-feather bed,
    with the sheet turned down so bravely, O!
For to-night I shall sleep in a cold, open field
    along with the raggle-taggle Gypsies, O!
                              (Old Song.)

# CHAPTER I

# CASTLES IN SPAIN

"I'M sorry I cannot attend the meeting : to-night I depart for Spain."

"Oh! but it is an important meeting, the committee wish to know your views on the teaching of Commercial Spanish."

"I tell you I have booked my passage on the Mail boat. I must leave Ireland to-night for important business in my Castle in Spain, and I shall be away until October; so I must bid you farewell."

With a muttered curse I sped my departing guest and busied myself in the task of paying bills and answering letters. This is the first day of the vacation and I am free to wander away from the tedious daily round of duty. Yesterday I did not feel as I do to-day, for I was still dominated by my conventional self. For months I had gone through life mechanically, paying meticulous attention to what my neighbours said of me. I enjoyed the monotonous rhythm of the daily task, for it prevented me from letting my thoughts dash recklessly away, like hey-go-mad.

Nobody who possesses a vagabond second self should ever put on his Gypsy clothes before the sun has set on the last day of term : they should be locked in the lumber-room with seven keys; otherwise they might behave like the magic shoes in the fairy tale and lead you a dance over the hills and far away.

This morning I felt that I could with perfect propriety bury my conventional first self and so I escorted him with all pomp and circumstance to the lumber-room and locked him in the chest, but I took good care to pour a bottle of Sherry wine over him to lay his ghost. Being full of Irish superstitions I always like to invest any momentous undertakings with a modicum of ritual : hence the pouring of the libation which would in addition be the baptism of my journey. The Gypsies when they set out in the spring from their winter-quarters celebrate wine-festivals in honour of their wandering. A Gypsy friend of mine once described how his folk set out in the spring from the east of Europe. " They have," he said, " a feast of the copper pans on the day of Saint George, April 23rd. For three days every Gypsy man, woman and child goes daft. They drink, they sing, they play, they romp, they drag out their tents into the plain, they harness their horses to the carts, they sacrifice lambs and wreathe the wine jars in flowers."

Now is the winter of my discontent made glorious summer—good-bye stiff collars—no Gypsy ever wears aught round his neck but a muffler—good-bye white shirts with breast-plated armour—good-bye dickies, bowler hat and spats and all the accoutrement of citizen number one and two. Back to the rough home-spuns of the peasant.

" I'm afraid the seamstress will have to let out the waist of those trousers of yours," said my wife. " You have added several inches to your girth since you raggle-taggled in Transylvania."

" My dear ! Do not stress my *embonpoint* : you know that I shall live like an ascetic in Spain and return to

you in the autumn as slender as a wraith—why, you'll
find your husband transformed from Sancho Panza into
a lanky Don Quixote."

To tell the truth, the question of my portliness never
gives me a moment's qualm, for I have long ago realized
that the world is divided into two camps—the fat and the
lean and I belong to the former. As a fat member of
society I am peaceable without a touch of splenetic
viperishness in my nature, but my wife, being a woman
of modern views, looks upon fatness as a crime against
the economy of Nature. As day by day she weaves and
unweaves Penelope's web awaiting my return, she will
pray that long days and nights of toiling over the plateau
lands of Castile, living on raw ham and garlic, will
change my squat, uncourtly figure into a bronzed
image of the Apollo Belvedere. Sweet illusion of the
female mind! What should we do if our wives ever
gave up the hope of their dreams? So, work away,
seamstress! Let out the girth three inches: I'll not
feel ashamed. Nay I'll console myself with the thought
that the best minstrels and story-tellers were gifted
with a pleasant rotundity of mind and body: they
were able to take the rough with the smooth and relish
the swift changes of fortune.

Now that I have my vagabond clothes before me, I
feel inspired to invent a host of tales to tell my children.
"Alma, my child, I am going over the sea to a far-
off country where I shall see the White Knight on his
horse, and I shall wander into the dark forest and gather
such a crop of strange adventures that I shall have
dozens of stories to tell you at bedtime. You see, I
must go away to collect some more tales, for I have
told you the same old Gypsy ones over and over
again."

"Mind you bring me new tunes to dance to," replied

my daughter Alma seriously—" tunes with stories about them."

" Certainly, my dear child : I'll bring you back tunes and stories, for my fiddle is going with me and he will remember all that I forget."

As I left the house I felt like a hardened old Irish minstrel of the fourteenth century, setting out on the boat for Spain, to wander along the way of Saint James to far-off Compostela, ready to play and sing his way, with his mind stored with ballad and dances.

" Where is your fiddle ?  Out with it, man !  Tighten your bow and play us a tune as the boat glides through the night——

" Faith an' you're the fine musicianer an' no mistake ! !  Is it to the States yer goin' ?

" No, sir, I'm off to my Castle in Spain."

Ah ! but I know a Spanish toast : I heard it in Valparaiso—come on, fiddler—drink up your whiskey and here's " *Salud y pesetas y* . . .  May your shadow never grow less ! "

The bibulous minstrel Villasandino himself could not have wished for a more auspicious beginning !

## CHAPTER II

# A KNIGHT-ERRANT OF FIDDLERS

*Paris.* Quai D'Orsay station on the night of the second of July.

WE are off to Spain! To-morrow morning will find me tramping along the road from Hendaye to San Sebastian. But before to-morrow comes there are twelve or thirteen hours of stuffiness comparable to the Black Hole of Calcutta.

My third-class carriage is crammed even to the corridors, most of the windows are closed and the night is sultry.

As the night draws its slow length along, the gentle courtesies of the initial stages wear away and the primitive instincts of man assert themselves. Portly travellers close their eyes and in the bland unconsciousness of sleep coil and uncoil their legs, bend their bodies this way and that, breathe heavily, and snore fitfully. Small children whimper and I curse myself for a hard-hearted wretch as I look at that pale, wide-eyed woman opposite with her three children whose ages range from four to seven years. I should be as hard-hearted as a gouty bachelor, but I remember that I have two children of my own. "Certainly, Madame, you may have my corner seat—*mais oui* . . . *enchanté*—the children will have room to sleep and you may close your eyes."

In the corridor I found a space untenanted and there I laid my *capa* upon the ground and settled myself for the night.

7

Alas, I could not sleep. The inexorable rhythm of
the wheels roused my mind to activity instead of lulling
it to sleep.

My head is like Uncle Toby's—" a funnel unswept
with the ideas whirling round and round." I must
take a pull at my wine-skin to steady myself and thread
my way through the maze of projects.

Here I am off to Spain to play the wandering minstrel as though I lived in the mediæval days of Villasandino or the arch-priest of Hita. I imagine the subacid
look on the faces of my friends as they shake their heads
and say : Our Walter has a slate loose somewhere. He
has been mixing too much of late with rake-hell and
skin-the-devil Bohemians for the good of his soul.

" Certainly, sirs, I admit my madness and I call Master
François Rabelais to witness that I hold it an honour
to be called and reputed a Merry-Walter and a Robin
Goodfellow."

It is only right that every traveller who approaches
Spain should have a tiny dose of Quixotic madness. At
home many say that I am a Sancho Panza, plodding
along the easy roads of life as placid in mind as plump
in body. Aye and let them say on ; I have no desire
to contradict them. I am content to go through eight
months of the year like Friar John—" in wanting
nothing but a cup of good wine, a good bed, my back
to the fire, my belly to the table, and a good deep dish."

But there comes a time when the shadow of the gaunt
knight of the sad figure falls across my path and withers
my placid mirthfulness like the first shrill blast of east
wind on an October day. All Spanish travellers express
their Quixotism in various ways : some have so dried
up their brains with what they have read of Spain—of
contests, battles, challenges, tortures—that they go to
Spain as to a Museum where specimens of the past are

set upon shelves and labelled : others set out upon the
journey with romance in their heart and their imaginations packed with enchantments, sheiks and sultanas.
Every girl they meet south of the Pyrenees will be a
dusky beauty with the East in her eyes, a tender Zaida
—flower of the Alhambra, and every man will be one
of the Abencerrajes.

My Quixotism will be of a far humbler kind, more in
accordance with the profession of minstrel fiddler.

I shall, however, proudly assume the title of Knight-
errant of Fiddlers, and my fiddle shall be my Rozinante.   In truth my fiddle has as many blemishes in it
as any Rozinante—but the blemishes are as the scars
on the front of a brave soldier ; " stars that direct others
to the haven of honour."   For honourable indeed has
been the career of my fiddle, I would have you know.

" Not much of an instrument," says the connoisseur
sourly, examining it as a Gypsy *chalán* would a spavined
mule at a fair—" What's the crack in the table—hem !
Good repair—must have been done by a Gypsy."

Don Quixote had not a more faithful companion of
his wandering in Rozinante than I have had in that
fiddle with all its blemishes—the only fiddle, I am sure,
that has been wounded since the old days when the
Gypsy minstrels of Hungary played the army into battle.

Let me tell the story—

One day towards the end of the War in Italy it was
stolen from me when I lay sick in my billet at Vicenza,
by a drunken sergeant of the Ordnance Corps, and found
two days later lying in the snow, by a British Major
who had more pity in his soul than music.

" I felt it was unlucky to leave a violin lying in the
snow," he said, as he handed me the piteous object.

" It must not die," cried I, as I gazed at its broken
neck and cracked ribs.

" The British Army will pay for its repair," quoth the Major ; " has it not been wounded on active service ? "

Other adventures it has had, for it is a Gypsy fiddle and it has vagabonded everywhere with me in fair weather and in foul. Sometimes I find it as irresolute as the ass of Buridano and as cross-grained under the bow as a tomcat, but on a moonlit night under the trees or else in smoky tavern by the fire you'll hear the devil's whisper cajoling the tunes out of it as though it were the enchanted violin of the old Spanish ballad, which the wandering rogue played at the foot of his gallows tree. At the first notes, the hangman let go the rope from off his neck, and began to dance with the judge and jury and Jewish usurer, as though they had turned into quicksilver, and they danced and danced while the sound of the wanderer's fiddle became fainter and fainter as he disappeared into the forest.

Gradually the monotonous sound of the rattling train began to hypnotize me into drowsiness in spite of my uncomfortable position on the floor. Sleep descended so gently upon me that when I began to dream it seemed but the prolongation of my previous thoughts. I felt myself jog slowly down a long dark passage towards a wide-open gate into a sunny courtyard planted with orange-trees. When I had recovered from the shock of dazzling sunshine I looked down and found that I was riding a queer brown horse which resembled in shape my fiddle. I was perched astride with my legs dangling on each side and, as I rode, an invisible hand guided a monstrous bow across the strings just in front of me awakening a storm of sounds. Round and round the courtyard with its orange-trees I cantered on my strange hobby-horse which possessed the devilish magic of a fairy broomstick. Then in one leap we vaulted the high encircling wall and I found myself careering over a vast, bare plain. The wind whistled in my ears and I heard the ghostly sound of fiddles being played in discordant sequence. My own fiddle responded even more furiously to the giant bow as it rasped across the strings, casting up such a cloud of white rosin in my face that I began to suffocate, and my clothes, face, hair were coated in sticky, white dust. Whether it was an effect of mirage I knew not, but in the clear air appeared countless other phantom riders seated astride on fiddles, all of them exact copies of myself. The music became more and more furious and demoniacal, but in the distance over the plain, I saw an opposing army of horsemen hastening towards us. In the distance they looked like bumble-bees, but when they came near I saw that they were horsemen dressed in red mounted on guitars. As they rode towards us they stood high in their stirrups and up and down the necks of the instruments careered a multitude of white hands. When the two armies came close together the cacophony was indescribable. The shrieking of the fiddles like a wailing storm could not drown the dull inexorable droning sound of the guitars.

I found myself in the midst of the tumult fighting hand to hand with an aged minstrel mounted on a guitar, and the fight became a contest of sound. My fiddle sobbed and shrieked in tones that soared above the tempest, and the countless white fingers careered up and down the guitar of my rival like hosts of white mice. I was helpless, because it had now become a battle between two devils and I was just the fascinated victim who knows that his fate depends on the issue of the contest.

Which of the two instruments would win—the fiddle or the guitar?

All of a sudden the music seemed to become transformed from discord into harmony. The figure of the old man riding on the guitar faded away. His grey beard faded away in mist, his white hair darkened as though someone had poured pitch upon his head: his eyes brightened, his pale, ascetic cheeks became touched up with colour. To my amazement he had become a young woman. The storm music ceased, all save a distant thrumming of the guitars. I felt myself glide gently, propelled by unseen hands towards the fair damsel; her arms were open to welcome me and her pale face and red lips were so near that I could feel her fragrant breath upon my face when . . . I was rudely awakened from my blissful dream by a sudden stabbing pain in my neck accompanied by a muttered exclamation. A fat woman trying to make her way along the passage had inadvertently trodden on my neck with all the weight of her big iron-heeled shoe. It was now four o'clock in the morning and a grey mist enveloped the land.

At Bordeaux many of the passengers left the train and I was able to secure a comfortable corner seat in one of the compartments. Then in a half-wakeful state I began to examine my dream to see if perchance I could discover its inner meaning. Surely it was all clear: I shall ride the fiddle which is my hobby-horse, my Rozinante, through the country, but I shall find myself defeated by the guitar of Spain in fair and open fight and meet with many a drubbing into the bargain; that fiddle of mine will be an interloper in the Spanish countryside and the guitars will buzz around it in angry mood seeking to drown its soaring voice. But who knows what surprise may await me at the end?

Perhaps in the discordant rhythms of Spain I shall discover harmony: perhaps too I shall meet, as the embodiment of that harmony, some damsel who resembles the lady of my dream—that fair Dulcinea whose lips I so nearly kissed.

## CHAPTER III

## THE TEMPLE OF FORTUNE

LISTEN to me, all you wandering fiddlers ! Shun Biarritz as you would the plague. You may saw your gut strings till you burst, but you won't get the price of a good dinner with wine and *pousse-café* in a day's playing at street corners. Why did I not continue my journey in my third-class carriage to the frontier at Hendaye ? It was the fault of a chatty Parisian who insisted that Spain since the Revolution began at Biarritz, not at Irún. " There are nearly as many Spaniards as French on the Côte d'Argent—why, the entire *noblesse espagnole* sits along the coast and looks with melancholy longing across the bay at Fuenterrabía."

But Biarritz is too blasé for a minstrel : after a day's hard work at street corners, I longed to meet my fairy godmother, for I should have begged her to change me into a jazz-band effects man, so that I might get a job in one of the hotel bands. Jazz on sea, on land, jazz everywhere. The only Spanish tune I have heard to-day came from a fat Spanish nursemaid who was leading two children by the hand in the park down by the sea.

After a six-francs dinner, consisting of a rough stew and a carafe of wine, I felt in a more optimistic humour. Now Biarritz is a famous centre for gambling—why should I not tempt the Goddess of Fortune ? Surely

13

nobody deserves to win her favours more than the poor vagabond. She would sooner be wooed by me than by the monocled gallant in boiled shirt who lives in the Hotel Palace. If I win I shall sleep in a luxurious hotel, if I lose I shall sleep on a bench in the park under the stars on this balmy July night.

There is an air of pompous solemnity about the Temple of Fortune in Biarritz and the usher in the entrance hall directed me to the ticket office with the air of a church-warden.

After paying my eight francs I was admitted to the gambling-room, which was crowded with people of every description. It was the only vital spot I had seen in Biarritz. Here at any rate there was an air of excite-ment and expectation. In the packed room every few minutes the buzzing conversation would die down and then all that could be heard was the toc, toc, toc, toc of the ivory ball scampering round the circle from one hole to another before finally settling on the winning number.

At first, I stood on the outer circumference of the crowd and watched the gamblers. The heat was suffo-cating and a fat man near me mopped his shiny bald head with a huge green silk handkerchief. Leaning on his arm was a painted-up siren with peroxide hair, dressed in a low-backed, purple evening dress. Just in front of them was a hunchback holding a bundle of twenty-franc notes in his hand, ready to wedge himself into the places nearest the board. I could not resist the temptation to touch his hump, for it seemed as if the Goddess of Fortune had sent that hunchback with the message that she was well disposed. I remembered Naples where a hunchback is a magic being, endowed with second sight. He can tell the numbers that will win in the lottery and women pay him for telling them what numbers he has dreamt of. Had I not been among a crowd of blasé, civilized unbelievers, I should have tapped him sharply on the shoulder and bowing I should have said—" Allow me to cast the first throw for you, Signore—just tell me the number ! "

As it was I followed the little man and stuck my blue five-franc counter on number seven.

" Messieurs, faites vos jeux ! " Round and round careered the ivory ball and all the heads swayed together in rhythm, and those who stood behind those seated at the table craned their necks and leant over as they followed every motion of the ball. " Rien ne va plus ! " The ball finally came to rest in number seven and the croupier pushed towards me my winnings. Bravo, hunchback ! Your hump brings fortune in other regions than Naples. All around me the people were standing silently as statues. Some had a vacant, hard expression, as they mechanically advanced their counters on the numbers. Others were a bundle of nerves. A fat lady in a green velvet gown with row after row of false pearls around her neck puffed asthmatically in the excitement, and a small squint-eyed gentleman by her side pushed counters over to her from a heap in front of him as she lost steadily. A florid, red-faced man with a big paunch licked his lips as he gathered in his winnings. Not one of those people was at ease. They all had some nervous affection or other : one squinted, another cleared his throat, a third blew his nose noisily, a fourth muttered to himself, a fifth whistled dolefully as the wrong number won. Every few minutes the croupier's voice sounded mournfully—" Messieurs, faites vos jeux— Rien ne va plus—cinq, noir, impair et passe ! " I followed my hunchback, but he began to lose, so I launched out on my own adventure, and I felt like some-one who after walking out as far as he can into the water begins to swim with vigorous strokes towards the open sea. The fever of gambling had gripped me and I played mechanically. Toc, toc, toc, toc! " Rien ne va plus ! " The sounds hypnotized me and made me oblivious of my surroundings. When I started to play I had vague ideas in my mind of the logic of gambling, and I imagined combinations of certain numbers. Seven, five, twelve fascinated me as a combination, and I would say to myself—Ah—number seven is my lucky star, if I do not weary its kindness—I must vary it with number five and number twelve. Gradually, however, the fever descended upon me. I played at random and the roulette circle became a blurred vision with blues and yellows and blacks assuming successive fantastic shapes before my tired eyes, like fragments of coloured glass in a kaleidoscope. I had entered the Casino, with the firm intention of limiting my losses to twenty or thirty francs. But after my luck with the hunchback's throw, I became reckless with my winnings, and by a strange whim of Fortune as I became more mechanical my luck increased. Again and again the croupier raked in the counters and pushed them towards me until I had a big pile in front of me. I felt as if some kind genii had descended to inspire me, and I had the sensation of walking along a tight rope Blondin-wise over a roaring torrent with thousands of spectators to witness my triumph.

When after about an hour of play I began to lose steadily, the scales fell from my eyes and I became lucid once more.

I rose from the table, cashed my counters, pocketed my money and rushed from the Casino.

I had in my pocket four hundred francs—untold wealth for a vagabond minstrel.

Half of this money I shall keep in the bottom of my ruck-sack as a reserve fund. It will be like the nest-egg of the Gypsy nomad or the silver coins which God ordained that the wandering Jew should always find in the bottom of his wallet at the hour of need. The other half I shall devote to material comforts of the moment.

After a Lucullian supper at a restaurant and a bottle of " Château neuf du Pape," I took a room in a moderate-priced hotel of the boarding-house type, and found myself lost in a cosmopolitan crowd of trippers from various countries. There were provincial Frenchmen with their wives and daughters, a few Italian young men, arrogant and Fascist looking, a Czecho-Slovakian fair-haired Hermes, a group of bright American girls on a European razzle-dazzle tour, an English party con-sisting of six Englishmen and two girls from Man-chester. I felt listless and dispirited. Nobody loves me here, thought I, when I saw how superciliously the gilt-braid porter and boots glanced at me. My clothes must be sadly out of tune with the red plush and gilt ornaments of this hotel. When I looked at myself in my bedroom looking-glass I felt disposed to agree with the minions of the hotel, though I thought them wanting in courtesy. I was unkempt. My khaki rough shirt had been made by a Genoese peasant in his mountain home, my boots were thick and hobnailed—the patch upon the seat of my trousers was indiscreetly visible—no, I had strayed into the wrong world and I could only blame my self-indulgent Sancho Panza nature. Here was I at the outset of my journey—right before the gates of Spain, playing false to the credo of the vagabond minstrel.

After a few glasses of vermuth downstairs I took a more rosy view. After all, is it not better to spend most of the money which has come as a windfall and reduce myself to the paltry silver coins of the wandering Jew, before I enter Spain? Besides, what could be more interesting than to study my hotel companions and gradually win their sympathy?

At first they looked upon me as an interloper—a queer suspicious fellow—one never knows whom one may meet nowadays—poor and down at heel into the bargain—perhaps a refugee from Spain in disguise. " Ah ! no—he is too fair for a Spaniard—he has blue eyes," I heard the English girl from Manchester say to her plain spinster friend. " Perhaps a Russian," whispered one of the American maidens—" drôle de type," grumbled the spectacled French *père de famille* not unkindly. The Italians stared fixedly but did not smile.

I enjoyed their perplexity and I started my campaign by telling the hall-porter my fake story—a rigmarole romance of wandering into Spain to gather news for a Royalist paper. " Je vous dirai un secret : je suis lié avec l'aristocratie espagnole," said I, blushing slightly from the emotion of weaving my tale. Whenever I start my story my blood courses lightly through my veins, my head seems to swell out like a crystal globe iridescent with all the colours of my fantasy. The French porter was incredulous, but polite. Anyhow, thought I, he will tell my story to the rest, and embroider it in his own colours.

My next plan was to call upon my *confrère* the fiddle to help me. My bedroom with its large bow-window looked out upon the verandah where the guests would assemble. In the calm evening at sunset I played all the ravishing tangos and waltzes I could remember—I trilled and fluted like a humming-bird, I languished with soft melodies in double stopping, drawing off the long notes until I could hear them echo in the courtyard beneath.

The first to fall was one of the American girls who

came up to me later in the evening, when I was sipping
a cognac in the lounge.

" I heard you play my favourite tune in the world."

" What was that, pray, Mademoiselle ? "

" ' Dark eyes '—it is a Russian Gypsy song."

" Russian, perhaps, but I am afraid it has come via
Manhattan."

" Anyhow, you brought tears to my eyes by that
tune—I remember the Russian boy who sang it to me
at Romany Marie's Café in New York."

After some minutes of banal conversation, she introduced me to her companions.  At her invitation I played
for the company, but not for long because with the
exception of the sentimental American girl not one of
them wanted my tunes.  The Englishmen still regarded
me as an interloper who had butted into the general
conversation : the women stared at my unconventional
clothes.  I have always found that music acts as stimulus
to conversation : it neutralizes shyness and enables the
tongue-tied to express themselves in more vigorous
language than otherwise, for their voices must rise above
the sound.  But music, though it is the great leveller
in society, yet does not confer any social benefits
on the minstrel who is performing for the company.
" Blooming fiddler—that's all he is," murmurs the
Britisher as he drinks his whiskey and soda.  " Buon
violino," snaps the Italian, that is the symbol for medio-
crity.  " Maldito violinista," says the Spaniard—he's
looking at my *novia*.  No : the minstrel only reaches his
glory when he plays to the solitary damsel—the lady
dressed in black velvet with Titian red hair parted in
the middle—the lady with the Madonna complexion and
eyes like stars—the lady with pale cheek whose pensive
expression fatally leads the player to guess that she
nurses some secret sorrow.

No—fiddle, you are out of tune to-night : I cannot play on your heartstrings for this audience. No more music, brother : go back to your case. It is best to lead the conversation back to roulette and baccarat.

Anyhow, I achieved a triumph of sociability with the aid of roulette. I told them of my winnings, discreetly magnified them and to prove my tale ordered a bottle of champagne to toast the company. For the American girl I wrote out on a card an infallible scheme of play based on the numbers five, seven and twelve. "I am sure the croupiers will bless me," mused I, as I went upstairs to bed.

Next day, after bathing with some of the party, I spent my time lying on the sands or sitting in the promenade café. Though I was surrounded by a gay throng of holiday-makers, I felt lonely and bored. Why is it that all watering-places are exactly the same? Modern civilization has created a depressing monotony of type. Among all those men and women there is hardly one face with character and personality stamped upon it. The girls all wear the same mask of fashion : their hair is done in the same way ; powder and rouge have moulded their faces according to the same pattern of boredom ; they walk with the same movement of the hips, they have the same gestures, their voices have the same metallic ring and in their conversation occur the self-same trite refrains. So little variety is there among all those women that I can only distinguish them as the expressionist playwrights have done by titles such as— the woman in grey, the woman in red, the woman in yellow. Among all the women on this strand at Biarritz there must be many interesting and striking individual-ities hidden away, but I cannot pierce the universal mask they have created for themselves at the dictates of fashion. As I see them here they have all taken as their model the frivolous and brittle *demi-mondaine* type. The ladies of the fashionable world wear their rouge and powder in the same blatant manner as the *cocotte* : their lips are fixed in the same hard, crimson line : their hair is waved in the same way ; they walk and talk and behave in public so that there is very little to distinguish them from their unacknowledged sisters.

Such were the thoughts that coursed through my mind as I sat alone in the open-air café, gazing upon the multitude of bathers ; such ungenerous thoughts as spring up in a lonely man who is out of tune with the world. If I only had some kind damsel to befriend me and awaken my sympathy.

After a while I saw two ladies enter the café and take a seat at the next table to mine. One of them was elderly—about forty-five years of age—the other was quite young—not more than twenty or twenty-one. Her face was one of those that Fra Angelico loved to paint—pale, oval-shaped with just the suspicion of blue veins beneath the fair skin at her temples. Her hair which was pale gold was parted and drawn back so as to mould her brow. A delicate profile carved from old-wrought ivory, thought I, as I watched her take off her white kid glove and display a tiny white hand. She was dressed in a white muslin dress with pale-blue spots upon it and around her waist she wore a blue silk belt. What I admired most of all was her graceful neck, just accentuated by the slender band of black velvet. Sometimes she smiled at her elderly companion—a demure smile with just enough of a hint of raillery in it to make me exclaim to myself—" What a dainty rogue in porcelain ! " Straightway my imagination began to work and I constructed a castle to enclose my fair princess. She must have led a cloistered life, thought I—probably in some ancient house near Tours hidden away in a vast

demesne surrounded by trees. I imagine her tripping
over the lawn beyond the marble terrace in front of the
house, throwing millet seed to hosts of ring-doves from
the neighbouring cot, or else pausing to gaze at the
slowly trailing peacocks. When I am launched on the
way of imaginative discovery I find it hard to be as
discreet as a courtier. I gazed at the lady, then at her
companion. I thought that she blushed and a slight
smile lit up the hard features of the elderly duenna, for
so she must have been ; the smile became a nod, the nod
a gesture—in a trice I was on my feet bowing as gallantly
as any Frenchman.

"Vous avez l'air bien triste, Monsieur," said the
elder lady, smiling ingratiatingly.

"Ah! Yes, Madame : a poor traveller is always sad
when he has no company but his own thoughts."

"Mais comment ! " she replied ; "lonely in Biarritz,
when there are so many beautiful women ! You are
jesting."

"Not at all, Madame : yours and Mademoiselle's are
the only *beaux yeux* that I have seen for days. Do allow
me to drink to them.

"*Garçon*—two cocktails for the ladies and a cognac
for me."

Germaine, for that was the name of the younger lady,
kept her eyes modestly lowered. From time to time
she gazed at me from under misty lashes. As the elder
lady prattled on about Biarritz, roulette, baccarat,
dancing, swimming, I tried to be silently gallant with
Germaine and convey deep meaning by my looks. I
wished she was a Spanish lady, for then she would have
understood the tiniest nuance in my *mirada*. From time
to time when her companion paused for breath she spoke
a few chosen words in a low, melodious voice—"My
aunt persuaded me to accompany my sister to Biarritz,"

she said, " on account of my health. Life in Paris is so fatiguing. My doctor said that I should fall seriously ill if I did not rest and breathe sea air."

Poor child! My sensibilities were touched and she began to take still more definite shape as the romantic heroine of my story. Perhaps she was consumptive— her pallor and the pink flush of her cheek inclined me to that opinion—perhaps she might be some delicate Mimi from the Latin quarter.

Fortunately Germaine seemed to divine my thoughts, for she laid her hand upon mine and I felt that there was no longer any need for telepathy to explain my meaning. After much skirmishing I led the conversation on to the beauties of Biarritz and I asked if Germaine had ever walked through the park and followed the path over the cliffs. It must be *ravissant* at night by the light of the stars.

" Oh! it is only fools who walk about *au clair de la lune*," interrupted the elder sister. " I prefer my own room—or else the cinema."

Germaine, however, in low voice accepted my invitation and we arranged to meet near the little shrine in the park by the sea.

At nine o'clock that night Biarritz seemed to me a fairyland. The sky was a deep sapphire blue with scarcely a cloud to hide the myriads of twinkling stars ; countless lights twinkled along the coast, as though one of the stars had fallen to earth and split into countless glowworms. As I stood alone by the little shrine I could hear in the distance the band playing in one of the hotels. On such a night of romance even a gross Silenus may become a lover and find a mate. I am not so hardened by the rough and tumble of life that I may not possess a touch of Romeo from time to time.

At last I saw her approaching in the distance. She

was wearing a dark-blue cloak trimmed with white fur. When she came up to me I kissed her hand, as tribute to her beauty, and we walked arm in arm along the narrow path by the cliff. The magic of her presence added to the night's enchantment worked upon me like a drug. I wanted to tell her all my story, to pour out words in an unending strain. Why is it that when a man is ruled by the gentler emotions he must pour out his thoughts? The girl listened attentively but said little. I suppose she realized that woman's part is to play the sympathetic listener and encourage her hero to uncover his heart. Now and then I pressed her tiny hand and when we sat beneath a leafy tree I kissed her pale cheek lightly, as I would have done my sister's. I was lonely and she was so sympathetic.

Few opportunities has a wanderer of meeting companions who will charm away his loneliness, and as a rule he is driven to bandy jests with crude wenches and women of the town, for he is the stranger.

Here was a charming girl, listening to my badinage without any fierce duenna at hand to point the finger of reminder.

Germaine became more lively when she heard my diatribes against modern women—Ah, Paris is such a heartless place for women. Nothing but *poules* everywhere—how I hate them. " Ce sont comme des bêtes— rien de plus, et elles ont perdu toute notion d'honnêteté dans ce métier là." She spoke with firm conviction like a good little French *bourgeoise* and her moral nature mounted high in my estimation.

The night was now becoming chilly and I did not want to linger by the sea until the grey-eyed morn, so I suggested that it was time for her to go back to her lodgings and I offered to call a taxi.

There was an awkward pause for a moment and I

began to wonder whether I had committed an indiscretion. She then blurted out quickly—"Eh bien, mon cher, j'espère que tu seras gentil pour moi."

"Mais, certainement," I replied, slightly perplexed by her use of "thou," which implied greater intimacy than she had shown to me before.

"*Voyons*, I have been very nice to you and I have stayed with you a long time. You cannot send me away like that."

Her voice had all of a sudden become harsh and more metallic.

I was still, as the French would say, *abasourdi*. Was she offended because I did not ask her to go with me to an hotel? Surely that could not be her meaning.

My illusions began to flutter about my ears like a gigantic house of cards. I then noticed that she had a hard, even a sensual mouth.

The girl continued inexorably—"You know I should love to have stayed the night with you for two hundred francs—come, be sporting—give me a hundred-franc note."

"But, Mademoiselle, I have not got such a sum upon me," said I, blushing, but setting my mouth grimly—"here is fifteen francs."

"Ah! You are not generous: *ce n'est pas comme ça que l'on traite une petite femme*. If I had only known I should not have wasted my time. My aunt was right. She said that you were a *farceur* and that I would not get even a *louis voyageur* out of you."

She pocketed the fifteen francs, however, and as I turned away she fired a Parthian shot by exclaiming in a shrill voice so that people promenading could hear—"Fichez moi la paix—sale espèce de maquereau!" and walked away in high dudgeon.

I felt deeply humiliated at the way I had been treated,

but the loss of my illusions caused me more pain than the insult hurled at me by the infuriated damsel. It is a sad destiny to have to go through life afflicted with an incurably romantic notion of women. I had idealized her because she did not look so hard and unsympathetic as the majority, but I had created my own image of her and flirted with that image like a member of the old-fashioned flirting-club of the nineties described by Paul Bourget. It was a sign that I was getting old. A good dose of Picaresque Spain would be necessary to cure me of my folly.

## CHAPTER IV

## SPANISH EXILES

WHEN I reached Hendaye one of my first thoughts was to visit my old friend Don Gonzalo. Don Gonzalo is a marquis and possesses sixteen quarterings.

There is no bluer blood in Spain than Don Gonzalo's : a long line of ancestors passed on to him the torch of nobility, but in addition he had striven all his life to be a worthy henchman of the monarchy. Thus it was inevitable that when the revolution broke out in April, Don Gonzalo should follow his Majesty into exile. But he had not the heart to wander far from his native land and so, in common with other noble families, he settled down on the silver coast at Hendaye, just across the border.

I visited him at his little villa outside the town, and I found him pacing sadly up and down the road gazing across the narrow strip of water at the castellated town of Fuenterrabía. I was shocked at his changed appearance. He was but a shadow of the vigorous old diplomat I had known : anxieties and disappointments had left their mark : his face was pale and drawn, and I noticed that his hands trembled.

"Ah, Marquis," said I to myself, "you look like a knight returning wounded from years of crusading. Where is your Castilian arrogance ? I remember how

minor officials used to tremble in their shoes when you
were angry : you were one of the martinets for discipline
in the services ; in civil life you maintained your military
dignity and your thick white moustache gave you the
air of a general of the old guard.  But as you pace up
and down gazing at Fuenterrabía you look like a crestfallen warrior : your figure is bent and your brow is
clouded.  Yonder Spanish town across the water is a
treacherous mirage for you, Marquis, so near and yet
so far, it will torture you unceasingly.  Now is the time
for you to show your true *nobleza* characteristic of your
race, and that *pundonor* which is your litany."

Don Gonzalo at first was stiff and formal and I felt
that since his exile he was determined to wrap himself
up in a cloak of impenetrable reserve.  Gradually, however, as I spoke words of comfort, he began to shed his
mask of bitter disillusion.  With flashing eyes and
excited gestures he told me of the burning of convents
and churches by bands of wild revolutionaries, led by
" irresponsible intellectual theorists."   " But," said he,
" Spain has witnessed those scenes of destruction before,
and such revolutions are but faint ripples on the surface
of Spanish History.  Don't for a moment believe that
the monarchy will disappear : it is impossible, for in
Spain the King is the source of law and justice ; he
is the *mayor alcalde*, the supreme judge who dispenses the
justice which he has received from God.  The Church
too, cannot fall in Spain, Señor, for the strength of Spain
has always been her religion.  Through her religion,
Spain evangelized half of the world; she was the light
of the Council of Trent, the sword of Rome, and the
cradle of Saint Ignatius.  If Spain falls now we shall
rebuild her as the builders of Jerusalem did, who raised
up the walls of the Temple with a hammer in one hand
and a sword in the other, defending themselves against

the enemy who attacked them unceasingly. Here I stand on this shore in sight of Spain waiting for another *Grito de Sagunto* which will announce the end of the Republic."

After his long tirade, the Marquis drooped his head sadly, and the grey mask of disillusion began again to spread across his features. While speaking of the Monarchy and Religion, he looked like one of the nobles of Velázquez, with his austere face, and his eyes blazing from their sockets. He should have lived in the days of spear and shield and coat of mail, when he could have declared himself the Knight-errant of the King of Spain. If he had been in the Royal palace on that day in April when the King decided to abandon the country, he would have put his back against the door and prevented his Majesty from leaving, uttering in a firm voice the famous words of Saint Martín de Hinojosa—" *Ahora a vencer o a morir. Si vencéis, Castilla os la premiará ; si morís, aquí tenéis un lugar de reposo, donde no os faltarán las oraciones de los santos* "—(" Now is the time to conquer or to die. If you win the day, Castile will reward you ; if you die you will have here a place of rest where you will never lack the prayers of the saints ").

The King would then have girt on his sword and followed the Marquis.

Spain would have been racked by yet another Civil War.

And then I remembered that before, in 1928, I had walked up and down that same road with Unamuno when he was in exile. He too had gazed across at Fuenterrabía and uttered the words—" I am standing here at the gates of Spain, waiting, waiting . . . how long will this all last ? " Unamuno had been exiled by the Monarchy and it was here at the gate of

Spain he prepared his campaign against the King, by preaching the holy crusade " to ransom the sepulchre of Don Quixote from the power of the scholars, priests, barbers, dukes, and canons who hold sway over it." Like many of the pilgrims to Spain, I had halted at Hendaye in 1928, to see the mystic. Not knowing his address I had wandered on a sultry afternoon into the biggest café in the square, when all the inhabitants seemed to be asleep, and there were no sounds, save the buzzing flies, but there alone, in the dim, vaulted room, I saw Unamuno. He was seated at a table reciting to himself his poems and making little animals out of stray bits of paper.

As a French writer said of him—" Here is the agony of Unamuno : a wrestler wrestling with himself, with his people and against his people ; a man of War, hostile, fratricide, tribune without a party, solitary exile preaching in the desert, provocative, vain, pessimistic, paradoxical, torn to bits between life and death, invincible, yet always vanquished." Yes, in 1928 vanquished—an exile vanquished by the dukes and canons, but a victor in 1931. Now it was the turn of the Marquis to tread sadly the path of exile, while Unamuno sallied into Spain to receive the plaudits of the multitude. Both men might be taken as symbols of that continual state of tension in Spain, or state of agony as Unamuno would have called it. And one in a way is the complement of the other. The Marquis with his coat of mail and shield represents the pageant of Spain as described by Velázquez and accepted by all the world as Spanish chivalry : Unamuno with his peering, owl-like eyes represents the ceaseless restlessness of the Spanish spirit as described by El Greco. For him, there is no relief in Kings or Churches. Man is the more divine, the greater capacity he has for suffering.

" Christianity has not brought us peace, but agony and struggle. Just like Christianity, Christ Himself is always in agony, and it was Pascal who wrote in *Le Mystère de Jésus*—' *Jésus sera en agonie, jusqu'à la fin du monde ; il ne faut pas dormir pendant ce temps là.*' " And so, says Unamuno, all the life of a true Christian should be agony, just as we see in Spain those tragic crucifixes, which represent the cult of Christ upon the Cross who called out : "consummatum est." The Marquis dreaded the victory of the Republic because it would disturb the pre-established harmony. Unamuno longed for Republican victory, because it would bring back the mediæval melting-pot, in which it would be possible to forge a new Spain, just as Siegfried forged his conquering sword Nothung.

Such were my thoughts as I walked back to the little Hotel Broca, where Unamuno used to live during his exile. The landlady, remembering my visits to the Maestro, gave me the room he used to occupy.

For hours I sat motionless in the lonely room recalling those days I had spent with my old friend, listening to him recite from those Biblical poems he wrote in exile here. When I awoke from my reverie there was no golden sun any more. Night had fallen and along the coast lights twinkled here and there through the thin mist.

# CHAPTER V

## THE GATE OF SPAIN

"HOW much will you charge for rowing me across to Spain?"

"A couple of pesetas, Señor," said the old Basque fisherman as he pulled his little boat down to the water's edge. With a scraping sound it slid along the shingle and the fisherman helped me to scramble in carrying my fiddle-case, my knapsack and my stick.

No more enchanting way of arriving in Spain could be imagined. Here we were far away from railway trains, buses, motors, customs officers, travellers, gliding gently over the rippling waters towards Fuenterrabía that shone like a magic city of burnished copper in the golden morning sun. In the distance it looked proud and sadly aloof, in strange contrast to the commonplace white villas of Hendaye. The old fisherman wanted to give me a good idea of his powers as an oarsman and he began to row with vigorous strokes, but I held up a warning forefinger.

"Don't row so fast: I have the whole of life before me. Come, I will give you four pesetas instead of two if you rest on your oars and let me admire the view."

"Certainly, Señor. Few travellers enter Spain this way : they prefer to dash over the bridge of Béhobie on to San Sebastian. But I tell you there are some who rush across this water like a flash by dead of night from

Fuenterrabía to Hendaye trying to avoid the patrols that
are after them."

I remembered then how notorious Fuenterrabía was
as a centre for smuggling, and the fisherman told me
lurid tales of refugees escaping from Spain to France at
dead of night in motor-launches, row-boats and even
by swimming.

"Many of them," he said, "were priests carrying,
hidden beneath their soutanes, church ornaments which
they hoped to deposit in some place of safety abroad."

The old fisherman is a typical Basque son of the sea
with a face furrowed with wrinkles and so covered with
bristling black beard that his eyes beneath their bushy
eyebrows looked like lamps seen through a maze of
jungle. In his body he resembled a gnarled oak-tree
with wiry, bulging muscles on his long arms and his
bow-legs. In manner he was as courteous as an hidalgo
and he declaimed solemnly for me the great traditions
of the Basque race of seamen.

"We have been born and bred to the sea from the
beginning of time. The sea knew our boats ere Spain
ever had a King. Aye, and our real King, Señor, is the
*alcalde del mar*, whose flag you'll see up there in a street
down near the harbour."

"Who is this *alcalde del mar* ?"

"What, Señor, do you not know who is the *alcalde
del mar* ? Why in this very month of July we elect one
for the following year. He is a powerful man, I tell
you, for every fisherman in Fuenterrabía puts trust in
him. He is King of the sea, I tell you."

The old man then gave me a long description of the
ceremony of election, when the fishermen of Fuenterrabía
meet in the town hall and the insignia of the *alcalde* are
carried in a basket by a girl dressed in white, and the
red banner embroidered with whales is hoisted over the

cottage of the mayor. The symbolism of the whales is a reminder to the world that it is probably the Basques who were the first to carry on the whaling industry.

The ceremony is one of propitiation to the sea, in the hope that Neptune may be generous in the coming season, and it reminded me of the custom among the fisherfolk of Calabria of welcoming by shouts and songs the return of the fishing fleet. The ceremony at Fuenterrabía closely resembles the ancient rite practised under the Venetian republic on the feast of the Ascension, when the city was wedded to the sea by the Doge. In his barge called the *Bucintoro* surrounded by all his courtiers, he would sail out to the Lido and then cast a gold ring into the sea, saying the magic words—" *Te desponsamus mare Adriaticum.*" So too by his ceremony of initiation does the *alcalde del mar* marry the fishing town of Fuenterrabía to the ocean.

" I suppose your *alcalde del mar* is King of the *contrabandistas,*" said I to the fisherman, with a twinkle in my eye.

The fisherman spat into the water before answering.

" In the old days, Señor, this was a paradise for smugglers, and my father could make a tidy sum out of this strip of water between France and Spain, but nowadays all is changed. Nobody minds his own business and goes his own way. Everyone must always be watching his neighbour. The government is run by a lot of lean policemen or *migueletes*; they are paid for spying and prying on the poor man who is hard put to it to feed his wife and children. Aye, and what is worse is that the police on both sides of the frontier give a hand to one another. Before, you could always be sure that a Spanish policeman would help a Spanish smuggler to avoid the French police; and a French smuggler could always rely on the help of his own countrymen against the Spaniards. But now the Spanish and French police tell one another every secret as if they were brothers, and they both combine to persecute the poor smuggler. I tell you, Señor, it is all contrary to the will of God to set up these barriers between the two Basque lands."

The old fisherman spoke so earnestly that I fancy he may have been a smuggler himself. The feeling of unity between the two sections of the Basque race was stronger in the dim past than it is to-day. The French Basques have become patriotic French citizens and were among the best soldiers of the army during the Great War. The Spanish Basques, of whom there are, according to Rodney Gallop, 450,000, are one of the most energetic and advanced sections of the Spanish nation in spite of their strong reactionary spirit.[1] It is natural that there should be smuggling along any frontier and the Pyrenean barrier is a paradise for the *contrabandista*.

After the declaration of the Republic, in July, the police on the Spanish side had to be always on the *qui vive* because it was rumoured that every night bands of royalists were escaping into France, carrying away all the money they could collect, and the Spanish republican government found itself obliged to introduce stern measures against them.

When our boat reached the shore of Spain and I had disembarked I started to walk up towards the town, but I was tapped on the shoulder by a policeman and told to go over to a booth to have my passport examined. Inside the booth was a portly little man, red-faced and asthmatic. After looking at me fixedly for some time he asked me in his wheezy voice, why I had come this way instead of going by train or bus. He seemed to consider me a suspicious character because I had chartered

[1] Rodney Gallop, *A Book of the Basques*, London, 1930, p. 24.

a rowing-boat. When I handed him my passport he
tried to read it upside down, then he scratched his head
and stuck the end of his pen into his ear. English was
not a language with which he was familiar, so he scrutinized every page and made a close examination of my
photograph, saying cryptically that it did not resemble
me. Then as he was handing me back my passport
stamped he paused to examine the first page of the
document, where it is stated that the Governor-General
of the Irish Free State begs the foreign governments to
grant free entry to the bearer. The request couched in
the long-winded courtesies of diplomacy was written not
only in English and in French but also in Irish (a little
touch of nationalist self-expression).

The official peered with his short-sighted eyes at the
Gaelic characters and said :

" That is Russian ! You are a Russian."

" Not in the least, Señor ; I am Irish and that writing
is Gaelic."

" Gaelic ? What in heaven's name is Gaelic ? "

" Gaelic, Señor, is the language spoken by the people
of Ireland."

" Why is your passport written in English as well as
in Gaelic ? "

" Why do you, Señor, speak Spanish as well as
Basque ? "

" Because if I spoke Basque you wouldn't understand
me."

" Neither would you if I spoke Gaelic. So you see
we are quits. We both agree to be international."

After a short walk uphill from the sea front, I came
to the main gate of the town with its coat of arms
proudly emblazoned above the arch. The archway and
the narrow street beyond seemed to be the synthesis of
all Spanish arches and streets : they reminded me more

of a Castilian than of a Basque town. The moment I
passed under the arch I knew that I was in Spain, for I
sniffed on all sides the heavy smell of burning olive oil.
At this moment the housewives in Fuenterrabía were
beginning to prepare the daily *olla* and from now until
three o'clock in the afternoon, the town would be
impregnated with the smell. Whenever a North European goes to Spain he must go through the preparatory
period of initiation into heavy olive oil before he enjoys
his meals. Eggs are fried in oil, meat reeks of it, French
beans, or *judías,* the everlasting solo vegetable dish,
float in it. After some days of heat-spots and rash it is
possible to pass through the narrow streets at dinner-
time without the feeling of nausea.

Fuenterrabía is a sleepy town which has watched
modern life dash by, without bothering to open an
inquiring eye. From the point of view of the contemplative traveller it has earned a mighty blessing, for he
knows that the energetic, alarm-clock traveller will never
find the town, because it is hidden in a nook just outside
the rushing tide of progress.

Fuenterrabía is a small town with not more than a
thousand inhabitants. In the Middle Ages it must have
been a stronghold for the King of Navarre, with its stout
walls and castle, but to-day it is sadly tottering. The
houses in the main street are very ancient and many
have the characteristic Basque decorated wood and
railings of worked iron. It is a sleepy town, were it not
for the hosts of romping children, whose shrill voices
echo and re-echo in the empty courtyards. One of the
first impressions the stranger gets of Spain is of un-
repressed children. In no country do children run so
wild as they do in Spain. In the other countries an
attempt is made to discipline the young and initiate them
at an early age into a life where even play must be

according to rules. In Spain the individualism of each child is allowed the completest expression : they frolic about the streets like kittens: they shout, they pester strangers with eager questions until he has to admit that they are the most charming children in the world. How is it that these wide-eyed, laughing lads and lasses will turn into the courteous, measured, taciturn Basque ?

Some travellers may cast doubts on my assertion that the most charming children come from Spain, but they cannot deny that the most picturesque beggars are to be found there. On that sunny July day in Fuenterrabía there were many beggars lolling about in the streets and I was immediately struck by their proud insolence. They were not energetic beggars, for in this southern country their needs were small. As the Sicilian proverb says, " *il sole è il pare dei mal vestiti* "—(" the sun is the father of the ragged "), and olives, bread and sardines are cheap. Begging will serve to obtain tobacco and an occasional glass of wine or *aguardiente* and even then—" paciencia y barajar" as the true vagabond would say. There are far more ragged beggars in Spain than anywhere else, but I often wonder whether they have not borrowed the hereditary rags for the occasion, just as Dicæopolis borrowed the rags of Telephus from Euripides in order to play the part of beggar.

One came up to me in the *plaza* at Fuenterrabía with his coat and *capa* literally in ribbons. He was tall and gaunt with pock-marked face, wild eyes and tousled grey hair, and his ragged costume hanging in strips gave him the appearance of a half-plucked vulture. But no nobleman could have shown more arrogant grace than that *mendigo* did, as he doffed his tattered hat and gazed at me haughtily saying—" Limosna por Dios ! "

My first instinct was to set my jaw and turn away, but I hesitated, for I saw that the beggar stood as still as a statue. I then remembered that in Spain the beggar looks on himself as a necessary institution whose services are needed by the Church for the salvation of rich men's souls. The Bible says that it is easier for a camel to go through the eye of a needle than for a rich man to enter the Kingdom of God. Beggars are necessary, and yonder ragged fellow knows that he is giving me an opportunity to salve my conscience. Hence the trace of *soberbia*. I gave him a few coins, and he bowed without smiling—*que Dios se lo pague a Vd.*

"I am surprised that you did not curse me," said I in a low voice, for I remembered the old Spanish proverb which describes the French, Italian and Spanish methods of begging :

> "*El Italiano pide cantando,*
> *El Francés llorando,*
> *El Español regañando.*"
> ("The Italian begs with a song,
> The Frenchman with a tear,
> The Spaniard with a curse.")

What way does an Irishman beg when acting the minstrel ? He should use a little of each : make a sing-song from time to time with a hypocritical look in his eye, then drop a few tears as he tells of hardships, and later on utter a few fiery Spanish oaths. But above all he should beg with a smile, for I have always found that the quiet smile of *bonhomie* works greater miracles than the most honied tongue. So I turned to the old beggar with a smile saying :

"I should not give you anything because I am a beggar too."

"What do you mean by that, Señor ? "

"I beg with this instrument you see under my arm. But I don't go up and demand alms. I play and then I pass round my *boina* to see if my tune wins a *real* or two."

With that I took out my fiddle and retiring into a shady corner of the street I started to play. The old beggar stood by, looking at me intently. As he saw nobody stopping to listen to my music, he shook his head and sat down on a stone. Fiddling in the public streets is at first a tantalizing occupation for anyone who has ever played in a concert room, because he imagines that at the first magic notes of his fiddle the traffic will stop and the great mass of public stand poised in silent expectation of his music. A street minstrel must learn in the bitter school of adversity to endure ingratitude. The carts lumber by, the pedestrians pass by chattering, the girls turn their heads the other way—all the world passes by without a thought for the poor *juglar*. After long experience, I came to the conclusion that the minstrel must play for himself alone.

In English-speaking cities the street-fiddler's job is heart-breaking, because everyone hurries past intent on business and there are but few loungers. But in Southern countries people do not move quickly through the streets in the brilliant sunshine ; they prefer to loiter and drag their feet as if they were waiting for some surprise to spring up at any moment, like a Jack-in-the-box. As I continued playing in the main street of Fuenterrabía a few loungers came over and stood before me and a minute later they were joined by three women carrying baskets. By experience I found that it is necessary to vary one's performance and introduce little quips and jokes to attract the public. After all, playing in the street is merely a comparatively legal form of begging and it is necessary to adopt subtle means of extracting money. A commercial friend would say that such methods were not begging but good salesmanship.

" Señorita, you must allow me to play to your face and to your two dark eyes. Come, come, don't blush and turn away: I know a melody which will bring you luck. If you let it enter your ears you will find a *novio* before two days are out."

Then to an oldish woman with a basket I would speak thus—" This tune I am going to play is one that pilgrims sing when they are tramping along the road of Saint James. Come, listen to it all of you because it will bring you luck." Sometimes my garrulous talk does not draw a murmur of interest or a smile out of the audience: but to-day I triumphed, for several women gave me coins when I passed my *boina* round. The old woman as she gave me the coin said: " You are a stranger: what are you doing here? "

" I am a stranger, Señora, and I am going to Santiago de Compostela, and when I get there I shall say a prayer for you." Meanwhile out of the corner of my eye I could see my friend the old beggar. I played in different parts of the town for about an hour and half, but he never let me go out of his sight. He would always walk behind me and when I started playing he would go a little distance off and watch the effect. At two o'clock in the afternoon when I had made two pesetas, fifty cents, I determined to cease work and retire to an inn. The beggar then came up and said—" How now, *compañero*, what about going shares? "

" Shares in what? You must be making a mistake."

" You should share with me: did I not leave the way clear for you? "

" Go along with you, my friend! You are joking."

" No, *compañero*: it is just that we should share. I left the coast clear because I said to myself: ' here is a stranger from over the river and I'll let him make a little profit.' Come, give me a peseta or two."

" To Hell with you," I cried and started to move away rapidly from the old fellow, but he followed me, gesticu-

lating and vociferating.   I then began to fear that a row
might arise.   If people gathered round, the old fellow,
knowing the ways of the town, might accuse me of
having tricked him.   The best policy was to give him
something.   So I gave him twenty cents, which he
refused with an obscene gesture, spat upon the money
and threw it upon the ground.   Finally I got free from
the old pest at the cost of fifty centimes more.   As he
was going away his wrinkled, pock-marked face twisted
into the semblance of a grin as he said—" Ah, *compañero*!
Your method of begging is better than mine, but you
have to work harder."   He went off swinging his iron-
tipped stick and laughing hoarsely to himself.   The
moral of that meeting was—" never tell a beggar that
you are one too : it is too amateurish."   I had made the
mistake at the beginning of giving him alms, so when
he saw me ask for money, he was determined to show
me that I had acted as a " black-leg " and poached upon
his preserves into the bargain.   If I had not given him a
share of the money he might have started a street row
or appealed to some trade union of Spanish tramps—
who knows ?   Anyhow, I was glad to have met one of
the true *pordioseros* as the Spanish picturesquely and with
a touch of irony call the beggars.   There is hope yet
in Spain for a lover of the Picaresque and the days of
Lazarillo and Guzmán de Alfarache are not over.

After a hearty meal in a dark eating-house in a side
street I settled myself down for a comfortable siesta.
Life south of the Pyrenees may still be a happy-go-lucky
business, at any rate, for a vagabond.   There is no need
for me to hurry.   I have no conscience driving me
according to schedule.   It is all the same whether I
snooze away for three hours or one hour and I have
no watch ticking a perpetual reminder.   This town of

Fuenterrabía during the early afternoon, when people are having their siesta, is like a city of the dead. Here in the tavern there is silence save for the fitful snore of the one dishevelled waiter who sprawls asleep with legs wide apart, waistcoat unbuttoned, mouth half open, with a toothpick in the corner.

Later on in the afternoon the tavern fills with people, all of them men—hardly a woman do I see. In France there would have been a good sprinkling of chattering girls, some of them unaccompanied and on the look-out for a cavalier, but in Spain one is struck by those solemn concourses of men who sit together wrapped in cloaks, for hours and hours, without saying a word. The old men leaning on their sticks resemble patriarchs seated on thrones, ready to be consulted upon any subject in the world. If I had been a fluent Basque speaker I might have broken down their reserve, whereas by speaking Spanish I proclaimed myself a foreigner. If I had not been accompanied by my fiddle I think some of those village worthies would have thawed more rapidly, but when they saw that I was a minstrel they looked at me with suspicion. Perhaps they were afraid that I might cajole the money out of their pockets by my tunes, and in their eyes being a foreign vagabond I was dangerous, for is there not a Basque proverb which says : " Heavy is the hand of foreigners." I was the foreigner in the town whose presence had not yet been explained and I was conscious of my isolation. " Good sirs," said I to myself, " let me stay here a week and I shall have all of you at my feet ; but, alas ! I have not the time, I must continue my way, trusting in God's mercy that I shall find less reserve in the next town where I make my halting-place."

I did meet one kindred soul in Fuenterrabía just as I

was about to depart. As I was walking down the street, I saw a small group of women gathered round a man who was selling ribbons and bead necklaces. In a loud voice he described the qualities of his wares, taking them out one by one and holding them up for the people to see. His tray which was suspended by a cord round his neck was small, but it was laden with an immense variety of knick-knacks—ribbons, laces, fans, silk handkerchiefs, brooches, bracelets, spools, thimbles, pieces of lace; it was a joy to see such profusion of colour.

The pedlar was a diminutive figure, not more than four feet ten inches in height, with a tiny, wizened, yellow face, black moustaches, side-whiskers, and a shock of unkempt black hair. He was dressed in a jaunty style with faded, grey, double-breasted coat, very greasy and out at elbow; tight, chocolate-coloured trousers, torn in places, faded tanned boots slit at the sides because of corns cut out of them. In spite of his bedraggled appearance he had a certain brisk jauntiness of manner and gait, which made him look like Tom Thumb aping the bullfighter. He possessed the true southern spirit of cheap salesmanship and he expended his energy on a wealth of gesture. He waved his arms, he gesticulated with his fingers, which I noticed were covered with cheap rings. At one moment when he thought that one of the girls wanted to buy a brooch, he opened his double-breasted coat, and lo, behold, he had quantities of brooches pinned on the inside and across his waistcoat. All the Basque reserve in the world was no match for that irrepressible, buoyant little man. In two seconds he had fastened three brooches on the girl's blouse and had put a necklace around her neck in spite of her mute protests.

At last after many flourishes and gesticulations he put on a broad-brimmed grey hat, shut his tray with a bang and stalked swiftly down the street. Out of curiosity

I followed him and soon caught him up. It was not difficult to enter into conversation, for he looked me up and down rapidly and said :

" I suppose you are leaving this town too : no use staying : there isn't a *céntimo* to be made here."

" You didn't seem to be doing badly just now," I answered.

" Oh, that was all foam and froth—not enough to pay for a night's rest. Where are you going with the guitar ? "

" I am off to San Sebastian."

" Well said, brother ! We'll make the journey together."

I was glad that my day in Fuenterrabía had been one of silence, for my pedlar friend's conversation rattled along at the rate of an express train. He was originally from Valencia and was Mediterranean in his sympathies, but he was now going to San Sebastian to peddle his wares, for during the summer season that city becomes the capital of Spain owing to the huge numbers of holiday-makers from Madrid. " Even the *Gitanos* from Madrid take their summer in San Sebastian," said he. " Why, you'll find every *tocaor de Flamenco* there, and you'll hear more *polos* and *martinetes* than *zortzicos* I tell you."

It was seven o'clock when we left Fuenterrabía to tramp to San Sebastian. Manuel the pedlar, for that was his name, jogged along at a jaunty trot, and I tried vainly to keep up with him. All the time he poured forth an incessant flood of conversation about his adventures in various ports of Spain. At first I answered by monosyllables as I plodded along, but soon I became too weary and too puffy even for that, and I lagged behind him, mopping my brow and cursing him inwardly. It was unfortunate to meet such an energumen at the outset of a tramping tour, for my feet had not had time to become acclimatized and impervious to blisters. Besides, minstrels are not supposed to have the powers of resistance of competitors in the London-to-Brighton walking race. " This is wrong," said I to myself as I gasped for breath ; " a wandering minstrel is master of his own actions and he may lie down and sleep under a tree when he feels weary." Still I struggled on through the dusk behind my indefatigable companion who was still talking. Many times I made up my mind to shout out, " Hell ! I am through," and sink down to rest in a ditch, but there is in every traveller an accursed doggedness which refuses to give in no matter how great the odds against him, and so I suffered on.

I was longing to call a halt at Pasajes and I hoarsely shouted out that it was a famous little town, for it was from there that Magellan sailed for South America, but Manuel was deaf to all the claims of history.

" Who was Magellan, anyhow ? " he asked.

" He was a famous sailor, an explorer who lived four hundred years ago."

" What do we want with explorers and sailors, and haven't we enough to-day without worrying about what happened four hundred years ago ? "

" Yes, but we might stop to see some of the fishermen and have a drink or two."

" No, Señor : it would be a mistake to stop now to drink, for a drink would make us chat and with the chatting we should never get to San Sebastian to-night."

" A plague on you," thought I, " you have never stopped chatting since we left Fuenterrabía."

At last I saw in the distance the bright lights of San Sebastian and my deliverance was at hand. When we reached the city it was nearly midnight and Manuel insisted on sharing lodgings with me. He brought me to a street off the Plaza de la Constitución. In a lodging-house on the third floor we were given a garret under the roof with two beds. The room was grimy, the floor covered with dust; there was dirty water in the tin basin and the bed was unmade, but I would not have exchanged its comfort for all the feather beds of Paradise. I sank down upon it fully dressed and in a few minutes I was as deep in slumber as one drugged with morphia.

Next day when I awoke the sun was streaming into the garret and I found that I had slept the round of the clock. Manuel the pedlar had risen at cockcrow and done a heavy day's work before I thought of stirring.

" Get up, you lazy bones," said he reprovingly, " you'll never sup off silver plate at the rate you're going."

" Leave me alone, slave-driver," said I—" I'm an artist, not a business man ; let me rest till the sun goes down and then you'll see me work like a demon."

With Manuel as guide I wandered through the length and breadth of San Sebastian until I was footsore. Up and down the streets we paraded, into the cafés, the bars and the bathing establishments. Manuel would not let me rest in peace. In his mind he was convinced that I needed a watchful guardian who would point out the opportunities for a minstrel. When we would come to a café, where there was no band of professional musicians, he would say in an eager whisper : " Remember this place to-night—you could easily make four or five pesetas here if you gave a small *propina* to the *camarero*."

I was grateful to him for his vigilant care, but I wanted to escape because San Sebastian did not attract me as a halting-place. It was too sophisticated and too near to Biarritz. The traveller is at once struck by the difference between this strand and that of Biarritz. At

Biarritz there is an air of frivolity and gaiety which is strangely lacking at San Sebastian. For one thing the bathers in France wear skin-tight bathing-dresses that show off every curve of their thin figures, but here every girl wears a skirt and the men too wear the most modest bathing-suits I have ever seen. There are not many exotic types : instead, I was struck by the numbers of fat complacent mothers surrounded by herds of small children, camped under voluminous red and pink parasols. Hardly a matron seated on the sands seemed to be possessed of less than eight or nine children.

San Sebastian is mainly interesting to the wanderer on account of its floating summer population, for it is the summer playground of Madrid. Since the Revolution there is a feeling of gravity and solemnity about the town, perhaps due to the closing of the Casino for gambling. Why is it that revolutionary governments always introduce an era of Puritanism? San Sebastian without gambling cannot compete with Biarritz and Hendaye : how long will it take Republican Spain to follow the free and easy notions of its sister republic across the border?

In the afternoon Manuel informed me that he was leaving San Sebastian for Zarauz and other coast towns, but he would introduce me to a friend of his—an old guitarist who would help me to turn over an honest penny. " Es un tipo raro," said he, " but he knows the ins and outs of this town and he'll keep you company, for believe me, *compañero*, there's nothing as bad in this world as being alone like Saint Peter's mother-in-law ! "

We found the old man in a café off the calle de Easo. It was siesta-time and he was dozing in the back of the shop with his head resting on his arms. His guitar lay on the table in front of him. When Manuel slapped him on the back he started up with a shout and let fly a curse.

"Come on, *tío* Lucas," bawled Manuel into the old man's ear : " I've brought a friend to see you."

The old man then peered anxiously into my face, saying in a mild apologetic voice : "Tanto gusto, Señor. What can I do for you ? "

"Now, Lucas," said my pedlar friend, " here is a stranger who is a friend of mine. He's like an innocent babe in arms. I want you to keep an eye on him and help him to pick up a few silver coins with the true ring about them."

" What can I do, Manuel ? " answered the old fellow. "Why I hardly make enough to keep body and soul together these days with Spain all *revuelta* as it is."

" Come on, old miser—none of your excuses. This fellow is on the rocks and you must help. For by God if you don't, I'll throttle you." With this he seized the old man by the back of the neck and pretended to carry out his threat.

"I was only joking, Manuel," said the guitarist. " I'll do my best for your friend, but not a cent have I made this day and not a drop of *aguardiente* has touched my lips though I'm as weary as a worn-out mule." As this was said with a sidelong leer at me, I clapped my hands and called out—" camarero ! " And then gave the order for three brandies. Peace was made and conversation progressed on a more familiar footing. To tell the truth there was not much in my new-found friend's appearance to awaken many happy thoughts of favours to come, for he had the most mournful face. No, he certainly was not prepossessing ; he had such a squint that I involuntarily crossed myself lest he might cast an evil eye upon me. " There is no doubt about his origin," said I to myself as I prepared to address him in Romany. There was no mistaking the glassy stare, the mahogany complexion, the raven-black hair.

" Come now, *plaloró*," said I, " you are going to help me, for I am one of the *Calés* and it is right for one of Egypt to help another."

" *Meclí*—may the sky fall upon me : so you are one of the roms : why didn't you say that before ? I thought you were a white mouth : with that fair skin of yours you would never pass as a true-born son of Egypt."

" Ah ! brother, as they say abroad—a *romí* suckled me, that is why I have wings. I can *chamuyar Caló* as well as any *chaval* of Triana."

" Faith and you can, *plaloró* : come, give me your hand. Go along with you, Manuel, my friend—order *repañi* for us and pay the bill. Let us drink confusion to-day, for to-morrow we die—as they say in Caló— ' *Retejos parchandrá, sos cayicó flacha sinará* '—(to-day it is carnival but to-morrow there'll be ashes) ; so come and let us drink confusion to the *Busnó*." After paying for the drinks, Manuel said farewell and departed, leaving me to the tender mercies of the old Gypsy. It was now evening and the cafés were full, so we both set out in quest of adventure.

Everywhere we went, Lucas insisted on acting the part of protector and impresario. He would address the people in the streets or in the cafés asking them to listen to my playing, and after every performance he would pass round the hat. Then at the end of the evening he handed me the whole amount saying— " To-night everything belongs to you by right of friend-ship. To-morrow we shall share our earnings." Not a penny would he take for himself in spite of all my protests, and I finally said good night to him outside his small apartment on the third floor of a house in the Plaza de la Constitución. At times the Gypsy character is most baffling. From the appearance of Lucas with his squint and his air, I should have inferred that he was a sinister rascal with all the tricks of Gypsydom to his credit, whereas he was a paragon of generosity. Never in all my experience among the sons of Egypt had I ever known them hand over the swag to me. Who knows what spell the old fellow may have put upon that money with that evil eye of his?

The night was balmy, so I sat on a bench under the trees in the park. There was hardly a sound anywhere save the distant murmur of the sea. While I was sitting there, gazing meditatively at the twinkling lights of the sea front, a girl came up to the seat and sat at the further end. I noticed that she wore a white bandage over her forehead, covering one eye. She sat there silently but after a while I heard a muffled sob and I saw her pull out a pocket handkerchief and hold it to her face. I then asked her gently what was wrong, but there was no answer and her sobbing increased in intensity. My heart was touched and I longed to console her as she sat huddled up in a corner of the seat. " Come, tell me, Señorita, what is wrong : you look so piteous and forlorn."

" Ah! Señor, I am very miserable," she said at length as she wiped away her tears.

What shall I do to console her, thought I. I feel so heartless and brutal. The best course would be to draw up closer to her and take her hand.

The soft pressure of my hand worked wonders.

The sobbing ceased and she began to tell me her story.

She was from Santander and she had left her home after the death of her parents to earn her living as a dancer—not a stage dancer but a simple dancing-partner, and she had come to San Sebastian to take up a position in one of the many dance halls that are opened in the summer season. A few days after her arrival she had slipped on the stone steps of her lodgings and fallen on her head—with the result that she had injured her face and eye. After three weeks in hospital she was turned adrift without a single prospect of obtaining employment.

"Nobody will have me at the dance hall," she said. "The manager has given my place to another girl and there are waiting lists in all the other dance halls. Do you know, Señor, that I have not eaten yet to-day? I have no money even to pay for a bed in a lodging-house. *Dios mío!* What shall I do?"

"Poor girl! Something must be done. First of all you must have a meal and a glass of wine—and then we'll see. Come, take my arm, Señorita—why, you can hardly stand upright—courage, don't give way to weakness or you will faint right off."

I took her to a small restaurant where she ate ravenously, like one who has habitually starved herself. Her hands as she held the knife and fork were pitifully slender and white with deep blue veins, and every moment a distressing cough racked her body. She was shabbily dressed but with a certain show of neatness and refinement as though she had made a brave attempt to face her bad fortune. "Ah! Señor," said she, "how can I thank you for your generosity? I should never have asked you to help me, for you might have misunderstood. When I left Santander I was a fool of a girl—I thought life was all plain sailing. I have learnt a bitter lesson and misfortunes never come singly, I tell you. For weeks I looked for work and then one day when I got a job as dancing-partner, I thought that my luck had turned. But it was not for long: five days after the start I had that dreadful fall and now I am in a worse position than ever before. To-night before I met you I even had thoughts of suicide. Women here used to say to me—'Why don't you go after men in the street?

If you wait about and speak to them they will take you to an hotel and pay you to stay with them. Ah! Señor, I could not do that, even if my dead mother arose from the grave and begged me. *No puedo, no puedo!* Back at home in the *pueblo* men would speak to me in the dusk and try to tempt me, but I would never listen to them. In the dance hall here it is not easy to avoid dishonest proposals, but I have never given way."

" What will you do for lodging to-night ? "

" God knows, Señor, I have not a *céntimo*."

I was in a difficult predicament. I had a little money, the remains of the Biarritz windfall, which I could have given the girl, but I was trying to harden my heart against any display of sentiment.

My reasoning was as follows : It was absurd for a wanderer to play the part of Lord Bountiful, unless he wanted to leave shreds of his heart at every turn of the road. A tramp witnesses sad events and hears sad stories in every village, but he must pass on without more than a momentary pause.

After a few minutes' meditation I exclaimed : "I know what I can do, Señorita : you shall come home with me to my lodgings. There is an empty bed in my room, for Manuel the pedlar has gone. You shall have it for the next few nights."

" Ah ! Señor, but I cannot accept . . ."

" Not a word : come with me. Don't be afraid. You will be as safe as in your mother's house."

When we reached the house we had to call the *sereno* or night watchman and I began to repent of my impulsive generosity. What would the landlady say if she saw me bring the girl up to my room ? She might not say much, perhaps, but even the slightest trace of a leer or even a bitter remark would be an agonizing experience.

" It is best to proceed as cautiously as possible," said

I to the girl in a low voice, as I gave the *sereno* his ten-cents tip. I made her take off her shoes and both of us crept upstairs in our stockinged feet.

"To-morrow morning you will be able to slip out early when no one is about," said I to her as I closed the door of our room gently. The next task was to create a line of demarcation between the two beds and assign to the lady her territory.

"Now, my dear girl," said I to her as she stood in the middle of the room silent and confused, "you must understand that this garret is going to be transformed into two rooms and one of them shall be yours."

Then walking down between the two beds I drew with my stick an imaginary line saying : "See how I am walling off your apartment. If you keep to that side of the line you will be as private as though you were locked up in your room at home."

Leading her out into the middle of the room I took her hand and kissed it saying : "There is your room. Good night, Señorita. It is time for bed. Remember that the sword of chivalry lies between us."

The poor girl looked as bewildered as if I had spoken Greek to her. She retired to her side of the room, while I turned my back on her and made preparations for rest.

I then put out the light and soon I was fast asleep.

How long my sleep lasted I know not, but I awoke suddenly, hearing an exclamation. The light was on and I saw a man standing in the middle of the room gazing down at us with a most sardonic grin on his face.

"What do you want ? " I exclaimed.

"I am sorry, Señor, but I was told that this was to be my room. The landlady, when she took the money, said that there was a vacant bed here. If I had known I should never have disturbed you and the Señora."

Here was a problem.

There were three persons and only two beds—one of which was occupied by a sleeping woman. The smile of the stranger seemed to shout out—" Go on, man. She's your woman : sleep with her and let me have the other bed." Though all he said was—" There's not another bed in the house vacant."

Another solution of the problem was for the stranger to get into the girl's bed. No sooner was it formulated in my brain than it was rejected with horror. Thank goodness she is asleep and blissfully unaware that she is the cynosure of neighbouring eyes. There was nothing for it but to adopt the third solution, which was to admit the stranger to my bed. After a certain amount of grumbling and sidelong glances at the sleeping girl he agreed to squeeze himself into my narrow couch. Soon his heavy breathing announced that he was asleep.

I lay awake, for I was planning to escape from the difficult situation which would surely arise in the morning when the girl would awake.

Yes, escape was the best course.

When the grey light of dawn began to steal in through the skylight I rose and dressed noiselessly. Then with my boots in my hand, along with fiddle-case, rucksack and stick, I made my way downstairs and out the hall door.

Before leaving the room I had left three pesetas at the end of the girl's bed.

# CHAPTER VI

## AGUSTINA THE GYPSY QUEEN

ONE day old Lucas said to me : " *Amigo,* I have
great news for you. Agustina Escudero has
come to San Sebastian."

" Who is Agustina ? "

" What ! Do you not know Agustina the queen of
all the Gypsies in Spain ? Why, man, she is so famous
that painters journey to Madrid solely to paint her, and
they say her face is worth thousands of pesetas to them.
Come, let us go and see her."

Queen Agustina lived on the top floor of one of the
houses in the Plaza de la Constitución. After climbing
a steep, winding stairway we came to the door of her
apartment. When we knocked, a little spy-hole in the
door was opened and a raucous voice shouted—" quién
es ? "

" Tell Agustina it is not the time for a siesta : I have
brought a friend to see her."

A dishevelled, slatternly woman with a towel round
her head then led us into a diminutive sitting-room and
told us to wait until her mistress was dressed. The room
was the essence of drabness : there was a profusion of
gilt-framed photographs and shabby antimacassars. It
was a broiling day, but the windows were tightly
closed and the atmosphere in consequence was heavy
and musty. Not much of a setting for a Queen of the

Gypsies, thought I, as I gazed at the array of cheap crockery stacked in a corner. Lucas then showed me a large photograph of a beautiful young dancer in mantilla and high comb, clicking her castanets. " That is her daughter—María del Albaicín, the famous dancer." Just as I was beginning to extol María's beauty Agustina tripped into the room.

Lucas bowed very low as he introduced me—" Here is Don Gualtero, Irishman and friend of the Calés, who has come all the way from his country to kiss your hand."

I bowed, too, and I kissed Doña Agustina's hand as respectfully as if she had been the Queen of all the Spains. " Yes, Doña Agustina, I have come to see you though I have known you for a long time. I have seen you in the pictures of Don Ignacio de Zuloaga, but no picture in the world would do justice to you, Señora."

One glance at Agustina explained to me why she was called the Queen of the Gypsies. No palaces were needed to show off her noble distinction ; why, if I had seen her standing dressed in rags outside one of the caves of the Sacro Monte at Granada I should have called out—" Hail, Agustina, Queen of the Romany chals ! "

She was not tall, but when she threw back her head with that proud gesture of hers, she looked like an Amazon. Her body was slender, but well formed, and when she walked she carried herself with such easy grace that you would have sworn she was a famous dancer. Her skin was olive-coloured with hardly the trace of a wrinkle though she was a grandmother, and her hair, which was black with blue reflections, was plaited in the Gypsy way, and so soft and lustrous that it resembled the raven's plumage. Of her eyes I am afraid to speak for they were Gypsy eyes and there was a touch of sinister witchcraft in them. They were not the eyes of a young Romany *chai*, for there was too much wisdom and cunning in them. Agustina was dressed simply in a black skirt and white blouse, but over her shoulders she wore a beautiful black mantilla ornamented with flowers; around her neck she wore several gold chains and from her ears hung long ear-rings of golden filigree work. When she spoke she would use a wealth of gesture, and her voice, which was low-pitched and slightly hoarse, became metallic when excited, and she would then smile, showing her brilliantly white teeth.

" Tell me, Lucas," said she, " something about the *caballero*."

" Well, Señora Agustina, he is a *tocaor*, wandering from place to place *a la buena de Dios*, earning a peseta here and a peseta there, without having to tighten his belt too much."

" Will you play me a tune, *amigo* ? "

" Certainly, Señora."

" Don't you think something is missing ? "

" Missing ? What do you mean ? "

" Have you never heard of a dry tune, *amigo* ? "

" Never to my knowledge ? "

" No Gypsy *tocaor* will play before he gets some *morapio* or *repañí*. Have you any money in your pocket ? "

" A little, Doña Agustina."

" Well then, take the hint, *amigo*, and bring us to a *taberna* where I can listen to your music at my ease."

Agustina then took my arm and Lucas walked ahead to lead the way. In the streets Agustina was an object of interest to the general public and many would turn round to stare at her, but she held her head raised and she passed through the midst of gaping crowds with a triumphantly arrogant air. As for me, I felt like a

timid prince consort, newly wed and facing his regal
wife's subjects for the first time.

In the tavern over our wine Agustina became still
more talkative and she catechized me upon my life past
and present. What were my parents like? How many
sisters had I? Was I married to a fair or dark woman?
How many children had I? Her curiosity was bound-
less, for she did not limit herself to those obvious
questions, but penetrated to details of a more intimate
and embarrassing nature. "Doña Agustina," said I at
last, "you are worse than a father confessor."

"Ah, Señor, we *Gitanas* have a special privilege.
Every Gypsy woman over forty can be a *bruja* whenever
she wishes. I like to question you because I know you
would tell me a lot of lies. But you can't deceive my
Gypsy eye, for I can see right through you without
looking at the lines on your hand."

"Come now, Señora Agustina, I am not a mere
*lilipendó Busnó* or stupid gorgio : I'm a Romany rye and
you can't fool me."

"God give me someone who will understand me, or
as they say in *Caló*—'*ondebel biya nu diñele, sar coin
nu chanele.*' I'm not out to fool you, *eray*. But I
don't believe all your story of your fair-haired wife over
the sea and your two children—may the Devil take me
if I do. With that roving eye of yours and those red
lips do not tell me that you go through the world always
thinking of your wife at home. *Juerguista*, or spreer,
that's what you are, and if we were in Madrid I should
find you in the Puerta del Sol with a *chica* on each arm.
Look at him—a *cara de Tenorio* he has to be sure."

"What about yourself, Doña Agustina? I too shall
answer with a proverb in Romany ; '*diquelas condarí on
aquí averí, ta na dicas a chiriri desquerí*'—('You see the
mote in your neighbour's eye but you don't see the

beam in your own '). What about your own husband—
I suppose he is all alone in Madrid ? Do you think of
him always ? "

Lucas interrupted me by kicking me under the table.

Agustina's sardonic smile died away and her mobile
face assumed a tragic expression. " Ah, Señor, you
have revived cruel memories by your mention of my
husband. Alas, many years have passed since he was
waked in Madrid. What a wake it was ! The bed in
which he was laid out looked like an altar with the
amount of candles that were burning around it. I can
see old Faraón at the head of the bed and beside him my
brother Ramón el Andaluz the greatest Gypsy *chalán* in
Spain. Aye, and all the horse-dealers from the *feria*
beyond the *matadero* were there, too, with El Pelao at
their head and they were weeping their eyes out for the
dead. Yes, Señor, we Gypsies have long memories, for
memory of relations is the strongest law amongst all
who are true Romanies of caste. When a Gypsy dies
and is laid in the ground he can still do harm to the living
if they forget him. The Gypsies say—' *O sos ne abela
enjayé, presas abele pinrés* '—(' He who has no memory
let him have good legs '), but swift as he runs he'll never
out-distance a ghost in a shroud."

" Why don't you," said I, " follow the examples of
the Hungarian Gypsies and pour wine on the grave to
lay the ghost, or else play music into the ears of the dead
man ? "

" The only wine we poured," replied Agustina, " was
into the throats of the funeral party. And as for music,
well, we had Lucas with his guitar, playing to us in the
dark morning with the dead body lying there and all
the candles guttering out one by one."

" Many Gypsies in other lands, Doña Agustina, burn
every chattel that belonged to the dead man ; why,

they even burn their caravans and become penniless beggars."

" Well, Señor, the true Gypsies in Spain make no end of mourning over their relations. When my *rom* died, I had to mourn as a true-born *romí* does. I had to cut off my hair, disfigure my face and dress myself in the filthiest rags. Never was I to wash myself or care for my body in any way, for the rule of the *Gitanos* holds that a woman who loses her husband should become an outcast shunned by all. When her *rom* dies, she is condemned to a living death and woe betide her if she breaks the Gypsy law. Lucas here knows how loyally I kept the command at first. I wandered about Madrid begging like the vilest *mendiga* in the Calle de Embaja-dores. Come now, Lucas, was I not the most wretched widow you have ever seen ? Many painters took pity on my lot, especially that *santo hombre* Don Ignacio : they were shocked to see Queen Agustina in rags, begging at street corners for a crust of bread. But I would not let them give me money, for I was afraid of Ramón and my other brothers. If they had known that the *Busné* were helping me they would have drawn their *navajas* and killed me. At last after some time one of those good painter friends arranged to kidnap me and hide me away from my infuriated brothers. How I trembled that night he came to fetch me. I feared the *olajai* or curse of Ramón el Andaluz and I was sure he would find me no matter where I should hide, for ' *os Calés abelan lachingueles pinrés* '—(' Gypsies have long legs '). However, thanks be to God, they never found me. After some years of hiding I heard that they were willing to forgive and forget, so I returned to Madrid to my family. Thus you see, Señor, how we Gypsies govern our lives by laws that are stricter than those of the *Busnó*. We have our own notions of *lachirí*, or

justice, which is different to that held by the governments
of the countries where we dwell. In spite of our
apparent submission we are independent of any law
made by white men, whom we hate. And here in
Spain we can still preserve our independence, for we
are not on any census roll. Hence we do not pay taxes,
and when the collectors come to look for us we have
already flown. I give you my address in Madrid as
number seven Calle Lombia and you may go there
sometimes to look for me, but I shall probably have
gone away and nobody in the whole district will know
where Agustina Escudero lives. All life to us is an
adventure which is always changing, and we cannot
understand those who build houses on their piece of
land and shun movement. As we wander over the
earth, we see beautiful things and we converse with
nature. Our word 'to work' is *randiñar* and our work
in life is to wander and wander until Death. We are
resigned to our fate, for our history has taught it to us.
I am proud of being a true-born *Gitana*, for my ancestors
have given me songs and stories which are the accumu-
lated wisdom of centuries, though I have had no
schooling in reading and writing such as they give the
children of the *Busnó*."

"But what about your daughter María del Albaicín?
Was she content to remain all the life a Gypsy following the rigid code?"

"No, Señor. María was a little rebel. She was
fated to fall for a mere *Busnó*. But the day she was
betrothed was a black one in the Barrio de Tetuan.
She was cursed by every Gypsy in Madrid for marry-
ing a white man, but she was a rebel and she did
not care; besides, María was born into the world
with a dancer's soul. She danced before she walked,
and when she grew up she thought of other countries

where she could win fame. Poor girl! the curse reached her only too soon, for there she is coughing her lungs to pieces. She is now in Switzerland up in the mountains. She says she will be cured, but I am afraid, for I fear the curse that came to her when she left her father's home."

As there was a fear that Agustina would fall again into one of her sad reveries, Lucas nudged me in the ribs saying—" Now, Don Gualtero, it is your turn to stand the round. Ho there, *camarero*! Bring three glasses of *repañi* : the *caballero* here has ordered them."

Soon Agustina had reverted to her old frivolous self and all painful memories were forgotten. Before taking leave she said to me—" Bravo, my friend—one who can *chamuyar Caló* as you can should become the *plaloró* or brother of all the Calés in Spain. You must meet Ramón el Andaluz, El Pelao and all the other Gypsies of Barrio de Tetuan in Madrid. We Gypsies cannot write letters of introduction, but we have passwords and I shall tell you them. When you arrive in Madrid go early on a Thursday morning to the horse-fair beyond the *matadero* and when you are among the Romany chals, shout out in a loud voice the names of ' Ramón el Andaluz ' and ' El Pelao,' then if the Gypsies look at you in cross-eyed fashion say—" I've no evil in my mind : I've come with a message from sister Agustina." Then the whole crowd of them will welcome you as if you were a *crayí*, or King."

After taking leave of Agustina for the night, Lucas brought me back to his lodging in the Plaza de la Constitución, where he rigged up a temporary couch for me in a corner of his garret.

## CHAPTER VII

## MARUJITA THE GYPSY DANCING GIRL

SINCE I came under the spell of Queen Agustina I feel as though anything might happen to me. Before I met her I was master of my actions, and I still lived in my own world. But Agustina led me by the hand into a new world and cast the evil eye upon me.

Anyhow, I feel bewitched since I have seen Marujita the Gypsy dancer and it is your fault—Agustina—no mere Gypsy witch possesses an ounce of the devilish sorcery that you store in those black eyes of yours. Why did you introduce me to Marujita?

I am a vagabond minstrel and I must follow my trail inexorably without halting by the wayside to lose my heart to a Romany *chai*.

It all happened because I gave a spree to Agustina. After a plentiful meal in the restaurant Victor, where our hearts were mellowed by a couple of bottles of *morapio* and three glasses each of *repañi*, Agustina in her sharp, metallic voice said to me:

" I'm going to take you to see a lovely *gachí*—one to make your mouth water."

" Don't tempt me, *Dai* : I have a *romí* and *churumbeles*, over in a foreign country."

" She won't let you be tempted : she's a *lachí gachí*

64

and besides, she has a witch of a mother—a *chuanjañí*—
with an eye that would wither the fiercest *chabó* that ever
drew near to pluck the flower. But still, *eray*, it costs
nothing to get your eye full of beauty : don't be afraid :
as they say in Caló—'*Na s'aqueró a anguin, somia dor
gel a mui*' ('Honey was not made for an ass's mouth').
It's an *eray* like you should look on such a jewel. Come,
pay your reckoning. *Debla santa!* you've still got some
*iayeré* I hope, so that we may have a good *juerga.*"

Agustina led me to a rendezvous down in the town
of San Sebastian, called the Teatro de Colón—a characteristic Spanish place of amusement. It was a small
theatre consisting of a *parterre*, a balcony, divided into
boxes and an upper gallery. On the ground floor were
many tables and chairs, and people came in at any time
and sat there listening to the show, which took place
on a stage at the end of the hall.

Such theatres are a paradise for the teetotaler, for
he may see dances and music-hall performances just for
the price of a cup of coffee. But anyone who is a
devotee of the god of wine will find the place a snare
and a delusion, for the bottles of wine cost three times
the ordinary price, and the stranger realizes that the
theatrical show is paid out of the money raised on the
consumption of alcoholic drinks. The audience was
mostly composed of men, but there was a good sprinkling of gaudy women of the *demi-monde*, linking arms
with their cavaliers. It was a pleasantly democratic
theatre : in some of the boxes I saw old men in evening dress and white ties, and in the *parterre* many rough
workmen still had on their blue work-smocks and check
caps.

The whole place had recently been painted from floor
to ceiling a violent blue and white, and it reeked of
turpentine.

The theatre was very full, and with great difficulty I secured a box in the balcony for Agustina.   To call it a box would be a euphemism, for it was just a space partitioned off from the next.   Agustina, however, entered her box like a queen and sat down in front, looking down on the public, flicking her fan with a dainty gesture and smiling graciously to some of her friends who were in the audience.   I have never seen a woman bear herself with more regal dignity than Agustina.   As soon as she took her place many women turned to look at her.   She had dressed herself in her best for the occasion, and in her black hair she wore a beautiful, elaborately worked tortoiseshell comb.   Over her shoulders she had draped a dark red shawl, which half revealed her bronze-coloured skin.   Her dress was black, but in front it was embroidered in red and yellow pattern : over her heart she wore a bouquet of red carnations, which I had bought for her.   I felt proud to be seen beside Agustina, for not a woman in the theatre could compare with her for beauty and majesty. Purposely I sat a little behind her so as to enjoy to the full the spectacle of her beautiful profile, the delicate contours of her chin, and her finely moulded ears from which hung the long golden filigree ear-rings.   When I ordered a bottle of wine she became vivacious with that vivacity of the princess at play : she beckoned to some friends of hers in another box and soon they joined our party.

The music-hall show was of very poor order—a mere excuse for exciting us to consume bottles of Rioja, Manzanilla or Jérez.

A very fat girl came on in a diminutive *cache-sexe* and began to wriggle her rolls of fat to the rhythm of an insipid *cancan*.   Her thighs resembled columns of tallow, mottled here and there with bruises, and above her knees were the red lines impressed by the garters she wore in the daytime. While she continued the rotating, vibrating movement of her loins, she sang an obscene song in a hoarse voice. The public laughed and roared approval for she was simply the *puta*, or whore, and she did not pretend to be anything else.

Another woman of mountainous bosom, who sang more ambitious songs in a shrill falsetto like a piccolo out of tune, received scant mercy. The people boohed and whistled her lustily, but she stood unmoved by the catcalls, simpering and airing her graces like a *prima donna*. Two Russian girl acrobats came on next and gave a wonderful display of tomboy dancing. The audience applauded them because they were foreign and because their closely bobbed hair made a subtly pornographic impression on the Southern mind. "Vayan las rubias—qué chicas," cried the youths in the pit as they tossed off their glasses of Rioja and Manzanilla.

Meanwhile Agustina had invited several friends into our box, including the manager of the theatre, a tall, dark and sinister man, in evening dress. Agustina tipped me an expressive wink. I understood. The shorthand might be explained thus : Take care of this gorgio : it is he who pays the piper. Give him some wine to soothe his spleen and he will smooth your path with Marujita. I immediately called a waiter and ordered wine of superior mark for the whole party. When it came I saw a smile of relief light up Agustina's face. Her smile could be translated thus : "Debla santa!" Now at last we are mounted and it is time to dig in the spurs—*olé* for the *juerga*, the *zambra*, or whatever else you like to call a spree in Spain. Her smile was like a shout of joy : "The *eray* has opened his purse. Hurray! Hurray!"

I saw a jealous old *romí* in the next box but one :

she was watching me and I fancied I could hear her mutter : "*Sat sonacai grel, o alcorabisa saré*" ("The ass with gold is the one that'll win the world").

After the acrobatic Russian girls had cartwheeled off the stage I heard the strains of Spanish popular music, and for the first time I became aware of the existence of an orchestra. It would be an exaggeration to call it a symphony orchestra for it only consisted of a few fiddlers, a 'cello, cornet, drum and cymbals. A scraggier lot it would be difficult to find. Most of them had a lean and hungry look, especially the two fiddlers who played in a shuddering, nervous way as though they were in perpetual fear. They wore their hats on their heads while playing, and had their coats buttoned up to their necks as a precaution against draughts. The cornet-player and the flautist were the living embodiments of digestive misery, and the only touch of colour in their sallow faces came from their noses, which by a curious coincidence were abnormally long and red. I suppose that many years of envious sniffing at the fumes of wine in the theatre had painted those two organs an optimistic red and given one luxuriant touch to lives that were sunk in mournful squalor. For the next number the orchestra was increased by the addition of two aged guitarists who sat at the back and thrummed their instruments in buzzing accompaniments.

Agustina clapped her hands when she heard the guitars and cried out : "Open your ears, *monró*. Now you will see our Marujita, the rose of Gypsy dancers. She is only a *chavala* but when they see her at Villa Rosa there's not an *eray* in all Madrid but will go daft. She has honey in her hips, I tell you, Señor, or as they say in Caló : '*Abela anguín andré as polomias—olé, olé !* '"

On buzzed the accompaniment and the men in smocks

and caps in the *parterre* stamped their feet in time to the rhythm.

Suddenly Marujita came out from behind the dark curtain at the back on to the stage. Agustina had not exaggerated her beauty. At the first moment I had a vision of two great dark eyes set in the crest of a long shimmering comet which flashed across the stage. Then, when my eyes became accustomed to her costume of glittering spangles, I saw that she was tall and slender for a Gypsy, with the most beautiful skin of that golden pallor which Gautier so much admired in the Andalusian Carmens. Even from my distant box, I was thrilled by the exquisite poetry of her skin. Its golden quality seemed to ripple and shimmer in the light like the delicate maple back of a golden-varnished Stradivarius. At first she did what was called a " presentation " followed by a *farruca* with a dignity and a languid grace that was intensely beautiful in its simplicity. " She is only fifteen, and as innocent as a child of ten," murmured Agustina to me. " But they say that she is as provocative as a *lumiasca* and diabolically enticing. If you went behind that dark curtain on the stage you would find her old mother sitting there keeping watch over her like a true Gypsy *dai*."

After dancing to Spanish rhythms, Marujita, in her second programme, performed the *tango gaucho* and North American jazz dances, but it was as if one wedded the tone of a Cremona violin to a blaring saxophone. It was desecration to contort and twist that lovely body to the jerky rhythms of the jazz, but Marujita's young body, like that of a young athlete, made the most exaggerated turns and twists seem graceful and every movement responded to some inner law of harmony.

As she stood alone upon the stage before that vulgar tavern audience she was like a goddess, conscious of a terrifying beauty that would drive men mad. She was the personification of the spirit of orgy—the embodiment of all the arts for one brief instant of excitement. She set all my senses on fire by her movements, but at the same time she quenched my fever by her classic dignity and innocence. In some dances like the *malagueña* she was languidly graceful, in others such as the *iota* she was heroic and the rattle of her castanets sounded like gun-fire heard at a distance.

For the *jota* she had put on a long black dress ornamented with flowers. There was nothing Gypsy about the dance, which was accompanied by guitar and drum, but Marujita possessed the peculiar Gypsy power of absorbing the essential characteristics of other races. She became as aggressive as a female Amazon and her large dark eyes shone malignantly. She was dancing to a hymn of hate and an intense one at that, and I remembered how the modern poet Salvador Rueda had said that in the *jota* we have the sound of helmets, the roaring of cannon, the neighing of horses, and the clang of swords. " Ah," said Agustina, " you should see her dance the *jota* opposite my nephew, ' El Gato,' and then you would see the sparks fly."

What struck me most about Marujita was her entire absence of self-consciousness. When she was dancing she seemed instinctively to improvise her movements. The preluding rhythms on the guitar seemed to turn her from an Oriental statue of marble into a living Maya. Between her performances she came up to our box and Agustina introduced her to me. At first she looked at me suspiciously, and only when Agustina told her that I was one of the *Calés* and could *chamuyar Caló* did she cast off her cloak of reserve. When she sat beside me I was able at leisure to examine her features. She had a beautiful forehead, broad and smooth as old ivory, and her eyes in the setting of her dark lashes were like deep pools of fire. Her hair was not raven black like that of Agustina but brownish in colour. Her slightly aquiline nose and her high cheek-bones gave a strength and nobility to her face which was contradicted by her large, sensual mouth and rather heavy chin. But in compensation when she smiled, which was frequently, she showed two rows of brilliantly white teeth.

What a contrast to the beautiful Marujita was her old mother! Outside the back streets of Triana or the caves of the Albaicín I have rarely seen an uglier or more unkempt Gypsy *dai*.

Beside her daughter clad in her shimmering low-backed dress she sat, looking like a grotesque scarecrow. Her dark dress was shabby and torn at the ends, and above she wore a dirty white blouse closed across her breast by a coarse safety-pin. On her feet she wore *alpargatas* or labourer's shoes.

"She is a disgrace to every *romí*," whispered Agustina to me, "for people think that all of us live in dirt and misery. The managers of the theatres try to refuse her admittance, but she will not be denied. She clings like a leech to her daughter to see that no harm comes to the child. If any *Busnó* were to make an assault upon that girl's *lacha ye trupos*, the old woman would pull out her *churí* from inside her blouse and rip him open where he would least choose."

Just at that moment we were interrupted in our conversation by one of the attendants who handed Marujita a note from a fat, grey-haired gentleman who was sitting in a box on the opposite side of the theatre. Marujita gave the note without a word to her mother. The old woman could not read and she asked one of Agustina's friends to spell out the message. "The gentleman wants Marujita to sit with him and drink a glass of wine."

" Where's the old fool ? " muttered the old woman, looking round the theatre.

" Over there, Mother—can't you see him ? " said Marujita.

" There they are—always after her like dogs after a bone—*malos chuqueles os jamen.*"

" Come now, Señora, you must be reasonable," interrupted the manager impatiently. " Marujita is engaged by the management of this theatre to dance and to make herself agreeable to any client who wishes to meet her."

The old lady gave a grudging consent and the girl went over to the old man's box. A few minutes later the waiter brought them a bottle of wine and Marujita's host, leaning his elbows on the table, began to talk more intimately to her. But not for one minute did the mother take her eyes off her daughter. She sat motionless as a statue, not paying any attention to the stage, with her dark eyes fixed on her.

" Ah ! Señor," said Agustina to me, " you strangers may laugh at Marujita's mother, and call her *charlá* or mad, but I tell you she is no exception among the true *Gitanas* of the race. A true-born Gypsy will guard the *lacha*, or virginity, of her daughter with her life, aye ! and against odds, for well she knows that when the girl's *rom* knocks at the door to ask her in marriage, she must be led out to him *sastí ta chachiperá*, with her white *dicló* hoisted on high to tell the world that she is a virgin. Small wonder is it that the women protect their daughter's *lacha*, when they find our men so mortally jealous. When my *rom* was alive he would never allow me to pose for any of those painter folk from Adalí or Safacoro unless he himself were sitting in the studio, and he would take the money from the artist. As for posing *rechipoti*, or in the nude, he would draw his *churi* if anyone so much as mentioned it."

" So Marujita's mother is a model of her race ? "

" Give over joking, *eray* : she's a poor creature and the whole family would die of hunger but for that young girl with her *meneo*."

" Ah ! So Marujita has brothers and sisters ? "

" Aye ! Seven all told, most of them brats that can't earn. The father does nothing but sleep, drink and scratch his fleas. Poor Marujita has to dance from sunset to sunrise to feed the lot of them. One day I'm sure they'll make her dance around her own coffin."

While Agustina and I conversed, the other guests had ordered further bottles of Manzanilla wine and the clatter of voices was deafening. Gypsies become excited at the sound of their own voices, and the volume of sound increases as each tries to shout down her neighbour. Finally, when the woman who possesses the sharpest lungs manages to defeat her opponent the voices sink again to normal pitch. Two of Agustina's women friends, mahogany-skinned with bright shawls and silver ear-rings, made loud remarks about me, asking was I a Gypsy because I could speak *Caló*.

" Of course he is," snapped Agustina. " He's a *rom* from abroad and he has come to visit the *Calés* of Spain."

In the next box to ours, the fat girl who had danced the *cancan* was now the centre of a group of intoxicated men who were pinching her naked thighs and hurling smutty remarks at the world in general.

Marujita devoted most of the time, when she was not performing, to the grey-haired old satyr in the box opposite. He ordered another bottle of wine but drank most of it himself, for the girl refused to take more than one glass. At the end of the show she left him

and came over to us. " Come, Señor," said her mother
to me, " you must dance with Marujita at the ball downstairs. You are one of us and she would sooner be
with you than with one of those *paillos*."

Before I left the theatre the waiter came up with a
tray on which lay the bill—a very large one for the
purse of a wandering minstrel. We had been a party
of seven or eight persons and the price charged was
twenty-three pesetas. As I took up my fiddle-case which
lay hidden in a corner of the box I could not help
saying a mute prayer to his satanic majesty to give me
the mysterious Gypsy power of extracting money out
of gorgios. An inner voice, probably that of the devil,
replied : " What is wrong with you is that you are
neither fish nor fowl. You want to run with the hare
and hunt with the hounds. You wished to play the
lordly Romany rye who acts as host to the Gypsies
in their spree. Small blame to them for leaving you
to settle the bill. If you wanted to play the Gypsy
why did you not remind them that you were a *tocaor*,
or minstrel, with nothing in your pocket but the silver
coins of the wandering Jew ? "

Never mind, thought I to myself. I am not yet
cleaned out of all the cash I won at Biarritz. Later
on to-night I shall play the Gypsy too.

I followed Agustina, Marujita, and the rest of our
party downstairs, into a small dance hall which was in
the theatre building. Here a jazz orchestra was playing, and it was now possible for any member of the
audience to dance with the music-hall actresses. Poor
Marujita ! How I pitied her, when I thought of her
life night after night exposed to the vulgar tavern
audience in the theatre, with the additional torture of
having to dance with drunken men until four o'clock
in the morning. No wonder she looked weary as

she danced with me in the midst of the jostling crowd.

" I am not tired, Señor, but I am worried."

" Why, Marujita ? "

" Look at my mother over there, sitting with Agustina at our table. When the manager sees her he flies into a rage. He says that many men will not come here to dance because they see her there. They call her a *bruja*."

" Why don't you dress your mother up in new clothes and put a black mantilla on her head ? People then would not call her ' witch.' "

" Ah ! Señor, you don't know my mother. She thinks there is a curse on people who dress up in fine clothes. She hates life in the town, and she longs to live dressed in rags in a tent as she used to do long ago."

" How did she ever let you become a dancer ? "

" It was my *sustiri* : I had to become a dancer, and it was my cousin who helped me to escape from home when we were in Madrid. But my mother followed and threatened to kill me if I did not return home. At last she consented to let me dance, provided that she could follow wherever I went. And I must dance, Señor, because my mother and brothers and sisters *pasan bocatas* without my help."

Poor Marujita ! Later on I assisted at a painful scene when the manager scolded her for not dancing with a drunken man who had asked her. At first her mother pleaded with the manager : he stormed at her and called her *bruja* : the old woman replied with a volley of oaths : Agustina sat still without a word, flicking her fan haughtily. Matters were approaching a climax, and people were watching us. I then lost my temper and shouted out that I had been insulted, for had I

not asked Marujita and her mother to be my guests?
"I am a stranger, Señor," said I, "and I should have expected more courtesy from Spaniards, who are reputed to
be the most courteous and hospitable people in Europe."

My words had a magic effect. The manager shook
me by the hand, and called for the waiter.

"*Camarero!* Four glasses of *aguardiente*. Your
health, sir, and a thousand apologies."

"Now," said I to myself, "my chance has come to
play the *Gitano*."

"Señor, you have given me a welcome *brindis* and
it is my duty to give thanks. I am a minstrel, or as
you would say in Spain a *juglar*, and I want to give
thanks in the traditional way by a song.

"Come, Agustina, hand me that fiddle-case over there.
I am going to play you all a Gypsy tune which will
bring luck to the whole company."

My ruse worked well. Most of the people gathered
in a circle round me at the request of the manager,
and I played a rousing Hungarian Gypsy dance just to
cheer them up from the start.

Then Agustina called out to Marujita—"What a pity,
child, you did not bring your guitar! You could make
a *mista sarsalé* to the *eray's* playing and give us a Spanish
*singa*."

"Oh! but Juanito over in the band has a guitar,"
said the manager. "Quick, Juanito, run for it."

In a few minutes Juanito returned with his guitar,
and handed it to Marujita.

After a few preluding chords she began to play a
medley of Spanish airs—*polos, boleros, tangos, malagueñas*.
I tried to follow her by ear, but it was like chasing
someone through a shadowy dream. Sometimes my
violin would catch up the tune only to find myself slipping behind as the guitar droned and thrummed and

raced along. Finally I anchored myself to the *malagueña*, a celebrated folk tune with which I had long been familiar—

" Otra vez ! " I cried to Marujita and we repeated the tune, introducing every Gypsy flourish and trill we could think of.

" Muy bien ! " cried the audience, clapping their hands.

Out of the corner of my eye I noticed that a fat man in the corner was applauding vociferously. I pointed him out to Marujita and she winked saying—" pajabaremos pa chuyó "—(" We'll play for the fat man "). I knew in my heart that he would be as they say in *Germania* the *barbalote*, or easy victim.

Marujita turned her Gypsy eyes upon him, alluring and provocative, and I gazed at him fixedly and sternly to prevent him escaping from the snare.

" You have not a chance, old boy," said I to myself as I played on, " the Gypsy spell will work here in Spain as well as in Hungary."

At the end of the night the old fellow, before leaving, handed us two duros each, making me promise to come back and play another night.

" Well done, both of you," cried Agustina, when he had gone. " As they say in Caló—' *dui empersó yes grel, simachí e mistó dañé* '—(' When two ride the same ass it's a sign that the year will be good ')."

At 3.30 a.m. we all departed on our way home to bed.

As I said farewell, Agustina murmured to me with a sardonic grin on her face : " Now put your hand on your heart, brother. Is she not fit for the bed of a King ?  Where would you find among the *Busnó* such charm, such innocence and such pride of race ?  No white-mouthed *rom* will take her *lacha*, I tell you."

In Lucas's garret I spent a white night.

I made a vow to see Marujita again.

# CHAPTER VIII

## TRIALS OF A TRAMP

AFTER leaving San Sebastian I began to feel a free untrammelled vagabond once more. It was a fresh, sunny morning and as I walked along the country road I conversed with myself in a loud voice. A wanderer is happiest in the morning when he sets out alone from his stuffy garret. When once he gets into the strong rhythm of tramping he is as free as the King of Nature.

As long as he stays in the town he is dependent upon others. In the *posada* I never felt alone. Once when I was murmuring to myself a man's voice from the dark corner of the room awoke me with a shock from my reverie by saying: " He who talks to himself is talking to the devil."

Out here in the country I am free from all hindrances : I can talk, shout, sing, wave my stick without anybody calling me madman. The sky is blue above my head, the roads are not dusty at this early hour, the air is fresh and there are birds singing.

The Basque country is nearly as green as Ireland and the cloud-capped mountains remind me that the weather may yet have surprises for me. In the morning I am an incurable optimist, for my frugal tramp's life has banished all gloomy, dyspeptic melancholy, and I am ready for any adventure that comes my way.

About five miles from San Sebastian I came to a
small house by the way and as I passed I smelled the
delicious scent of roast meat and onions. After my
walk in the morning air that scent was like a swift
vision of paradise. A woman in a blue smock was
roasting a rabbit over the fire and around her were
five children.

" Buenos dias, Señora. How good that rabbit smells
—my mouth waters." In two minutes I was inside
seated at table beside the master of the house. I preferred that simple meal of roast rabbit and onions to
the most gorgeous meal the Ritz Hotel could offer me.
Then after loitering a while in friendly conversation,
toothpick in hand, and after distributing a few pence
as presents to the children, I said farewell and continued
upon my way.

The sun was now hot, for we had passed the hour
of noon. The day began to be oppressive and thoughts
of the siesta entered into my mind.

Spain shows its superiority to our Northern nations
by this tradition of the siesta. We are rapidly becoming a nation of dyspeptics owing to our habit of rushing through our meals and dashing back to work.
Many of us snatch a cup of tea and a bun at a counter
in the intervals of feverish work. When we order a
solid meal we do so with a shamefaced expression as
though it was wrong to linger lovingly over the details
of such a sensual pleasure as cookery. Rarely do we
enjoy a dinner in English-speaking countries because
we are surrounded by wan-eyed, wrinkled men, the
embodiments of digestive misery, and by women who
hold the mistaken notion that slimness spells grace and
beauty. The Spaniard studies his dinner as though it
was a long and subtle work of art—a poetical drama
to be followed by the siesta or period of divine con-

templation. The poorest peasant or tramp on the roads, when the hour for dinner arrives, will say in a majestic tone as though reciting a magic formula : " Ahora vamos a comer "—(" Now we are going to dine "). He stresses the word *comer* and pronounces it with a flourish of the tongue. Then though he has only a few coins in his purse he will choose his dinner with care and artistry and the innkeeper will not give short measure. In our inns and restaurants, dinners suffer from the evils of mass-production : how many of us lose all desire for food when we hear the slatternly damsel behind the counter bawl down to the kitchen : " Three steak-and-kidney pies and three vegs ! "

In Spain in the humblest *parador* each dinner is a separate individual entity and the tramp, if he sees his neighbour order veal, will order rabbit and will say in a low voice : " Amigo, add in a few *pimientos* with my portion for I like it hot." And our tramp when he has finished his stew, drunk his carafe of wine, sipped his coffee and perhaps (if he has had a good financial morning) an extra glass of anisette, will not rush away into the hot streets.

" Only a madman would walk about in this heat," he says as he lolls back in his seat. " *Camarero*, bring me a toothpick." Toothpicks are frowned upon in our genteel countries, but I should like to sing a pæan in their honour, for they are gentle reminders that the siesta-time has arrived. Look at that red-faced, sweating man with protruding paunch who sits opposite to me. Not a word has he spoken for the past hour, for he has been dedicated heart and soul and body to the goddess of the table. Now he gazes at me with a far-away look in his face as he uses his little wooden shaft with nimble efficiency, and soon we enter into a bland conversation.

In this hour of siesta we do not excite ourselves with any fierce subjects of argument : we talk affably until we reach the blissful state of sleepiness when it is time to retire. I then take leave of him and go out to the yard where I know there is a snug barn. Lying in the hay I may sleep through the heat of the day and there is no one to rebuke me for my snores.

In siesta-time, too, I make the acquaintance of the women of the establishment, for when you go into the courtyard you will find them all sitting in the shade with their workbaskets in front of them. Most of them are fat or as the Spaniards would say—" Jamonas." While I am in Northern Europe I dream of the slim, clean-limbed Nordic maiden with the curveless body of young Hermes, but after a few weeks wandering in the south my thoughts fly away to the dark-eyed, black-haired damsels with opulent curves. In my meditative siesta in the hay-loft, between each bout of sleep, I see you, Mercedes—the young servant of the *posada*. You are fat and you are as deep-bosomed as a Homeric goddess, but you move as swiftly and arrogantly as a race-horse and there is a roguish twinkle in your eye. The day is hot, Mercedes, and I have still the devil of youth in me : don't come too near my hiding-place, Mercedes, I warn you. The flesh is weak and a vagabond who yields to temptation can slip away in the cool of the evening without anyone being the wiser.

"What soft white skin you have, Mercedes, and what fiery eyes ! But I see a gold chain on your neck and a little crucifix on the end of it which hangs between your breasts. You are a religious girl, don't tempt me any more. I shall save myself from you by flight without even seizing a kiss."

" Let me have a companion of my way," says Sterne, " were it but to remark how the shadows lengthen as the sun declines." As I go on my way through the country in sunset I too feel the need of a companion —someone to whom I could translate my sympathies. Perhaps it is the subtle influence of Mercedes, but I feel full of gushing sympathy with the world in general as the sun goes down. In the morning when I tramp through the country I feel as hard as steel and as firm a lord over myself as Julius Cæsar. But towards evening I become more mellowed and more full of human kindness. My eyes sometimes fill with tears when I think of the swift-fading beauty of the world and I long for a companion in my loneliness. As night advances the melancholy deepens to depression and it is time to take the fiddle out of my case and play for myself. Many a time out in the wilds I have come across old flute-players and fiddlers seated under a tree playing to themselves to drive away the demon of melancholy. In the evening I am less hardened against the slings and arrows of misfortune. Early in the day I can enter a village with as much arrogance as a Picaresque knave of the Golden Age ; no bands of urchins throwing stones at my portly figure dismay me ; no yelping dogs make me tremble ; I can swing my stout stick and beat back the mangy curs with the nonchalance of a Romany chal. But when night falls, even the sound of barking terrifies me and I wonder what tricks some of those irrepressible boys may play upon me.

Sometimes I deliberately avoided the village at night-time and camped outside. But I had made the mistake of dressing too lightly for the Basque country in that treacherous summer. When I left England I expected to sleep out of doors in the sultry nights of Spain, forgetting that the Basque country is mountainous and open to the squalls from the Bay of Biscay.

The day I left San Sebastian was sunny and there

was every prospect of being able to camp out under
the trees. After passing through the town of Zarauz
I searched for a comfortable nook where I could pass
the night. At last I discovered a sheltered corner off
the road at the foot of some trees. It was about ten
o'clock and not a sound could I hear save the distant
barking of some dogs in the farmhouses. After lighting a fire of twigs I laid my cape upon the ground and
prepared for sleep. How simple are the needs of a
wanderer who tramps through the world by himself.
My cape of black and white plaid was given me by a
shepherd—a rough cape it was, but it was an efficient
wrap on a summer night provided there was not too
heavy a fall of dew. There is a Spanish proverb—
" *Debajo de mala capa suele haber un buen bebedor* "—
(" Beneath a shabby *capa* you'll find a good drinker ").
My *capa* is a poor one, but I have my wine-skin handy.
Nobody should ever sleep in the open in Spain without a full wine-skin, for there again the Spanish proverb
warns—" *A mala cama es bien un colchón de vino* "—
(" When you've a hard bed lie on a pillow of wine ").
When I left San Sebastian my wine-skin was bulging
like Silenus's paunch, but during the toil of the day I
had visited it assiduously and now at night it was flaccid
and woebegone. A plague on my thoughtlessness :
why did I not fill it at Zarauz ? There is no companion
fit for the lonely watches of the night save the *bota*.

Whether it was the lack of wine to mellow my rest
I do not know, but I could not sleep. The night was
heavy and sultry and the heavy smell of the earth and
the thick vegetation filled the air. In the distance I
heard the monotonous murmur of the waves beating
upon the rocks below the cliffs. At last, after tossing
about on my hard couch, I snatched a brief period of
rest.

When I awoke, the fire had burnt itself out: all was dark around me. Then drops of rain pattered upon me and a slight breeze shook the branches of the trees above. Soon there was a heavy downpour. In a few minutes I was drenched through and I began to fear that the rain would even soak through my light violin-case and injure the instrument. Gathering up my belongings I struggled out of my leafy den and made for the road. The wind had risen now and was blowing the rain in my face as I struggled, and there was not a light anywhere. I had one crushed cigarette in my pocket which I tried to light, but alas my matches were soaked! Not a drop of wine in my *bota*, not a crumb of bread or cheese in my rucksack—I was in a state of mournful misery. Then my Sancho Panza personality cursed my Quixotic nature with all the expletives at his command. " Next time you go vagabonding," said he, " mind you don't forget to buy the Hiker's Annual or ' Tramping without Tears.' Why, any boy scout who has attended a jamboree would laugh you to scorn."

But then my Quixotic companion answered: " Out on it, man; get thee behind me, pot-bellied Sancho: the true vagabond is no hiker who has visited Woolworths and bought all the gadgets for his tour. I am a knight-errant: I long for hardship. Few adventures come to the man who lies in slothful ease upon a feather bed. Rage on, wind, and let the skies pour rain in pailfuls. I'll rejoice."

" Adventures fiddlesticks ! " said Sancho. " You'll find them and no mistake. But the principal one will be double pneumonia if you go on tilting at storms."

After walking aimlessly on for a while I came to a house shuttered and bolted. I knocked at the door— timidly at first but then with ever-increasing sound.

No reply. I threw pebbles at the windows—no reply.
Then in a little window on the second floor I saw the
light of a candle. I shouted. Then suddenly the light
went out, but I could see a white face pressed against
the glass.

"Open the door, open, please," I cried in Spanish.
The pale face stared at me but did not move.

The rain ran down my face and neck in streams. I
was desperate and I gesticulated in excited fashion; I
threw pebbles up at the window; I rushed over and
knocked at the door.

Five minutes, ten minutes, fifteen minutes passed, but
no one descended to open the door. The white face
still stared at me from the window, without moving.

To this day I still wonder whether it was a real face
at the window or whether it was my hallucination.

After leaving the house I went to two others, but
I met with no better success. Decidedly the fates were
against me that night. Perhaps in the storm the inhabitants of the village thought I was afflicted with the
*begisko*, as the Basques call the evil eye.

After knocking unsuccessfully at the third house I
gave up trying to appeal to humanity and I searched
for a shed where I could lie in shelter until dawn.

My teeth were chattering with cold, I was drenched
to the skin and there was no possibility of obtaining
a light. At last I discovered a rough outhouse with
some straw in the corner, where I was able to divest
myself of some of my drenched garments. Then in
order to restore my circulation I practised Swedish
exercises with as much vigour as a sergeant-major.

In all such uncomfortable predicaments our guardian
angel does not leave us altogether forlorn. At the moment of blackest despair there is always the ray of hope.
As I was searching in my soaked rucksack for even a

particle of dry clothing I suddenly discovered a little bottle.

It was a flask, half full of Martell's brandy which I had stored away in case of emergency.

No nectar or ambrosia ever tasted so sweet as did that four-franc brandy.

It was the softest pillow I have ever slept upon.

# CHAPTER IX

## A VISIT TO ZULOAGA

NEXT morning the sun shone brightly, and the
storm had brushed away the clouds, leaving
the sky pale turquoise blue.  Though I felt
stiff and rheumatic after my wet night I tramped along
and soon reached the small town of Guetaria.  I did
not linger in Guetaria, for my halting-place was to be
Zumaya, about ten kilometres farther along the coast.

Before I set out for Spain I had determined that I
should visit Zumaya because it is the home of Spain's
great painter, Don Ignacio Zuloaga.

"Go to Don Ignacio," said the Spanish Ambassador
in London, Ramón Pérez de Ayala, "and ask him to
map out your vagabond route through Old Castile."

So here I was on my way to Santiago Echea, the
palatial dwelling of the painter, which is situated on
the Bay of Zumaya.  "Santiago Echea" means the
house of Saint James and that name was given to it
because in the demesne is the ancient chapel wherein
pilgrims of the Middle Ages, trudging along the road
of Saint James towards far-off Compostela, used to halt
and rest their weary bodies.

As I walked up the shady avenue towards the painter's
house I felt misgivings.  I was hot, dusty and dishevelled after my tramp and I was unshaven.  "But,"
said I to myself, "Zuloaga is the great friend of the

88

Gypsies—why, some of them look upon him as a *crayi* or King. He will welcome me all the more if I knock at his door as a penniless, ragged minstrel. Yes, he will understand a *picaro*, but what about his butler and footman?"

With trepidation I lifted the huge bronze knocker that looked like a relic from a feudal castle and tried to knock softly.

The sound echoed and re-echoed through the hall and porch. At the same moment a gigantic wolfhound sprang out of a corner at me. "I am lost," said I to myself as I warded off the brute with my stick. "None of the mediæval writers tell how the minstrels avoided being torn asunder by dogs at the castle gates." Seeing a little statue of Our Lady in a niche in the wall I mumbled a prayer. I then discovered that the wolf hound was chained to his kennel. After a moment an old woman came to the door, but when she saw me she muttered what I am sure was the word *mendigos* and disappeared.

"Why not try the traditional way?" said I as I pulled out my fiddle and started to tune it. I then played as a tune of salutation a good old Basque song.

Before I reached the end of the tune I heard a loud roar of laughter and Don Ignacio Zuloaga came towards me with open arms.

"Welcome, *amigo*, welcome to Santiago Echea. Now that the Celt salutes the Basque it is time to call for wine." In a few moments I found myself drinking golden muscatel wine with my host.

Don Ignacio Zuloaga is a tall and sturdily built man, with the muscular shoulders of an athlete. He is over sixty years of age, but his ruddy complexion and moustache give him a youthful appearance. On his head he wore his *boina* or Basque cap at a rakish angle and I compared him mentally to a well-known *pelota* player I had known at Saint Jean de Luz. Don Ignacio, I may add, is a very good *pelota* player and has beaten some of the champions. The real secret of his restless agility, his bright eye and his rhythmic poise is his skill as a bull-fighter. One of the first souvenirs he showed me was the collection of bright posters announcing his performances as a *matador* in various bull-rings of Spain. All his longing for the feverish excitement of the *corrida* with its varied colours and intense drama has been translated into his paintings, many of which hang in European galleries. And after the *corrida* Don Ignacio would go off to visit his Gypsy friends in Villa Rosa, the haunt of the Madrid " cantaores de Flamenco," or else Triana in Sevilla. In his Gypsy and bull-fight scenes he has always disdained to show the false exotic Spain *de pandereta*, as Juan Valera called it, for he knows the true life of the Romany chals in the Albaicín or in Cádiz. As a true Spaniard he knows that the dancing of a Pastora Imperio or the bull-fighting of a Gitanillo de Triana is as striking a symbol of Spain as a play by Lope de Vega or a " romance " by Góngora.

After my ascetic life of the past few days, I was able to appreciate to the full the generous hospitality of Don Ignacio. A succulent banquet was served to us in the big porch which looks out on the Cantabrian Sea. *Sopa de almejas a la pescadora*—a soup of mussels richly flavoured and tasting of brine, followed first by *Sar-*

*dinas a la asturiana,* then by *chuletas a la leonesa,* with plenty of red Rioja wine to mellow the feast.

"At such a feast as this, Don Ignacio, I should play a hymn of thanks between the courses and dance when the fumes of the wine go to my head."

"*Hombre,*" answered Don Ignacio, "you have come to the right country if you are a minstrel. Here in Guipúzcoa we have a host of wandering singers and poets who roam from one village to another, reciting ballads and improvising songs. If you were one of those *bertsularis* or improvisers, you would meet a rival in a *posada* and then you would stage a contest with him. The crowd in the inn would give the theme for each of you in turn to improvise upon. And after a long struggle the judges would declare the winner. Yes, my friend, if you were a good singer you could make a mint of money with *canciones de maldecir* in the traditional style for reviling your enemies, or else *canciones de amigo* for extolling the hospitality of your friends."

The mention of bardic traditions awakened memories in Don Ignacio's mind and he began to tell me of his early life in the small town of Eïbar in the heart of the province of Guipúzcoa. Eïbar, he told me, was a miniature Toledo of North Spain, inhabited by a population of metal-workers. "Go to Eïbar," said he, "and you will meet the dwarfs of Velázquez.

"I have never forgotten those forges of Vulcan with their fires lighting up the faces of those grotesque smiths."

Don Ignacio loves to recall Eïbar because in that town stands the old house of his father Placidio Zuloaga, the Spanish Benvenuto Cellini, who more than any artist contributed to the Renaissance in Spain of the ornamental incrustation upon metals.

Such were the surroundings in which the famous painter was reared. In early childhood he worked as an apprentice in the art of damascening, but a chance visit to Madrid led him to the Prado Museum. Henceforth his mind was made up; he would be a painter. Velázquez thrilled him to ecstasy, but it was El Greco who profoundly influenced his life.

"All my life," said he, "I have had a passion for El Greco. When I was a young student in Paris in 1889 I was as poor as Lazarillo de Tormes. You might have seen me walking about Montmartre with my friend the sculptor, Paco D'Urio—a tattered pair of Bohemians we were. Often I went without food, not because I was short of money but because I saved it all to buy an El Greco. In those days people would laugh at me scornfully for my apostolate of El Greco, but instead of paying attention to their gibes, I would tighten my belt, stint my food, borrow money and rush off to buy another masterpiece. El Greco is my god. Some of us like Meier Graefe and Maurice Barrés felt that we had the vocation to sing through the world the message of Theotocopuli the God-hatched bird. Come now with me and you will see one of the last works of the enigmatic master." So saying he led me from the house to the lofty studio, which stands at the other end of the garden. Then telling me to shut my eyes, he drew out the picture from the strong-room and set it at one end of the studio. "Now open your eyes," said he, "and gaze upon the Apocalypse. Remember the words which the painter's friend Góngora engraved upon his tomb:

"Esta forma elegante, oh peregrino,
De pórfido luciente dura llave,
El pincel niega al mundo más suave,
Que dió espíritu al leño, vida al lino."

On the vacant wall of the studio the frame of the picture was a window. Through the window I saw a pallid ghostly vision. Saint John the Evangelist, a giant in stature, dressed in flowing habit, was praying over the débris of the world. With face uplifted in ecstasy and arms outstretched he knelt transfigured by his vision, for the Lamb had opened the seventh seal and there was silence in the sky and on earth after the storm. The four horses of War and Hell had galloped through the air bringing the legions of hell in their train. But now there was a deathly stillness and from the sky a ghastly white light illuminated the desolate scene. As the Evangelist in this lonely waste implored God to descend in judgment, men and women rise from their tombs, cast off their shrouds and join their imploring voices to that of the Saint. In the dark, threatening clouds moving across the firmament the shadowy figures of angels are seen.

The strained figure of the Saint and the small ghostly figures are dwarfed by the infinity of the space surrounding them. The whole picture is a sudden vision of the feverish personality of El Greco at the end of his life when he was conscious of his approaching death and wished to dash on to the canvas the strange, deformed shadowy presences that haunted his dreams. In such a dream world there are no classic proportions of normal life. Those livid, wild-eyed figures moving through shadowy immensities all form part of a gigantic harmony that resounded through the mind of the painter who was the contemporary of Don Quixote. Like the knight of the sad countenance he deformed the exterior world of the senses so as to raise it to a symbol. Instead of painting the life he saw around him in Toledo he painted thoughts and associations of ideas such as arose in the minds of the mystics of sixteenth-century

Castile—Saint Teresa and Saint John of the Cross.
"Remember," said Don Ignacio, "one significant detail that we do know of that mysterious artist who shut himself up far away from the prying eyes of his contemporaries. Music thrilled him and he had in his service a permanent band of musicians to play to him while he painted."

"Yes, Don Ignacio, many of those strange pictures with their element of cosmic endlessness suggest music. El Greco as he advanced in life seemed to be for ever trying to illustrate harmonies floating through his mind."

After showing me his El Greco, Don Ignacio led me out into the garden. It was a relief to pass from the shadowy world of El Greco into the golden sunlight once more. The grass was so green, the trees rustled gently and the birds sang sweetly.

"How good it is to be alive, Don Ignacio, and have a rollicking Pagan life again after all the tortured melancholy of ancient Castile. Lead me over to your rose garden where the fountain bubbles up and flows over the tiles ornamented in ancient Moorish pattern."

Seated beneath the trees we drank wine and conversed pleasantly like two shepherds out of the pastoral eclogues of Garcilaso de la Vega.

Don Ignacio then said: "You are wrong to think of Castile as a place of melancholy black shadows and sadness. It is true to say that the Castilian is obsessed by the idea of Death but that is only because he worships life with passion."

"Ah, yes, Master; Spain was the truest home of the Dance of Death where the skeleton danced merrily with the king, queen, knave and the bride on her wedding morn. Spain is the only country that ever erected a supreme monument to death—the majestic Escorial which rose out of the Castilian landscape as a perpetual *memento mori* at the very moment when Spanish vitality was at its highest.  Remember, Don Ignacio, that the greatest poem on death in the Spanish language was written by that dissolute vagabond the archpriest of Hita whose mirthful slogan was 'gather ye rosebuds while ye may.'

"'Ay Muerte! muerta sseas, muerta e malandante!
Matásteme mi vieja : matasses a mi enante!
Enemiga del mundo, que non as semejante :
De tu memoria amarga non sé quien non se espante!'

And yet those lines were written as a lament by the reveller on the death of his disreputable pander, the old hag Trotaconventos.   The Spanish conception of Death springs from that racial *nobleza* and dignity of man who is dethroned by Death."

"Yes," answered Zuloaga, "that is the eternal paradox of Spain.  To-day when you wander through the country-side you will find in close juxtaposition symbols of life and death.  Take the bull-fight with its pageantry of colour, movement, music, leading up to the death of the bull.  Watch the *torero* in his *traje de luces* performing the part of high priest in the blood sacrifice.  Then take our *coplas* with their wild poetry always obsessed by the swift approach of death.  Come, let me show you how I once expressed the antithesis in the Spanish soul."

He then led me back into the studio and brought out three of his pictures which he arranged in a row so as to form a triptych.  The central picture which was called "*los flagelantes*" describes a custom which, the painter told me, used to be performed in Holy Week in some of the villages near Segovia : while the ceremony of the Descent from the Cross is carried out in the open air, the penitents flog themselves in turn.  In the picture we see some of the penitents lowering down the figure of Christ from the Cross by ropes while one of the flagellants kneels at the foot, naked to the waist, with face masked, and in his hand he holds the lash ready to flog his back as soon as the figure of Our Lord touches his head. Already the statue has touched the flagellant, for from his white back streams blood, and the congregation of villagers with their priest in full canonicals gaze devoutly upon the scene. In the distance we can see the village houses and the mountain ridge.

"*Los flagelantes*" shows one phase of the Spanish soul which appears throughout the history of the peninsula. The wizened faces of those peasant men and women of Castile, the old houses, the melancholy sadness of the scene give a mystical interpretation of ancestral Spain.

Don Ignacio, without saying a word, pointed to the two pictures of narrower dimensions standing at each side of "*los flagelantes*." In one was an arrogant *torero*, dressed in a green *traje de luces*, and in the other was a beautiful Spanish *maja* dressed alike in green, but with black mantilla over her head and shoulders. In the two lateral figures the painter intended to symbolize the joy of life and in the central picture the sadness, but in looking at the *torero* and the *maja* it was impossible not to discover beneath the gay exterior an intense melancholy expression. Though they were both sprung from the people there was in their features and expression an air of aristocracy as though they were the offspring of an ancestral line.

Don Ignacio would not pause to discuss his pictures, but he began to show me them one after another in rapid succession. I had the sensation of passing swiftly through the whole social history of modern Spain. I saw portraits of famous writers such as Unamuno, Ayala,

Ramón del Valle Inclán; scenes among the fishermen of the Basque coast or else the inaccessible Batuecas : vivid *fiestas* in Sevilla. Like Goya, Zuloaga is large-hearted and generous in sympathy. Every type of humanity interests him, from the dwarf of Eïbar to Agustina the Queen of the Gypsies. His sympathy does not stop with human beings but also includes animals. One of his most beautiful pictures called " The Victim of the Feast " shows a horse that has been gored by the bull being led out of the ring by a *picador*. The scenes of Gypsy festivities with their visions of bright mantillas, high combs and castanets were the most brilliant and exotic, but I preferred the scenes of Castile where the painter interpreted the intensity of that hard-baked land with its unending variations of brown and grey. When I told him of my preference he replied : " Though I am a Basque and a patriotic one at that, I am most active in my work when I live in Segovia, for there I never fail to find queer grotesque types as models. Here in this Basque garden life is too soft and easy. In order to feel pulsating energy of mind and body I must go to my castle at Pedraza, not far from Sepúlveda in the province of Segovia. In the ruin of the ancient castle on top of a mountain I have built a studio and from its windows I can gaze upon a great stretch of Castilian sky and landscape. Up there I lead an ascetic life. I am far away from the modern world and I can live the timeless existence of the traditional Castilian. For you should remember that though I am born a Basque from Eïbar yet I refuse to sacrifice my universal heritage for any regionalism. It was Castile made Spain and every one of us whether we are Basques, Galicians or Andalusians must go forth from our narrow regions and become Castilian, for it was Castile that made the Spanish world."

Before I left Zuloaga's house the shades of evening had begun to deepen. The painter with pen and paper carefully traced out the route I was to follow in my tramp through Old Castile and he did not forget to point out villages where I should have opportunities of meeting Gypsies.

"Whenever you come across a tribe of *Canasteros* or basket-making Gypsies," said he, "don't trust any of them except the old man who is chief, for they are rascals most of them, and in these lean days of revolution a fat, juicy *forastero* is always a tempting morsel."

With rucksack well stocked and full wine-skin I said farewell to the hospitable painter and departed on my way.

## CHAPTER X

## THE HOUSE OF LOYOLA

A S it was dusk when I left Zuloaga's house I did not walk for many hours. My next objective was Loyola, but it was impossible to reach it on the same day, so I halted at Cestona, about eleven kilometres from Zumaya, and foraged for sleeping-quarters. The weather was dark and chilly and I did not want to repeat my damp experience of the previous night. In the Café-*posada* of Cestona I was graciously received by the proprietor—a tall, muscular bruiser of a man with no collar to his shirt and a fortnight's growth of beard on his sallow face. There was a *tertulia* in the café and my fiddle was welcome. After serving me my *cocido* and some wine the host pointed to my case saying: "Why not play a tune for the company?"

"Certainly, Señor. As many as you wish. Let us go shares in the profits."

From experience I have found that this profit-sharing scheme is an admirable method to adopt in *posadas*, public-houses and bars, for the whole performance depends for success not so much on the talents of the minstrel as on the encouragement given by the landlord or waiter. Watch my landlord of Cestona; how he goes up to the groups of men arguing or playing cards or dominoes. He is a subtle manager of publi-

99

city—an effective producer who sets the stage for Hamlet. I was wise to offer him thirty per cent. of the takings, for he has awakened the interest of those dour Basques. Without his help I could not have excited that cold audience even by standing on my head as I fiddled. As it was I had a most successful evening financially, and the landlord gave me a snug room at the back of the house at the price of a peseta.

When I entered the Basque country I had the fixed idea that the Basques were fierce defenders of their religion. But in Zumaya and in Cestona if one could judge from the *tertulias* in the *posadas* there is still the eternal struggle between Carlist and Clerical on the one hand, and Liberal and Republican on the other. Every *tertulia* was a superb illustration of Spanish individualism. " Yes, every Spaniard is a Satanic rebel," said I to myself as I watched two men at Cestona shout at one another across a table. Both were flushed with anger, and sweat was trickling down their faces in streams. I was afraid of sharp oaths followed by the glint of steel, but I was misjudging the Basques. It is a tradition in these parts to indulge in fierce verbal encounters into which the opponents put all their muscular energy.

" It is good for trade," said my confederate the innkeeper as he brought frothy bottles of beer to the thirsty warriors. Political discussion in those Basque villages takes the place of dramatic performances, for each man acts his part. He knows that he will never sway his opponents, for it would be unmanly for a Basque to yield even to the most irrefutable logic, and so again and again the tavern *tertulia* becomes the scene of the same frenzied dialogue. Sometimes unwittingly I found myself dragged in as a weapon for laying low an opponent. It all arose because I meekly informed the company that I was going on foot to the shrine

of Saint Ignatius de Loyola.   The religious warrior of
Carlist tradition—a haggard, grey-haired man, blear-eyed
and toothless—then said in a wheezy voice : " Bravo !
Here is your health, stranger !   I like your spirit.   Why
don't all the Basques follow your example and tramp
as pilgrims to Loyola ?   When are we all going to revive the chivalry of Saint Iñigo de Loyola and drive
all those false heretics and pagans like swine into the
sea ? "   The old man was straightway cut short by a
ruddy-faced cattle-dealer in a blue smock who snapped
in a sharp tone :  " The curse of the whole Basque land
is that it is priest-ridden.   Please God they'll not last
long, otherwise the Revolution was mere foolishness.
And as for the Jesuits, the sooner they take to their
heels the better, for they were nothing but *señoritos*
aping the nobility.   Aye, rank capitalists, every man of
them.   Keep away from Loyola, *amigo*, I warn you.
They say the government in Madrid will drive the
Jesuits out and turn it into a *manicomio* or asylum."

Finding myself fully launched into a choleric dispute
I thought it most prudent to retire, for a stranger is
never in a safe position in the political and religious
quarrels of a country.   But the difficulty is to choose
a subject of conversation which will be perfectly inno-
cuous, for even a sport like *pelota* arouses the fiercest
discussions.   In England when conversation is flagging
among my men friends and they begin to yawn there
is only one remedy :  start a discussion about women.
Such a remedy would not be efficacious in the Basque
country.   If I were to talk in a flippant way about
Basque housewives or marriageable maidens the two
political adversaries would snap off their wordy warfare and gaze at me in shocked surprise.   They would
then make me understand the enormity of my conduct.
Women are kept far away from the scandalous tongues

of men, that is why one sees so few of them in the *tabernas* of Guipúzcoa. I have not seen a single skirt in Cestona this evening. Where are they hiding? Behind close shutters they are tending their multitudes of children, for each Basque mother seemed to have at least six children. It is only eleven o'clock and the night is balmy but not a serenade do I hear—no twang of a guitar outside a lady's casement—no distant sound of the *irrintzi* or savage primeval shout of the Basques from the hills. However, Mari, the drudge of the *posada*, did rescue me from complete disillusion by her delicate attentions. She was a tall, bony girl with fair hair, pink and white complexion and red, puffy hands, but she was as deft a seamstress as I have ever met. In climbing over a jagged wall that night I tore the seat of my one and only pair of khaki trousers. They had resisted bravely many an escapade, but now at last they were defeated. My position was desperate, for I could not appear next day on the road at the risk of being pelted by the natives for indecent exposure. There was nothing to do but to go to bed until the trousers were repaired. "Now, Mari," said I to the girl when she came up to my room, "here are the trousers. It rests with you whether I can start to-morrow on my journey. I must reach the monastery of Loyola in the morning, so use all your skill, Mari, I am at your mercy." Early next morning there was a light knock on my door. It was Mari with my trousers patched up as though they had never suffered at all. In one of the pockets I found a little blessed medal of Saint Ignatius which the girl had put there for luck.

The scenery from Zumaya to Azpeitia reminded me of the glens of Scotland, owing to its melancholy. As I approached nearer to Loyola the panorama became more harsh and rugged, with rows of frowning mountains encircling like Giants. The sky was dark and threatening; the huge storm-clouds descended upon the peaks and in the valleys there was mist. After passing through Azpeitia I perceived the majestic pile of the monastery protected by chain after chain of mountains in the background.

I followed a procession of women dressed in black into the *Casa Santa*.

My first impression was one of disenchantment. The rugged scenery led me to expect austerity in the dwelling-place of the Saint, but I was shocked to find that the original fortified building was hidden away in the huge, baroque building of 1681.

The original building, dating from remote antiquity, was a grim fortress overlooking the valley of the River Urola.

The original walls were built of huge boulders, sometimes nearly two metres in thickness, and at each of the four corners of the building there were castellated towers. In the Middle Ages such a fort was a secure retreat for the fierce warriors of the Loyola family, whose heraldic emblem was the wolf. So fierce were those barons of Loyola that in the fifteenth century the King ordered the upper storeys of the house to be razed to the ground.

Such were the warlike traditions that echoed through the mind of Ignatius the gallant soldier when he inhabited this house. But in later centuries when the Society of Jesus had grown in wealth and power it was decided to make the house into a gorgeous sanctuary and reliquary in honour of the Saint's glory.

And so the lonely pilgrim who goes to Loyola to discover the austere spirit of Saint Ignatius will wander, as I did, disconsolately through room after room overgilt and over-ornamented. The chapel of the reliquary,

I was told, was during the lifetime of the Saint the dining-room of the family, but to-day there is nothing to remind us of a baronial hall. There is a profusion of white marble, and the walls are studded with innumerable niches where relics are preserved in tiny sculptured shrines of gold and silver. In this bejewelled chapel there was just one pathetic relic of the dim past —a worm-eaten door leading to the ancient Oratory.

The Oratory was erected in 1498, when the Saint was only seven years old, to commemorate the marriage of his elder brother to Doña Magdalena de Araoz, a maid of honour of Queen Isabel the Catholic. It was here that Saint Ignatius spent his days when he was recovering from the terrible wound he had received in the defence of Pamplona. One of his legs had been fractured by a cannon-ball and the other injured by a splinter. After being captured by the French he was by them taken to Loyola where he spent a long period of painful confinement. When he recovered from his wound he found that his fractured leg had been badly set, and with grim determination he consented to the painful operation of having it rebroken in order to be set again. Once again he had to undergo a long period of convalescence, lying on a couch in this room.

It was here that his conversion took place.

He read with intense interest the Romances of chivalry describing the fantastic exploits of a host of knights-errant, who rode out in quest of adventure. Granada had only recently been captured and the spirit of chivalry still glowed white-hot in the hearts of the Spaniards.

Ignatius, however, had lived to satiety the life of a knight of fortune and he had become disillusioned with the purposeless, warring episodes. It was then that he turned to the only other romances that were then known in Spain—the lives of the Saints. As he read of Saint

Benedict, Saint Francis and others who had renounced the pleasures of the world he became fired with zeal to follow their example. But he was a warrior—a knight sprung from Spanish chivalrous tradition. He would continue to be a knight, but a knight of Christ, bound by the rigid discipline which he would impose on his obedient followers.

As I was meditating over the wonderful conversion of Saint Ignatius, which had taken place in that very room, I noticed a young Jesuit, kneeling near me praying devoutly. To guide me in my meditation, I gazed in my mind's eye at the portrait by Sánchez Coello which shows the Saint not as a knight in coat of mail but as a haggard ascetic, with deep-set eyes, though the moustache and grim mouth remind us that he was still a soldier. When I observed carefully the young Jesuit I noticed that he bore a close resemblance to the portrait. He was if anything still more haggard, with parchment skin and deep-set eyes beneath dark eyebrows. There was the same sharp aquiline nose, the thin pursed lips, but there was no moustache. He was about thirty years of age, the same age as the Saint when the great crisis in his life took place. I pretended to pray, but merely in order to have the opportunity of studying his features at my leisure. At last he made the Sign of the Cross and stood up to go. I followed him out of the Oratory and as a pretext begged him to show me round the house.

"With great pleasure, Señor," said he; "have you seen the Reliquary?"

"Yes, father, I have seen it: in fact I have seen the whole house, but I want to walk up and down with you and listen to you talking about Saint Ignatius."

The Jesuit smiled at my exacting request and without saying a word led me down the stairs and out into the open air. Up and down we walked in the space below the steps leading to the Basilica.

"When I saw you praying in the Oratory, father, I thought you were the Saint himself."

"Ah, Señor, you were influenced by the *ambiente*. Everyone who goes in there feels the invisible presence of Our Saint and founder."

"What will happen to all this monastery, and indeed to all of you now that the Republic has been declared ? "

"Quién sabe ? Loyola is crowded with members of our order who have had to flee from the incendiarists in the cities. We are ready to leave at any moment. Who knows when that will be ? But be certain of one thing, Señor : we shall return to this *Casa Santa* of our founder one day soon, even if they scatter us to the ends of the earth."

"Why does the government attack you so bitterly ? "

"Because we are the sword of Rome."

"But surely Rome to-day does not need the sword but rather the olive branch of peace. We hear too much of war and rivalry. Why don't you all preach toleration and sweet kindliness ? "

"I am a Basque, Señor."

"So was Saint Ignatius."

"I tell you, Señor, that in this hour of peril for Spain, the Church looks to the Basques to fight for their faith. And in this Basque land there is only one hero and knight to lead us—Saint Ignatius. Now is the time for him to appear and found an order of eager youths living in the world who will arm themselves and fight for the protection of the ' Society of Jesus.' "

"But, father, the Socialists call you *capitalistas* and they accuse you of devoting yourselves exclusively to educating the caste of nobles, and instilling doctrines of subtle casuistry. To-day your enemies still hawk about the *Monita Secreta* or ' Secret Instructions ' for advanced members, though they were proved forgeries over three centuries ago."

" Remember, Señor, the adage—' *corto en palabras, pero en obras largo.*' We do not waste our time on idle words, for we are soldiers of Christ, and soldiers do not speak, they act. The Socialists speak truly when they say that we educate a caste of nobles. Yes, we still believe in the age of chivalry. When Saint Ignatius started upon his mission after his conversion he set out as a knight-errant, accompanied, so Padre Ribadeneira tells us, by two servants, and he undertook his life of adventures for Christ's name with the firm intention of seeking always the most difficult enterprises. And one of his first actions was to hang up his arms in the monastery of Monserrat and watch over them like any mediæval knight.

" In this way he signified to the world that he was renouncing the war of blood and iron and undertaking spiritual war. To-day we need a noble caste to carry on such chivalry, but it is not nobility of blood we seek. As the proverb goes—' *Cada cual es hijo de sus obras* '—(' By his deeds you'll know him '). It is not birth that counts but service to the ideal of chivalry. Alas, Señor, Don Quixote, the ideal Knight of Spain, was chaste and left no descendants, whereas Sancho Panza has begotten children in every corner of our country."

" Nevertheless, father," I replied, " we need loving charity, toleration and the simpler virtues more urgently than austere discipline and obedience. Forgive me for preferring the gentler and childlike spirit of Saint Francis *il poverello* of Assisi, who called poverty ' his bride.' As I speak to you I hear in my mind the soft tolling bells of Assisi calling the people to prayer. His ' Hymn to the Sun ' is of greater moment in the world to-day than

all the ' Spiritual Exercises of Saint Ignatius.' Saint
Francis preached the brotherhood of man in terms of love
—in his ardent song he called upon brother sun, brother
sea, brother birds, brother wolf—all the world was his
brother. But nobody in our storm-tossed materialistic
age remembers that hymn, and it needs some mighty
singer to chant it in tones that can be heard from one
end of the world to the other.

" Saint Francis could never be called the silent nightingale for he was always singing. He would never
have permitted his brothers to close their ears to music,
for music is a spiritual aid to prayer, and song is the
doctrine of the heart. Saint Francis did not disdain to
compare himself to the humble minstrel—the *juglar* who
wanders from village to village. ' We are *joculatores
Domini*,' he would say in his sermons, and when he
had raised his listeners up to a pitch of ecstasy he would
pretend to draw the bow of the lute across the strings,
and he would end his lesson with a song. Then Brother
Pacifico would say in a loud voice to the people : ' We
are minstrels of the Lord and for payment we ask you
to do true penance.' "

My praise of Saint Francis nettled the Jesuit and he
drew himself up proudly saying : " God has given to
every age of the world the Saint it needed. In the
twelfth and thirteenth centuries the world needed a
beatific visionary like Saint Francis to preach love and
charity. But in the days of Saint Ignatius far greater
issues were involved. The whole essence of the Roman
Catholic religion was threatened and it was necessary
that a warlike spirit should appear on earth to protect
the faith. Saint Ignatius sounded the call to duty and
iron discipline. Those who followed such a Knight of
Christ had to lead lives of sacrifice and renunciation.

" Saint Ignatius too wandered through the world,

curing the sick and helping the poor and humble of heart : Saint Ignatius was not a mute nightingale. He said on one occasion that to listen to sacred music was the greatest consolation, but when it was necessary to save the Church from 'the all-prevalent evils of the Pagan Renaissance, Saint Ignatius shut his ears even to the music of the Cathedral.

" Discipline and renunciation were his two watchwords. And to-day in this tragic Spain of ours, I say that Saint Ignatius alone will save us from annihilation. Upon the banners of Spanish youth I would embroider those two words, ' discipline ' and ' renunciation,' in letters of gold."

" Alas, father," said I, " in these days of universal crisis what good is it to talk of renunciation ? What good is it to tell the millions of starving people huddled together in cities to renounce ? What can they renounce, when they have not a crust with which to feed their children ? If Saint Ignatius came on earth to-day he would preach a stirring crusade among the richer classes and he would discipline the young men beneath his banner, but would he stir the masses of hungry humanity in the great industrial cities so profoundly as ' Il Poverello ' with his sympathy for the poor ? Wherever Francis went he would radiate peace and his smile would comfort mankind in their suffering."

The Jesuit was about to answer my arguments when another priest came up to him and drew him aside. He then turned to me saying : " I must say farewell, for duty calls me. Some other day, please God, we shall take up our argument where we left off. Meanwhile I wish you good fortune in your wanderings as a *juglar* through Spain."

After leaving the monastery I found myself surrounded by four little girls of ages ranging from eleven to thirteen, who evidently considered me a strange creature, for they all laughed and pointed at me, making rude remarks about my personal appearance. In the Spanish villages a stranger is an object of curiosity, and the children, not possessing the taciturn courtesy of their Basque parents, express their feelings in hilarious fashion. When they were wearied of laughing at me, one little girl—aged twelve, with black hair and eyes like Carmen, left her frolicking companions and came up to me, smiling ingratiatingly. When she was close to me she put out her hand and gave me a slap on the face.

Loud chorus of laughter.

The little minx then said in a loud voice as she looked at my khaki trousers : " Tienes pantalones color de mierda de niños ! " Renewed laughter and blushes from me.

" What is your name ? " I asked the little girl.

" Lucía Gomez," she replied.

" Who is that fair-haired friend of yours over there, who is sticking out her tongue at me ? "

" That is my friend Carmen Aguirrezabal."

" Well, Lucía, bring your friend Carmen whatever her name is over here and we'll all go and buy sweets."

Lucía, however, looked on me as her personal property and she would not share me with anyone else. She snubbed her companions and took my arm to lead me over to the sweet-stall. Then in a solemn voice she announced : " I want to present you to my mother."

The mother, a corpulent, good-looking matron, was occupied in selling medals, post-cards, book-cutters, vases, knives, studs—all with miniature pictures of the monastery of Loyola upon them. " I hope that child of mine has not been pestering you : she has no shame. Why, she even cheeks the *curas* when they pass."

Noticing a group of five motor-buses drawn up near

by I asked the woman whether they were for tourists returning to San Sebastian.

"No, sir, those buses are from Durango and Bilbao. They are bound for Ezquioga."

"Is there a *fiesta* at Ezquioga?"

"No, sir, but there are apparitions there."

"What do you mean?"

"Have you never heard of the visions of Ezquioga? Why, it is the talk of all Spain. Yesterday it is said that fifty thousand were praying on the hill at Ezquioga, with their arms outstretched, and four people saw Our Lady."

"What do the priests say about it?"

"Oh, they don't say much, yet, Señor, but they will approve. You must go there, Señor, and see for yourself. You may even see 'La Dolorosa' yourself— *quién sabe?* Though you have a *cara de hereje* like a guitarist I used to know at Iraeta."

The woman's words had excited my curiosity.

Why not go there immediately? It was some distance from Zumárraga, the woman said. With luck I could reach the village in time for the evening celebration on the hill.

"Take me with you," said Lucía. "I want Our Lady to appear to me as she did to the two children of Ezquioga."

With a hurried farewell to Lucía and her mother I departed on my way towards Zumárraga.

## CHAPTER XI

# THE VISIONS AT EZQUIOGA

I

BY the time I reached Zumárraga dusk was falling and I felt weary and crestfallen. Everybody I met on the road told me different stories about Ezquioga : some said that I should go to the left, others urged me to take a short cut over the hills to the right : some said it was four leagues away, others said two and a bit. As I was ambling along I was accosted by a youngish man who was carrying a sack on his shoulders.

"You look footsore, stranger. By the instrument you are carrying I infer that you are a *tocaor* or minstrel. Ah, well, minstrels never have good legs."

"How so, sir," I replied ; "good legs I have, for to-day I've tramped all the way from Loyola's shrine."

"*Caramba*," replied the young man ; "you must be one of the pilgrims of the old days : precious few you'll find to-day since the republic has been declared."

"Well, Señor, in a way I am a pilgrim, for I am off to Ezquioga, but devil a bit can I find the way."

The young man became thoughtful at these words and paused before he answered : "I know where Ezquioga is, but what do you want with Ezquioga ? Leave that to the *beatas* and clerics. 'Son cosas de monjas!' I don't hold with the Ezquioga fairy-tale at all : I am a Spanish republican and I say : ' To hell with the Church, the clerics and all their machinations.' Come, sir, follow me to a tavern in Zumárraga, and we'll drink to the prosperity of new Spain."

On we walked chatting gaily and soon we came to a small bar where we stood one another several penny rounds of *chiquitos*, or small glasses of red wine from Rioja.

The young man's name was Juan José and he was a comb-maker by profession and came from Legazpia, six miles from Zumárraga. He was a thickset youth, above middle height with ruddy face and a great shock of untidy black hair escaping in bushy masses from under his *boina*. He was dressed in a coarse blue jacket ; around his neck he wore a big tie of violent red : his trousers were tightly shaped to his leg and so short that they did not altogether reach the top of his tan boots.

After a few drinks, Juan José became a brother and told me all his family history. I was feeling worried, for I wanted to move on to Ezquioga, but when I timidly mentioned the word, Juan José would burst out into fierce invective against the wiles of the Church and say : " It is all a conspiracy of the Jesuits." At last he said : " Señor, I shall accompany you to Ezquioga and take you there by the shortest route, but on one condition : you must promise to stop for drinks at every tavern we pass."

I accepted his terms with alacrity and off we went.

Juan José had no intention of setting off into the wilds at once : from one bar to another we roamed until we had completed the circular tour of Zumárraga. In some of them he would introduce me to the company as a *un gran tocaor*, and I had to take my fiddle from its case and play the "Guernica Tree" song and zortzico dances until I was tired. Juan José danced up and down the bar, sang Basque songs, Galician songs, Seguidillas—all in a hoarse, cracked voice. Then he would walk up mysteriously to the landlord and whisper in his ear that I was a foreigner—a famous foreigner from a far-off country, say America, and I was on my way to spy on the *barbaridades* that were being committed in Ezquioga by aristocrats and clerics—for I was " un buen amigo de la República."

At last I managed to draw him away from the bars of Zumárraga, and we began to plod our way up the mountain road.

The night was dark and stormy : the sky lowered threatening with masses of scurrying clouds and the rain at moments lashed our faces as we walked on. But rain or wind did not trouble Juan José as he lurched tipsily forward singing songs at the top of his voice. Though I had drunk a great deal I felt dispirited and sad as I walked along in the gloomy night trying to keep up with my companion. Suddenly he stopped dead in the middle of the road and when I came up, he said to me in a low voice : " Have you any money on you ? " When I answered in the affirmative, he continued : " Then put it in your trousers pocket." " Why ?" I asked in some alarm. " Because there are a lot of robbers about."

I trembled, thinking of highwaymen lying in wait for unsuspecting pilgrims, and for a moment I thought of turning back but Juan José's next words tranquillized me. He had only wished to warn me against the pickpockets at Ezquioga who concealed themselves amid the crowd of praying pilgrims and filched their purses when they were in the ecstasy of prayer.

After we had gone a little distance Juan José turned off the road to a farmhouse and knocked loudly. After a while a slatternly woman came to the door and Juan

José insisted that she should give us some drink and
in addition fill my wine-skin. Thus fortified we continued on our way.

From being dejected, I began to enter the full-blown
Rabelaisian stage of drunkenness under the influence of
my volatile companion. He sang *coplas* at the top of
his voice, about his *novia*, intoning a whole litany of
praises in her honour. I began to call to mind all the
proverbs I had ever read about pilgrimages—" *Si fueres
a buscar novia que no sea en romería* "—(" If you go to
look for a bride don't let it be at a pilgrimage ") : or
else " *romería de cerca, mucho vino y poca cera.*"

On the road we met bands of peasant girls and children
returning from Ezquioga to Zumárraga. When Juan
José saw them approaching he would stand in the middle
of the road to bar their way shouting—" Have you seen
the Virgin ? " Some of them shouted back " Yes," and
laughed gaily, but one woman cursed us roundly and
shouted—" A plague on virgins."

When we arrived within a kilometre of the village of
Ezquioga, we found row after row of cars and buses
packed along the road and in the fields, and everywhere
we could see little lights burning like fairy lamps in the
woods. Here and there were countless drinking booths,
each consisting of just a table with many bottles on
it and a candle or two in glass jars to light up the
scene.

We halted at a good many of them to drink *chiquitos*
and Juan José became more and more blasphemous.

Then suddenly in the distance we heard the sound of
singing that seemed to float down to us from the sky
above. I could hear it in the far distance above the
laughing and chattering of the wine-sellers and the
whistling of the wind in the trees. Some moments it
would sound near and at other moments it seemed to

be blown away into distant echoes. Then I saw lights moving high above on the top of a hill on our left and descending slowly. Soon there was a confused murmur like a distant flood of water, and in a few minutes we were engulfed in an excited throng. Down the people came in serried ranks scattering here and there like hosts of crawling ants. The roadway was full to overflowing of gesticulating and shouting men and women : on all sides sounded the honk of motor-cars and buses.

Ezquioga is a tiny village in the valley, of not more than twelve houses, and on this night there were certainly thirty thousand pilgrims, many of whom had come from distant Basque and Navarre towns. After pummelling and pushing our way we reached the central house of the village which combined the functions of inn and tavern. In the bar we struggled like demons in a crowd of sweating peasants. Juan José had now arrived at the critical stage of inebriation—it just needed the *coup de grâce* to put him definitely out of action. Luckily, in the serried throng, his blasphemous sallies passed unnoticed and soon he was surrounded by his personal friends who did their best to calm him. In the hazy depths of his consciousness he wanted to do me a good turn, so he went up to the proprietor of the inn and told him I was a *forastero muy importante*, that I had come to study the apparitions and I was to be given a room and food. The proprietor then called for one of his daughters and ordered her to give her bedroom up to me. When I returned to look for my friend Juan José I found him in the middle of the road surrounded by a host of girls : he was dancing away in tipsy fashion and stopping every now and then to hurl an obscene joke at the world in general. At last his friends seized him by both arms and dragged him away. I finally saw him lurching away in the dark on the long road to his native village. I wished his guides luck on their ten-mile tramp.

The house where I was to stay was the most important in the village, because it was a tavern and had a telephone. All the richer pilgrims halted there and the priests, the doctors and the journalists. When any of the faithful saw visions on the hillside, they were brought to this house and their accounts were examined by doctor and priest and written down by zealous secretaries. At the moment of our arrival I saw a girl carried in by four men, unconscious, and deposited in a room upstairs. A big crowd of women followed weeping and wringing their hands as though the girl was dead.

Downstairs there was a scene of great activity. I found the proprietor of the house, old Simón, serving drinks to his customers with methodical efficiency A characteristic old Basque peasant he was—crafty and hardbitten, with a roguish sense of humour. He was not a monarchist or a clerical—oh no ! he was a full-blown Republican, but a bit of a cynic. His moral was : " Let us encourage the apparitions at Ezquioga—that will bring the shekels in and soon we shall have enough to build our Basque *casa solar*, buy a good many adjoining fields and pile up a big balance in the bank." Old Simón is a courtly old man but as cunning as the devil, and in his opinion his Satanic majesty is no match for a Basque in bargaining and money-making. Old Simón has a large family : most of them lived abroad, earning their living, but as soon as they received news of the apparitions they hurried back to Ezquioga, to help their father and mother. I had a long conversation with one of the sons called Florencio who was helping as bartender. Florencio was an elegant young man of brown complexion, with curly black hair well oiled, wearing a lilac shirt and a purple tie. He had been learning hotel business (that is to say, following the profession of waiter) in Paris and he preferred to speak French, for it was more modern and up to date. Florencio had come back to give his daddy a hand in making money. I asked him for a glass of brandy and he advised me to drink Domecq cognac instead of the ordinary stuff which was only fit for muleteers. Incidentally he charged one peseta for a glass, though in the dearest bars of International San Sebastian it cost no more than forty cents. Florencio was a man of the world and a romantic, with his *patillas* or side-whiskers and his waisted, double-breasted coat *a lo torero*. He thought there were possibilities to be exploited in Ezquioga, for it might turn out to be a Spanish Lourdes. " Mais pour ça, Monsieur, il nous faut un miracle." Florencio's one obsession was the miracle that must take place. Every day he spoke of it and every visionary carried unconscious to the room upstairs was an object of interest to him, for on the morrow he might be the instrument of that wonderful miracle which would transform the squalid peasant village of Ezquioga into a town of brick and marble.

" You know, several rich gentlemen who are pilgrims here have promised to give thousands of pesetas towards the erection of a basilica. Why, the old tottering Conde de X. insists on leaving in his will a million to such a scheme. When the basilica has risen, it will be necessary to plan out the town and set up industries, and build houses, hotels, inns, theatres, cinemas. But before all that happens we must make it easy for the people to come here. You know, sir, the main railway line from Paris—San Sebastian to Madrid runs through a cutting only a few kilometres away.—We might get one of our local bosses to make representations to the government to have an *apeadero*, or halt, made and a road constructed

linking up the village with the railway station. Already
we have arranged an efficient service of motor-buses
between San Sebastian, Pamplona, Bilbao and Ezquioga.
The main thing is to join Ezquioga up with the great
world. And, sir, I assure you no place will ever prosper
until it is controlled by business men and artists as well
as clerics. I am an artist in my profession. I was a
waiter in Paris, but in my spare time I studied all the
technique of the hotel business : I know the secrets of
French *cuisine* and the wine-cellar. I can use them to
good purpose here, for I have drawn my own con-
clusions from observing the worthy pilgrims. After
their prayers and their genuflexions they want a tasty,
varied dinner with wine and a good *pousse-café* to crown
the meal. Imagine this dirty, squalid village with its
cabins, its lazy, ignorant set of peasants, transformed
by God's grace into an attractive town with marble
basilica up on the hill, built over the four trees where
Our Lady appeared : row on row of attractive modern
apartments with a Cinema theatre over there where you
see the cowshed.. There in the middle a *parc des eaux
vives* with flowering shrubs and a bandstand with an
orchestra playing to a crowd of people seated beneath
the trees sipping ices and cooling drinks."

The young man continued speaking in a dreamy
voice, expanding his vision like the Barber's sixth
brother. I then said to him :

"What about your republican anti-clerical government ? Surely it does not look with favour on all this
revival of religious observance ? "

"Ah! Monsieur, you forget the Spanish proverb—
'When two fight, it is the third who wins.' The
Basques are divided on the subject of religion. The
people of Bilbao are socialist and anti-clerical but those
of Guipúzcoa and Álava are religious to the core. They

will follow the priests to a man and even if the government made an end of all the clerics, the people would continue to see visions and apparitions out on the hillside. The government will go far in their attempts to conciliate the Basques and they will let Ezquioga alone, especially if everything is run on businesslike lines. My father is a Republican and I am a *libre penseur*, but my mother and sisters are *beatas*, and we have thus an ear in both camps. But, remember, Monsieur, *nous attendons le miracle*."

At half-past eleven, when the hubbub had died down, the girls in the kitchen began to prepare the supper for the guests staying in the house. I went into the dining-room and sat at a small table in the far corner so as to be as inconspicuous as possible. At the large central table three women were seated. One of them was very fat and florid with a deep booming voice and was laying down the law to her two companions. She was what the Spaniards would call a *mujerona*, but we in the English-speaking world, wishing to be polite, would say that she was a woman of commanding presence. At first sight, she reminded me of those plump female members of the Royal House of Spain that Goya painted with malicious glee, and whose faces stare arrogantly at the visitor to the Prado gallery, but there was also a touch of the Velázquez about her. Her face was originally hard and rugged, but the adipose tissue of advancing years had invaded it and filled up the seared crevasses. Her nose was the Bourbon nose but exaggerated by a carbuncle on one side : her hair was parted in the middle in the Madonna fashion and gave an appearance of chastity to a face that had no more mysticism in it than that of Juliet's nurse. She had as strong a jaw and chin as any Spanish warrior, but their strength was diminished by the sensual mouth, the thick moist lips and the tendency to gulp her words due to the loss of her upper teeth. One of the daughters of the house told me in a whisper that she was Doña Carmen de Medina, sprung from one of the old noble families of Spanish aristocracy and a sister of the Duquesa de Tarifa.

Her two companions were a contrast : one of them called Doña Julia was tall and thin, grey-haired, a bundle of nerves, with the precious and mincing air of an old maid on holiday. The other was a young lady doctor— good-looking, efficient and dressed in serviceable tweeds. Doña Carmen, in the intervals of putting Gargantuan morsels into her mouth pontificated about everything. She apostrophized the girls who were serving the dinner : she abused the cook ; she asked for the priests ; she criticized the behaviour of some of the young people at the religious service : her resonant voice echoed and re-echoed through the house. I tried to crouch in my corner, but I knew that sooner or later I should be dragged within her sphere of influence and become a butt for her inquisitive questioning. She began by pointing me out to her two companions and they all three gazed at me simultaneously : then she put a pair of silver-rimmed spectacles on the end of her nose and scrutinized me at her ease. Finally she lumbered to her feet and came over to my table, addressing me in perfect English.

"Ah ! sir, excuse me for introducing myself—I am Doña Carmen de Medina. Señor Simón has told me about you. Now I know why you have come to Ezquioga—I know—you are an Irish Catholic. You come from that little emerald isle which has more true love for our Holy Mother the Church in one of its glens, than there is in all the rest of the world."

"Ah ! Condesa, I am, as you say, an Irish Catholic,

but an unworthy one—not a true pilgrim from that land
of Saints and Scholars."

It served me not at all to be diffident of my religious
qualities, for Doña Carmen had already permanently
classified me in one of the shelves of her capacious mind
as an Irish Catholic. For her, Irish Catholic meant
saintliness and mysticism, and I was sorry that I had
not a rosary with me, for she suddenly extracted her
own voluminous black beads and turned to Doña Julia
saying : " Let us say a few Hail Marys." The three of
them in a low sing-song voice said their prayer and at
the end Doña Carmen suddenly blurted out to me :
" Now tell me about your life—what are you doing in
Spain ? Why have you come from your beautiful
island of Faith to this land of Sin and blasphemy against
God ? Here we need soldiers with stout hearts to
fight the battle of the Church against the forces of
Satan."

Beneath the inquisitorial eyes of the old lady who was
taking shape in my mind as Doña Perfecta, I felt troubled
and timid. How could I confess to her that I was
following the route of Alonso of the Many Masters, the
Arch-priest of Hita and other merry vagabonds ! Luckily
Doña Carmen did not expect any answer, for she was
one of those imperious women who declare their views
but never wait for an answer. Such people's whole life
is so rooted in assertion, that they only hear their own
voices. Destiny fortunately deafens them to any other
sound. When she had delivered, for my benefit, a
magnificent tirade against the Spanish Republican
Government—against Maura for playing false to his
family tradition, against Azaña for undermining the
army, Alcalá Zamora for pretending to be a good
Catholic and leading the Republicans : she relapsed into
a moody silence. Then for the first time I was able to

hear the squeaky voice of Doña Julia. Doña Julia with her mincing manner rhapsodized over everything whether religion, music or omelets. She was hysterically religious, and she got on my nerves because she never sat still physically or mentally, but hopped about from one subject to another like a blackbird, or thrush, prattling about generalities. On her arms she wore a great number of thin silver bangles, and whenever she made an excited gesture the bangles jingled like bells on a restive mule.

It was interesting to study the attitude of both women towards the apparitions. Doña Julia was merely hysterical and gushing. She said that she was frequently just on the point of seeing Our Lady, but she had never actually seen her—only a great brightness in the sky. Doña Carmen had the Spanish realistic mind : she longed to see, but her matter-of-fact character would not allow her to delude herself, and so she stayed on day after day at Ezquioga, hoping against hope that one day she would see the vision.

# CHAPTER XII
## THE VISIONS AT EZQUIOGA

### II

ON the following day, which was Sunday, I awoke early and accompanied Doña Carmen to Mass at the little country chapel.

It was a fresh morning with radiant sun and the birds sang sweetly as we walked along the road.

Doña Carmen carried an enormous black leather prayer-book : as for myself, I had made frantic attempts to clean up for the occasion, but I was conscious of my raggedness beside the severe grandeur of the Condesa and I felt like a reformed Gypsy who has had to shave off his side-whiskers, pare his nails and put away his iron-tipped stick. Doña Carmen touched me by her piety : though she was a daily communicant and spent a great part of the day in prayer, she was a very active and practical woman, and directed many organizations connected with the Church and the exiled monarchy. As we walked along the country road she gave me a terrible picture of the excesses committed by the Revolutionary forces in other parts of Spain, but she placed all her faith in the Basques. The Basque province and Navarre, in her opinion, would rise before long in defence of their religion. In my own mind I felt quite convinced that she was doing her best to use Ezquioga apparitions as a political lever. With glee she told me that the government in Madrid was intensely worried about the wave of mysticism that had swept over the people in this part of Spain, and it was rumoured that even the famous Doctor Marañon, one of the important men in the revolution, had come to Ezquioga disguised, in order to see the effect of the apparitions on the people. "Ezquioga is a symbol in Spain to-day," she said: "the government may call it hallucination, obscurantism or whatever it likes, but Our Lady is appearing in order to inspire the people to defend their religion.   And, I tell you that in many cases she is appearing, holding a sword dripping with blood."

In spite of her warlike views, Doña Carmen was a kind woman, for I saw her do many deeds of unselfishness and genuine charity.   On our way back from the Chapel, she stopped to speak to every peasant she met and later in the day she visited sick women of the parish, and gave money for the children of the poor, but she was a fighter, who should have lived in the good old days of the Queen Isabel, or mad Queen Joan: she should have been fighting Moors at Granada and raising the Silver Cross above the minarets of the Prophet, instead of wasting her energies in our prosaic days.   She longed for battle, and I saw her nostrils dilate like those of a war-horse when she described how civil war might come in a few weeks, with the Basques as the leaders of the revindication of the Church of Rome.

After breakfast I accompanied her and Doña Julia to the top of the hill to visit the hallowed spot.   Poor Doña Carmen found it a superhuman task to climb the steep banks, and every few steps we had to halt while she tried to recover her breath.

Up above we came to the four trees where Our Lady appeared first to the two children.   The scene reminded

me of a war-scarred area in France during the War.
Though all the country around with fields, trees, and
encircling mountains was as green as Ireland, the sacred
hill was desolate and bare of all vegetation.  The earth
had been churned up by the feet of thousands of pilgrims
and the four slender trees had been despoiled of every
leaf and the bark stripped bare by the souvenir hunters.
The four trees were pathetic sights in their nudity, like
waifs and strays that had survived from a terrible war.

As we sat near the trees, peasant women dressed in
black continually went up to them and knelt down in
prayer : then they would kiss the trunk of one of the
trees before they departed.  One woman told me that
the four trees were sent by God as a symbol : they
represented the four provinces of the Basque Kingdom :
Guipúzcoa, Navarre, Alava and Vizcaya.  Doña Carmen,
meanwhile, in a loud voice started a decade of the Rosary
and all the peasant women around joined in the repeated
prayers.  The sun was shining brightly and birds were
singing in the trees of an orchard on our left.  In front
of me stretched the glorious panorama of the Basque
mountains, for the village of Ezquioga below us lay in
a valley.  At the end of the prayers I saw a little girl
and a little boy climbing up the hill.  Doña Carmen
turned to me excitedly.  " Now, Señor, you must meet
those two children, for they were the first to whom Our
Lady appeared in the shadow of the four trees."

The little boy, Andrés Baracierta, was about nine or
ten years of age—chubby and round-faced with hair
close-cropped—as mischievous a little urchin as I have
ever seen.  When he saw us he put out his tongue and
cocked snooks with his fingers : then he threw pebbles
at Doña Julia as she prayed.  He was in fact the personification of boyish impudence.  Doña Carmen coaxed him
with a sweet, and he crept over on all fours and stood

timidly in front of us twiddling his *boina* in his hands. His sister was about eleven years of age—small and slender with black hair and great dark eyes. I have rarely seen such a tragic expression on a child's face. She looked as if she had already borne the brunt of a whole life's sorrow. Doña Carmen told me that she was very sad, because the Blessed Virgin had not appeared to her lately, though she had appeared to many other pilgrims. And so the poor little thing shut herself up in her room and refused to play with the other children.

I asked the little girl to tell me how the Blessed Virgin appeared to her and to her brother. At first she would not answer my questions, but under the persuasion of Doña Carmen and Doña Julia, she began to speak in a low monotonous voice. While she was speaking, her little brother pulled her hair and made grimaces at us, then he lay on the ground and kicked his legs up in the air. The little girl said that one day in the preceding month of June, at dusk she and her brother were leading the cows down the hill towards the stables. When they got to the foot of the hill she looked back and saw a great light between the four trees, and above the light the form of Our Lady. She then cried out to her brother : " Look, there is Our Lady between the trees." The little boy then cried out : " Yes, I can see her too." Our Lady had a white veil with stars in it and her face was very sad. She beckoned to the children and then slowly disappeared. When the children reached home, they told their parents, and soon the news of the apparition spread like wildfire through the country round. A few weeks later it is said that sixty thousand people came in the evenings to the hill and recited prayers with arms outstretched.

After the little girl had finished her story, all the women around crossed themselves and uttered a chorus of " Jesús mío." Doña Carmen in her portentous matter-of-fact voice, then started to tell a series of amazing stories of cures and conversions caused by the apparitions. She told me of a chauffeur who drove people for hire to Ezquioga to assist at the ceremonies. " He was a drunken, dissolute sot and he used to jeer at the people praying. But one night this reprobate was waiting down by his taxi, when suddenly the Virgin appeared to him out of the sky, and since then his whole life had changed and he had become a model of holiness."

Later on, when I told Doña Carmen's story to a man in the village, who was a cynic, and a republican, he gave a different interpretation. He said that all the chauffeurs in San Sebastian, Bilbao and Pamplona were very tired of Ezquioga because they had to drive for hours through the night, and after all their trouble the passengers would give them a paltry fifty-centime tip. The different motor companies reaped the golden harvest, but the poor chauffeurs were given no advantages. And so a body of them went to the chauffeur who had seen the vision and told him that on no account must he see the Virgin again because the whole business was against their interests !

During the day the hours passed very slowly at Ezquioga, for I had too restless a temperament for a pilgrim. So I used to set out on foot to visit the neighbouring villages. One day I went to Ataún, which is about eighteen kilometres south-east of Ezquioga—a characteristic old Basque village where there were houses of a type known in the Basque language as *dorreak*. The word *dorreak* is derived from the Spanish *torre*, and the houses do resemble stone towers built on narrow foundations. In those houses the main living-room or kitchen (called in Basque *sukaldia*) is on the ground floor beside the cattle-sheds. Above the ground floor is a large attic or *gambara* under the sloping roof in which the vegetables such as onions, turnips or red peppers are stored. Ataún, I may add, has an unenviable reputation among the Spanish Basques, for there is a local proverb which says : " *tonto como uno de Ataún* " —(" mad as somebody from Ataún "). Perhaps this proverb was applied by other villages to the mystic visionary nature of its inhabitants ; I met certainly more people in Ataún who said they had seen the apparitions than anywhere else. At Ataún, too, I met a visionary of a more sinister kind who assured me with a wealth of detail that he had seen the Devil appear on the hill at Ezquioga. " God help me, Señor," said he, " but I saw him with these two eyes of mine. I saw him appear above the trees—tall he was, with red hair, dressed in black and he had long teeth like a wolf. I wanted to cry out with terror, but I made the sign of the Cross and the figure faded away slowly." The devil-seeing visionary was not prepossessing in appearance. In fact he looked like the village idiot of Ataún, village of madmen. He was low-sized, bow-legged and his big head was too big for his ungainly body. His eyes had a vacant stare and his mouth was twisted into a grotesque grin when he spoke. He insisted on accompanying me on my way towards Ezquioga, though I tried innumerable times to shake him off. To tell the truth I was afraid that he might insist on climbing the hill at Ezquioga with me. What should I do if he started his devil-seeing beside me ? However, to my relief he halted at Beasaín and I continued my journey alone.

The road from Ormaiztegui to Ezquioga at this hour of sunset was crowded with people wending their way to the pilgrimage : there were buses of every description, many from places as far away as Bilbao and Miranda :

there were pony traps and carts driven by trains of mules : there were lorries laden with men, and private motors.  When I arrived back at my inn it was nine o'clock and just the hour for the celebrations to begin. Doña Carmen was surrounded by relations and was chattering away.  She introduced me to a cousin, the Duke of Kleis, an old man of eighty-four, and to various aristocrats.  She then said to me excitedly : " To-night you must climb up near the four trees, because Francisco Goicoechea, the famous " Chico de Ataún," is coming and you will see wonderful things I tell you.  He is the miracle of Ezquioga.  He becomes entirely unconscious and holds long conversations with Our Lady and she tells him things that the whole world should know. Ah ! Señor, if you only saw him : his eyes shine like stars when he is gazing upon her, and his whole face is as pale as that of one at the point of death."

" El Chico de Ataún " was a tall, strapping peasant of twenty-four years.  When he came first, he used to mock the crowd of his men friends he saw worshipping, but then one night he saw the vision and from being a coarse, brutish fellow he had become a veritable Saint John of the Cross for piety, as Doña Carmen said.

On this night, as it was generally known that he would attend, thousands of extra people came, attracted by his fame and merely to watch him.  When I was leaving the house by the back-yard to climb the hill, one of the daughters of the house ran after me to present me with a thick newspaper to prevent me from soiling my knees in the mud when praying the Rosary.  As I started to climb, the last rays of the sun lit up the mountain at the back with gold.  It was an extraordinary concourse of people : I saw every type imaginable : there were old and young, ugly and fair, aristocrat and peasant, rich and poor.  I saw a great many infirm : near me was a paralytic who had been carried up to the foot of the hill by his relatives and now three of them were upholding the poor wreck as he tried to grope his way up. There was a whole host of blind men with long sticks in their hands : some of them with little boys to guide their footsteps, others alone, stumbling and groaning as they clutched at rocks to steady their faltering steps. One blind man had a dog on a lead to guide him. There were a great many lame people on crutches striving with superhuman energy to climb the hill. Near me as I climbed, was a fat old woman who had taken off her shoes and stockings, for, as she told me, she had made a vow to climb the hill every night barefoot. Poor old woman ! Her apoplectic face became each second of a deeper hue, her soft white flabby hands grasped a diminutive umbrella to steady herself, and her mountainous bosom heaved in anguish. I assisted her a little way up to a tree against which she halted for breath. The whole hill and surrounding spaces were black with people in serried ranks. Here and there were old women selling caramels and biscuits before the prayers began.

When I struggled up to the summit of the hill I found that the space around the four stark trees had been railed off by wire, but many had climbed over it into the enclosure. The women selling biscuits did a roaring trade, and everyone was chatting gaily : scores of little boys tumbled over one another, scandalizing the older and more sedate pilgrims. One woman remarked to me sadly : " Jesús mío, qué chicos ! " " Para ellos todo esto es una corrida ! "

It was a beautiful night and all the mountains around were clearly outlined against the dark-blue sky : the moon rose and the stars twinkled through the trees. As I looked back behind the four trees I could see in the orchard the priests and altar boys with their white cassocks. Suddenly all the chattering died down and I could hear the resonant voice of the priest begin the prayers leading to the Rosary. They were said in Basque and the vast concourse of people answered back, just as a mighty chorus answers the solo singer. The Basque language has a harsh, barbaric sound : it is a man's language and has none of the softness of the Galician dialect or Portuguese.

Gradually as I heard the words : " Holy Mary, Mother of God, pray for us now and at the hour of our death, Amen," repeated again and again with the curious marked rhythm, its monotony hypnotized me into drowsiness in spite of my intensely uncomfortable position, for I was kneeling in a rut and every few seconds somebody jostled me out of position and made me fall forward on my face. The people near me were very devotional, especially the women, and they spouted the prayers as fast as they could, but every now and then they looked round anxiously as though Our Lady might descend upon them at any moment.

After the Rosary there was silence for a few minutes— one of those eerie silences that herald the approach of a moment of crisis—and then came the Litany to the Blessed Virgin which had to be recited kneeling with arms outstretched in the form of a cross. I had to give up the attempt as my kneeling position in the rut was too uncomfortable. I felt ashamed because all the old and infirm around me had their arms fully outstretched.

The Litany in contrast to the Rosary was recited in Latin, and right from the start I felt that curious sensation of collective excitement. The air had become sultry, and high above the trees in front of me I saw a thin white cloud. " Rosa mystica, Turris Davidica, Turris eburnea, Domus aurea " resounded in a vast void studded with stars. I felt as if the devotional excitement of those thousands and thousands of people had enveloped me and lifted my soul out of my body. Suddenly I heard a cry piercing through the buzzing rhythm of the Litany. All those who were kneeling near me started up and looked around. Many rushed towards the place whence the sound came, and stood in a cluster above the kneeling masses : then there was another cry and the word " Ama, ama, ama," repeated again and again spasmodically. It was a young woman who had seen Our Lady. The crowd pressed round and suddenly I saw her lifted up on the shoulders of five men and carried down the hill as though she were a corpse. Then again I became conscious of the inexorable rise and fall of the Litany—" Regina Virginum ora pro nobis," and then I heard a high-pitched voice on my left among the trees. It was the voice of a child addressing the Virgin. At times the voice continued pitched on a high note and then the child would weep frantically as she implored the favour of Our Lady. Everyone near me hushed their answers to the Litany in order to hear the sad little voice wearying itself in its anguish. The child was seeing the vision of Our Lady; she was not interceding for herself, but praying that sight and hearing might be given to her blind and deaf father who was by her side. The passionate pleading, moving because it sprang from the purest faith and expressed the intense longing of the child for the all-bountiful Mother who will bring her consolation for the sorrow of her world. All the people, whether rough men of the fields or timid little children, long for the great Mother to appear in the sky—a beautiful vision as " La Dolorosa," dressed in black and white, with radiant white face and stars shining in her hair. The little children put no calculation in their prayers— life has not yet closed the windows of their souls : Our

Lady is to them a wonderful Fairy Godmother who will unlock a magic door and lead them away from the squalor and cruelty of the world. In the trees under the silver light of the moon, they will see visions any night of sylphs and fairies, but then one evening Our Lady comes to them as the greatest vision of all, filling them with joy instead of terror. Such was the mood of little Andrés and his sister, when they saw the Blessed Virgin at dusk as they were leading back the cows.

Meanwhile the Litany had ceased and some of the pilgrims were singing hymns. The moon had disappeared behind a cloud : and in the distance up above I saw the torches of the priests and altar boys. Suddenly there was commotion among the people near me and I heard people murmur—" aquí está El Chico de Ataún." He was surrounded by a bodyguard of four young men dressed in black. One was at each side and two others walked in front carrying flaming torches. Behind followed a big mass of people struggling to keep up with him and jostling the kneeling crowds out of their way. " El Chico " himself took no notice of anybody : he looked up into the sky and around anxiously on all sides—then he muttered thickly : " No veo nada." For a while he would pause and pray and then he would move on to another place. Everybody near him began to pray in a loud voice and he suddenly sank down on his knees and remained motionless for a long time. Then he began to cry out the words " Ama, ama," and he sank back into the arms of the two men behind him. His face was the colour of wax and his mouth was half open like somebody at the point of death. Though he seemed to be completely unconscious his eyes were open and staring. For a long time he would lie motionless in the arms of his two companions, and then all of a sudden, as though some superhuman power had gripped him, he would spring up into the air and mutter a few words before sinking back again on to the ground. His trance lasted for full three-quarters of an hour and then he was carried still unconscious down the hill into the house of old Simón and put on the bed in the room where the priest and the doctor were waiting. With great difficulty I managed to keep close by the four young men and I accompanied them into the room. When lying on the bed Francisco Goicoechea looked as if he was dead. The pallor of his face, his half-open mouth, his emaciated nose and sunken cheeks would deceive any ordinary observer ; but then his wide eyes starting from the orbits seemed full of wild vitality. The doctor, who was standing by in his shirt-sleeves, told me that his pulse was quite normal during those trances and his breathing was regular, a proof that he was not suffering from any hallucination or cataleptic fit. When he recovered consciousness he began to speak in a deep, low voice, half in Spanish, half in Basque, and give an account of his vision. Our Lady had spoken to him for a long time and had told him many things that he would not tell them then, but at a future date. She was, he said, surrounded by twenty-five angels, dressed in white and blue and with swords drawn. Saint Michael the archangel was standing by, holding out to her a big sword dripping with blood. Our Lady, who was dressed as " La Dolorosa," was wiping the blood from the sword with a white cloth. " She told me," said Francisco Goicoechea, " that there would be Civil War in the Basque country between the Catholics and the non-Catholics. At first the Catholics would suffer severely and lose many men, but ultimately they would triumph with the help of twenty-five angels of Our Lady."

At 11.30 p.m. we all had supper in the large dining-room and Francisco Goicoechea sat at one end of the table surrounded by his bodyguard of four austere-looking young men dressed in black—fervent members of the " Acción Católica."

Francisco in ordinary life looked a sloucher : he was a handsome peasant and massively built, surly and gruff of speech, and his mouth was coarse and sensual. If I met him by chance in the village, I should describe him from his appearance as a *juerguista,* or spreer, and a cave-man where women were concerned. But there was a far-off melancholy look in his eyes : at times he would lose himself in his reflections and not answer a word : at other times he had a queer mad glint in them. His old mother was seated near him : a beautiful old lady, well over seventy years of age, wearing the characteristic Basque peasant costume, and a black *coiffe* on her head which gave a classical outline to her sad, wrinkled face.

When I spoke to her, of her son, she told me that she was very worried about him, for she was afraid that God would take him away from her. " At times he comes back from those visions so exhausted that I'm afraid he will die. At other moments it seems to me he will go mad, and I'm afraid, I'm afraid. However, it is all God's will." She then told me that his life had broken up since he had begun to see the visions : before, he had been a hard-working farmer and he was engaged to a young girl with a good dowry : but now he would not look her way at all and he would say again and again that he longed to die, for then would he see the Blessed Virgin for ever. " Since I've seen Her," he cried, " I have nothing more to live for." At the other end of the big table sat Doña Carmen and her aristocratic friends chatting about the effect the visions would have upon the political situation in Spain. She introduced me to a charming young man called Llorente from Pamplona—a strong member of the " Acción Católica," who informed me that I might expect any day a rising of the Basque province and Navarre against the Republic in defence of their religion.

" I am a soldier," he said, " and I have fought in the Morocco campaign, but I shall be overjoyed to draw my sword again in such a glorious cause as that of my religion." His sister, who had been educated in England, then turned to me and said : " If Spain has a religious war, may we not count upon the sympathy of England who gave Spain her Queen ? " Beside me at the table was a pale-faced priest wearing very large and thick spectacles—a member of an order which devotes itself to teaching the children of the poor. He was very insistent that I should not be led into exaggerating the importance of the visions. " Remember," he said, " the Roman Catholic Church does not necessarily approve or uphold all this performance that you have witnessed. It is all very striking and it is wonderful to watch the simple faith of the Basque peasants, so long as you do not exaggerate. A great deal more is necessary, before the Church will approve." I then ventured to tell him the story of the Archbishop of Vitoria in whose diocese apparitions once occurred. When the prelate was told about them he exclaimed : " What ! Apparitions in my diocese, without my permission : that will never do ! "

The monk laughed loudly. He then pulled out of his soutane a postcard and handed it to me. It was all covered with the most minute writing I had ever seen— so minute that a magnifying-glass was necessary to read it. He told me that he had been able to write the whole of Saint John's Gospel on the postcard in the minute caligraphy. "I might just as well spend my time thus, as in any other way nowadays : I am not allowed to have my school : Spain does not want me. What is there to do ? "

Later on we all said good night and I went off to my room, but to my surprise I found two girls seated on my bed eating their supper at a table. When I tried to talk to them, not a word could I get out of them, for they were both deaf and dumb and they had been put in there as there was no room anywhere else !

Downstairs I found Florencio showing the last inmates out of the bar. Over a *copita* of brandy I described the evening's experiences and Florencio's parting words were : " C'est très bien, Monsieur, mais ce n'est pas le miracle—nous attendons un miracle ! "

# CHAPTER XIII
## THE VISIONS AT EZQUIOGA

### III

EARLY next morning Doña Carmen knocked at my door and said that she and Doña Julia were hiring a motor to go to San Sebastian and she would be pleased to take me with them and bring me back in the evening. The car was ordered for 9 a.m. and we rushed through breakfast, and Doña Carmen fussed and swore at Doña Julia who was not ready. For a long time we stood on the doorstep, but no one appeared. At last at eleven o'clock a sleepy, red-haired individual drove up in a battered Ford car and we set out on our expedition. Off we drove on a sunny day through Villafranca and Hernani, where we halted to see some relations of Doña Julia —through Astigárraga, the town where the best cider in Spain is produced, and we arrived in San Sebastian after one o'clock.

During the drive the two ladies spent most of the time in prayer : first of all they recited aloud a decade of the Rosary, then the Litany to the Dead in honour of a mutual friend recently deceased, then the Litany of the Virgin Mary. At times they would suddenly interrupt their prayers and hurl some remark at me about the scenery, or Doña Carmen would explain to me the history of various towns and castles.

When we arrived in San Sebastian I took leave of them at the gate of a convent in the Calle Easo, and went off to find my friend, Lucas the Gypsy.

I went to his lodgings in the Plaza de la Constitución, but though I knocked and knocked, nobody answered. At last, after a long search through the town, I found him in a small café.

" Where have you been these eight days ? " said he.

" I have been away at Ezquioga, watching the apparitions."

" Apparitions indeed ! They are not the affairs of Egypt. What do you want with all that flummoxery of *paillos* ? I thought you were a better *Calé*."

" Ah ! but, you know the proverb : ' *perro que no anda, no tropieza con hueso* '—(' The dog that doesn't roam will never come across a bone '). I roamed far and wide to make some cash, and at Ezquioga there are folks from San Sebastian, Pamplona and Bilbao."

" Ah ! You are wrong, *plaloró* : only a *diñeló* would play at a *romería* ; it would be worse than playing for the ' cinema.' You wouldn't get a piece of *longaniza* out of a pilgrim—the *curas* would see to it that every *céntimo* went into their boxes."

" Oh ! but I have been to Zumaya, Cestona and Azpeitia as well, and I have made some *jayeré*. To show you I'll invite you to drink at my expense : come, what shall it be—*repañi* or *morapio* ? See, here are four good solid *duros*—enough to *armar una gran marimorena* and drink destruction to the *paillo*."

After a few drinks of brandy the old man became more alert, and his mournful face smoothed itself into a smile. " I want to go roaming with you, young man : what do you say to a jaunt to the *feria* at Villafranca which is in full swing ? "

" Certainly, brother : when shall we start ? "

"To-morrow, for to-night I must play for a *juerga* of young Frenchmen from Biarritz. They want me to play some *Flamenco* to excite some of the *putas* they have invited."

I took leave of the old man after lending him a *duro* and promising to meet him at a certain café in Villa-franca the afternoon of the next day. We arranged also to visit together some of the small coast towns on the way to Bilbao. " That all depends if I can escape from Ezquioga," said I to myself doubtfully : " Doña Carmen has nearly converted me already and I shall not be able to break away from the atmosphere of religion ! "

At 6.30 p.m. I met the two ladies and we set out for Ezquioga. We first of all drove in the direction of Tolosa, for Doña Carmen wanted to call upon a certain young girl, Dolores Nuñez, who had seen visions of Our Lady at Ezquioga, and bring her back with us if possible. Dolores lived with her sister in the main street of the town in a small apartment on the second floor. They were poor members of the bourgeois class. When we called, the elder sister received us rather coldly, I thought, and she did not respond to the cordial effusions of Doña Julia or the verbosity of Doña Carmen. She told us that since the apparitions of Ezquioga had started she had had no peace with her sister, for the girl was living in a continual state of nervous excitement. She would not sleep at night or take nourishment and all her thoughts were centred on Our Lady at Ezquioga. Since she had begun to see the apparition, she had been like one distracted, and there was grave fear that she would become a nervous wreck. The doctor, she said, had warned her repeatedly not to allow her sister to go through the exhausting ordeal again—" And now, Señora Condesa, you come along and take my sister away with you and you never think that I might lose her for ever." Hardly had the sister finished her tirade than the girl Dolores entered. She was very young—just barely eighteen, with very pale face and thin aquiline nose and small mouth with very red lips. Her hair was fair-sandy colour and her eyes deep blue. At first sight she was a very pretty Spanish girl from the North, of the refined, rather exotic type, with a certain exterior light-heartedness and joyous movement. She was graceful in her body with beautifully moulded shoulders and hips, but in her pale face her blue eyes were so big, that when you gazed at them, they gave an entirely different character to her mobile features. They were wild eyes with a far-off dreamy expression and in the setting of her dark eyebrows they were like strange blue lamps, throwing fantastic lights upon the rest of her countenance. Then when her eyes led me to examine her restless face, I noticed that her white forehead was abnormally broad and prominent.

"Dolores is a mass of contradictions," said I to myself. She has one conventional and frivolous personality, with merry smile and graceful, kittenish gestures of the young stenographer of eighteen : but there is that other personality hidden away in those sombre, deep-set eyes, with blue rims under them—like two lakes surrounded by bushy foliage—what kind of a Spanish mystic are you, my girl ? "

Doña Carmen, after a great deal of heated discussion, managed to persuade the elder sister to let Dolores come with us, and at last after the tearful entreaties of Dolores herself, the girl was allowed to pack her shawl and nightdress in a parcel and set out.

Soon after we left Tolosa the sky clouded over, the rain fell in torrents and thunder and lightning raged. When we arrived at the village, we found that fewer pilgrims had come on account of the stormy weather, but at eight-thirty in the evening a big crowd was assembled on the hills around.

At nine o'clock Doña Carmen came up to me and told me to look after Dolores because she had to go off with her relatives. So Dolores and I started to climb the hill in the pouring rain—no easy task, for the ground was as slippy as ice and in some places there were great pools of soft slush, in which one sank to the ankles. It was a weary climb with the rain and wind lashing our faces: Dolores was dressed in a white muslin dress with a light cape over it and on her feet she wore thin sandal-like shoes: she slipped nearly every step and I as her cavalier tried my best to hold her up when she fell, but I was slipping myself. The Rosary had started before we had managed to climb quarter-way up the hill. Dolores, as she tottered and slipped and fell against me, kept muttering the Hail Marys to herself punctuated by exclamations:

" Jesús mío—no llegaremos en tiempo ! Madona mía—Ten piedad de mí."

At last, when we were about half-way up, the Litany began and I determined to halt. I was just arranging some newspapers for her to kneel upon when she cried out loudly in ecstasy : " La veo—la veo : Madre mía te veo."

She had risen to her feet : her face was deathly pale, and her eyes were like those of a mad woman. She went on talking to herself in a passionate voice. By this time a dense crowd had gathered round us trying to see Dolores. She went on speaking in more and more excited tones :

" Virgen, Virgen, díme lo que quieres que haga : lo haré todo, todo ! No me importa morir—Ah ! sí que quisiera morir ahora mismo "—(" Holy Mother,

Mother of mine, tell me thy will : let me die now at this moment ").

As she was talking I was holding her body upright, for it seemed as if at any moment she would collapse in my arms. Suddenly I nearly dropped her in terror, for a great gaunt figure appeared before us with a large black cloth in his hand. He bent down over the girl and held a black veil over her face saying : " It is not true—can you see Her now ? " He was a tall monk dressed in a black soutane, with the pale, cadaverous face of an Inquisitor. As he stood there threatening with the black veil, there was silence, and it was only in the far distance that I could hear the ejaculations and answers of the Litany. The girl's voice faltered for a second and then burst out again in high-pitched tone :

" Sí que es verdad—la veo—la veo—la veo " (" I see her—I see her—I see her ").

Then the monk disappeared in the black mass of humanity around us. Dolores then began to weep despairingly as she described to herself the vision she was witnessing—" Ah ! Blessed Virgin of mine, why is your face so sad—why are you dressed as ' La Dolorosa ' in white and black—now do not leave me—you are fading away into the bright light —lift up your hand and bless the crowd." She then began to pray in a lower voice to the Virgin asking her to save Spain and preserve it for Christ and his Holy Church.

Since the beginning of Dolores' vision I had felt myself gradually sink every second more and more under the domination of her emotion. I forgot all about her, under the sensation of terror which she had awakened in me. My ordinary, everyday logic deserted me and I felt the unreasoning dread that some sudden blaze of light would burst upon me and kill me by its brightness. I was afraid to look up into the sky above the dark hill lest I should see the vision. When I did look up, for a second the sky seemed gradually to open out as though rent in twain and a strange light appeared. If I gazed long at that strange light I should discover a face . . . a vision. Just for a second, no more, I felt myself swept away by its force, but then through my dream I heard the high-pitched words of the girl. I became conscious of holding her frail body in my arms. I could feel the strain reacting upon her : every now and then a powerful shock seemed to pass quivering through her and galvanize her into energy and she would toss in my arms and try to jump forwards. At last she sank back limp and when I looked down at her white face moist with tears I saw that she was unconscious. With the help of two other men I carried her down the hill—no easy task, for crowds of people jostled us in their attempts to gaze on Dolores : in the distance I could hear the melancholy hymn sung, as it were, as a dirge over the girl we were carrying.

When we reached the house I found the doctor in his shirt-sleeves waiting, and a priest standing motionless behind the bed. " Ah ! here is the girl from Tolosa again," cried the doctor as we laid Dolores on the bed. He then took out his stethoscope and prepared to examine her. A big crowd had followed us into the room and stood round the bed. There was a death-like stillness, for everyone wished to hear what the girl would say on recovering consciousness. When she came to her senses she began to weep convulsively and speak, keeping her eyes shut, repeating over and over again the phrase—" Our Lady has told me that I must come here seven days following and I must depart from here and sing for joy in the streets."

Then after a pause she opened her eyes and cried out : " More air, more air, more air ! " But nobody made a move, so intent were they to hear her story. As the girl seemed about to relapse into unconsciousness again, I pushed my way out of the room and fetched a bottle of soda water from the kitchen which I held to her lips. When I reached her bedside again, I found a woman in black, kneeling by the bed, disconsolately weeping. She had come all the way from Burgos in Castile to Ezquioga to pray to Our Lady for a daughter of hers who was dying of consumption. She had met Dolores on another occasion, when the girl had seen the vision and she had begged her to ask Our Lady to save her daughter. And now the weeping woman in black was kneeling beside the girl bathing her hands in tears, asking her whether she had remembered to ask Our Lady. All the other women in the room were now sobbing and I was weeping too, and the whole of life seemed to be blotted out by the emotion of the moment. Doña Carmen, Doña Julia and an old Duchess friend were holding handkerchiefs to their eyes : the two daughters of old Simón were crying freely in a corner : the four young men from Ataún, the bodyguard of Francisco Goicoechea, stood in the corner, pale, motionless like corpses dressed in black shrouds. Everyone, rich and poor, mighty and humble, was living his vision and constructing his own dream-world : not a sound in that room but the muffled sobs from time to time and the sound of heavy breathing. We were afraid to move away and enter life again, afraid to break the thin-spun texture of our vision. Time in that small room ceased to beat imperiously as the heart-beat of the world, and we were like a group of people sculptured in stone by Medusa's power. Then a cry from Dolores lying on the bed—

" Tengo sed "—brought us all back to the world and Time came rushing in upon us, dissipating in one second the fabric of the dream-world. Doña Carmen asserted her practical self and became the imperious countess. She dismissed every man and woman of us with a wave of her hand and turned to administer to the needs of Dolores. . . .

Later on, the supper *en famille* was a very tame affair, for we had passed through such a storm of emotional experience that we were all jaded. Everyone tried to be jocular and make a point of not mentioning the night's experience. Doña Carmen bellowed at the daughters of the house and at Doña Julia, who was on the verge of hysterics, wiping her red eyes and jingling her bangles until all my teeth were on edge. Next to Doña Carmen sat a very fat-bellied priest who made puns every few minutes in the intervals of noisily consuming his *arroz*. The doctor, who also was an amateur humorist, engaged in the pun competition and made jokes about the young girls whom he had to attend. His spirit of levity reduced me to the depths of depression and I felt as if the only relief would be a *borrachera*, but whom could I select as my drinking companion in that company ? Dolores then entered the room and sat down at the table with us. She was still very pale, with deep-blue lines under her eyes, but she entered like the heroine of a play and was received with acclamation.

Whether it was the result of being jaded after all the excitement I know not, but I felt the chill shock of disillusionment when I saw Dolores enter into the light *persiflage* and conventional frivolity of the company. I had held her in my arms up on that gloomy hill-side, and I had felt all the acute terror of the unknown, the sensation of being overwhelmed by something far mightier than my human reason. I had seen her pale face illumined by her eyes that seemed to blaze with blue fire, and I had heard her passionate voice in anguish as she addressed Our Lady. But here she was now, tidied up, with trim hair and clean white frock and silk stockings, acting, as it were, the *prima donna* for the company. The doctor, as he passed the wine-jug to her, asked her if she had a headache and if she had a better appetite than on the two last occasions when she had seen the vision. " I don't want to send the little girl back all skin and bone to Mamma—or she'll be out for my blood," he confided to me. Poor Dolores, for many of those good people you are like Francisco Goicoechea—a purveyor of nightly stunts, and you act as a thriller for them. Dolores now did not seem to be a great tragic heroine with the wild mystical yearning in her eyes : she had dwindled again to the fair typist with a good dose of coquettishness and pose.

Perhaps subconsciously I was slightly jealous that she should unbend to all these people, for I had seen her in her raptures and I should have preferred if she had continued her life on a different plane to the rest of us —breathing a purer air, living on a hill-top amid cowslips and daisies and wild violets. I had looked upon her as a troubadour looked upon the lady of his dreams —one soaring far away from the maidens of his feudal castle. Dolores had become worldly : there was a touch of slyness about her as she confided to me that she had a *novio*, but she had told him nothing about the visions (though her name had appeared in the paper more than once) because he would be frightened. She said that she had no intention of becoming a nun, and she appealed for support to the fat, red-faced priest,

who replied : " Yes, my daughter : you are quite right
to marry. God may be served in many ways and your
way will be to bring into the world several pairs of
angels whom Our Lady will bless."

After supper I could endure my depression no longer
and I asked Doña Carmen for permission to play a few
tunes on the fiddle for the company before they retired
to bed. Then they all arranged themselves in a semi-
circle with Dolores in the middle. Some called for
Basque dances, others asked for tangos and popular
melodies from zarzuelas and operas. I adopted the
Hungarian Gypsy's plan of playing to the face of the
lady, and I played to Dolores' eyes. "Ah, Dolores,
Dolores, I could knife you for ceasing to be my wild-
eyed visionary : I could plunge my *navaja* into that
white muslin frock of yours, and watch with glee the
red blood gush like a red wine in the snow. Why
do your actions belie those great blue tragic eyes ? O !
if I could only call back again that voice of yours I
heard on the hill-side." For once I did not play as
the ordinary *jongleur*. I played to Dolores' eyes, and
instead of a bolero or a tango it was a Hungarian
death song I drew out from my violin—a slow, meandering, heart-rending tune of wandering over the Puszta :
she closed her eyes to listen and I knew that the sound
was working its influence. At the end she remained
motionless and the rest clapped and made banal remarks,
calling again for tangos and boleros, but I paid no more
heed to them than if their voices were the rain on the
window-panes. I then played a *Saeta* followed by an
*Asturiana*, always in the same sad minor key. Dolores
put her hands before her face and started to sob. At
the end she rose and left the room. " Poor Dolores
is weary and overwrought," explained Doña Carmen ;
" she should not listen to music when she is in that

state. Doctor, you must give her some bromide or else a soothing sleeping-draught. And now, gentlemen and ladies, it is time to go to bed." I didn't, however, let them go until I had played a luscious tango and a rousing grand finale *Vito* to express my joy at having momentarily saved Dolores from her company.

In bed that night I reflected on the whole question. Could I endure to talk platitudes to Dolores next morning over coffee and rolls? Could I endure seeing her play the sly puss with the fat, red-faced priest? Was it not better to dash away at dawn, preserving within me intact the vision of the tearful Dolores with the wild blue eyes? What more was there for me to see at Ezquioga after such a night of emotion? No, it was best for me to remember that I was a *jongleur*, a wandering minstrel—a rolling stone that must gather no moss—better to leave Ezquioga as a memory, a slight fragrance in my mind.

At 6 a.m. I said good-bye to Florencio and wended my way along the road to Villafranca.

# CHAPTER XIV

## THE *FIESTA* AT VILLAFRANCA

" *L ACHÉS chibeses*, brother," said Lucas when he met me in the square of Villafranca de Oria. " You have arrived just in time for the *chibe-baró*, or festival. First let us go and watch the dancers." The town was full to overflowing with a gaily dressed, festive crowd : the streets resounded with flutes, fiddles, guitars and concertinas. There were throngs of girls walking about, sometimes four and five abreast, laughing gaily at the bands of young men. Not a trace anywhere of the characteristic Basque taciturnity. No matter how solemn a Basque may be in his everyday life, he sheds all reserve when the *fiesta* comes round. During the week of celebrations he puts on, as it were, the mask of carnival and kicks over the traces. There is a proverbial expression—" Time is money "—which foreigners always apply to the English character, as if everyone of us measured it in hard cash. We can quote the Spanish one—" *El tiempo es fiesta* "—(" Time is festivity "), which certainly describes the Spanish character. The Spaniard, and especially the Basque, puts much more energy into his *fiesta* than we do into our merrymaking. At home when I have a holiday, I like to devote myself to simple pursuits, far removed from my busy, active life of every day : I play a leisurely game of golf or I do a little mild gardening. The

151

Spaniard, on the contrary, puts every ounce of energy into his holiday amusements. He runs races, he climbs greased poles for a prize, he watches bull-fights, he plays *pelota*, and he dances acrobatically.

When we had drunk a few glasses of wine as an " eye-opener," Lucas and I wedged our way through the crowds in the square to get a view of the dances. First of all the young men trooped into the square from the Town Hall, with their *novias*, and the drums began to beat for the *aurresku*. The *aurresku* is surely far more than a mere dance—it is the national symbol of the Basque race. As I watched the solemn expressions of the youths as they danced in front of the girls, I was conscious that this dance was part of the ritual of Basque life. The reception of the young couples by the Mayor of the town, the procession into the square, the dance itself, were all parts of a national dramatic spectacle. In this spectacle the men play a preponderant rôle. The leader is called the *aurresku*, or " first hand," and he sends four men to fetch his *novia*. After he has performed in front of her he leads her into the dance. He and the *atzesku*, or last hand, who is at the end of the line, direct the various complicated figures. As each lady is invited to dance by her cavalier a special leitmotif is played :

The whole dance seems to have been expressly created to show off the strength and grace of the triumphant hero who is wooing his fair lady. He makes incredible jumps and performs acrobatic feats in opposition to any rival who may want to become her suitor and finally he carries her off as his prize. The lady's part is to watch discreetly and bestow favours. I noticed too that the young man when dancing with his *novia* did not clasp her by the hand, but he held one end of a white silk handkerchief while she held the other—a delicate proof of the modesty of Basques.

After we had seen the *aurresku* we saw the " Sword-Dance " which is characteristic of the province of Guipúzcoa. I had expected to witness a performance similar to the brawny Scottish sword-dance where the weapons are crossed upon the ground and a kilted warrior dances fiercely between the blades. The Basque sword-dance is more of a pageant than a dance. The young men were dressed in white shirt and trousers with red *boina* and sash. When the band played a march tune they all formed up four abreast and the leader danced solo in front of them kicking his legs high up in the air. The music, which was slow and heavily accented in $\frac{5}{8}$ time, gradually increased in tempo as the rest of the dancers followed the example of the leader. Each of them had a sword in his hand covered with a handkerchief and as the lines closed in and opened out, the swords crossed as in battle. I have never seen a more martial dance or one more calculated to excite men to battle : the music blared, the drums beat the inexorable rhythm, the sword-blades shone in the sun, the people in the square shouted with enthusiasm. One of the dancers suddenly fell to the ground amidst the forest of gleaming blades and straightway he was raised up by his companions as though he was a chief who had been killed in battle. Since it was originally a warrior's dance, it is customary to divide the dancers into two camps—one called the Christians—the other the Moors.

As a stranger taking part in the Basque *fiesta* I was fascinated by the irregular rhythm of the dance music. Musical historians say that the irregular rhythm of $\frac{5}{8}$ or $\frac{7}{8}$ is a mannerism which crept into Basque music

during the last hundred and fifty years, and they think
that it was due to the tendency among the professional
instrumentalists to hurry the second half of the ⅜ bar.
There is no doubt, however, that the irregular rhythm
suits the improvised singing of the people. The *Bert-sularis* take well-known tunes from other parts of Spain
and even from other countries and sing them in their
free and individual way, making them irregular in the
process. I had many opportunities of testing myself
during that day of *fiesta* in Villafranca when Lucas and
I performed in the streets and in the cafés. Anywhere
we went we were welcome visitors, provided we played
a *Zortziko*, for, as one of the youths told me, " A Basque
can dance a *Zortziko* in his sleep." The rhythm must
be sharply marked in ⅝ divided into 3 and 2. From
experience I found that my most successful tune was the
following, which I remembered from Pablo de Sarasate :

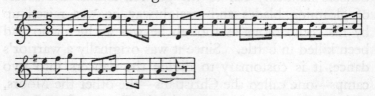

" Play on, play on, brother," said Lucas to me as he
thrummed his guitar—" that tune will rouse anyone in
Guipúzcoa—why, it is even played in the church."

Then after a round of drinks we passed into another
tune which Lucas taught me—

The *Zortziko* is the most restrained dance I have ever
seen, for the performer only moves his feet, and his

---

[1] Rodney Gallop, *op. cit.*

arms remain limp by his side. As we play, a boy with a drum approaches and begins to beat in time with the tune. The peasant who is dancing to our playing is of medium height, black-haired with sallow complexion and wild eyes. As he dances he reminds me of a Red Indian I had seen performing the orgiastic eagle dance in New Mexico. He is supercilious and not a muscle of his face moves, but there is a devastating energy in his wiry body and his eyes are like those of a vulture. He is not a young man, but he has become seasoned by toil in the fields and he is tireless. In the Basque country I was struck by the numbers of old men who danced with greater energy than the young, as though old age had hardened their muscles. I was reminded of the Roumanian villages where it is the old men who can out-dance the young in the energetic dance called the *Braû*.

In the afternoon Lucas and I, instead of taking a siesta, went to the bull-fight. With great difficulty we secured an outer seat, a good way distant from the ring. The bull-fight of Villafranca was a homely, local affair without any of the majesty we attribute to Spanish *corridas* in general. When I go to bull-fights my mind, nurtured on Henri de Montherlant, visualizes scenes of barbaric splendour recalling the arenas of ancient Rome. The bull becomes the symbol of Mithras and his death is the sacrifice to the god by the *matador* who is the high-priest. The *toreros* Belmonte and Gitanillo de Triana are romantic heroes of the most colourful pageant in the world in which blood sacrifice comes as a great climax. But in the bull-fight at Villafranca both the bulls and the *toreros* seemed determined to try their best to add a touch of grotesque humour to their performance. When the gates of the *toril* were opened I expected the wild gallop of the bull into the ring—

always the most exciting part of a bull-fight. Instead, a flabby bull trotted in sheepishly and then looked round the arena as much as to say—" Dear folks : this is a *fiesta* and the sun is shining. You are all gaily disporting yourselves : why kill me ? Let me off this boring exhibition of myself and send me away to a quiet meadow where I can chew the cud." The bull-fighters too, with their cloaks, seemed loath to disturb the drowsy animal. They flapped their cloaks at a distance, but rather as one waves a huge fan on a sweltering day. I expected that the crowd would rise up in rage and vent their feelings in the usual way by throwing objects at the *toreros*, but they remained surprisingly calm.

" This is not a Madrid crowd," said Lucás, " otherwise you would see *banderillas de fuego*, I tell you." Poor bull ! I pitied its destiny. After the cloak-wavers or *chulos* came the *picador*—a pathetic, oldish man, mounted on a wretched old horse. In a bull-fight, the only character who arouses my affectionate pity is the *picador*. He is like Don Quixote mounted upon Rozinante. He has to ride into the ring before all the people, lance at the ready, and engage in an enterprise which he knows is impossible. He must ride up to the bull, knowing that he will be thrown upon the ground amid the scornful laughs of the crowd. All the others, whether *matador*, *banderillero* or *capeador*, receive their due meed of glory and success, but not the *picador*. He is the eternally vanquished one like Don Quixote. In the profession of bull-fighting he is the victim of the feast—butchered to make a Roman holiday. Poor old *picador*, as I saw him fall heavily on the ground when the bull gored the horse, I could fancy him muttering to himself as he tried to raise his aching, rheumatic body—" A few seasons more of this and I shall be selling matches outside the bull-ring. I should be glad to be free of the tosses, but what about my sick wife at home and my children?"

And what was Rozinante thinking? "Poor frenzied victim lying on the ground, kicking your hoofs despairingly while your red blood drenches the yellow sand!" A dangerous symbol for Spain I call this unhorsing of Don Quixote—and the death of Rozinante. What will happen when all the knights-errant are unhorsed and all the Rozinantes are dead?

After the *picadores* had disappeared the melancholy bull had to submit to the indignity of the *banderillas*. A diminutive bull-fighter, holding the two darts with pink ribbons entwined round them, tripped lightly towards the bull and planted them in its neck. But even the *banderillas* did not excite the animal from its lethargy and it was now the turn of the *matador*. With his red *muleta* and sword in his hands he tried to coax the bull to attack him, but in vain.

"Es un buey—no quiere," said Lucas, and the public began to express their disapproval of the bull and *matador* by catcalls and whistles. Then the *matador*, who was behaving like a governess trying to coax a naughty child to approach so that she may give it a whipping, suddenly aimed with his sword and lunged forward. The sword flashed in the sun, passed over the horns of the bull but glanced off the backbone and fell to the ground. Another sword was brought and the *matador* tried again, but this time he only pierced the skin of the animal and the sword hung out like a *banderilla*. It took four swords to lay low that melancholy bull, and then the little dagger had to be brought into operation before the corpse could be dragged away by the team of horses.

There was only one exciting moment in the *corrida* and that was unrehearsed. As the third bull—a more

energetic fighter than the first—was careering round
the ring, scattering the *chulos* in all directions, I saw
a small boy of about fifteen years of age spring over
the barricade into the ring and run towards the bull.
He was a ragged urchin, barefoot, with a long mop
of hair that waved as he ran, and in his hand he held
a red rag. The cloak-men tried to stop him, but he
motioned them aside, and continued his race towards
the bull. The bull gave one look at him, and charged
straight at the red rag. There was a shout from the
audience. I shut my eyes, fearing to open them again
lest I should see the body of the street-arab being tossed
from one horn to the other before being shot into the
corner of the ring like a bundle of blood-stained rags.
But to my astonishment the imp stood his ground with
as much coolness as a trained *torero* and with his *muleta*
performed a perfect *verónica*. The bull turned and
charged again and his horns just missed the boy's chest,
who with a slight movement did another *verónica*.
The public now applauded vociferously and the boy,
after making a few more passes, ran away to the side,
climbed the barricade and disappeared.

"That is a 'capitalist,'" said Lucas.

"Why call him a capitalist?" said I.

"A 'capitalist' is the name we give to one who
wants to become a *torero*. That is the only way a poor
devil can bring himself into notice."

"Who will bother about that boy?"

"Many bull-fighters start their careers as 'capitalists.'

"Most of them are wild little scamps playing about
the streets of Triana. They haven't enough to eat and
they haven't a whole shirt on their backs, but they are
as agile as monkeys. As soon as they reach the age
of twelve they hang about bull enclosures, picking up

all the information possible concerning bulls. Then one day their chance comes at some *corrida* or other. They jump over the barricade as that kid did and face the bull. They do it with a light heart, for they haven't much to lose. They are fatalists like all *toreros*. If they are *valientes*, then you'll see one of the promoters or managers speaking to them afterwards and soon they find themselves learning seriously how to become *toreros*. If you meet Belmonte, *amigo*, ask him to tell you the story of how he started to *torear*. Why, it's an epic poem. He was a street-arab like that boy you saw to-day—aye, as nippy a brat as ever came out of Andalucía. He used to creep into the bull enclosures by night with some of his ragged companions and when the guardians weren't looking he would secretly entice away a bull and fight it. One night while the guards were asleep he and a companion fought a *toro bravo* for a long time in the moonlight, but the bull at last caught him and gave him a bad *cogida*. There he was, lying on the ground, oozing blood, but afraid to call the guardians. As for his companion, he had fled shrieking, thinking Belmonte was dead. The guards then awoke in alarm, and jumped on to their horses and set off in pursuit. Belmonte in the moonlight saw them riding straight towards him, so he raced for all he was worth, towards the river, though he was weak from loss of blood. Then after swimming across he escaped from their clutches.

" The only school for *toreros* is poverty and hunger. As we say in *Caló*, ' *Aor sauyó y aor bedoró, a ortrica postañí y o solibar grasnó* '—(' For a colt or a boy loosen the crupper strap, but tighten the bridle ')."

" The reason why we Gypsies produce most of the great *toreros* is because *pasamos bocatas*, we go hungry more often in a month than any *Busnó* in a year. That is why you won't find a Gitanillo de Triana north of Madrid, unless by the grace of God."

After the bull-fight Lucas and I continued our tour of the streets and cafés of Villafranca. It was a red-letter day for us; the streets rained wealth upon us and there was no café proprietor who said us nay. The only difficulty that arose was when we found rival musicians in our path. Lucas, however, had infallible tact, and never the ghost of a dispute arose between us and the few roving minstrels who visited the *fiesta* of Villafranca. At the end of the day in our room in the *posada* Lucas the treasurer pulled out of his pocket the knotted handkerchief containing our earnings and made a division of the spoils. We had made a total of twenty-one pesetas on our day's work. By arrangement Lucas took fourteen pesetas or two-thirds of the swag on account of his superior experience, and I was left with seven pesetas to add to my small nest-egg. Next morning we took the train from Villafranca to Zumárraga, where we changed trains *en route* for Zumaya.

# CHAPTER XV

# THE THREE GIRLS OF MOTRICO

JUANITO the *picador* travelled with us. Dressed in grey, with a big felt hat and puffing a big cigar, he looked even prosperous, and I hardly recognized in him the woebegone figure I had seen in the bull-ring the day before. A bull-fighter does not need to wear his *traje de luces* for you to recognize him. Anybody could see that Juanito belonged to the confraternity. His clothes were cut *a lo torero* or *a lo Gitano*, for the bull-fighters have so modelled themselves on the Gypsies, or vice versa, that I sometimes mistook a *tocaor* for a *matador*.

Juanito wore his clothes with a rakish air: his trousers fitted tightly to the leg and were so long that the ends fell over his brown buttoned boots. He wore his coat double-breasted like all bull-fighters and so closely cut that it seemed as if he had no hips. His tie was a flamboyant red, his black hair was curled and his brown, wizened face was framed by swarthy *patillas* or side-whiskers. Though he came from Valdepeñas and was a Manchegan by birth, Andalucía was responsible for his education. He swaggered like a Sevillian and spoke with a lisp, using a wealth of expletives that savoured more of Triana than anywhere else.

"Two is company and three is none," thought I, as I watched Juanito and Lucas talking excitedly together as if I did not exist. There you are, Lucas the Gypsy and

Juanito the bull-fighter—both of you nomad entertainers, making your livelihood out of the *juerga* or spree of Spain.   For what is bull-fighting except a *juerga*, and what is the word *juerga* or *juelga* but a dialect form of the familiar word *huelga* which means a holiday or strike ?

Yes, both of you, Lucas and Juanito, you are the purveyors of holidays—Spanish holidays with plenty of colour, excitement, energy, shouting, dancing, orgy. No wonder you are both alike in features and in dress, for your functions are complementary.   When you, Lucas, start to play in a tavern, you treat your guitar as though it was one of the bulls of the Marquis de Veragua —as you play your *polos, martinetes* and *garrotines* you look as if you were throwing a good *verónica* or planting a fine pair of *banderillas*.

You are a *picador* among guitarists, Lucas ; your body has gone to flesh, you become a little breathless, your eye has a squint and it is not as bright as it used to be years ago, when the Flamenco fans called you the *caballero de la guitarra*, but when the Jérez or Manzanilla runs through your veins you can achieve the impossible, or, as they say in Spain, plant a lance in Flanders like the bravest *picador*.

At Zumárraga, Lucas insisted that we should drink the health of Juanito who was going to Bilbao for a *corrida*.

" Long live the wandering life, Juanito, my friend. You are a good man and *muy serrano* : believe me, the greatest joy in the world is to live *serranamente*."

Lucas, whenever he wanted to sing the praises of anyone, would call him *serrano*.   The phrase to live *serranamente*, he explained to me, meant to live as nomads like the Romany chals.   Juanito had a strong dose of Gypsy nomadism in his composition, but it only appeared when he was out on a spree with friends.   He explained to me in great detail that he followed the profession of *picador* not from love or adventure, but simply because it was the only way in which he could earn enough to feed his wife and six children. " This Gypsy," said he to me in a low voice, " thinks I am one of the bull-fighting *gentuza* or rabble who rush from the ring to the *tabernas* and later on in the night visit the brothels in their *traje de luces* to dazzle the whores. A plague take the whole lot of them, say I ! The whole business of *toros* stinks of capitalists. What can poor devils like myself do when the directors, the matadors, even the bulls are capitalists ?

" What good has the Revolution done me ?

" When the King disappeared I said to myself—' Aha, Juanito, my boy : your time is coming. We'll found a trade union of bull-fighters and we'll keep the capitalists from putting their finger in the pie. No more Belmonte, no more Lalanda, no more Domingo Ortega ; no more golden cigarette-cases flung into the ring by film stars. The Revolution has come and it is our turn now.'

" But, Señor, it is worse under the Republic than before. I am leaner than I was in the days of Miguelito Primo de Rivera. I wander from one bull-ring to another ; I wear the same *castoreño* ; I ride the same old, worn-out horses ; I fall to the ground and scramble out of the ring somehow, when the band strikes the note for the *banderillero*. What do I get out of it all, except a wretched pittance which hardly keeps my wife and children from hunger ? Aye, and most of my time I'm far away from home, roaming from one place to another, thinking of my wife and the children, who are running wild about the streets of Madrid.

" And yet there was a time when I had my hopes for the future. I could dance and side-step and go down on my knees before a *toro bravo*, without turning a hair. Those were the days when I used to hear the applause, and the caps would fly into the ring, and sometimes the *golfos* on the *barrancas* would squirt me from head to toe, with rich, red wine from Valdepeñas.

"Nowadays I'm like a man born dead when I am in the arena : I see nothing but my own wee corner of the job and when it's over I sigh with relief saying—'there's a few *pesetejas* for the children,' and I go back to the *posada* to sleep."

At Zumárraga a girl entered our third-class carriage and sat down opposite to me. She was black-haired, dark-eyed, with pale skin, chubby red cheeks and rose-bud mouth. Lucas and Juanito were still arguing together, so I was entirely free to feast my eyes on the young lady's beauty. She was dressed in the smartest navy blue costume, with grey kid gloves, and I noticed at once that she had the daintiest little foot in patent leather I had seen for months. In England the girls pull down a blind when you look at them. "They are afraid your evil eye might turn them sour," said an aged witch of an aunt once when I had been so rebuffed. Not so the Spanish girl—you may gaze into the depths of her dark eyes without making her lose her wide-eyed watchfulness.

"I have seen you before, Señor," said the young lady, wishing to put me at my ease, after I had stared fixedly at her for some minutes.

"You confound me, Señorita, for it is I who should have seen you first, had I been a true cavalier."

"You could not see me because you were too much engrossed in the girl who saw the visions at Ezquioga."

"Ah, Señorita, I too was seeing my vision."

"People told me, Señor, that you were an Irishman and I wanted to meet you, because I was educated at a convent where there were Irish girls."

Then, to my surprise, the young lady mentioned the

name of the daughter of one of my dear friends in Dublin.

Surely the world is small and coincidence's arm is a long one !

The girl's name was Carmen Alberdi and she was the daughter of a rich magnate of the Basque province, owner of the cement works at Zumaya. As far as I could gather, most of the land we traversed belonged to her family and the railway too was her father's property.

" How democratic of you, Señorita, to travel third class with vagabonds like myself. Let me introduce my two friends."

Both Lucas and Juanito stood up and tried to bow majestically to Señorita Carmen, but the inopportune swaying movement of the train threw them off their balance and they subsided on the floor.

Señorita Carmen had been most gracious and pleasant to me, but her manner changed suddenly when I introduced my companions. A shadow of haughtiness dimmed her sunny smile and she became transformed into a Spanish princess, conscious of her dignity.

Lucas and Juanito, following my example, paid compliments, to her or, as they say in Spain, *echaban piropos*, but she did not respond. With a foreign vagabond she could be as pleasant and intimate as with a companion, but when she met one of the vagabonds of her own country all the old traditions of caste and class appeared.

Poor girl, thought I, you should not travel third class : no, you should travel first accompanied by a severe duenna and you should be heavily veiled. Though the Republic has come to Spain, bringing the modern ideas of hiking maidenhood, you will still remain attached to your feudal traditions.

At Zumaya Station, a severe-looking young man, dressed in black, was waiting for Señorita Carmen.

Hardly deigning to bow to us, she walked away with him.

" They're as haughty as Queen Isabel la Católica," said Lucas in his mournful voice.   " But one day a man comes along, who won't put up with any of their fancy notions."

" Yes, friend Lucas, as the proverb says : ' *Juanica la pelotera ; casarás y amansarás y andarás queda* '—(' Juanica the shrew, when your wedding comes along, you'll become soft and gentle ')."

Lucas and I took leave of Juanito at Zumaya and we walked along to Deva, a distance of about fifteen kilometres.   Deva is a beautiful place for the holiday-maker and it may contain, for all I care, a multitude of objects of historic interest, but I shall only remember it as the town that gave me the best *bacalao a la vizcaína* (*cod a la biscayenne*) I ever tasted.   When we entered the restaurant we saw behind a curtain at the back of the room the cook skinning the tomatoes for the sauce, and mashing them with a wooden spoon.   The air was impregnated with onions as she chipped them up and scattered them on the red sizzling mass in the pan.   At home I eat cod with the family as a penance in Lent, but in the Basque land it is a meal for the gods, especially when the *pícaro's* hunger adds its sauce.

" Come on, Don Gualtero, eat your banquet in calm : this meal touches my pocket.   When we get to Motrico you can do the work.   Drink up your wine, brother, and let us order brandy.   There's time for us to reach Motrico before nightfall : so come on—let us swallow the brandy to give us legs."

Slightly tipsy, we took to the road again and in an hour we had reached Motrico.

Motrico is a fishing town, one of those gnarled, weather-beaten Basque coast towns, where all the inhabitants have from time immemorial been dedicated to the sea. On the flag of the town there are whales—a proud reminder of its prowess centuries ago. The town is built into the cliffs of the bay. The houses mount tier above tier and some of the streets are at an angle of sixty degrees. There are countless narrow dark passages with steps leading from the harbour level, where the fisher-men dry their nets, to the dwelling part of the town above. The whole town is clustered around the gloomy castle perched on a huge rock, dominating the bay.

After mounting the winding street we came to a small *plaza*, where there was a café-restaurant. Seated outside were three girls.

Lucas said to me in a whisper : " They are called the three girls of Motrico. In the whole of the North coast of Spain you won't find three more impudent hussies." The three girls were certainly exotic plants in this small fishing town, for they were dressed in the flashy style that we associate with Paris *midinettes* rather than with daughters from the sea. Their faces were heavily pow-dered and rouged, and they wore an abundance of lip-stick : their blouses were v-shaped, revealing plenty of white neck and throat : their dresses were short and as they sat with their legs stretched out before them I per-ceived a vista of sleek silk stockings, pink garters and lace-edged crêpe de Chine. The curious part of it all was, that the three girls were dressed, rouged and stock-inged in exactly the same way. Their hair, too, had been Marcel-waved to the identical degree of perfection, but whereas the two elder sisters had black hair, the youngest was fair.

Lucas and I sat down at one of the tables outside the café and waited for one of the three to serve us with wine. But though we waited and waited, not one of them turned her gaze our way.

Lucas clapped his hands.   The fair-haired sister turned
to look at us, and then continued her conversation with
her sisters without bestirring herself.

"They always act like that," confided Lucas ; "they
are princesses, I tell you, and they wish to assert their
authority, but, believe me, they are not haughty when
they take a fancy to you.   They are the talk of the region.
Their father is the skipper of fishing trawlers, and spends
all his time on the sea.   Since the mother died the three
girls have gone their own way and there's no one to say
them nay."

"Why don't they marry, Lucas ? "

"Marry whom ?   None of the fishing youths here
would dare bring one of those painted lassies home to
his mother.   Besides, they are too dainty and they would
turn up their noses at a man in oilskins, and would hold
their hands to their noses, saying—' Ugh, fish !   I can
smell it—fancy a girl with a *novio* who stinks of fish,'
and the poor man would go off crestfallen."

"What do they want, then ? "

"Bless your heart, they want the fine *señorito* from the
city with creased trousers and high collar.   Their paradise is Bilbao, and they would rob their father to get the
money for a week-end there with some temporary *novio*.
But they dare not go, for even the old man's patience
has a limit.   He would go off and fetch them back and
give them the biggest hiding they have ever had.   The
Revolution has turned their heads.   They imagine that
women now have rights to do whatever enters their
heads.   You'll hear them talk of lovers and divorce,
and such devilment as never entered the minds of Spanish
women."

Lucas then went over to the three girls and gave his
order.   The fair-haired girl snapped out—" Who do you
think you are—God Almighty ?   I'll serve you when

I'm ready." She did, however, serve us, though with bad grace, and she then resumed her seat beside her sisters.

"I'm afraid we are not in favour, *amigo* : we are too ragged and down-at-heel for such a *señorita de pan pringado* (dainty miss). Do not, however, be cast down, Señor Don Juan Tenorio. I know a way to bring them to you like wasps to jam. Leave it to me, brother ; I'll catch you kissing the fair-haired *gachí* yet."

To tell the truth, I was attracted in a distant way by the three girls. They appealed to my sense of mystery. It was refreshing to find three girls hidden away in a primitive Basque town, pitting their strength against the solid mass of inherited convention. A Nora Helmer trio struggling together against the bolts and padlocks of their doll's house. They were all three pretty. The two black-haired sisters attracted me by their tall, lithe figures and big passionate eyes, but I mentally chose the youngest with the fair hair and buxom beauty. I made a pact with Lucas. I was to disappear from view for a while and he was to prepare the way for me with the fair damsels.

So I left Lucas and went for a stroll down to the harbour. As I descended the steep, narrow streets and the countless steps leading to the harbour level I marvelled at the multitude of dark passages and cubby-holes. It was like a town of pirates, full of dens and hiding-places, where freebooters could hide the treasures they had seized from galleons out in the open sea.

Down in the harbour I found myself in the midst of a crowd of women, who were collecting the sardines and packing them into lorries. The whole atmosphere reeked of fish, and such a medley of excited female voices I have never heard. Most of them were dressed in blue-striped smocks and their sleeves were tucked up. Fair, vigorous women they were too, with brawny arms like Amazons. Some of them were good-looking, but plump, rollicking, sensual like Maritornes, the Asturian wench.

When I walked into the middle of such a crowd of women, I thought that there were other men present. Then suddenly, it dawned upon me that I was the only male, and I tried to escape discreetly, but it was too late.

A few women had noticed me, and they pointed me out to their neighbours.

Soon there was a hum of curiosity. I was the stranger, and a stranger is always an object of ridicule. They then began to close in upon me, talking, laughing, shouting. As most of them spoke in Basque, I could not understand what they said, but I felt sure that the words described my personal appearance.

It was a most embarrassing experience.

Nearer and nearer they approached and the air was thick with the smell of perspiration and fish. Some of them then began to jostle me : one woman pulled off my *boina* and ruffled my hair—another dug me in the ribs—a third tickled the back of my neck—a fourth pinched my thigh so hard that I slapped her fat, naked arm. They all roared with laughter, and then, to add to my discomfiture, they began to say things to me which sounded to my ears like obscenities. To my horror I realized that I was being mentally undressed, weighed and valued as a specimen of the male species, and to my greater dismay, I was evidently found wanting, for there was a ring of scorn in the laughter.

What position could be more distressing ?

It was all like a fantastic nightmare.

I was in a worse plight than Orpheus, for though he was torn in pieces by the Thracian women he had the consolation of having estranged their husbands. But here was I at the mercy of these viragoes, who were comparing me unfavourably with their bronze-limbed, Herculean fishermen.

I looked around quickly for a means of escape, but there was none. Everywhere I looked I saw the barrier of mountainous bosoms.

Finding myself sinking to a condition of helpless rage, I determined to make use of rough words as my muscles were of no avail. " The Basques are bilingual," said I to myself, " and they will surely understand Castilian expletives. There is one oath in Castilian which moralists of the nineteenth century said should never be written or pronounced, but which the lonely traveller in Spain hears every day—the word *carajo*. According to Richard Ford, the word is a sovereign remedy against the evil eye, because it terminates in *ajo*, or garlic, the magic plant. So now I'll loose the whole artillery of that oath upon the Amazons without emasculating it to any mild *carai* or *caramba*, and in this way I'll show them that I have at least as virile a tongue as any of their coarse menfolk."

No sooner had I fired the oath, than the magic spell worked.

The women fell back in astonishment, for it was the first word of mine they fully understood. Hurrah for the Phallic abjuration ! May it never lose the power it received by the waters of the Nile.

With a hop, skip and a jump I cleared the barriers and hastened on my way up the steps in the direction of the upper town.

When I arrived at the café-restaurant I found a transformation. The three sisters came up to me with their faces wreathed in smiles. Lucas, who was sitting in a corner of the café, winked at me with his squint eye. The eldest girl handed a key to her youngest sister, telling her to show me to my room. The fair-haired girl led me under an arch into a long corridor, and opened a door with the key and ushered me into the room which I was to share with Lucas. It was a fine airy apartment with a window and balcony looking out on the lower town and harbour, a hundred feet below.

The girl took my rucksack, opened it, unpacked its contents and arranged them in order on the table. Then she tucked in the blankets on one of the beds and turned down the sheet at the head.

After performing these delicate little attentions she left the room and returned a minute later with a bunch of wild flowers, which she arranged in a vase on the table beside the bed, humming all the time gently without saying a word.

Amazed I could only murmur to myself—" Never before was knight so honoured by ladies as Don Gualtero after his departure from his native village." The damsel then reclined in a steel swing-chair which was near the window, and, swaying gently to and fro, she spoke to me for the first time.

" The old man said you were a *forastero* and were travelling for pleasure."

" Yes, Señorita, call it pleasure if you will. I call it taking the rough with the smooth."

" Why do you go around with that old tramp ? At first sight I thought you were no better."

" Neither am I, Señorita. I'm only a *vagamundo*, here to-day, gone to-morrow."

" I don't believe you, Señor. The old man said you were really a foreign gentleman with money too, but disguised."

" Now, Señorita, you must not give me away. Otherwise, I might have the *guardia civil* on my track."

The girl smiled triumphantly at having found me out.

She then relaxed a little more languidly in the rocking-chair and the swings to and fro became longer as she gazed at me.  The lines of a mediæval ballad came into my mind as I melted beneath her gaze.

> "Fuerte qual azero entre armas,
>   Y qual cera entre las damas."
> ("Like steel among weapons,
>   Like wax among women.")

"What is your name, Señorita?" said I at length.

"They call me Paquita," she replied.

"You have green eyes, Paquita."

"Cat's eyes you mean, Señor.  That is not a compliment."

"You misunderstand me, Miss Paquita.  Green eyes in Spain are aristocratic.  I like your eyes and your impudent little upturned nose.  If you understood Italian, I should say that you were *una birichina*."

"What things you say, Señor: I can't understand the half of them."

"Nor should you, Paquita.  A young girl like you should be serious and reserved."

"How can I be otherwise in this boring place?  I wish I was a man so that I could slip away from home and see the world."  As she said this, Paquita stretched herself lazily like a young panther, giving me thus full opportunity to admire her supple figure beneath her muslin frock.

"Have you never been away from Motrico?"

"Occasionally, Señor, my sisters and I go to my aunts' at Bilbao, but not for long.  Papa will not allow us to stay more than a few days, because we must look after the café.  Ah, how I love Bilbao!  When I am there, every night I go dancing *como una loca* with young men friends of mine.  What sadness to have to come back to this hole where there are only rough fisher-men."

" You should have a *novio*, Paquita."

" Not a Spanish *novio*, Señor : a Spaniard is too jealous. If you look sideways at a man he frowns : if you made *ojos blancos* (glad eye) he would draw his *navaja*. A girl has a right to be free, Señor, and that is why I won't have a *novio*—unless perhaps a foreign one."

As this was said with a toss of her head and a twinkle in her eye, I drew nearer to her and took one of her hands in mine. The warmth of her hand passed like fire through my veins. I stood up ready to escape, but my legs trembled with excitement and refused to obey. The girl stood up too, and she was so close to me that I could feel her breath on my face. Her eyes were closed and there was a look of expectancy on her face. It would have been cruel to resist the temptation alto-gether. I am not made of stone, Paquita, but of wax in your hands.

When I kissed her, she blushed and struggled in my arms, and without a word she dashed from the room. I rushed to the door after her, and out into the passage, but she was gone.

To my surprise I saw at the end of the corridor a sallow-faced, black-haired man gazing at me. There were so many daggers of hate in his looks that I slipped back immediately into my room and locked the door.

When I ventured out a little later there was no sign of the ferocious man, so I went back to the café, where I found Lucas seated in a corner talking to Paquita's two sisters. Every evening the three girls of Motrico hold a veritable court in the café as though they were princesses. The old skipper of a father should bless his exotic daughters for attracting all the young men into the café to spend their money on wine, coffee and *aguardiente*. Without their disturbing presence, the little town would indeed be a dull place. Grimy fishermen, brawny, *pelota*-playing youths, cobblers, chauffeurs, mule-drivers, all bowed humbly before the imperious girls.

When dinner was ready I was served by Paquita herself, and when no one was listening I whispered to her : " You must let me serenade you to-night, Paquita—but tell me first—who is the ferocious youth with the black hair and wild eyes ? "

" Oh, that is Ramón—he is always hanging after me. Don't mind him—es un tonto (he is a fool)."

Somewhat tranquillized in mind I tucked into my meal, which consisted mainly of *calamares en su tinta* (squids in their own ink). In England the sight of squids with their tentacles and swollen ink-bags would give me nausea, but in Spain, cooked in white wine, sprinkled with parsley and pepper, and floating in their own black liquid, they are food for the gourmet.

Next to me at the communal table sat a commercial traveller who ate his dinner without saying a word. When he had finished he said to me : " Allow me, Señor, to offer you a *copita*." Over the brandy he told me he was a travelling salesman in ladies' underwear, and to illustrate his remarks he pulled from under the table a portmanteau from which he extracted an abundance of camisoles, knickers, silk stockings and coloured ribbons. " They all know me here, especially the three daughters of the house—eh, Paquita ? " said he, winking at the girl as she examined closely a pair of flesh-coloured silk stockings. When she had gone he began to speak in a low voice, making sardonic remarks about the three girls. By the time he had finished describing them they had not a stitch to cover their nakedness, moral or otherwise. I wondered in my heart whether perhaps it was the nature of commercial travellers to be cynical about women, for never had I met such a rank materialist. Perhaps a wanderer, when he is a salesman, has to bear more than his share of the slings and arrows of outrageous fortune, but why should selling women's underwear lead a man to look upon the gentler sex as a cattle-dealer does upon heifers at a fair ?

" Your idea of love, my dear sir," said I to myself, " would better suit the eighteenth century, where, according to the author of *Tom Jones*, gentlemen thought love was no other than that kind of affection which, after the exercise of the dominical day is over, a lusty divine is apt to conceive for the well-dressed sirloin or handsome buttock which the well-edified squire in gratitude sets before him, and which, so violent is his love, he devours in imagination the moment he sees it."

" Look at Paquita, Señor," said the traveller, scratching his scraggy black beard, " she is well covered and her skin is silky, I grant you, but *re-Dios*, Señor, she is not appetizing enough for one accustomed to plump Spanish girls. She has fine thighs, but I tell you she would not be as expert in the love game as her sister Lolita, who is as sinuous as a snake in the grass and has wider hips."

With all his cynicism the salesman was a melancholy individual. Commercial travelling, he told me, was not what it had been in the past. It was very difficult to interest people in anything, and since the Revolution there was always the political difficulty in the towns and villages. Like most commercial travellers I have met, he was a bit of a trimmer in politics and he tried by devious questioning to ascertain my views. At first he thought I was anti-republican and he began to praise the Basque autonomy party, but then a chance word from my lips gave him the suspicion that I might be a government agent, and so he started to parade his freedom of thought and his detestation of the religious orders. After some time I became wearied with his talk and I left him seated at the table drinking with two of the sisters.

It was now time for me to serenade Paquita.

The night was soft and balmy with strange, varying effects of light and shade over the dusky sea, but not a ripple on the water. Not a sound could I hear save an occasional distant shout of fishermen in the harbour. Paquita had said that she would slip away unobserved from the café to the house of a friend in a neighbouring street where I could serenade her. I avoided the promenade along the battlements, where groups of fishermen strolled up and down, and turned down a narrow passage which brought me to the house.

The door with its ancient heraldic emblems sculpted above made me conscious of my deficiencies as a serenader. My fiddle was a good instrument with which to serenade a Dulcinea, but a guitar would have been more classical in Spain. Besides, I was not dressed for the part. I should have worn a big hat and a cloak which I could have pulled over my face so as to be *embozado* in the traditional Spanish manner. I should also have had a squire to hold my fiddle-case, stick and a torch to light up the scene.

The street was deserted: not a sound anywhere. In the deathly silence, I became acutely conscious of the smell of seaweed, stale fish and open drains, but I suppose Don Juan Tenorio or any other refined gallant must have had as keen a nose back in 1620. Two cats crept noiselessly out of a dark corner and flashed their phosphorescent eyes at me like spirits of evil. Paquita had told me to wait under the barred window or *reja* on the left of the door. The window, to my dismay, remained obstinately shut.

I took out my fiddle and tuned it.

The sound echoing and re-echoing in the narrow street sounded macabre to my ears. The two cats at the first note scampered away scared.

I then took up a few tiny pebbles off the road and threw them up at the window. After a few minutes, the casement opened and I saw a woman's face, but it was not Paquita's. This must be the *dueña*, thought I. Truly this serenade is developing along traditional lines with a Celestina to keep watch while Calixto and Melibea invent their sweet devices. The woman was old and ill-conditioned, and muttered in a low voice that Paquita was coming, so I continued playing my tune—a *Siguiriya Gitana*.

At last Paquita appeared and leant her elbows on the window-sill, as she listened to my playing.

After a while I stopped and she said : " I could listen to you all night, Señor : you make the violin speak."

" Yes, Paquita : I would play the live-long night for you, but it is beginning to be chilly down here. When are you coming down to me ? "

" Ah, Señor, I feel so happy up here listening to your music." The little minx, being an incurable romantic, enjoyed having an admirer down in the street to play to her. I heard the sound of neighbouring windows being opened : various heads peeped out at me and there was much whispering.

" Put on a cloak, Paquita, and come for a walk with me," said I again.

" En seguida," replied the girl, and the window shut gently.

In a few minutes, she reappeared in the doorway, muffled up in a dark cloak and we walked down the street towards the main road leading into the country. When we had turned the corner, Paquita took my arm confidingly and I began to utter all the pretty compliments in Spanish I could think of, for romantic girls of Paquita's type are not satisfied with silent, calf-eyed flirtation ; compliments and pretty phrases flatter their vanity and are in fact the breath of life to them.

After a long-winded disquisition on her charms I recited in her honour a Gypsy *copla*—

> " De tu pelo rubio
>   Camelo un cabeyo
>   Pa jaserme—una caeniya
>   Y echármela al cueyo."
> (" One of thy fair locks I crave
>   To fashion a chain of gold
>   And wear it round my neck.")

We were alone under the trees. No one was about and Paquita was in a languid mood.

All of a sudden I heard in the distance a whistled sequence of notes which made me start in dismay, for I recognized the leitmotif.

It was a danger signal.

Lucas and I when we travelled in the country had arranged between us a regular code of signals by means of which we could warn one another. The whistled leitmotif was a sign that something was amiss, so I waited in trepidation for my friend. Soon I heard his heavy uncertain steps as one leg drawled after another. When he came up to us, he could hardly speak so breathless was he. He muttered in a low voice—" Get away as quick as you can, and go straight back to your room in the *posada* : I'll follow. *Chapesca* (run), or the fellow with the *navaja* will catch you here. He's been drinking and he's in a dangerous mood."

" But, Lucas," I remonstrated, " what about——? "

" Don't argue, man—run for it and lock yourself into your room, otherwise *aquel gorrón te pintará un jabeque.*"

There was no arguing with Lucas, though I had my little relic of masculine pride which I wanted to save. It was, to say the least of it, exceedingly undignified to flee like a poltroon from a village clod-hopper, even when he was armed with a *navaja*, and Paquita looked so mutely appealing under the trees.

I hesitated, wishing to explain my position to her, but Lucas pushed me away, and so with heavy heart I made my way, as quickly as I could, back into the narrow streets of the town, and after a long *détour* I reached my room.

As I thought over the incident, I felt glad that I had taken Lucas's advice, though it had showed me up as a coward. At home in my native city I should stand up to an insulting rival and defend my rights, but in a foreign country, as La Celestina says—" Travellers have many ends and few friends, for in so short a time they can never fashion friendship with any : and he that is everywhere is said to be nowhere." I was not armed and, besides, what could I do against a man who could probably cut my face into an ornamental pattern, as Lucas had said? And so I consoled myself with the Panglossian thought that all was for the best, though I could not help feeling a vague, gnawing sense of shame at the inglorious part I had played before the girl.

When Lucas knocked at the door I was already in bed.

" You narrowly missed a fine *chinga* (quarrel), brother," said he.

" What crime did I commit, Lucas ? My conscience is clear."

" Have you never heard the expression *soplar la dama* ? That is what you did, brother : you snatched his girl."

" But Paquita told me he was *tonto* : she didn't want to have anything to do with him."

" She always says that, brother, for she is a vixen. Nothing gives her more pleasure than to see two men at one another's throats all for the love of her."

" But I wasn't up to any mischief, Lucas. Surely it is not a crime to serenade a girl in Motrico."

" When a man has drunk too much *morapio*, brother, he begins to see red. Next time, remember that men serenade girls with revolver and knife in their belts."

Next morning Lucas and I left Motrico early to walk to Ondárroa. When I passed through the small *plaza* I saw the three sisters seated in front of the café. When they saw me, they turned their heads haughtily away, and the fair-haired Paquita gave me a look of withering scorn, that burnt into the marrow of my bones.

# CHAPTER XVI
## THE TREE OF GUERNICA

Guernikako    arbola    da    bedein catuba

THE tree of Guernica is the blessed symbol of the Basque race all over the world, because it recalls the independent days of old, when the Biscayan *Junta* used to deliberate beneath its branches. More than a thousand years ago, tradition tells us that it was planted by God to unite the four sister provinces—Vizcaya, Navarra, Guipúzcoa and Álava. Beneath the Guernica oak, the King received the personal homage of his subjects and the *Juntas* ruled according to their *Fueros*, or charters.

Before I went to Guernica I had majestic visions of the ancient oak. It must resemble, thought I, the King's oak in Windsor, which sheltered William the Conqueror. I imagined a broad expanse of green sward and in the middle, the huge, gnarled tree standing like a giant with extended, writhing arms. I mentally compared the Basque tree to the Yggdrasil or World Ash of the Edda in whose shade the gods held their court and whose sap conferred immortality. When I visited the tree of the Basques in its scrubby, imitation Greek temple at Guernica I regretted the loss of my illusions. The tree of Guernica is a pathetic relic of the past and its branches are tenanted by innumerable souls of Basque heroes seeking to escape from the prison-house. If the tree stood under the open sky on a lonely heath you would see those spirits descend and wander through the land.

Biscayans, look how your tree is drooping in that shrine ! Among the ancient Romans, when a passer-by noticed that the sacred fig-tree of Romulus was drooping, he set up a hue and cry which was echoed far and wide, and a crowd rushed with buckets and water to revive the tree.

" But we revive our tree," replies the Biscayan, " by singing our national song—' Guernikako arbola.' Wherever we are in the world, North, South, East or West, we have only to sing that song to bring it to life before us clad in all its leaves."

Under the Guernica tree I gazed in retrospect over the ancient history of Basques, when they guarded their privileges by force of arms. Who can read the history of Spain in the nineteenth century without being thrilled by the tragedy of those grim, fanatic men, fighting desperately for their Carlist dynasty which symbolized their Faith and their *Fueros*? In the villages of Guipúzcoa where I had halted on my way, the old men still talked of those days of battles, skirmishes and ambuscades, when the phrase " a la montaña " (go into the mountain) was the synonym of going up the line. Even to-day the ghost of the ferocious priest Santa Cruz rides through the valleys leaving behind him a host of legends. But the day of the *Fueros* is gone and all that is left to remind the people of them is this melancholy tree. Where formerly there were guerilla warriors to-day there are smugglers. The Basque adventurous spirits find relief in outwitting the Spanish and French governments. Their mountainous valleys and above all their secret language enables them to evade the sharpest detectives of the modern world with as much ease as if they were nomadic Gypsies speaking Romany. It is for this reason that the Basque country has been in modern days the paradise of the artist and man of letters. Some like Loti in " Ramuntcho " have been inspired by the wild beauty of those glens and mountains : others like Pío Baroja were fascinated by the strong virile qualities of those men who slept with their guns by their sides.

As I look back over the vast panorama of modern Spain three Basques spring up in my mind as the incarnation of the spirit of Spain with all its stress and struggle. The three are—Miguel de Unamuno, Ramiro de Maeztu and Pío Baroja.

First of all there is Unamuno, the living Spaniard of most importance to Europe, because he proclaims the significance of faith, of blood, of Don Quixote as the highest symbol of man.[1]  In appearance he resembles an oak-tree with an owl's head. In his dress he shuns adornment and his coat is buttoned right up to the neck. Put him into a rough smock and give him an ash-plant and you would swear that he was one of the rugged, white-bearded mountaineers of Biscay, were it not for his strange, owl eyes, which are those of a soothsayer. Hence the name Teiresias which has been given to him by his disciples. With him walks Maeztu, who is as majestic as a Spanish nobleman of the seventeenth century with cape and sword. He possesses the strength and the solemnity of a *conquistador* ordered by the Catholic King to sail upon uncharted seas to distant lands. After Unamuno and Maeztu comes Baroja dressed in a shabby suit, with an old cap pulled down over his forehead. His boots are dusty, for he has walked all the way to Guernica from the province of Guipúzcoa.

If I asked those three Basques to a banquet there

[1] Keyserling, *Europe*. London, 1928, p. 87.

would be no interchange of dialogue, no *eranos* or contribution-feast, for they would not listen to one another. Each of them would straightway affirm his truth and their minds would fly out in three parallel lines without ever meeting. Unamuno proclaims his doctrine of Spanish Quixotism, calling it the despairing struggle of the Middle Ages against the Renaissance.

Baroja the humble wanderer, as he calls himself, proclaims the philosophy of the *pícaro* in opposition to Unamuno's Knight of the Sad Countenance. The Picaresque Knave is the antithesis of the Knight, but he possesses the same courageous qualities, the same lust for adventure as the *conquistador*. "I have," says Baroja, "the same desire for the nomadic life as my hero Silvester Paradox : I wish to see new faces and new scenes : I cannot vegetate in a village in Guipúzcoa, for I have within me a restless, insatiable imp that drives me on."

After hearing Unamuno's long tirade on Saint Ignatius, the great captain of the Basques, Baroja would shrug his shoulders and grunt his dissent as follows : " Great states, great captains, great kings, great gods, leave me cold. They are for the people who dwell in plains watered by rich rivers, for Egyptians, Chinese, Indians, Germans and French. We Europeans of the Pyrenees and Alps love small states, small rivers and small gods whom we may address familiarly."

" But, Don Pío," I should ask timidly, " whom do you understand by Europeans ? "

Then Baroja would answer gravely : " At times I think that the Alps and the Pyrenees are the only European part of Europe. Above them I seem to see Asia and below them Africa."

To which Unamuno would murmur dreamily : " And I should not be ashamed to be African, yes, as African as Tertullian and Augustine."

All this time Don Ramiro de Maeztu had kept silence, stroking his powerful, clean-shaven jaw. His function was to hold the balance and reconcile the militant faith of Unamuno with the nihilism of Baroja. He rises and says in a loud voice : " Don Miguel, you cry out— ' Unhappy countries, indeed, those wherein men do not continually think of death,' and like Ibsen's Brand you build your church up in the snows where no one but Don Quixote can follow you. On the other hand, you, Don Pío, are as great a sceptic as Lazarillo de Tormes or the Semitic *converso* Rojas, author of *La Celestina*. Both of you have led Spain astray. You, Don Miguel, cherish the memory of those ascetics and mystics who taught us to despise the world we live in and turn away our eyes from it. You, Don Pío, cry out that ' Evil is the root of life,' for you have lost your faith in humanity and your literature is a terrible accusation. You have generous sympathy with the waifs and strays who float helplessly through life, but there is in your work too much rancour against society. I am an optimist and I say to both of you that we Spaniards must put away those thoughts of death and try to give eternal significance to our actions in this life. We Spaniards are excellent losers and we resign ourselves to the thought of abandoning the works we have begun; our wise men have told us again and again that this world is nought but dust and ashes, and alas we are too easily disposed to hearken to them. To-day we need to live for our country, not to die for it."

Such was the imaginary conversation of the three Basque writers. Each of them was Basque by race but Castilian by tradition, for Castile is universal Spain—the Spain that exists not only in the Iberian peninsula but over the sea in the New World.

## CHAPTER XVII

## BROTHER CELT

Tanto bailé la jota gallega ole, ole, ole!

"LET me welcome you to Bilbao, brother Celt."
The words were spoken to me by a Galician
friend of Lucas called Tío Anselmo, whom we
met in a bar on our arrival in the city from Guernica.
Tío Anselmo, being a Gallego, was convinced that the
Celts everywhere belonged to the noblest brotherhood
in the world. He was a tall, white-haired old man with
flowing white beard, dressed picturesquely in a flowing
cape and broad-brimmed hat. Tío Anselmo was a
fierce partisan of the Galician separatist movement, for
Galicia, he said, the land of the Gods, must stand alone.
His ideas of Spanish politics were hazy, but of one thing
he was certain : the future of the Spanish republic could
only be settled by a Galician as president. "We Galicians have always held our tongues in Spain and let
Basques and Andalusians do the talking, but we have
worked. It is time for us to copy the Catalans and cry
out for independence." Tío Anselmo played the concertina, and as soon as I pulled out my fiddle a Herculean contest began between Irish and Galician music.
Lucas and the bar-tender sat as umpires while we played,
and glasses of wine were set in a row upon the counter

to quench our Gargantuan thirst. When I played
" Emer's Farewell to Cuchulain " and " The Lament of
Owen Roe O'Neill " old Anselmo played one *alalá* after
another, but I won that part of the contest, for in slow
melody the tone of a fiddle conquered the wheezy concertina.   To show there was no, ill feeling, I played an
ancient *alalá* set by Felipe Pedrell—

An *alalá* is sung to four-line *coplas* and the Galician
singer gives free reins to his improvisation, introducing
grace-notes and trills *ad libitum*.   Every kind of emotion
enters into the *alalá*.   There are cradle-songs, ploughing
songs, muleteer songs, but in all of them there is a sense
of melancholy, or *morriña* as a Gallego would call it,
such as we get in the Irish songs.   After a few glasses
of wine the old man started to play a *muiñeira*, or " dance
of the miller's wife," which made me feel as though I
had been transported back to a harvest *Ceilidhe* in Ireland.
The tune he played was as follows :

Hurrah for the *Gaita Gallega*, Galician bagpipe—native
instrument of the Celtic race !   Come on, Tío Anselmo,
stop your instrument a while till I deafen your ears with

jigs and reels from Ireland that you would swear were *muiñeiras*. First I played " Young Tom Ennis "—

—followed by the "Kinnegad Slashers," "The Rakes of Mallow," "The Antrim Lasses," and a host of other jigs that came into my head.

"Brandy," I shouted to Lucas; "bring it to us quick as you have no *poteen* in Spain."

"Señores," said the bar-man, "this drink is on the house."

Old Tío Anselmo then told stories of Galicia and recited folk poems in a nasal, lisping voice. His stories were all autobiographical and rambled along endlessly. He described *romerías* or pilgrimages to shrines in the country where everyone brings wine-skin, tambourine and concertina so that there may be dancing beneath the trees. Then he went on to tell us of queer beliefs of the peasants in wizards called *nubeiros* and witches who can wither up children by merely gazing upon them.

" They say, Tío Anselmo, you have wakes in Galicia just as we have in Ireland," said I.

" Too true, Señor, and the more the guests eat at those funeral feasts the more content will the dead man be."

" What do you mean by that?"

" Every piece of bread you eat and every glass of wine you drink at a wake means a sin the less in the load the deceased carries on his back into the next world. But it is not enough to eat and drink at a wake : you must do the *Abejorro*."

" What is the *Abejorro*, pray ? "

" It is a kind of bees' dance. The guests must join hands and circle slowly round the corpse, making a buzzing sound as though they were bees. But you must take care never to stop buzzing while the dance lasts, otherwise you would die within the year."

From wizards we passed to minstrels. " Galicia is the paradise of the bagpiper," said he ; " you will find them in every village : queer fellows they are, full of malice, most of them blind too."

" In my country, Tío Anselmo," said I, " we have bagpipers as well as harpers and fiddlers. Many of them are blind, for the blind man is best at remembering the songs. Consequently everyone in Ireland reverences the blind player, for they know that he possesses the last remnant of the great ancient tradition of the bards. In the past the blind singer with his poor tattered garments was able to cheat the vigilance of the enemy invaders and wander among the people, keeping alive the old songs. Ragged as he was, he could always boast of his descent from ancient Gaelic bards, who dressed in five colours and wore the blue cap adorned with a gold crescent. Every great family in Ireland had its own minstrels : they would play at all feasts and marriages and they would follow their masters into battle as Dermot O'Dugan, the harper, did the Earl of Desmond—the famous " Sugan " Earl.

" In Galicia," replied Tío Anselmo, " we have never allowed the bardic tradition to die. Why, to-day in Pontevedra and Coruña you will hear as fine minstrels as in the days of the troubadours. No *romería* would be complete without a bagpiper and a tambourine-player."

Tío Anselmo then proceeded to challenge Lucas to a musical contest. It was fascinating to watch the two old men sitting side by side in the Bilbao tavern with their carafes of wine beside them. Tío Anselmo, being a chauvinist, played nothing but Galician on his concertina, and he supplemented the defects of his instrument by his hoarse, mournful voice. Lucas, being a Gypsy, humoured his friend and pretended to play Galician, but little by little he would make the music veer round towards Andalucía and in the end we heard *Soleares* and *Polos*. His Gypsy temperament showed itself in his playing. He would embroider one of Tío Anselmo's Galician themes in such a way that it lost its diatonic character and became Andalusian.

Galician music is a fascinating subject of investigation for the musical historian as well as the folklorist, because there is an unbroken tradition of minstrelsy back to the period of the " Cántigas de Santa María " of Alfonso X. El Sabio and the " Seven Love Songs " of the Galician troubadour, Martin Codax of Vigo. In the manuscripts the music is given as well as poetry, and it is instructive to note that the poets of Castile of that period wrote in Galician dialect, because it was the language of the troubadours.

In Galician music the most characteristic dance is the *Muñeira* or *Gallegada*, a lively six-eight rhythm. There has always been a tradition among the Galician minstrels to introduce as many trills, scales, flourishes, arpeggi as possible into the simple original tune. In this they are as unrepentant as any Gypsy guitarist from Puerto de Santa María. Julián Ribera in a study on Galician music,[1] quotes as the original theme of the *muñeira* the following, entitled " La Molinera " (the Miller's Wife). It will be noticed that it is in two-four time.

[1] J. Ribera, *De Musica y Metrica Gallegas*. Hom. Menéndez Pidal. Madrid, 1925, Vol. 3, p. 11.

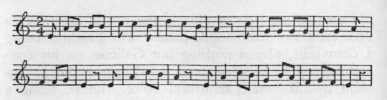

The above *muiñeira* is a famous old tune in Galicia, but the minstrels play it in six-eight at a quicker rate, change the accents and decorate it gaudily with variations. According to Julián Ribera, it is not exclusively Galician, for it belongs to other parts of Spain as well. The Galicians always declare that it was originally Galician and from that region passed to the others, but Ribera says that its minor key, its rhythm, its initial notes and its cadence stamp it as the classical type of Andalusian *soleares*. The true *muiñeira* of Galicia is a kind of gay parody of the sad songs of Andalucía. No *tocaor* from Triana or Cadiz would spontaneously play a *muiñeira*: he would prefer to revel in the tragic sadness of the ancient *soleares*. In Andalucía you rarely find Galician players, for they would meet with scant sympathy from the audiences there. The Gallegos in Seville and Cadiz own fried-fish shops, but they are not minstrels.

It is the bagpipe which has given Galician music its flavour and drawn it away from the music of the rest of the country. A wandering fiddler who wants to extract money from hard-headed Gallegos has to play a droning lower note on the open string in accompaniment to his tune. He must imitate the bagpipe or go without his dinner.

Tío Anselmo taught me one *muiñeira* which has brought me luck on every occasion that I played it. With the exception of the original *muiñeira* none is as famous as this tune, which rejoices in the title, " Tan-

tarantán que los higos son verdes " (" Tantarantán for
the figs they are green ").

Whenever I have played it in Ireland, Scotland or
Wales the Gaelic lads and lasses stamped their feet and
danced to it as if it had sprung out of the soul of the Celt.
I have always thought that it was the most Galician mill-
danced tune of all until I read Ribera's study on Galician
music.   He states that it must have been very popular
in other regions of Spain before it was considered the
exclusive possession of Galicia.   The theme is well
known in Catalonia, and in the sixteenth century it was
sung in Castile.[1]   Even the rhythm, which seems so
characteristically Galician, was very common among the
Spanish Moors in the days of Salinas, the great musician
of the sixteenth century.

According to Ribera, the influence of Spanish minstrels extended far beyond Spain in the Middle Ages—
even to Ireland, where one of the oldest traditions of
music in Europe existed.   In the Middle Ages there
was continual intercourse between the two countries.
Spanish Knights came over to the Purgatory of Saint
Patrick if we believe Viscount Perellós' account of his
journey ; Irish Knights went over to Spain as pilgrims
to Santiago.   As soon as they landed in Spain and began
to wend their way towards Compostela they would fall
in with many a Moorish *juglar* on the road and exchange
tunes as well as courtesies.   Through the influence of

[1] J. Ribera, *op. cit.*, pp. 19–20.

the wandering *juglares* tunes travelled widely, becoming modified according to the musical idiom of the various countries.

Tío Anselmo was very insistent that I should change my route and visit Galicia. " You are a Celt, Señor, and you will find more sympathy in Pontevedra than in the whole of Castile. Remember that Galicia is the land of minstrels."

" But I am not a Celt, Tío Anselmo."

" What are you then, Señor ?   I thought all Irishmen were Celts."

" So they are, Tío Anselmo, but only when they live in exile in the United States, just as you Gallegos do in Argentina."

" Ah, yes, Señor, we feel *morriña* and we sing *airiños de miña terra.*"

" Tío Anselmo, many of us are not Celts by race, but by emigration.   We need poets to create for us a Celtic twilight full of vague, mythical gods and heroes to console us in our bitter struggles.   Fortunately you Gallegos have Rosalía de Castro and we have our Dark Rosaleen—

    " ' O my dark Rosaleen,
        Do not sigh, do not weep !
        The priests are on the ocean green,
        They march along the deep.
        There's wine from the royal Pope,
        Upon the ocean green ;
        And Spanish ale shall give you hope
        My dark Rosaleen.' "

Tío Anselmo sighed when he heard the name of Rosalía de Castro and wiped away a tear as he recited from one of the Cantares gallegos—

> " ' If the sea had a bridge, there would I pass
> To Brazil, across the sea,
> But there is no bridge o'er the sea, my love,
> How shall I come to thee ? ' " [1]

Lucas the Gypsy spat on the ground and interrupted our dreamy tearfulness :

"Devil take both of you with your moaning poetry and tears. As they say in Caló, ' *goles e ternoró, ne aupran aor charó* ' (an ass's braying won't reach heaven). You, *plaloró*, should know better than to let that old fellow dribble over you. Those are not the affairs of Egypt, brother. You should be tough as Castilian leather, not *bostán* (soft) like a tear-stained *dicló*. Come on, brother, order three glasses of *repañí*. We'll drink to your journey to Castumba (Castile)."

[1] A. Bell, *Spanish Galicia*. London, 1922, p. 175.

## CHAPTER XVIII

## TRAIN-VAGABOND—THIRD CLASS

"YES, Señor, there is a *tren mixto* to Miranda at 15.55, but I warn you it is very slow. If you wait until 17.10 you will catch the *rápido.*"

"Give me a ticket for the *mixto.* I prefer it."

The *tren mixto* or mixed train is a unique institution and one to be recommended to the contemplative traveller, who has left his watch at home. It is one of the great contributions to the Spanish philosophy of life, but, alas, its beneficial lessons are not understood by the great band of globe-trotters. If I were a powerful statesman in England, or the United States, I would make an arrangement with the Spanish Government, whereby all Speed Aces and Road-Hogs should be sent to Spain for some months every year to undergo a course of " Mixed Trains." The Spanish Government would supply them with third-class kilometric tickets. What is a kilometric ticket? they would ask sourly.

My dear sir, a kilometric ticket enables you to buy one, two, three thousand kilometres of Spain. Here is the document duly signed and stamped with your photograph in the corner. Quick, sir! The train waits—Good-bye—*hasta luego !*

The Road-Hogs would then run to catch the mixed train and I should see them fade away into the distance over the vast steppes of Castile and La Mancha in their puffing, jolting, slowly winding train as though they had ridden off on camels into the Sahara. Weeks of crawling, delaying, shunting would chasten their proud spirits and, in consequence, the roads of England and America would be safe again for man and beast.

When I entered the mixed train at Bilbao I regretted that I was a tramp. I should have preferred to be a kilometric vagabond. There is a subtle thrill in presenting the brown passport with its countless little coupons at the ticket office for the clerk to tear off the kilometres. As our lengthy wandering progresses, the land of Spain seems to flutter away in a trail of tiny scraps of paper, as though we were laying a paper-chase.

A mixed train is a combination of the goods as well as the passenger train. The greater part of ours was given up to cattle and casks of wine and oil. At the beginning of the journey there was great excitement: the cattle lowed, the women chattered shrilly; some men sang and others whistled. The corridors of the third-class carriages were full to overflowing, not because the train was full, but because many Spaniards never decide where they will sit until the train has been for some time under way. Standing in the corridors they spy out the land and then pounce for the best seats.

It is remarkable how heavily laden Spanish peasants are when they travel. There are three women in my compartment, who carry enough luggage to set up house in a desert. There are baskets of clucking hens and quacking ducks; a sewing-machine, which is perched perilously on the rack; sacks of vegetables, not to mention a paper bundle smelling strongly of fish, which is placed on the rack above my head and begins after a few minutes to drip at regular intervals upon the back of my neck.

Soon it is meal-time and one of the men draws out a battered case from which he extracts various portions of garlic-scented *salame*, hard-boiled eggs, *chorizo* or sausage, and bread. At first I felt inclined to be stand-offish, for I want to keep to my own meditations, but at such a communal banquet it is impossible to play the outsider. Homer would have called it an *eranos*, for everyone in the carriage contributed some delicacy except myself. One brought sausage, another cheese, another beer or wine, and an old fellow in the corner passed round a bottle of *aguardiente*. I felt ashamed that my wallet and *bota* were empty, for I was given royal hospitality. As the French say, " l'appétit vient en mangeant," and I am afraid I was indiscreet in my visitations to the wine-skin of my neighbour, and his white cheese. But do not imagine for a moment that any of those good people looked askance at me. " Good appetite " was all they said as they watched me tucking into huge slices of bread and ham, in the intervals of squirting the red wine into my mouth, when the skin was passed to me.

After the meal the carriage looked like a battlefield the morning after. There were crumbs everywhere, greasy bits of paper with pieces of ham and sausage adhering to them, and orange peel, while in the air floated a symphony of smells, with fish and garlic as the leading motives. After cigarette-rolling and cloudy puffing, the digestive period began. I could retire into my shell once more, for the majority of the passengers passed into beatific slumber. Even the hens in the hampers stopped clucking, and the cat that had been miaowing and scratching restlessly at the lid of the basket under the seat, relaxed into rest. There was a rhythmic sound of snores—loud and assertive from the old man in the corner—timid and high-pitched from the melancholy woman on my left, whose head leant trustfully on my shoulder. The only wakeful person was the woman opposite to me—a pale-faced, frightened widow with a black veil over her head who kept on continually murmuring prayers to herself—decades of the Rosary, I think, for her lips moved in a sequence, and every few seconds I heard the accented final syllable of amen.

I was in a reminiscent mood and that short journey by rail from Bilbao to Miranda awakened recollections of past adventures in trains. In the twelve years I had been visiting Spain, how often had I lived this life of the vagabond train, watching the panorama of Spain flit past. It was in 1920 that a Spanish friend said to me, " There is only one way to study Spain and that is the way of Pérez Galdós, the greatest novelist since Cervantes. When he was writing his books on contemporary Spain he wandered through Spain in third class, talking to the peasants, shopkeepers and vagabonds of all kinds, whom he met between one station and another." As Azorín said of him, " He appeared silently. With his little eyes that pierced, his cold, scrupulous glance ; he appeared, looking at everything, examining everything."

As a result of my friend's advice my wife and I spent a long honeymoon in Spain, armed with kilometric tickets for three thousand kilometres.

An incident stands out in my mind as characteristic of Spanish railways. One day we had a two-hours' wait at a small station in North Spain and we wanted to visit the town, but, warned by experience in other countries, we were afraid to leave our luggage unpro-

tected on the platform. As we were deliberating, a
Spanish *caballero* who was travelling on the same train,
came up to us and bowing courteously said : " Leave
your luggage there on the platform : no one will touch
it. Remember that in Spain no one robs the stranger."
We had many opportunities of verifying the truth of
the *caballero's* boast.

It is curious that when a kilometric wanderer looks
back over his long range of experience he rarely thinks
of the majestic towns, castles or landscapes he has seen.
Instead, he thinks of some particularly bleak station
miles from anywhere and he remembers the dreary restaurant, with its stacks of bottles, the loud ticking
clock, the strange, dilapidated lavatory with unusually
picaresque examples of graffiti scrawled upon the walls.
Years afterwards when the vision of the cathedral of
Burgos or the Mosque at Córdoba have begun to dim,
the traveller will remember the dim-lit platform of
Venta de Baños, or the sound of trains shunting at
San Fernando.

This is all due to the obstinate cussedness of the
human imagination.

As soon as I feel cross-grained and angry with my
surroundings, straightway my imagination begins to
weave their ugly drabness into a wonderful pattern, as
though to do so were the prime pleasure in the world.
When I travel by train through Spain I do not think
of Madrid, Seville or Barcelona, but I feel a genuine
affection for such stations as Bobadilla, Baeza and
Medina del Campo.

They are oases in the vast desert of Spanish railways.

Bobadilla never shone in history. It is the junction
for Granada, but none of the Abencerrajes ever halted
there, and no dark-eyed Zorayda gazes from a watch-
tower. It is just a railway station, but its significance

is deep, for it guides the modern mind to the past.
If the junction had been at a place of great historic
interest like Ronda, it would have distracted my attention and made it impossible for me to approach the
Alhambra in the right spirit. Bobadilla I shall remember too, because there I met the most famous Irish railway porter in the world. " You are the guide to the
Arabian Nights," said I to him once, " and if you
understood Greek I should call you the ψυχοπομπός or
guide of the ' Souls ' who were weaned on Washington
Irving."

Then take Baeza, where many a " mixed-train "
traveller spends long hours waiting for a connecting
train for Córdoba. Though I have been there many
times I have never walked to the town, so fascinated
was I with the passengers I met in the station *fonda*.
The dyspeptic waiter in the *fonda* knows the power of
music since the day when Aurelio the cross-eyed, my
Gypsy friend from Cadiz and I played for our dinner
of arroz, chuletas and a bottle of Manzanilla.

Finally, to come to Medina del Campo, let me relate
another touching example of Spanish honesty. One
day when we were waiting in the *fonda* there for the
train to take us to Salamanca, my wife left behind her
an umbrella with a silver top to it. When she discovered her loss in the train, she said : " Alas, I shall
never find it again, for who knows when we shall pass
Medina del Campo again ? Besides, there is no morality
or honesty in the world as far as umbrellas are concerned."

Two months later on our return from Salamanca,
the train stopped at Medina del Campo, and just for
curiosity I asked the waiter in the *fonda* if a silver-
handled umbrella had been found. " No, Señor, not
to my knowledge," he replied. Before I left the room

I went over to the corner where I remembered that
we had dined two months before, and to my surprise
I saw the umbrella leaning against the back of the sofa
exactly in the same position as my wife had left it.

During a train journey in Spain I become fascinated
by the vast monotony of the landscape. The earth
yellow, red, brown, stretches out without a break to
the horizon ; hardly a tree to vary the scene. Occasionally I see a horseman ride away into the distance.
Above there is not a cloud.

As a contrast to the monotony of the scene, the life
in the train is varied and multi-coloured. At every
station queer wandering sellers board the train. There
are knife-sellers, with trays full of the ferocious daggers
from Albacete in La Mancha. They are the classical
*navajas* used by the Gypsies in their brawls, and described by Goya in his famous drawing of the two
duellists buried up to their knees in the sand and slash-
ing at one another. Then there are water-sellers with
big jugs made of porous clay, sellers of *sandías* or water-
melons, sellers of wine and pastry.

As the train runs along, the ticket collector balances
like an acrobat on the footboard outside the carriage
as he passes from one separate compartment to another.
On the way to Sevilla there is a great increase in the
numbers of itinerant sellers and beggars. I have seen
a cripple who had lost both legs at the hips carried
round the third-class carriages on a tray in order to
beg alms. Those who do the biggest trade are the
sellers of prawns (*camarones*) and other shellfish. Most
of them come from Puerto de Santa María, and speak
a very exaggerated Andalusian with as much *ceceo* or
lisping as a Gypsy from Triana. With them come the
vagabond guitarists and lottery promoters. Do not
imagine that to win the lottery on the train will bring

you in a fortune. Those lotteries are the thinnest camouflage for begging in the world. The men rush along the train, if it is a corridor one, with little coupon tickets and, by fair means or foul, pester the traveller into paying for a number. When they have sold sufficient tickets they announce the winning number and the prize is a rather bedraggled box of chocolates. On several occasions I have taken a hand in running those train lotteries between Córdoba and Sevilla, but the talents required for rapid salesmanship were greater than I possess. It is essentially a *métier* for the full-blown *Gitano*.

During the day in the Spanish trains there is plenty of amusement, even excitement, in spite of the sun which beats down upon the wooden carriages, and scorches us into coma. But then comes the compensation at sunset when we pass through gigantic mountain defiles, where jagged, beetling crags overhang the train.

It is at night that the contemplative traveller needs to possess his soul in patience. Night-travelling in a *tren mixto* was meant for a race born to be ascetic. Many times I longed for the silent fortitude of those saints Ribera painted, with their emaciated faces and wiry muscles quivering under self-inflicted torture. In the crowded compartment my diminutive portion of hard wooden seat, after five or six hours, became like the torture of the "tripod," or *veglia*, as it was practised under the Inquisition. There are no glass windows on the carriage, but at night wooden shutters are pulled up which effectively shut out the air, for fresh air, it should be remembered, frightens the primitive man. In the night air fevers roam about, so shut the window, Señor, *por caridad*, and let us sleep. Yes, fresh air is a sign of decadent modern civilization.

Nobody who travels a long distance in a *tren mixto*

need expect any sympathy, for his Spanish friends would say sharply : " *Hombre*, don't be a madman—you are not a mule or an ox that you should travel in such trucks and vans. Why don't you take an express ? "

On one occasion, some years ago, I thought our train bewitched because it played such antics. We had set out at night from Madrid *en route* for Baeza and Córdoba. The carriage was old, unpainted and dilapidated, but it had a small open-air platform at the rear which made me choose it. When we gathered speed the walls of the carriage began to roll and rock in the most alarming fashion. Every jolt threw me with the rest of the passengers from one side to another. " Jesús mío," screamed the women and blessed themselves. The men swore and spat noisily. When the fear had passed, the antics of the carriage became a theme for jokes, and every fresh jolt caused roars of laughter. It was like Alice's journey in the Looking-Glass World when the train jumped the brook. As for me I felt very ill, for I had eaten prawns in Madrid, and the jolting, steeple-chasing motion of the train made them bob up and down in my inside like corks in a rough sea. At last I closed my eyes and sank into uneasy slumber, for the train had become a mare and I was riding her like mad over fences, hedges, water-jumps. All of a sudden I heard a shrill scream from an engine and I saw that my mare was riding straight along the track towards an oncoming train. The engine whistled : I screamed, and, in desperation, I tried to throw myself from the mare, but my foot caught in the stirrup and I dangled on the rails—helpless. . . . I shrieked and shrieked. . . .

When I awoke I found three men and a woman pinioning my arms while the rest of the passengers gazed at me as though they had seen a ghost.

" A nice scare you gave us, Señor," said one of the men. " You shrieked as if all the demons in hell were after you, and then you jumped up and made a spring for the door over there : we thought you were going to throw yourself out on the line."

Just then the train began to slow down, so I asked the man what station we were stopping at.

" This is Cinco Casas," said he, " where you change for Argamasilla de Alba."

" Argamasilla, cradle of Don Quixote de la Mancha," I murmured dreamily.

Then all was as clear as daylight to me.

The train was a Quixotic one, and who could blame it for frisking and curveting through the plains of La Mancha ?

Many were the recollections that passed through my mind on that journey from Bilbao. When I arrived at Miranda de Ebro, it was dark, so I halted for the night in the station *fonda*.

# PART II

PART II

# CHAPTER XIX
## THE GATEWAY OF CASTILE: THE CAVES OF THE MOORS

WHEN the gods created the kingdom of Castile they ordered the race of giants to build a gateway of boulders wrenched from mountainous peaks. "It is like Wotan's Walhalla raised by Fafner and Fasolt," said I to myself as I approached the Pass of Pancorbo.

All the sixteen kilometres from Miranda de Ebro to the pass had been a gradual preparation for this mighty scene. The landscape began to cast up strange rocks like sentries guarding the approaches. There was just room for the narrow road to pass between the lofty, jagged crags that formed the titanic gateway. High above my head on the edge of the precipices hung huge masses of granite, threatening to crash down any moment with terrible roar and close the entrance for ever.

When I had passed through the tunnelled passage I came to the *pueblo* of Pancorbo—a straggling village of decrepit houses with red roofs, cowering at the base of the grey rocky fastness.

My first thought was to climb the rocky mountain above the *pueblo*, so instead of continuing on my way towards the *posada* I began to make preparations for my climb. In the tavern where I halted, the men told

me that at the summit of the mountain there were deep
caverns called the caves of the Moors. " Don't spend
the night up there," said one man, " or you might have
to fight one of the *Moros*."

It was about two o'clock in the afternoon when I
began to mount the winding path. I had my rucksack
on my back and I had fastened my fiddle-case around
my shoulders with a strap. I was too heavily laden
for a climber, but what odds ? One must endure the
crosses to win the crowns. All discomforts are insig-
nificant in comparison with the joy of playing the fiddle
on a peak overlooking Castile.

The sun beat down upon me remorselessly, but I
plodded on. The winding path had become a goat's
track over slippery rocks and crumbling earth. I had
not been educated to be a mountaineer, for I had wandered mostly in the plain throughout my life, so my
feet were clumsy : I slipped, fell back, fell forward,
fell sideways, but there was no one near to hear my
blasphemous cursing as I struggled, sweating, up that
rocky escarpment. In the far distance on the steep
slopes I saw frisky, brown goats leap from crag to crag
and I envied them.

When I reached the summit of the mountain the heat
of the afternoon was past.

I wandered about in a maze of jagged rocks. It was
like a torrential stream, suddenly petrified by a Gor-
gon's eye. Sometimes the impish fantasy of Nature
had carved the stone in the likeness of queer ante-
diluvian beasts and birds.

One spur of the mountain was cut in the shape of
a gigantic Moorish warrior lying on a bier. I saw his
broad forehead, his aquiline nose, stern chin and the
enveloping *burnous*. Here and there dotted in the
mountain were the caves, some of them as much as

thirty to forty feet in depth. As I lay at the edge of one of the caves with a sheer drop of a thousand feet, I saw below me the panorama of Castile. In the golden sunlight the plain resembled a huge brown quilt patched up here and there in red, purple and yellow. Brown is the colour of Castile, but it is shot with innumerable variants of red and purple, and in the distance it fades away to the colour of straw.

Deep below I could see the red roofs of the houses of Pancorbo, and here and there over the plain little *pueblos* like tiny clumps of red poppies.

Not a soul about, not a sound.

I saw a vulture with wings outstretched floating below me, and in the distance a tiny white puff of smoke from the train reminded me that while I was poised in the midst of this silent immensity there were others below dashing along through the noisy chaos of the world. As the sun sank lower, the distant mountains became bluer, and my grey cliffs turned to red and gold. I then remembered how a Spanish writer once said that the landscape of Castile was in the sky. However hot the sun and blue the sky there were always clouds forming and reforming, disappearing and re-appearing. The broad plain below with its tiny clusters of villages remained motionless, but overhead there was constant change and movement. I saw thin wisps of vapour float through the yellow sky on the horizon and join with a pink cloud to form a fantastic palace, with tier upon tier and terrace upon terrace ending in a cluster of minarets. Sometimes the clouds flitted through the air, at other times they moved majestic-ally, casting shadows upon the earth beneath.

" Clouds," said the poet Campoamor, " are ideas that the wind has condensed." As I watch their vague, ever-changing shapes, I feel that they are the tenuous creatures of my imagination.    From their unstable shapes I may interpret my own mind.

When I climbed up the mountain I was obeying a deep impulse within me.    At certain periods of our life we long to stop the inexorable ticking hand of time and meditate upon our whole destiny.    But alas, in the turmoil of to-day it is wellnigh impossible to drop out of the line and halt a while.    Our sense of honour and duty forbids us to be laggards in the fierce race.    In the olden days, when life was not such a mass of complexities, it was easier to retire from the fierce struggle and change the active life for the contemplative.    Many of the greatest thinkers retired to the cloisters where there were none to disturb their meditations.    But to-day our duty to the State forbids us to renounce the burden of life in the world, and everywhere youth is being educated to the idea that it is selfish and unpatriotic to relinquish obligations and retire from the struggle.    The tyranny of the State and society will soon deprive us of all the individual's greatest rights. We must live amid the noise and shouts of the world, and our houses must be open for all the world to see. Soon it will no longer be allowed to possess a secret room closed by a hidden key, for then the guardians of law and order would cry out that it was Blue-Beard's closet.    " He is like the cat that walks alone," they will cry, " and we are sure he is a suspicious character." And yet never was there a time when humanity needed its moments of silent meditation.    The greatest reformer of to-day will be the man who founds a League of Silence.

My greatest joy in my wandering springs from my sensation of silent solitude.    During my working days at home I rarely have the time to think, for I am then, as it were, under military discipline and a soldier must never think. But when I wander away from my world, I am free to converse with my different personalities and I even allow each of them a little freedom of expression from time to time.

When I set off to climb the Pancorbo Sierra, I wanted to reach the domain of silence in the upper air and purify myself after my life in the plain. For, as Unamuno says, a mountain rises towards the sun like a naked body that has cast off its garments. In this kingdom of silence I can make my examination of conscience. When I look back on my days of wandering, I feel a sense of profound melancholy as though the scenes I had witnessed, the fugitive melodies I had heard, the personalities I had met for a fleeting instant were all part of a vague dream. When I was following my humble life as a vagabond minstrel in the villages I lived for the moment without a thought for the morrow. Up here in my present melancholy mood, with the sun sinking behind the mountains on the horizon, I feel a sense of helplessness in face of the cruel universe. Two more vultures have flown to their nests in the rocks above the caves. They are sinister watchers like the ravens of Wotan. A yellow feather flutters down from above and falls near my feet.

The sun has sunk and the rocks begin to turn to a violet tinge in the dusk. Like a lonely Indian rock-dweller, I longed to worship the dying sun. All the world around me was full of mystery. Not a sound anywhere. So still was the scene that I fancied I could hear the dew fall. The rocks in the dim light looked strangely watchful and I thought I saw a figure gazing at me. I sprang to my feet and stumbled across, only to find that it was a big piece of quartz.

I then collected some sticks and weeds and lit a fire at the entrance to the cave. The flames lit up the grim vaulted cavern and cheered me.   After drinking a little *aguardiente* I took out my fiddle and started to play. The notes of the instrument floated through the stillness of the night and the cavern echo harmonized the single notes.   With a bright fire and a fiddle to keep me company I should snap my fingers at all the spirits of the universe, but still I could not shake off my attack of the shivers.   I do not believe a traveller who tells me he never suffers from an attack of the shivers, even though I know he is as courageous as Achilles. Sometimes I fall victim to them without a moment's warning.

I still had the eerie feeling that someone was watching me.   The flames of the fire lit up the cave, and as I drew my bow to and fro across the strings, my huge, warped shadow quivered on the wall.

Suddenly I heard a rustling sound behind me and I turned round swiftly, dropping my bow in terror.

There was not a sign of any living being, but the unearthly stillness increased my shivers.   My teeth chattered and a cold sweat broke out upon my brow.

After a few minutes I heard a rustling, scratching sound again, and in addition a faint wheeze.

What could that wheeze be ?

It sounded like the heavy breathing of an old man hidden away in the pitch-dark recess at the back of the cave.   I then recalled an experience years ago in an ancient castle in Wexford, when I had heard a similar sound.   One night when passing the haunted tower of the castle, I heard a strange wheezing sound and I thought the ghost was abroad.   So I searched up and down, but not a trace of the ghost could I find.   At last, when climbing up the winding stairway to the roof of the tower, carrying a lighted candle in my hand, I suddenly saw two big eyes staring at me from the top step. It was a big white owl, wheezing and blinking at me in the light of the candle.

I searched everywhere in the cave, and among the rocks outside, but not an owl did I find.

Perhaps the sound came from one of the vultures that nested above. I have always looked on vultures with horror, ever since the day I saw them perched in a row, gazing with sullen eyes at the carcase of a mule which a Gypsy was flaying. No sooner had he departed with his hide, than there was a whirr of wings and a swoop down on the carcase. In a few minutes there was nothing left of the mule but a heap of smooth white bones. Hence my fear lest those " living tombs," as Æschylus called the vultures, might take it into their heads to join me at my camp fire. I was afraid to leave the fireside and walk about outside in the dark because many rocks looked to me like pale silent faces, and yet when sitting by the fire I was frightened by my shadow on the wall.

Few human beings possess enough powers of concentration to endure complete silence. I was too conscious of my pounding heart and too restless a victim of my riotous imagination.

I tried to make my mind a blank so that it might become hypnotized by the silence, but instead, I found that my ear detected the minutest sounds around me and each one flashed disturbing thoughts through my mind.

Not a wink of sleep did I get that night in the cave, and I felt like a mediæval noble of Castile watching over his armour on the night before he was dubbed a *caballero*.

I saw the gradual approach of dawn.

First of all there was a long, dark, sullen period; then came the faint grey light with green reflections in the sky. Then there was a hush before the first slender rosy finger of dawn appeared on the horizon leading to the outburst of sunrise which I saluted with music from my cave. During the long period before the sunrise I had felt a sense of oppression as though the air was heavy with dew. Then all of a sudden there came a slight rustling breeze as if somebody had opened a window in the sky to purify the earth and brush away the cobwebs of the night.

I rose from beside the fire and went outside to gaze upon the panorama.

In the nippy morning air I felt invigorated. All my pessimistic thoughts of the night fled as though by enchantment, and I was eager to continue my wandering through the plain. There before me lay Castile of the Cid Campeador, national hero of Spain. Over that plain the warriors had galloped on their chargers, clad in coat of mail, to fight the Moorish infidel, shouting the Christian war-cry—*Santiago y cierra España* (Saint James and close, Spain !). The slender ribbon I see winding over the brown expanse is the famous way of Saint James.

Along that road thousands of pilgrims through all the ages journeyed towards the distant western shrine of the Apostle. Kings rode over that plain with their retinue ; powerful lords and ladies too, as well as humble minstrels, bringing with them the pageantry and songs of France and Italy. From my mountain cave I could have seen their thousands advance like crawling ants over the road towards Briviesca and Burgos. Who could travel to-day over that plain and not feel that from its brown earth sprang all that was noblest in the Spanish race ?

As I was clambering down the rocks from the cave, I came suddenly face to face with a shepherd who was leading his goats to pasture. He was a small, wizened-faced old man, with black hair and stubbly beard. My sudden appearance at that early hour must have terrified him, for after darting one look at me, he shouted and fled down the path followed by his goats, as though a herd of spectres in white shrouds were after him. Stumbling and muttering to himself as he ran, he soon disappeared from view.

I continued my descent calmly, and in less than an hour I reached the village.

## CHAPTER XX

## THE INN AT PANCORBO

AFTER my alfresco night in the *sierra* I murmured to myself in the words of Falstaff, " Shall I not take mine ease in mine inn ? " The inn at Pancorbo was outside the *pueblo* between the main road and the railway. From outside there was little to suggest feather beds and Lucullian banquets ; in fact the building was a rather ramshackle Castilian farmhouse and I asked myself mentally the usual question that comes into the traveller's mind as he crosses the threshold : " Into what category of Spanish hotel must I set this example ? "

The language is rich in words for " hotel," because the Spaniard, being a true individualist and a nomad, takes pleasure in distinguishing subtly the various types of resting-place. The genuine inn is called the *posada*, which means a place of repose. Richard Ford, in his classical description of Spain in 1846, says that the *posada* ought to be compared to its type the " khan " of the East, and never to the inn of Europe. " If foreigners, and especially Englishmen," he says, " would bear this in mind, they would save themselves a great deal of time, trouble, and disappointment, and not expose themselves by their loss of temper on the spot, or in their note-books."

After many rambles through Spain I have acquired

some of the Spanish fatalism with a good dash of curiosity. It is a *posada* said I to myself as I entered the wide-open door of the house behind a man who was leading a mule. In accordance with true Castilian tradition the ground floor was given up to the mules and cattle. So dark was the interior that I had difficulty in groping my way, and I slipped perilously in cow-dung before I reached the stairs leading up to the first floor. Here I was agreeably surprised by the air of comfort of the inn. Along the wall of the landing which went from one end of the house to the other there were old Spanish chairs, and a carved chest ; the kitchen had many resplendent coffee pots and pans ; there was an attractive *comedor*, and my bedroom with its window looking out on a kitchen-garden boasted of a fine double-bed with fresh sheets and a gaudy quilt.

It is not a *posada*, I murmured, for then there would be no dining-room and the landlady would mumble the eternal refrain : " We have no food. There is just enough for the *arrieros* (muleteers). If you buy some meat at the butcher's out in the *plaza* I'll cook it for you." No, it was not a *posada*, nor was it a *parador*, for a *parador* is a mere halting-place, whereas my comfort-able bedroom tempts me to stay here a week at least. It is more like a *fonda*, but the Italian word calls up too many visions of Lombard and Venetian inns, whereas this place is essentially Castilian. I prefer to call it a *venta*, which, according to Richard Ford, is an isolated country inn, a house of reception on the road.

Gautier, in his *Voyage en Espagne*, relates how he halted at this Pancorbo inn and had to pass behind the mules to get to his room. To-day, as a result of the advances of modern civilization, the inn has many more benefits to offer the traveller. The wine was excellent and did not taste of goatskin as it did in the time of the

good Théophile. The improvement, I am sure, is due
to the Spanish artists and writers such as Zuloaga,
Ramón Pérez de Ayala and Unamuno, who visit the
*sierra* frequently and induce the fat old landlady to raise
her standards of comfort. And so the inn tempts the
Falstaffian traveller to take his ease and at the same time
it preserves its ancient tradition of *posada* which appeals
to all modern lovers of the picturesque.

The landlady, whom I mentally labelled "Tía Fermina,"
is an imposing figure and deserves the title *tía* or aunt
which is given in Spain to a married woman who is a
personality. Tía Fermina remembers all famous guests
who have halted here : she will tell you what Don
Ramón said to Don Ignacio and how Don Alejandro or
Don Calixto quarrelled every evening over their wine, or
how Don Rafael always travelled about with a girl of
nineteen—fair as the sun. "Yes, Señor, I know she was
not his wife, for some of the others told me that his wife
was black-haired and lived in Madrid with the eight
children. *Es un escándalo,* but what business is it of
mine ? Still, I did sometimes want to cry out at the
hussy, *mala mujer !*

Economy is the watchword of Tía Fermina. Not a
crust of bread or a *garbanzo* is wasted in her inn. Every
evening when the work was done she would put on her
spectacles and work out her accounts until far into the
night. I was sure that she rationed the amount her
ancient, good-humoured, apathetic husband might spend
in the *tabernas* of Pancorbo. She gave him a few coins
with the air of a harassed mother sending her small
boy to buy sweets in order to keep him out of her way.
Yes, Tía Fermina was the soundest of economists.
Nothing was wasted in that inn : even the sanitary and
the drainage system of the house and stable was utilized
to fertilize the vegetables at the back. Tía Fermina,

being a stern economist, would not spend any money on personal adornment. Hence her slatternly, slovenly appearance with her torn rag-shoes, her dirty apron and dishevelled grey hair, which, added to her mountainous bulk, and coarse features, gave her the air of a good-natured ogress.

During my stay at Pancorbo I spent most of my time in the village tavern, because there I was able to meet the society of the village. No traditional dried branch was hung up over the door of the Pancorbo tavern to attract the thirsty villager. When I entered I had difficulty in seeing the assembled *tertulia*, so dark was the room. A Castilian tavern is built on the cellar or catacomb principle, as a refuge from the sun that beats down on the streets. In the dark cellar sit a group of men, with *boinas* or black, broad-brimmed hats on their heads. Not a word is spoken but the *porrón* of wine is passed from hand to hand. The *porrón* is a squat-bellied glass vessel with a long spout, and each man in turn holds it up to his mouth without letting his lips touch the spout. All the village worthies were there: the chandler, the grocer, the saddle-maker, the tailor and the cobbler. Who knows how long they had sat in silent conclave before I arrived upon the scene ? They all gazed at me without saying a word. Many questions, I am sure, were on the tips of their tongues, but they possessed too much Castilian dignity to give way to mere curiosity. It was the woman behind the counter who broke down the barriers, for woman in Castile is allowed the privilege of indiscretion. She questioned me unmercifully, and as I answered, all the silent men continued to gaze upon me, summing me up, weighing me in the balance, testing me by all the laws of man and beast.

At length I was found acceptable.

The saddle-maker—a tall, portly man, with red face and grey hair, like an aged, prosperous Sancho Panza—made place for me beside him and the *porrón* of wine was passed to me.

No people in the world possesses more courteous manners than the Castilian peasant. The reason for this national trait springs from the innate individualism of the Castilian. So conscious is he of his own solitary loneliness that he respects it in others. He knows that he is a desert-dweller in the midst of this immense brown steppe and that he must live out his life like a lonely watcher. Hence his cult of manliness and his particular concept of honour : the honour of the Spaniard, as many have shown, is the " pathos " or the passion of the lone individual. He neither offers nor seeks pity because he wants to be as Unamuno says, " nada menos que todo un hombre," a man who can stand on his own feet and fight for himself. Hence the long-drawn gaze in which he weighs and tests the stranger. The offer of wine pleased me more than gifts, for it meant recognition by the village : " Tell me who's your drinking companion, and I'll tell you who you are," should be the Castilian equivalent to the more commonplace proverb.

" Tío Martín is becoming madder and madder every day," said the saddle-maker.

" Why, what has happened ? " said the rest in chorus.

" I met him this morning near the church and he was as pale as a corpse, muttering to himself."

" His child is sick, they say, since last week," said the chorus.

" It wasn't his child. He said he had seen a ghost in the *sierra* up above near the caves."

I pricked up my ears as the saddle-maker continued.

" He says he was leading his goats up the path when he heard in the distance the sound of music—very faint,

says he, but not a bit like a shepherd's reed pipe—no
—something much softer. It was like angels' music
floating in the sky. Then the sound disappeared and
he climbed up towards the caves. When he had nearly
reached the top, suddenly from behind a rock a spectre
appeared. 'I thought I was going to die,' says he, 'and
I made the sign of the Cross, but it kept advancing towards me. So I turned on my heels and ran down the
path.' While speaking to me, the fellow was shivering
in every limb as if he had the fever. I think he is going
daft."

"Yes, we've noticed him queer this many a day,"
murmured the rest of the company, shaking their heads
mournfully.

"Did Tío Martín describe what the ghost was like?"
said I timidly.

"Yes, he did," answered the saddle-maker. "He
said it was a man, *muy feo* (very ugly), with long hair and
eyes like a vulture, and it was carrying a big shepherd's
stick in one hand and in the other a *caja* that looked like
a small coffin."

"Surely none of you believe in ghosts," said I.

"No more do we," answered the cobbler quickly.
"But those shepherds become mad after years of
watching their sheep and goats in the *sierra*. In the
night they imagine they see apparitions, and I don't
blame them : I wouldn't climb among those rocks in
the dark, no, not for a thousand pesetas. In the summer
they see ghosts and in the winter wolves. But Tío
Martín has shouted 'wolf' so often that we don't
believe him."

"Well, I slept last night in the cave of the Moors and
I saw no ghost," said I with a faint tinge of pride in my
voice.

My statement was received with incredulous astonishment by the company. It was unbelievable that I should choose of my own free will to sleep in a cave when there was a *posada* in the village ready for the stranger. I too must be mad, they thought, and they looked at me with some misgiving, but then with a fatalistic shrug of the shoulders and a few trite remarks on shivering in the dark, vultures and mists on the mountain heights, they passed on to other topics. I had become again in their eyes the incorrigible stranger, wrapped in a cloak of mystery. Perhaps I had my secret reasons for sleeping out on a mountain : if so, then it was none of their business.

I was sorry that I had not the opportunity of meeting Tío Martín the shepherd face to face again, that I might convey a less sinister impression of my personal appearance.

As it was my turn to stand the round I went with the empty *porrón* to the back of the shop where the huge wine-skins were stored. There they were in a row, huge, bloated pig-skins, brown, like the earth of Castile, but blackened here and there with pitch. Some of them were so bursting with wine that they stood up, ears, feet and all, like a living pig. Others began to droop pathetically as the woman bled them.

That bulging pig over there has all the humour of Sancho Panza, the glutton, who was really a wine-skin, full to the brim of good, mellow Manchegan wine ; this one here that drips into my *porrón* has been wounded, and I shall flush and grow merry with long draughts of that gore. Spiritual gore, that is what I should call it, flowing from those pigs that have come to life a second time to rejoice mankind.

Such were the big-bellied monsters Don Quixote the ascetic slew in the Manchegan inn, thinking they were giants. Tragic adventure indeed ! Who but the Knight

of the sad countenance would have sacrificed such
streams of gore even in his dreams ? Many times in
Spanish history has that adventure repeated itself, while
thirsty Sancho Panzas ruefully watch the earth drink
up the blood that has been poured in vain.

Before I left the village, the saddle-maker presented
me with a fresh *bota*, for my own was leaking. Selecting
one from about twenty that were hanging in a row in
his shop, he filled it with hot water and sugar to soften
its shrivelled skin and take away the smell of pitch,
and handed it to me with a gesture, saying : " Fill it
to the brim with wine and you are ready for a long
journey, or as we would say—' Está Vd con bota y
merienda.' "

From Pancorbo, my headquarters, I set out to scour
the countryside, following the road towards the River
Ebro. After eight kilometres, I halted at the village
of Encio, on a small hill, some distance from the main
road. At first I thought it was a village that had been
suddenly deserted by its inhabitants in time of plague.

Not a soul was to be found in any of the houses.

I walked up and down the main street and the narrow
lanes, but no sound did I hear save an occasional bark
of a dog. The doors of the houses were open, the tables
were laid and there was food in the larders. Furtive
cats gazed suspiciously at me from dark corners as I
wandered in and out of the cottages.

Where were all the inhabitants ?

Had they been suddenly spirited away by enchantment ? From the top of the hill above the village
where I rested a while I heard a distant sound of voices,
and I saw down in the fields a great crowd of people
harvesting. There was the whole village—men, women
and children, shouting and singing as they worked.
Not until the shades of night fall will the heavy, mule-

drawn carts lumber over those cobbled streets, followed by the excited throng. About nine kilometres farther on, I came to the village of Santa Gadea del Cid, a more imposing village, for it possessed an arched gateway like a fortified town. Who knows why it was called by the same name as the Church in Burgos where the Cid made King Alfonso VI swear before the nobles of Castile that he had no part in the treacherous slaying of his brother Don Sancho at the Siege of Zamora? The inhabitants of the village are convinced that the Cid stayed in their town, and they keep his memory so fresh in their hearts that he might have died only yesterday. A poor, decrepit village it is: the brown houses with their red roofs are for the most part wretched hovels: the narrow roadway and winding lanes inside the village were so clogged with mud, manure and drainage that I sank nearly up to my knees in the slush. But the citizens of Santa Gadea del Cid consider all those material ills of no account, for they are buoyed up by their association with the national hero of Castile. They may throw back their heads arrogantly and cry out— " Somos Cristianos viejos rancios," that is to say, genuine old Christians as opposed to the base renegades of the neighbouring villages. When I asked questions about the Cid, I was surrounded in a trice and a furious argument began of which I was the innocent cause. An old man tottered up to me, leaning upon a stick, and proceeded to give me a long disquisition upon the hero, how he had fought the Moors and had raised some of his bravest champions from this part of Castile. " Every stone of this region is historical," said he, " for it was the frontier and bitterly contested by the enemies of the Cid and his father." Then all of a sudden a man cried out from the group—" The Cid never came this way— there is not a word of truth in the tradition." For a moment there was silence and a gasp of horror rose from all the men. Then a chorus of excited voices broke forth against the renegade who disputed the authenticity of the tradition. "Why, Señor," said they to me, "that man is a madman and jealous into the bargain. He comes from the neighbouring village of Puentelarra and he is jealous of the men of Santa Gadea del Cid." Then the old man raised his stick, saying solemnly: "This is one of the towns of the Cid, and it is right that it should be so, for here may be found the flower of Castilian manhood."

In Santa Gadea I made the acquaintance of a queer little old witch called Cristina. She was eighty-nine years of age but as active as a woman of forty. She was only about five feet in height and as thin as a wraith, but her eye was as bright as a hawk's, and her bony, wrinkled face was twisted into the most malicious smile imaginable. The women of the village pointed her out to me saying—"There goes our Cristina—the worst tongue in the town. Nothing is hidden from that old ferret's gaze. She unearths the secrets of man and wife—why, she even turns the cow's milk sour if she goes near the women when they are milking."

Cristina then came up and joined in the conversation. As she smiled, every wrinkle on her parchment face puckered up with malice. "Yes, young man, they all hate Cristina, and if looks could kill they would all have laid me six feet under the sod long ago. But never mind, Cristina can turn them inside out. She knows all their secrets—eh, María, my dear? You wish your poor Aunt Cristina was over there in the graveyard, so that you might get her pesetas. But Cristina will cheat you—yes, if God is kind, she'll cheat you yet for some years to come."

Saying this the old witch raised her stick and waved

it in the direction of a fat matron who was sitting sewing outside a hovel surrounded by a numerous progeny. The fat matron said to me in a low voice : " She's a wicked old woman, Señor. Wherever her shadow falls, there's sure to be evil. She goes round the place creating trouble. God knows, we give her whatever there is in the house, but she is never content. She is always thinking that she has been robbed ; why, at night she sleeps with a bag of money under a pillow like a miser. Yes, miser, that it what she is—Vaya la roñosa ! "

Then began a long wordy dispute in which both children and grown-ups combated against old Cristina, but she fought like a demon and, flourishing her stick like a wizard's wand, she soon vanquished them all. As I walked away I heard her squeaky, querulous voice in the distance showering abuse upon them. In those tiny, out-of-the-way villages there must be many wizened old witches of our Cristina's type. They wield the powers of a tyrant in the community : old and young fear them, for they have outlived all the kindness, softness and weakness of human nature. In the midst of that crowd of women and children, Cristina was like the skeleton of the Dance of Death—a sinister figure, always present to mar the joyful feast of youth.

By the time I reached Pancorbo it was dark. Tía Fermina had prepared the *cocido castellano*, which was no other than the classical *olla* of Don Quixote. According to Richard Ford, a cook must throw her whole soul into the *puchero* if she would make a good *olla*. The soul of the *olla* in my opinion is the *garbanzo*, or chick-pea, which, scholars tell us, was the staple food of the country even in the days of the Carthaginians. The whole success of the dish depends on the cooking of those elusive chick-peas. If they have not been patiently soaked, they will bob up and down like pellets in the guest's inside. Tía Fermina's *olla* had the classical flavour of sausage, partridge, carrots, garlic, and she had not forgotten to season it all with plenty of bacon, for as the Spanish proverb says—

> " *No hay olla sin tocino,*
> *Ni boda sin tamborino.*"

(There is never an *olla* without bacon nor a marriage without a tambourine.)

But for many hours afterwards the *garbanzos* rattled within me like grape-shot and kept alive the memory of that historical dish.

In the inn I made the acquaintance of a commercial traveller called Gabriel Ureña, who was touring the villages of Castile, accompanied by his son. Don Gabriel was born in Chile and spoke Spanish with a mellifluous and, to my ears, exotic accent, but he was Castilian to his finger-tips. His home was at Burgos in the shadow of the venerable church of San Gil, and for the past ten years he had driven over the roads of North Spain in his battered Citroën car. He was a small, bald-headed man, courtly and pompous in manner like a nobleman of the old school. His son Pepe was so strikingly beautiful that for an instant I thought that the ghost of Rudolph Valentino had returned to life. He was tall and slender, with black hair and thick eyebrows. His face was moulded in classical proportions and his great dark eyes gave a look of tragic intensity to his pale, aristocratic face. There was a touch of effeminacy about him which became more marked when he became excited in conversation, for he would then make expressive gestures with his white hands with their long pointed fingers.

Father and son were the exact antithesis to one another in their opinions. Don Gabriel, who belonged to the old school, was a loyal monarchist and a fervent Catholic. Pepe was full of vague yearnings for a revolution that would sweep away the crumbling relics of the old world. Don Gabriel loved all the churches and castles of Old Castile because they reminded him of the glorious past of Spain. Pepe looked upon Spain with all the superiority of an arrogant South American. " My father is Spanish," he would say, " but I am Chilean : I was born in Chile and my education was South American: Spain is like a far-off dream to me." When travelling about together father and son would agree to differ and life was harmonious, but as soon as I the stranger took part in the discussion each would try to enlist my sympathy. The father would describe the burning of churches and convents, ending up with a pious hope that God would send destruction upon the wicked republican atheists : Pepe would then talk of lands held in mortmain by the Church, and he would discuss Doctor Vallina and the agrarian disputes in Andalucía until his parent would interrupt him indignantly with the words—" Enough, my son, you have wearied our friend by your irresponsible talk. Go and fetch that poem you were writing. Read it out to us and we shall criticize it." This was an unkind thrust, for, though Pepe was at the age when young men lisp in numbers, he objected to reading aloud his efforts to his father whom he considered an old-fashioned critic and entirely unable to appreciate the finer points of modern verse. Pepe was a snob in literature and he looked upon his father as the philistine business-man who is completely illiterate.

For a while I listened attentively to his sing-song voice as he read out to me a long poem on the Andes, but I had spent a long day tramping and I was weary.

My head began to droop and the poet's droning voice lulled me into slumber.

I awoke suddenly with a start, conscious that I had emitted a loud snore. Without a word I rose to my feet and with a hurried " good night " I went off to bed.

## CHAPTER XXI

## CASTLE CRAZY

DON GABRIEL'S Citroën car would have graced a Harold Lloyd film, for it possessed all the bone-shaking qualities necessary to provoke the mirth of the public. As we dashed along the road, it creaked, groaned, rattled and snorted so that I thought any moment it would disintegrate. While we coughed our way through clouds of dust I regretted having accepted Don Gabriel's invitation for a day's motoring.

Pepe was an erratic driver, but it was mainly the fault of his father. The old man kept up a continuous flow of critical comment which must have been maddening to the impulsive Pepe. To vent his spleen the latter would clench his teeth and scorch more fiercely, while Don Gabriel peered cautiously in front, trying to spy out through the dust any stray animals, whose presence on the road might be a grave danger to us.

As for me, I was resigned to my fate. I had seen a black cat just before we started—to me an unlucky sign, and I felt that some misfortune would befall us before the day was over. As the car jostled and swerved I shivered with apprehension lest Pepe's irritation might tempt him to take still greater risks. After crossing the Ebro we reached a tiny village, Espejo, and a little farther on we halted in a beautiful oasis by a stream. Here were trees and shrubs to give us delicious shade in the fierce heat of the day. The air was fragrant with sweet-smelling herbs, and over the softly murmuring water hovered myriads of white and blue butterflies. After a bivouac meal and a siesta we regretfully departed from the enchanting spot and resumed our bumpy journey over dusty roads. All went well throughout the day until it was time to follow the way home. Then, alas, the fates were against us. When turning a sharp corner the steering-gear went astray, Pepe jammed on the brakes, the car wobbled, Don Gabriel and I shouted, there was a crash and we all found ourselves lying in a heap in the ditch. The car was on its side—a piteous sight. "If we could pull it up on the road I could mend it," said Pepe with youth's impulsive optimism. But in spite of our Herculean efforts the car remained embedded in the ditch.

The road was deserted; Santa Angosto, the nearest village, was ten kilometres away.

What were we to do?

Don Gabriel then said that he knew of a castle three or four kilometres away where we might receive hospitality.

At the mention of the name, Pepe laughed sarcastically, saying: "Strange hospitality we'll get in that castle— I'd as sooner go straight to the asylum."

In spite of Pepe's protests we abandoned the car and set out on foot. Don Gabriel told me that the castle belonged to two sisters of noble family who lived alone. The younger sister suffered from an incurable complaint and the elder was her devoted nurse and guardian. For the past twelve years no one had seen the sisters, and many strange stories were told about them in the neighbourhood. Don Gabriel had known the elder woman many years before in Madrid when she was a young girl.

"She is a true chip of the old block," said he, "and

upholds an heroic tradition. In the olden days the women of that family were famous throughout Castile for their bravery, and a story is told how one of them put on the full armour of a knight and rode into battle to fight for the King. Such was the girl's valour that the King conferred a marquisate upon her. But to-day Doña Remedios does not ride out in coat of mail. Her heroism is to live like a hermit in the desert, sacrificing herself for her unhappy sister."

When we reached the castle dusk had fallen, and as we mounted the winding path a chorus of barking dogs greeted us. The castle stood on a small hill surrounded by a plantation of trees. It was more of a manor-house than a castle, but its battlements, loopholes and tiny moat gave it an air of feudal dignity. Seen through the trees in the fading light it looked like a fantastic mansion conjured up all of a sudden by a magician in a deserted place.

We crossed the moat by a little bridge and pulled a rusty bell by the side of the massive, iron-barred door. The jangling of the bell echoed through the building and the chorus of barks began again. Above our heads dozens of doves and pigeons nesting in the battlements cooed and gurgled. After some minutes we rang again, but there was no answer. At last, after twenty minutes of waiting, footsteps shuffled through the stone hall and we heard the sound of heavy bolts being drawn. The door opened and a small, white-haired, wrinkled old man peered out furtively at us. When Don Gabriel spoke to him he shook his head and tried to shut the door in our faces, but Pepe thrust all his weight against it and pushed back the little man into the hall. After a long argument the old man agreed to admit Don Gabriel to the lady's presence, but Pepe and I were to walk up and down outside in the meantime.

For half an hour we stood by the edge of the moat, gazing down into the still, black water. Not a soul, not a sound anywhere : we might have been in a city of the dead.

At length Don Gabriel rejoined us and led us into the house, saying : " Make yourselves at home, if you can, in this ghostly house : I was afraid she would not give us hospitality at first. She says her sister is in a very disturbed state and she is afraid of letting strangers near her. I know that the girl is mad. I confess I am beginning to feel scared already, for everybody in the house seems to be a lunatic. Look at the old servant." I saw the old man who had opened the door standing in a corner of the hall, gazing at us with a crazy expression. He had a candle in his hand which quivered as he held it and dripped grease upon the floor.

" They do not appear to welcome visitors," said I to Pepe, as we followed the servant down a dark passage. He led us into a lofty room which must have been the ancient banqueting hall. In the middle of the room was a long, narrow table with a three-branch candlestick at each end. These the old man lit, muttering incoherently to himself as he shuffled over the stone floor.

In the dim, flickering light, I found it difficult to observe the details of the room. There were old tapestries on the walls, torn in places and ragged : between them were ancestral portraits looking like pale ghosts in the flickering light ; at one end of the room were two suits of armour standing like silent warriors on guard. The furniture in the room was of the seventeenth century : there were presses of elaborately carved wood against the walls and around the long table were sixteen chairs—seven at each side and one at each end.

" How often do they give banquets here ? " I whispered to Don Gabriel.

"Not for many years past," he replied. "Look at the dust."

I then noticed that the table was thick with dust. The velvet of the chairs was torn and across some of them the spiders had spun huge webs of fantastic pattern.

"It is a mausoleum," said Don Gabriel, "enclosing all the memories of Doña Remedios and her ancestors. She has shut herself and her sister up in this tomb, where not a single ray of modern life can reach them. Our arrival from the outer world has disturbed and terrified everyone in the house, for it has made them conscious of their tomb."

After a long wait we heard a rustling in the passage and the light of a candle advanced slowly towards us. It was Doña Remedios herself. She entered the room and stood before us without saying a word.

Don Gabriel then took her hand and kissed it—"Señora, let me introduce my son and our friend whom you are good enough to entertain to-night."

I then bowed and went through the formality of the *besamano*, expressing my deep sense of gratitude.

The lady then said in a slow voice : "Gentlemen, I am pleased to welcome you to my castle and offer you hospitality for the night. I have forgotten the usages and conventions of the world in my secluded life, but I do remember that none of my family ever turned away a lonely traveller from the door."

In the light of the candles, Doña Remedios looked like a ghost. She was a tall, gaunt woman of about forty years of age; a drooping figure and a pale emaciated face with sharply cut features. Her black, flowing garments with long sleeves, and her veil draped round her head, gave her the appearance of a queen of night. Her waxen face resembled a mask of death, were it not for her deep-set eyes which shone like fire. They were the eyes of a fanatic and they made me think of Queen Joan the Mad. After a pause, Doña Remedios went to the door and clapped her hands loudly. A little wizened old woman came scurrying along the passage. Doña Remedios then said in an imperious tone, that it was time to serve food to the guests.

I have never been present at a stranger dinner-party. There was not a trace of the convivial hospitality which you, O Epicurean traveller, expect from palaces.

The conversation was mainly in monosyllables.

As we ate in silence I felt like a guest at a Borgian banquet: the rather tasteless soup might contain some subtle poison : the wine was sour and my glass was very dusty, but I dared not adopt the Spanish habit of wiping it thoroughly with my napkin, for I might have condemned myself in the eyes of this noble lady as a frequenter of pot-houses.

My dinner was spoilt for me right from the outset by my evil star. Hardly had I sat down upon my red velvet, seventeenth-century chair when with a crackling noise it broke under me, throwing me heavily upon the ground. No mischievous Puck could have played a more sinister prank upon a shy, fat stranger. Red with confusion, I scrambled to my feet with profuse apologies. To my surprise not a word was said. Not a muscle in Remedios' pale, emaciated face moved. Don Gabriel and Pepe, though their eyes sparkled with merriment, did not betray their feelings, beyond a short cough. The old servant silently removed the broken chair and drew up another. I sat down gingerly upon the edge of it.

It is curious how tasteless all the food is, thought I, as I vainly looked around for the salt-cellar. I remembered the old folk-legend of the peasant who was asked to dinner by the Devil in disguise. Dish after dish was served to him, but none of the food contained salt because his Satanic majesty rejects salt like poison. When the peasant called for salt there was consternation, and when in fear he made the Sign of the Cross the whole banquet, Devil and all disappeared into thin air. Fearing that the same might happen to me, I held my peace and continued eating my tasteless mutton.

While we dined the old woman-servant stood behind Doña Remedios' chair, and from time to time spoke into her mistress's ear. Meanwhile Don Gabriel, Pepe and I tried to keep up a conversation in order to cheer ourselves, but every few minutes Doña Remedios would rise from her place and walk to the door of the hall and listen intently.

Suddenly we heard a prolonged, moaning cry which seemed to come from an upper storey of the house. It started as a low moan and rose to a shriek. At the first sound Doña Remedios stood up and called the old servant to her side. The latter hurried out of the room down the passage. The moaning stopped, but we then heard the sound of stamping and banging of doors above. Doña Remedios stood silently in the middle of the room waiting. After a long pause we heard the sound of struggling outside and all at once a young woman came running into the room pursued by the servant and another old hag.

Rushing up to Doña Remedios she cried out excitedly : " Sister, they tried to prevent me coming downstairs. He has come, he has come." She then turned and looked at us wildly. " Where is he, sister ? Lead me to him at once." She went over to Don Gabriel and looked at him, muttering to herself, " No, it is not he." She passed on to Pepe, still muttering. " No—no." When she came up to me she stood looking at me for a long time, then she touched my face, passing her hands over my eyes. At last with a sob she turned away, saying : " Where is he, sister ? Where have you hidden him ? " She then went over to where Doña Remedios was standing and put her two arms about her, weeping as if her heart would break.

When my shock at this apparition had passed I observed the girl closely. She was about thirty—tall and thin, like her sister, but more ethereal : whereas the elder sister was emaciated and wrinkled, with traces of deep suffering in her face, the younger had a simple, childlike expression and her eyes had a vacant stare. She had put rouge on her pale cheeks and this gave her a look of hectic excitement. Her fair hair, which was parted in the middle, hung in two long plaits down her back. She was dressed in a white silk dress, but it was tattered, torn and stained. No stockings had she, or shoes, and I noticed that her white feet were tiny and delicate. Around her neck she wore a quantity of gold chains that shone in the candle-light.

Doña Remedios at first tried to persuade her sister to return upstairs to her room under the guidance of the two old women, but the girl pushed them away, crying out : " Let me stay, let me stay ! Can't you understand that this is the greatest moment of my life ? "

Doña Remedios led her sister over to a chair and made her sit down. She then stroked her forehead, talking to her gently in a mild, reproving tone—" Now, my dear Asunción, rest a little while. He will come, he will come."

The girl, after a short pause, suddenly sprang up, wrenched herself away from her sister and ran across the room, crying out : " I heard the door slam ; there he is—there he is." Her face was deathly pale, except for the two blobs of rouge in her cheeks ; in her frenzy she had bitten her lips and her mouth was covered with blood. "There he is," she repeated, and with those words she disappeared, followed by the two sinister hags. Doña Remedios turned to us, saying: "Gentlemen, you know my secret now. I had hoped to conceal my poor sister Asunción from you. You now understand why I live here in this lonely castle. When we are alone here no one knows of her madness but these faithful servants of the family, who have been with me since childhood. Here I can devote myself entirely to my poor sister and give her moments of rest." Wiping away a tear, Doña Remedios continued her story.

"Twelve years ago," said she, "my sister and I lived in Madrid. Our parents died very early and I was mother as well as sister to Asunción. She was then eighteen and very beautiful but, alas, delicate and highly strung. Even in those days, I feared for her. Then one day, a young friend of the family paid his court to her. He was a fine *caballero*, handsome, of noble family, and Asunción fell in love with him. But I was grieved at the thought of his taking away my beloved sister. I hated him because I had grown to look upon Asunción as part of myself. I was jealous of him, yes, I was jealous, and now I feel that my jealousy was perhaps the cause of all the sorrow God sent upon us afterwards. Poor Asunción could read my innermost thoughts and she suffered, but she was determined to marry her lover. All had been fixed for a certain date when he would arrive in Madrid from Barcelona. Asunción's trousseau was ready, the guests were invited for the wedding, when all of a sudden news arrived of his tragic death. He had been killed on his way to Madrid. The poor girl collapsed in a dead faint. For a long time, we all thought she would die. The shock had been too great. Her mind clouded and she became again a little child as I used to remember her in the old days. We left

Madrid and retired to our castle in this desolate spot. Here, there is no prying eye to watch my poor sister when she raves as you have seen her to-night. She is not always in that state : most days she is calm and trusting like a tiny child, but when she gets her periodic fits of madness she becomes violent, and I must soothe her and play up to her tragedy."

Doña Remedios stopped suddenly, rose, took up one of the candlesticks and silently disappeared from the room. The old man entered bearing three small candlesticks and handed them to us. Without saying a word we followed him out into the corridor and up a creaky staircase to the bedrooms. He then led me to my apartment—a musty room with the windows hermetically sealed. With a curt " good night " he departed, slamming the heavy door behind him. The evening's excitement had wearied me more than if I had tramped thirty miles. I climbed into the lofty four-post bed with its thick curtains and soon fell asleep.

After a short rest I awoke suddenly hearing a tempestuous chorus of barking dogs beneath my window. I also heard a long-drawn-out sound of moaning as though someone was keening over a dead body. The moaning in the still night was as dismal as the cry of a banshee, and around the house the watch-dogs kept up their incessant barking.

" Asunción has a troubled night," thought I. " The presence of strangers in the house disturbs her and accentuates her delirium." I heard the sound of footsteps in the corridor outside my room and through the cracks of the door I saw lights passing. What has happened ? The moaning did not stop but continued on the prolonged, keening note. I dressed hurriedly and crept softly out of the room in my stockinged feet. Down the creaking staircase I went, along a dark corridor

towards the back of the house where I saw lights.
Hiding in a corner, I was able to observe without being
seen.

The three servants were standing in the yard with
lighted candles in their hands. In the middle was
Asunción so transformed that I hardly recognized her.
She was clad in a long black cloak, her hair was dishevelled, and she waved her arms up and down in
rhythm to her long-drawn-out moan. The three servants
stood there motionless and kept their eyes upon the
ground.

Then Doña Remedios went up to Asunción and taking
her by the arm she led her out of the courtyard, followed
by the three servants carrying their candles. I followed
the procession at a distance and watched it pass out of
the castle grounds into a small wood. After walking
about three hundred yards they halted at a small mound
on the top of which was a rough wooden cross.

Doña Remedios then took out a prayer-book and
recited some prayers in Latin while the three servants
chimed in with the responses. Asunción prostrated
herself at the foot of the cross and wept convulsively.
For a long while she remained there crying, muttering
incoherently to herself fragments of prayers, and every
few minutes she would raise her arms to heaven in an
imploring gesture and call out the name of her dead
lover. After the girl had worn herself out by weeping,
she buried her face in her hands and fell forward with
her forehead touching the mound of earth.

After a long pause Doña Remedios lifted Asunción
to her feet and led her away, followed by the servants.
The girl was now in a dazed condition. Without a
word she allowed her sister to direct her tottering steps
towards the castle. When they had entered, I crept
back into the castle as softly as I could, hoping to reach

my room upstairs unobserved, but when I mounted the
creaky staircase in the dark I suddenly came face to face
with Doña Remedios, who was gliding through the
corridor silently like a ghost. Paying no attention to
my confused explanation, she waved me aside, saying in a
loud voice, as if to herself, " illusions, illusions! I must
preserve her illusions. She now thinks that he lies
buried in the wood beneath the cross, and so for a short
while his spirit will cease to torment her. While the
spirit sleeps," she said in a weary voice, " I too may rest."

Next morning Don Gabriel, Pepe and I departed early
from the grim castle. Everyone seemed to be asleep
except the little old woman who opened the door for
us. Soon we were following the road back to Pancorbo.

# CHAPTER XXII

## THE PILGRIM OF SAINT JAMES

THE next day as I was plodding my way along the dusty road from Pancorbo to Briviesca a long, mule-drawn cart piled with sticks passed me, and the driver, seeing that I was red-faced and perspiring, invited me to jump up beside him. Mule-drivers are the chief friends of the lonely pedestrian in the roads of Spain. They are a good-natured race and they cannot understand why anyone in the world should walk farther than the distance between the stable-yard and the tavern. A traveller may always appeal to their aid when he is drooping from fatigue, that is to say, if he can attract their attention, for I know of no drowsier men in the world than the *arrieros*. They doze away their days on the Spanish roads, lying in the bottom of their slow-moving, jolting carts, while the docile mules plod along for ever to the same steady rhythm.

At Briviesca I forsook the muleteer and attached myself to two *peones camineros* (road-menders) who were walking to Villamorico, a village on the lower main road to Burgos. After the muleteers I should place the road-menders next in order as the great benefactors of the wanderer. They belong to the true brotherhood of the road and behave as knights-errant to the distressed traveller. They know where the inns and taverns are, and where there is a fresh spring of water. No traveller need fear that he will have to sleep in the open if he meets a *peón caminero*, for the latter knows where the road-menders' shelters are to be found.  Those shelters are merely huts by the side of the road, where the *peones* store their tools.  They are the resting-places of every nomad, and the walls are scrawled with initials and signs of those who have camped by the way, and on the earthen floor there are the ashes of many a fire that cheered the tramp during winter nights.

The road-menders in Spain are a race of knights-errant because they descend from the Prince of Spanish roads, Saint Dominic of the Causeway, whose name deserves to be engraved in letters of gold.  He was the great protector of King and Lord as well as humble pilgrim in the eleventh century when there were few roads and hedges.  Saint Dominic for the love of God gave away all his wealth to the poor and became a Benedictine monk.  But instead of retiring into the seclusion of a cloister he built a cell and chapel in the midst of forests and bramble-bushes by the pilgrim way.  After clearing the forest he built a causeway and established hermitages where pilgrims might halt and be refreshed before they continued their journey towards Burgos and far-off Compostela.  King Alfonso VI gave Dominic land and money which the Saint devoted to this great work of road-building.  Not only did he feed and clothe the poor palmers but he also nursed them when they were sick, and buried those who fell by the way.  To-day in Castile every *peón caminero* acknowledges proudly the Saint of the Causeway as his patron.  One of the two who walked with me came from the village of Villalobar, near the town of Santo Domingo de la Calzada, called after the Saint, and told me a legend of the town.

" What, Señor, have you not heard of the white chickens of Saint Domingo de la Calzada, which crew after

they were carved ?   It was a miracle performed by our
saint to show that he can protect the poor devil of a
pilgrim who is the victim of a pair of dark eyes.   It
was a girl in the *posada* who gave him loving glances,
but he was a serious fellow, always thinking of his
rosary :  he turned a cold shoulder on her and she
determined to revenge herself.   So in the night, she
stole a silver cup, hid it in his scrip, and then raised
the alarm, saying that the pilgrim youth had robbed it.
He was seized and brought before the judge, who condemned him and he was executed.   Then the parents of
the youth came to the town and asked the judge about
their son.   ' With my eyes I saw him executed ;  he was
as dead as those two roast chickens over there,' says the
man of law, pointing to two fat capons on the spit.
But lo and behold, the cock on the spit claps his wings,
stretches his throat and crows to remind the people that
to a Saint all things are possible.   And to the joy of the
parents and the amazement of the judge, the son appeared
in the flesh again."

Following the River Oca we passed four or five tiny
hamlets on our way to pick up the main road to Burgos.
Before we reached Zalduendo my two companions made
me turn aside from the road to visit the shrine of San
Juan de Ortega (Saint John of the Nettles), who continued the great work of Saint Dominic of the Causeway ;
he was as active a bridge-layer and road-builder as his
master, and in this calm retreat he built his beautiful
Romanesque church and the hermitage near by where he
lived until his death in 1163, devoting himself to the
needs of the pilgrims.   After his death, in common with
other saints of the Middle Ages, his spirit performed
miracles from his tomb, but, strange to relate, those
miracles were chiefly worked upon women.   Saint John
became the patron of women who wished for a child.

Even the great Queen Isabella did not disdain to pray at the shrine of the Saint for increase, and in answer to her prayers she was given three children, all of whom were destined to misfortunes—Prince John who died in youth ; Queen Joan the Mad ; and the hapless Queen Catharine of Aragon.[1] But in spite of Isabella's evil luck, Saint John has never lost his reputation among matrons and many go to-day into his chapel to pray for son and heir. It was of Saint John of the Nettles that they tell the lovely story of the white bees with fragrant odour that rose from his tomb when it was opened in the fifteenth century. In folk-lore bees are unborn souls and Saint John kept hosts of those bees ready in his tomb for women who should beg for babies.

After saying farewell to my road-mending companions at the village of Villamorico I continued my way towards Burgos in the glow of the setting sun. As I walked along, the lines of Antonio Machado came into my head—

" Castilla miserable, ayer dominadora
　　Envuelta en sus andrajos desprecia cuanto ignora.
　　Espera, duerme o sueña ? La sangre derramada
　　Recuerda cuando tuvo la fiebre de la espada ? "

In a few days' tramp I had seen many ragged villages where in former days proud heroes dwelt. Castile, as the poet says again, once so fertile in captains, is to-day the stepmother of humble labourers without a trace of decadence. How long will this land of memories continue its sleep and dreaming : when will modern civilization come to this great Castilian people which still clings to the Middle Ages ?

With these thoughts in my mind I was not surprised

[1] G. G. King, *The Way of Saint James*, London, 1920, Vol. I, pp. 431–7.

to meet a pilgrim on the road of Saint James. I came across him just outside the village of Zalduendo. He was resting by the side of the road cooling his feet in a stream. For a moment I thought that I had been spirited back to the Middle Ages, for here was the living embodiment of the pilgrim as described by the Arch-priest of Hita and other writers. He was dressed in a brown habit and walked barefoot : his feet were cut and lacerated after many a weary mile. In his hand he held a long staff and from his shoulders hung his scrip and a wooden cup for water. His hat was broad-brimmed and around it were the traditional shells that pilgrims to Saint James used always to wear as a sign that they had come from afar. He was a man of about thirty-five to forty, pale-faced with black beard. For years he had been wandering about the country as a pilgrim and he was now tramping on foot all the way to Compostela. " When I have prayed to the Saint Apostle," said he, " I shall set out from Galicia on foot and walk all the way through Spain, France and Italy to Rome. I made that vow long ago—on the day when I gave up all my claims to property and distributed among the poor all I had in the world. I come of noble family in the South of Spain and at first I studied for the priesthood, but I chafed under discipline. I could never have stayed motionless in a cloister : I longed to wander through the world from one shrine to another, praying for those who have no time to pray. Yes, Señor, all my life I wish to pray against the evil that is in the world."

As night was drawing on I asked the pilgrim whether we could share lodgings together in Zalduendo or in some neighbouring village, but he informed me that he never would sleep in a bed, nor would he accept any money. " I have made the vow," said he, " to walk barefoot, sleep in the open and live by charity." At

Zalduendo he knocked at the door of a cottage and asked
for some food. The woman gave him a piece of
*longaniza* and a chunk of bread, and filled his wooden
cup with water. After finishing his meal he sat beside
me on a wall and talked to me while I tucked into my
raw ham, bread and garlic. " Con pan y ajo crudo
anda el mozo agudo " (" Bread and raw garlic sharpens
a youth's wits "), said I, offering him a few sprigs.
Though he refused to take a swig at my wine-skin the
pilgrim did not refuse the gift of garlic, because of its
medicinal properties, as he said. He had such a touching
belief in the efficacy of prayer, that I told him the Asturian
legend of the lost soul that went on the pilgrimage to
the shrine of Saint James. It was a gloomy night and
not a star was shining to guide the soul along the way.
Then a knight came to a window and said :

" If thou art of the Devil I conjure thee to depart ;
if thou be of this world tell me what thou dost need."

The soul then answered : " I am a sinful soul
journeying to Santiago, but there is a deep river in front
of me and I cannot pass."

" Trust to the rosaries thou didst say in thy life,"
answers the other.

" Alas, woe is me, I said none."

" Trust to the fasts then or to the alms thou didst
give."

" Alas, I gave none."

But the Knight was charitable and he pitied the soul,
so he lit the sacred candles at the window and the soul
crossed the river and went on.

The same night the soul returned from the holy
pilgrimage singing—" Blessed be the Knight who by
saving my soul saved his own as well." [1]

For many hours that night we talked of the pilgrimage

[1] J. Menéndez Pidal, *Poesía Popular*, Madrid, 1885.

to Saint James and my head resounded with tales of miracles that took place all along the Way of the Saint from the day when, as Archbishop Turpin said, " The stars in the sky revealed themselves to Charlemagne and led him to Galicia in pilgrimage, so that all peoples should follow even to the end of time."

The night was warm without a breeze and we made ourselves a comfortable couch at the foot of some trees. Next morning we continued our journey towards Burgos and the ancient Hospice of the King where pilgrims used to halt long ago. I said farewell to the pilgrim of Saint James.

# CHAPTER XXIII

## A CITY OF MEMORIES—BURGOS

THE lace-work spires of Burgos Cathedral which caused King Philip II to exclaim, "It is the work of angels," awoke in me a host of sleeping memories. Thirteen years ago my wife and I had spent three months of our honeymoon in Burgos and our arrival in the city coincided with the solemn celebrations in honour of the seventh centenary of the Cathedral. In July of that year, we saw the national hero of Spain laid to rest in the Cathedral beneath a red marble slab before the high altar in the presence of the King of Spain and a vast concourse of nobles. Burgos initiated me into Spain. No other Spanish city possessed such an appeal for me as Burgos, because I had wandered through its narrow streets and explored its hidden beauties at an impressionable moment of my life. Burgos resembles a haughty princess who will not confer her favours lightly. She must be wooed by lovers who are ready to possess their souls in patience. There is nothing flashy about her: she prefers solemn grey to the warm yellow tones of her sister Salamanca. At first she repels the wanderer, for he may only be a globe-trotter who is content to give her a hasty glance before he continues his journey in the express to Madrid. I well remember our arrival in July 1921 from Irún. The train halted at Burgos before dawn and we des-

cended half asleep upon the long, deserted platform.
Not a soul to be seen anywhere but a solitary bleary-
eyed porter, who led us to a primitive horse-bus.    In
that decrepit vehicle we bumped our way in the dark,
beneath trees, under arches to our lodgings in Llana de
Afuera, a square behind the Cathedral.    As soon as I
thought of the house in Llana de Afuera I visualized
our dear Doña Leocadia.    Many years had passed since
I had given a thought to Doña Leocadia, and yet
she is attached to many delightful memories.    For a
moment I held my breath in agonized suspense : ten
years have passed and who knows if she is still alive ?
I could not even remember her full name : all I knew
was that we called her Doña Leocadia, that she was a
widow and lived at No. 5 Llana de Afuera.    Straightway I went to the square and with trepidation rang
the bell of the house.    An aged dame, evidently the
charwoman, opened the door and eyed me suspiciously
from head to toe.

"Is Doña Leocadia at home ? " I asked timidly.

"Who wants to speak to her ? " said the woman
gruffly.

"Tell her Professor Starkie wishes to greet her."
When I said this the woman looked so frankly incredulous that I regretted bitterly I had not cast off
my picaresque clothes and put on a black suit, bowler
hat and spats.    A continental professor is always smart
and *soigné*.

Grumbling to herself, the old woman went off to
deliver my message to her mistress.    After a few
minutes Doña Leocadia appeared.    I was delighted to
find that she had not changed in ten years.    Her figure
was as plump and matronly as ever : her hair was just
as black, her face had still that air of breezy good-
nature.    She was if anything more prosperous.    To

my dismay she did not recognize me when I put out my hand. Her straight glance seemed to say—" I don't know you : at first sight you look to me a tricky customer and I'd better be on my guard—one never knows nowadays."

" What, Señora : do you not recognize me ? Surely you remember the young *matrimonio* from Ireland—the bride was fair-haired, the young man played the fiddle."

" Y cómo no ? Of course I remember them," said Doña Leocadia. "The lady was *rubia* and the man was young and thin. Ah, surely you cannot be——" Poor Doña Leocadia broke off her sentence, and blushed in confusion, for it was on the tip of her tongue to add : "You can't be the same person, Señor : you are too squat and double-chinned and too unkempt. Why, that young man was dressed as a perfect *caballero*—with neatly pressed trousers, tan shoes, and his hair plastered down like a *señorito* straight from Madrid." All the good lady actually said was : " Well, Señor, ten years have passed and time changes every one of us."

Doña Leocadia none the less hastened to kill the fatted calf for me. She gave me the best room in the house—a combination of bedroom and drawing-room, with a balcony looking on the street. It was the same old room I knew so well. The bed was still covered by the red-embroidered quilt; the same old print of Don Quixote brandishing his spear as he spurred on Rozinante, hung upon the wall.

Doña Leocadia is a discreet woman and not given to prying into what does not concern her. She did however peer into my rucksack, and to my dismay she began to unearth its secrets. With shame I watched her pull out begrimed shirts, torn socks and handkerchiefs and drop them gingerly upon the floor. She then said : " I remember your wife, Señor : how she

used to mend your socks and iron your ties. You
need a wife or a mother this moment to look after
you."

It was pleasant to be mothered after living the life
of a tramp, so I submitted with good grace. My meals
were served in solitary state as if I had been an emperor. Doña Leocadia would not eat with me, but
after I had finished my five-course banquet, she and her
niece and a few crony neighbours would troop into
the room and form a circle around me. I was expected
to talk while the women sewed or embroidered, but
before I could utter a consecutive sentence one of them
would interrupt with excited comments. Doña Leocadia was a fierce conservative and she felt nothing but
loathing for the new republican government. She was
aided and abetted by the two old cronies who nodded
assent to everything she said. But Doña Leocadia's
young niece was the rebel, and every evening the battle
would rage between the old and the new, whilst I as
the much-travelled stranger was expected to hold the
balance. Doña Leocadia's niece was eighteen years of
age, black-haired, brown-eyed, and vivacious—a tempting morsel for Don Juan Tenorio, if he existed in a
town so far north as Burgos. But Don Juan would
have had to tread the primrose path warily as far as
Isabel was concerned, for Doña Leocadia watched over
the girl as if she had been her daughter. Having no
daughters of her own, the good lady centred all her
maternal impulses in Isabel. When I gazed at Isabel
I was conscious of the passing of time. I remembered
her as the little girl eight years old who used to romp
about on the floor of our sitting-room. In those days
she was being prepared for her first Communion and
my wife helped Doña Leocadia to make the white dress
and veil for the ceremony. I had seen her sitting in

a pew in the Cathedral with her little companions and
I had compared them to a bunch of snowdrops.  To-
day she was grown up and waiting for a romantic *novio*
to carry her away on his horse as if she had been Rapun-
zel.  Isabel fretted under the severe discipline of her
aunt.  Doña Leocadia possessed a strong personality
and she wanted to quell the rebellious nature of her
niece.  " Ah, Señor," she would say to me, " why can
I not cure her of all this day-dreaming ?  Her head is
full of romantic nonsense that she has read in books.
I have asked the *cura* to talk to her, but she says he is
too old and does not understand youth.  What are we
coming to, Señor ?  the world is upside down."

Isabel longed for dancing and excitement, but she
was not allowed to go anywhere without her aunt, for
in Spain it is not right for a young girl to be seen walking alone in the street.  There was perhaps a little
touch of selfishness in Doña Leocadia's love for her
niece.  She could not bear to be without her, for Isabel
was the soul of the house : she did most of the cooking, she made the beds, she mended the clothes, and
as she worked she sang the whole day long.  She was
usually laughing and singing, but at times she would
become serious and go over to the balcony to look
down at the *plaza.*  Then she would sigh, saying :
" Ah, Señor, how I wish I was a man : I should jump
down into the street and dash away so fast that my
aunt could not catch me.  Here I feel like a caged
bird.  Why can't I be like the girls in your country,
Señor, who are independent and live their own lives
without interference ? "

" But you are very young, Miss Isabel, and it is not
yet the time for you to spread your wings and fly away."

" Even if I was twenty-five, Señor, my aunt would
keep me a prisoner.  She says that a girl should be

locked up like a precious jewel which no one must see except the *novio*. But how can a girl find a *novio* if she never has the chance of meeting any man?"

Isabel then confided to me that she had a *novio*, but he was not officially betrothed to her, for her aunt knew nothing about him, and so the courtship was secret. She had met him one day when her aunt was away and it was a case of love at first sight. The young man used to leave notes for her hidden in a secret place, but she was mortally afraid of their being discovered, for Doña Leocadia had an eye like a hawk.

From the first I realized that Isabel had marked me down as her confidant. I became the sympathetic listener to whom she unburdened her heart. I have never seen a more serene girl. She had not the smallest trace of self-consciousness, as she prattled artlessly of her lover. He was the epitome of every masculine virtue.

" I wish you could see him, Señor : he is tall and *moreno*, with such soft, dreamy eyes and a broad forehead like a philosopher. He is so strong and manly like a soldier. I feel like a little child when I am with him and I like to play pranks on him and pull his moustache."

As far as I could make out, Isabel had only actually spoken to her *novio* on two occasions, but innumerable letters had passed between them and her imaginative temperament had already woven a romantic courtship with full details.

As we lived behind the Cathedral, some of my day was spent there. I used often to go to Mass with Doña Leocadia and her neighbours—all of them dressed in black and carrying big prayer-books.

I would always return to the Cathedral at noon, when

the streets were at their hottest, to enjoy the cool atmosphere. There are two mystical hours in such a cathedral—the hour of noon and the hour of dusk. At noon you may see all the colours of the Cathedral : the sun illuminates the beautiful, fourteenth-century glass of the great rose-window and creates a mass of dazzling jewels. Rubies, sapphires, emeralds, flash mingled with an all-pervading amber glow. The light of the sun dances upon the grey walls here and there, bringing to life strange statues hidden in corners and chiselled reliefs. At noon the sculptured figures of the Cathedral play their part for us in the light of the sun. At that hour there is only a sprinkling of people praying in the immense edifice and most of them are beggars and cripples. One old man kneeling with his head bent forward murmurs audibly to himself, and his voice echoes through the nave.

At the hour of dusk the aspect of the Cathedral changes. The statues and grotesque reliefs sink back to rest in their shadows, all save a few here and there whose features lit up by the neighbouring candles become sinister in the flickering lights. This is the hour of meditation when you will see many women dressed in black enter silently and seat themselves in the gloomy nave. Doña Leocadia comes here every day at dusk. I see her seated with her hands on her lap. Is she following Saint John of the Cross's journey of the soul and climbing the mystic ladder, wearing successively the three colours of Faith, Hope and Charity—white representing Faith, green Hope, and red Charity ? Or is she content to sit there motionless with mind at rest, having banished from her life all struggles ?

Doña Leocadia's pale face is a mask. What goes on behind that mask ? Who knows ? Once she was a laughing, rebellious girl like her niece Isabel, but years of tribulation have closed the windows of her soul one by one.

Three memories of the Cathedral of Burgos will always remain in my mind. First of all there is the chapel of the Condestable of Castile, Pedro Fernández de Velasco and his wife Doña Mencía de Mendoza, created by Simón de Colonia. Husband and wife lie side by side in the centre of the octagonal chapel, and so exquisite is the work of the artist that he has breathed life into the marble figures. They are not dead, but only sleeping. Pedro de Velasco was one of the most famous warriors of his age and deeply religious. When he rode into battle he always carried a tiny ivory altar which may still be seen in the sacristy. The sleeping figure with its elaborate carving calls up before us a vision of the Castilian hero of the late fifteenth century, when chivalry had become more spectacular. Pedro de Velasco was a Knight of Ferdinand and Isabella and belonged to that period when the Kingdoms of Castile and Aragon, through the marriage of their sovereigns, combined to create a spirit of chivalry with romantic trappings.[1]

Pedro de Velasco belongs to the age, described by the contemporary chroniclers, Diego de Valera and Fernando del Pulgar, culminating in the capture of Granada in 1492, and portrayed by the German artist in his carvings on the choir-stalls of Toledo Cathedral.

My second memory is a contrast to the gorgeous chapel of the Condestable. In a room off the cloisters, hanging from the whitewashed wall by a chain, is a battered old iron-bound chest called the " Cofre del Cid." When the *Campeador* was exiled by his lord and master, Alfonso VI, he was in desperate need of money

[1] A. Pastor, *Essay on the Chivalry of Spain*, pp. 109–40 in *Chivalry*, ed. by E. Prestage, London, 1928.

to pay his retinue, so he determined to borrow from Raquel and Vidas, the Jewish money-lenders. But, alas, he had no security. Then an idea flashed across his mind. He sent his friend Martín Antolínez to the Jews with two chests covered with gilded leather and studded with bright nails. " These," says he, " are full of gold, and the *Campeador* leaves them in your power as security for six hundred marks. But take heed of one condition. They must not be opened until his return." The Jews believed the word of the Cid and handed over the money, but later on, to their dismay, they discovered, upon opening the chests, that they were full of sand. According to tradition, the " Cofre del Cid " is one of those two chests by which Spain's National Hero cheated the sons of Israel. The story is often quoted as an illustration of anti-Semitic feeling, but surely such an idea is erroneous. The Cid was in a desperate plight through lack of funds and it was only as a last resource that he played the trick upon the Israelites. The Epic Poet makes him say " amidos lo fago " (" I do it against my will "). Besides, later on Minaya tranquillizes Raquel and Vidas by telling them that they will reap much benefit for what they had done for the *Campeador*.

The chest and the story attached to it remind us not to look upon the Cid as the French did upon Roland. Roland was god-like in his magnificence and when he fought he could always call upon the supernatural to aid him. The national hero of Spain unlike Roland did not belong to the highest aristocracy, but to the squire class and derived his income from his mills on the River Ubierna. Instead of an arrogant hero with feudal wealth and privileges we find a tender husband and father driven into exile by an ungrateful monarch. In this sense one of the most moving passages is the description which the epic poem gives of the hero riding with his men sadly through the streets of Burgos on the first night of his exile. No one will open his door or receive him for fear of the King's wrath, but he meets a child of nine years who consoles him and bids him godspeed.

As I wandered through the Cathedral examining the wealth of ornamentation and carved figures round the choir I wondered how the sumptuous church would appear to the ghost of the Cid were he to rise from beneath the red marble tomb. Would he not feel ill at ease if he found himself greeted by an arrogant knight such as the *Condestable*? Would he not sigh regretfully for the former chivalry of Castile when the simple rural knights ate garlic and indulged in horse-play?

My third memory of Burgos Cathedral is the Santísimo Cristo of Burgos, which is renowned through the whole country. When I tried to enter the little side chapel which contains the Crucifix I found that it was full of praying women. According to Doña Leocadia, the statue works miracles and the people of Burgos pray to it whenever they are in trouble. Never in my life have I seen a more terrifying representation of the Passion of Christ. The Figure on the Cross is said to be covered with human skin and to possess real hair and nails, and real thorns in the crown on its head. The bleeding wounds have been so well imitated by the artist that it is believed that the statue bleeds and the flesh sweats. There was even a tradition that it had to be shaven and have its nails cut from time to time. In the light of the candles the eyes move, the leather skin shines, and the whole body seems to quiver in agony upon the Cross. The Figure is dressed in an embroidered petticoat which by its ridiculous incongruity increases the effect of horror and makes me recall those mummified martyrs dressed up in satin and brocade, with white gloves on their skeleton arms, that are shown to travellers in some of the Italian churches.

The Santísimo Cristo de Burgos is an object of a profound cult in Spain. It represents the cult of Christ in agony before death, whom we adore upon the Cross, the Christ of agony who cries out : " Consummatum est." Agony is struggle and Christ dying upon the Cross brings us struggle not peace.

After half an hour's meditation in front of the macabre crucifix I began to feel like one who has spent all night in a closed cell waking a corpse. The air was heavy and there was a slight musty odour of decay. It was time for me to escape into the courtyard, away from Spain's cult of death. In order to clear my thoughts of visions of agonizing death I tried to recall epitaphs from the Greek wherein quiet figures say farewell to the world and depart with calm faces and undisordered raiment.

As I said before, Isabel made me her confidant and I had to listen to her while she read out to me long love-letters which she received from her impressionable admirer. I felt like a confessor, and while she read to me I would hold her little hand and pat her cheek. Doña Leocadia left us alone together because she had complete confidence in me as a married man and a foreigner. If she had only suspected the scheming brain of her niece she would have been more wary. For Isabel did not limit herself to asking me advice, but began to use my services as a chaperon or go-between. When she accompanied me to the Cathedral at noon, I discovered that it was not for the purpose of explaining the statues or sculptures, but of meeting her *novio*. Alas, Isabel had exaggerated his personal beauty. He was small instead of tall, with sallow, pimply complexion instead of healthy tan, and he wore spectacles. When we met, I thought that I could leave the two lovers together in the vast nave and disappear to my own devices, but Isabel was most indignant. It was my duty, she said, to accompany them and thus countenance their clandestine meeting. In spite of my protests, I was forced to follow the two around the Cathedral while they spoke together in a low tone. Not only did I feel mortified by my undignified position of " Celestina," but I also trembled lest Doña Leocadia might have taken it into her head to visit the Cathedral for a noonday prayer. Before long, Isabel made further demands on my good nature. I had the best room in the house, for it possessed a balcony looking out on the square. One night Isabel whispered to me when Doña Leocadia's back was turned, that she had a secret to tell me.

" What is it, my child ? " I asked with some alarm.

" He wants to see me to-night."

" But that is impossible, Isabel : you can't get out after dark."

" Oh, but, Señor, you have such a lovely room for a serenade : could you not lend it to me just for this evening ? "

" Your aunt would kill me if she found out that I was aiding and abetting you."

" Ah, Señor, she will be sound asleep. She always takes a sleeping-draught because she does not sleep well. To-night I'll give her a good dose of it and then she'll sleep."

In spite of all my arguments and protestations I had to give in to the imperious little damsel. After Doña Leocadia had gone to bed, Isabel waited until the worthy

lady was fast asleep, then she came into my room and
sat at the balcony talking to the young man who was
down in the street. As for me I sat at the back of
the room near the door, ready to warn the lovers as
Brangäne did Tristan and Isolde. To my dismay I
heard a sound of scrambling and I suddenly saw Isabel's
young man jump into the room. I left the lovers to
themselves and went over to the balcony in search of
the moon. Not a soul was in the square. In the
sky a spire of the Cathedral gleamed white under the
moon like a slender piece of silver filigree; below,
the huge mass of stone lay concealed in the shadow
like an ominous presence. I said to myself: " When
the moon sinks behind a cloud and the silver spire
disappears into the shades of the night, the fabric of
the lover's dream will crumble and draw them both
down to earth again."

As long as I stayed in Doña Leocadia's house I had
to play a double rôle. For part of the day I acted as
the gentleman of leisure, devoting my time to sight-
seeing in the town and visiting the Cathedral. But I
had to think of my finances. Burgos in summer-time
is thronged with visitors, and the beautiful promenade
called the *Espolón* is crowded at various hours of the
day. So I used to escape with my fiddle on some
pretext and make my way to the promenade and play.
At first I had very scanty success, for my audience
under the trees was mostly composed of nursemaids
and chattering children. Burgos in summer must be
a children's health-resort, for I have never seen so many
anywhere. Beautiful children they are too, and richly
dressed, for in Spain many parents stint themselves and
wear rags so that their children may be dressed in silks
and frills. In normal times I love audiences of children

who prattle artlessly and make personal remarks, but it is a different matter when one's purse is beginning to hang loose. Then it is time to avoid children and especially nurses, for they do not pay for minstrelsy. By experience I have discovered that the most unmusical creatures in the world are those buxom wet-nurses dressed in white, with white streamers to their caps. They are the personification of rosy, ox-eyed healthiness, but they have not as much ear for music as a heifer listening to a milkman's song. I saw more than a score of them in that shaded avenue at Burgos, and I made mental notes as I played. They were all mountainous in shape with distended breasts like well-filled gourds.

The mothers choose them, thought I, for those luxuriant orbs to which the infant may cling like a barnacle to a ship, but Rabelais and Sterne have told us the consequences of employing such nurses.

" The length of a nose," they say, " depends upon the softness and flaccidity of the nurse's breast."

In my journeys through Spain I had been struck by the number of Spaniards possessing long noses. I now realize that this peculiarity may be due to the ministrations of those voluminous nurses, for the nose of the child sinking into their soft breasts as into so much butter becomes as Sterne said, " So comforted, nourished, plumped up, refreshed and refocillated as to be set a-growing for ever." As a consequence you will rarely find a Spanish girl choosing a lover with a short nose. A long nose is the sign of manly worth, and if she is disappointed she will cry: " Nose, thou hast deceived me ! "

In our Northern countries where there are no wet-nurses and where woman is slim and hard-breasted, children have their noses so snubbed, rebuffed and rebated as never to reach their appointed length.

In spite of their plump, good-humoured exterior, those nurses are hoydenish tyrants, coarse-mouthed, loud-tongued and viperish in disposition. Rich families buy them for their houses as they would a milking heifer, but as soon as the woman crosses the threshold, she makes her master and mistress quail before her. Henceforth her word is law in the house. Give her this dainty, give her that and you'll hear her still grumbling. "Baby is pale to-day; the food must not have been tender enough for nurse."

"Baby cried all night: I could not sleep," says the father.

"I know why, dear," answers his wife. "Nurse says she cannot sleep in the nursery: it is too noisy. We must put her in the best spare-room."

When you look at those pampered, florid females, think of the wretched, rachitic infants they have cast aside to be brought up motherless in the Foundling Hospital.

In the cool of the evening, when the promenade was crowded, I obtained a fairer measure of success. Burgos is a big military centre and the streets are thronged with soldiers. From experience I found that the best points of vantage for a minstrel were the street in front of the barracks, and the *plaza de Prim*, a square which was always crowded with people waiting for buses to the distant villages. In one of the cafés I came across an old friend of mine—a waiter who ten years before used to serve drinks and ices in the Casino. When he saw me enter the café and ask the proprietor for permission to play a tune for the company, he came up and immediately recognized me. After the usual banalities he suddenly said: "Well, Señor: time has not dealt any more kindly with you than with me. I remember you as a rich man with a beautiful wife on your arm and I used to say to myself—there is one happy and contented man in the world at any rate. But *quién sabe?* This is a world of ups and downs and I see you have fallen on rough days."

Pablo, for that was the name of the waiter, had always been a confirmed pessimist, but his gloominess had increased with age. His hair in turning from jet black to iron grey had given him a more solemn appearance, but in manner he was as much an aristocrat as any grandee of Spain. In 1921 I had heard him exclaim passionately against the maladministration of the country, so I imagined that now, at least, he would be satisfied with free republican Spain. To my surprise, however, he waxed just as bitter against Alcalá Zamora and Azaña as he had done against the King. After a long harangue he wound up prophetically : " Mark my words, Señor ; Spain will soon be just an island of memory. Pilgrims will come here from every quarter of the world to see its beauties and dream of the wonders that have passed away. They will come to Burgos with flowers in their hand to cast them upon the grave of the Cid, saying, ' This was once Spain,' and they will depart weeping."

" Come now, Pablo," said I, " you are too pessimistic. Bring two glasses of Manzanilla and let us drink to the newly awakened Spain ; may she never prove unworthy of her ancient glories."

After leaving Pablo I returned to my minstrel work in the *plaza.* A band of young girls shouted out to me in chorus to play " La Marseillaise." All over Castile in 1931, even in the smaller villages, I found that the national anthem of France awakened enthusiasm among the young. The atmosphere of revolution still clings to that rousing song, and in modern Spain it has become the symbol of the struggle for liberty. The young men and young girls who surrounded me applauded vigorously, but I noticed some scowling faces among my audience, so I hastened to play *peteneras* and *boleros*.

After a while I handed round my hat. A good shower of coins jingled in it as I passed.

All of a sudden on the outskirts of the crowd I came face to face with Doña Leocadia. There she stood amidst a group of old women dressed in black and stared at me reprovingly.

With biting sarcasm she said, handing me a peseta: " In return for your Spanish songs, Señor, here is the image of my King."

## CHAPTER XXIV

## GYPSY CAMP FIRE

AFTER saying farewell to Doña Leocadia I set out
to look for the Gypsy *patrin*.

Where are the raggle-taggle Gypsies ? I
have not set eyes on one of them since I hatched my tan
in Burgos. When an English Gypsy is lost and cannot
find the camp he cries out in the night the magic words
" Romany joter ! " and gives the Gypsy whistle on the
two notes ; but here in Spain the *Gitanos* are more elusive.

Lucas said to me : " You won't find them in the town,
brother : they're not always welcome there. Go up to
the arch of San Esteban at sundown and you'll find some
of them loitering about near by."

The arched gateway of San Esteban is in the oldest
part of the city, on the way up to ruins of the old Castle
of Burgos. It is a Moorish horse-shoe arch of stone
surmounted by an open gallery of small arches, forming
part of the ancient city walls of Alfonso el Sabio. As
soon as I reached the gateway I saw two ragged, brown-
faced fellows leaning over the parapet gazing at the roofs
beneath. Approaching softly I suddenly shouted out
in Romany :

" Lachés chibeses plalorós : where are the tents ? "

The two turned round suddenly with one accord and shouted back in surprise : " What ? You one of the *Calés* ? " " Why, we thought you were a *Busnó*."

After the introduction it was necessary to say the password and mention the name of other Gypsy chiefs, for in that way I might enter the tribe as a guest.

" Yes, brother, I have come from another country, but I bring news of the Heredia clan, and Lucas el de la sonanta (guitar), so you must welcome me." Among Spanish Gypsies nicknames often perform the functions of passwords, and if the Romany rye knows them he may go from one end of Spain to the other and find the Gypsy tents and houses open to him.

After leaving the arch of San Esteban with my two companions we set off for a camp which was in a lane at the back of a neighbouring hill.

As I walked along with the two ragged youths I remembered the words of warning of an older Romany rye, a friend of mine : " Whenever you meet a tribe of Gypsies in the deserted country, don't trust the younger members, for they might pick a quarrel with you and tear the clothes off your back and leave you stripped in the ditch with a wound in the head, especially to-day when Spain is topsy-turvy after the revolution. The best course is to inquire at once for the *puro Rom* or old man of the tribe, for he is the *crayí* or King, and his word is law. Once you have told him the password you will be as safe as in a church."

The old man of the tribe is the grandfather : he leads an enviable existence, for all the men, women and children serve him, and he is a dictator.

When we reached the camp we found him lying asleep in the grass with his broad black hat down over his eyes and his *chuquel* or hound beside him. One of the youths

kicked him to awake him and he scrambled to his feet
with an oath and peered into my face, muttering : " You
are not one of the *Calés*—Why, you've a white face."
Among the English or Welsh Gypsies the phrase *pawno
muy* or white face is an expression of scorn and used by
them to designate the *Busnó*. This is not a good beginning, said I to myself, but when I mentioned the name
of the Heredia clan, Agustina and Faraón, he became
affable and invited me to sit by the fire outside his tent.
He was a fine-looking old man in spite of his rather
ragged clothing : tall and lanky in figure with long wiry
arms and legs. His hair was black, and a tousled black
beard covered up most of his face except his flashing
dark eyes. As soon as he had drawn up a low stool for
me he turned to my two companions and cursed them
roundly for not having brought back a rabbit or a hare,
saying to them : " Where are your catapults—you lazy,
rascally louts ? "

The youths then extracted from their pockets two
of the most villainous examples I had ever seen. The
catapult is a Gypsy weapon all over Europe and I had seen
them in Hungary and Transylvania, but the catapults of
those Gypsies at Burgos would have slain Goliath first
blow. Instead of answering the old man, each youth
picked up a pebble and pulled back the sinewy elastic.
There was a simultaneous whizz, and the two pebbles
embedded themselves in a tree fifty yards away. The old
man then murmured the word *mol* and I took the hint
that wine was required. A tiny child seized the money
from me and rushed away with the old man's wine-skin
to the nearest tavern. When a Romany rye pays his
first visit to a Gypsy camp he would do well to double
the wine ration whenever he can, and add in from time
to time a dose of *repañí* : nothing loosens the tongues
of Gypsies more than brandy, for it whips the sluggish

body up to vigour. For that reason the Spanish slang phrase for having a drink is " darle un palo al burro " (" give the mule a taste of the stick ").

When the wine-skin returned full, the men of the tribe gathered round as if by magic. The six tents of the tribe were arranged in a row against a crumbling wall. They were not picturesque painted tents of world nomads, but rough, improvised contraptions. Some of them were triangular resting on one long stick and two short ones, others were fixed to the wall. Outside each tent round the fires women sat basket-making and as they worked they sang songs in a lilting rhythm. The wine-skin passed from man to man and warmed up their hearts. I was the *lachó quibilero* (good companion) whose health should be drunk by the whole company not once but many times. I then began to hazard a few timid phrases in Romany for now was my chance to be a word-taster and add to my store. The men with their big ash-plants tipped with iron crowded round me and patted me on the back. It was a fantastic scene. I saw in the fitful glare of the fire wrinkled crones, buxom, naked-breasted women suckling babes, golden-skinned maidens dressed in red skirts with golden earrings and bracelets on their arms; swarthy, bearded men with wild, bushy locks; lean and mangy dogs skulking in the background. It was the old *romi* of the tribe who tested me first—the wrinkled spouse of the chief, but the words she used would not be found in any school book, for the Gypsies like to shock the *Romany rye* in case he might have some remnants of *Busnó* modesty. Obscenity after obscenity—the gross words bespattered me like a fusillade of dung pellets and between each shot the old hag cackled with mirth, and the other women swayed to and fro with laughter. Fortunately I had been well coached in Romany swear-words and obscenities after long nights in Transylvania and in Spain, and I answered back. Words were bandied to and fro, shrieks of Gargantuan mirth arose. The men cracked their fingers like castanets, the naked children squealed, the dogs barked. Such was the prelude to the Gypsy-student's conversation in Romany. As I listened to the strange lilting tones of the language I began mentally to catch the fluttering words as a naturalist does butterflies in his net. Many of the words were as nomadic as the Gypsies themselves. They were like a magic *patrin* leading me back over the Gypsy trail to the East. Indian, Persian, Greek, Slav words flitted here and there in a maze, mingled with Spanish until my brain reeled. A paradise for the etymologist, thought I, but how can I write them all down in my notebook with all this shouting and confusion going on? The conversation in a Gypsy camp is wildly inconsequent and dashes from one subject to another, for Gypsies have not logical minds. Their language is based upon certain fundamental words which express their nomadic existence. There are few words signifying the organization, stability and steadfastness of the peasant who ploughs and reaps, and such a multitude of synonyms for action and movements. The Gypsy will say: "God condemned our race to sterility, hence we are for ever fleeing from deserted wastes towards a land of plenty. When we discover an oasis for our halting-place we mark it with the Indian swastika, but we do not tarry there long. As soon as it has given us its fruits we pack our tents and slip away in the night to fresh pasture."

"Accursed parasites," replies the civilized man, "you sow not neither do you reap, but you prey upon the worker of the soil. For this reason God condemned you to wander like poverty-stricken gleaners over the plains of the world."

While I was talking to the men the women had been stirring the *pirriá* or stew. "What are you going to give me to eat?" said I to the old man; "don't follow the Spanish proverb and give me cat instead of hare." "*Jojoi* (rabbit), that's what you'll get," replied the old man with a smile. When the food was ready, the old woman brought out a big dish and the three of us in turn spiked the best pieces of meat with our knives and passed the dish on to the younger members of the family. The wine-skin had been replenished again at my expense, so there was hilarious festivity in the camp. While we ate, the small children scrambled for dainty bits and the hungry dogs sat a little distance away eyeing us enviously. The chief then told me his name. He was called Pedro de Castellón and he came originally from the Province of Valencia, but he and his tribe spent most of the winters in Logroño. "Burgos is our halting-place for the moment," said he, "but we are always on the move through Old and New Castile, aye and down through La Mancha into Andalucía."

"How do you eke out a living?" said I.

"Querelando cornichas (making baskets)," he replied. "We are *Bajirinanós* (basket-makers), but there isn't much we wouldn't turn our hands to, in order to earn a *chulé* (dollar). Times are bad, *eray*, and there's nothing so vile as poverty. You are lucky because you have your *sonanta* (guitar). If I had such an instrument I could go up to Madrid and make money like Antonio Heredia or Pipindorio as we call him."

"Who is Pipindorio?"

"He is a cousin of the *chavala* you saw dance at San Sebastian. He plays and his wife Grañita dances. To-morrow I'll send for both of them and we'll have plenty of *jaleo* in the camp."

" Why don't we have some *jaleo* now ? I'll play for you." No sooner said than done. I took my fiddle out of the case, tuned it and started to play.

A minstrel must choose his melodies and dances warily if he wants to work the music on nomads. When I was among Hungarian or Roumanian Gypsies I played Hungarian or Roumanian music, taking great care to improvise in the different national styles. If I was in Andalucía I preluded pizzicato on the violin as if it was a guitar and played Flamenco. In Transylvania it was easy to be a minstrel in the countryside, for the fiddle among the Gypsies is associated with the *Beng* or Devil and many witch dances are dedicated to his Satanic majesty. Once the music starts, the orgy proceeds apace and the Gypsies become like demons when they dance. In Spain it is more difficult for the fiddler to work up the orgy because in that country the guitar not the fiddle is the magic instrument. Often in my wandering I remembered my dream at the beginning of my tour and wished I was a knight-errant of the guitar in preference to the fiddle. At first when I played an *alalá* and a *gallegada* and a *zortzico* my playing produced little effect beyond a low murmur of comment in my audience. The notes of the fiddle sounded hollow and empty in the laneway. As soon as I began the Flamenco style the murmuring became a stamp of feet and a clapping of hands in rhythm with cries of *olé*.

The Gypsy method of musical performance is closely allied to incantation, and the rhythmic phrase is repeated again and again until it hypnotizes the audience. Then

as a contrast to the brilliant first theme I made the
second subject as alluring as possible—

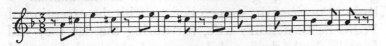

In Hungary, I know that the tenderness of the theme
would have fascinated the Gypsies, and I should have
held my audience in silence by my bow, as if it was a
wizard's wand, but not so in Spain. The Spanish
Gypsies are the noisiest people in the world when they
make *jaleo* or whoopee. They worship noise for its
own sake. It is not the melody which counts with them
but the rhythm. And the rhythm, once they have
stamped it and clicked it into their brain, serves as an
incentive to further noise-making. To a minstrel who
has been brought up in Anglo-Saxon countries, where
audiences listen in silent, polite boredom to the fiddler,
such clatter and din is disturbing. For he timidly
imagines that his playing is not producing its desired
effect, nay worse still, that it is causing an orgy of fury
among the audience, and he prepares to duck his head
at the first sign of a carrot or potato whizzing through
the air. After experience he realizes that the noisier the
audience is, the more successful is his playing.

When I played my tender melody nobody paid any
attention to it, so busy were they stamping in tune to the
three-eight rhythm. The same was true of the singing of
the Gypsies. It was not singing but hoarse meandering
on the same note, which they accompanied by clicking
castanets or else knocking stones together in rhythm.
As I played on, the moon arose and I felt that I was
playing the fiddle on a fairies' ring in the forest, but,
strange to relate, as I continued playing the men receded
into the background and the women came forward and

formed a ring around me.   In the moonlight their loose smocks looked like witches' shifts and I expected to see great cats clinging to their backs as in the Sabbat.   I had not noticed the women before, with the exception of Pedro de Castellón's wife, for during the day they had kept in the background, but now I observed them as I played, and I picked out one as the heroine of the dance. She was about twenty years of age, with a mass of untidy black hair falling over her pale face.   She had on only a remnant of a torn shift and her breasts were naked and her legs bare up to above the knee.   Encouraged by my remarks and perhaps by my hypnotic eye, she began to dance in a strange, wild way, as though she was responding to some fierce impulse within her.   In the light of the moon her skin looked a ghostly alabaster, but as she turned, the glow of the fires would suddenly kindle her face into burnished copper.   I then noticed that she had a fiercely sensual face, with large animal mouth and brilliantly white teeth.   The gold and silver chains and bracelets she wore sparkled in the light of the fires, giving me the illusion that flames sprang from her body as she moved.   It was an exciting experience to play for the young savage as she danced.   So fascinated was I by her presence that I forgot to be a minstrel. It was as if my music-playing personality had disappeared down a long corridor leaving me standing there amazed. When I ceased playing I determined to say some pretty compliments to the girl and carry on a little harmless flirtation, so I followed her over to one of the tents, and taking her dusky hand I kissed it, reciting as a compliment a *copla* in her honour—

> " Ven acá, almacén de gracia,
>   Cuerpo de sal y salero ;
>   Que eres más agraciadita
>   Que la flor que echa el romero."

The girl smiled and turned away.

Just at that moment a tall Gypsy came up to me, and stood looking at me fixedly for a moment; then he spat on the ground, and pulling out a sinister-looking knife from his *faja* (sash) he bent down and stuck it into a low table which was standing at the entrance to the tent. Not a word was said. I looked at the knife stuck in the table and the Gypsy looked at me. No need for an explanation : I had learnt my lesson.

The girl stood at the back of the tent looking at us with a sardonic grin on her face.

The incident, however, impressed me so deeply that it was as if the man had spiked it to my heart with his villainous knife. Later on when the chief and I were sitting by the fire I asked him why the Gypsy had drawn his knife in my presence.

" That is her husband José el bulero. He married her a year ago and he is *odoroso* (jealous)."

" But, *plaloró*, I was merely paying her a compliment. Surely you Gypsies allow us to utter a *rebridaque* (compliment) in honour of your women."

" We distrust those who pay compliments, unless the women who hear them are deaf as a doorpost. A woman hears all the compliments before she is married, but once her *dicló* has been hoisted, her place is in the tent *querelando cornichas* or feeding the *chabós* (children)."

Pedro de Castellón then proceeded to give me a severe moral lecture upon the *lacha ye trupos* (corporeal chastity) of the Gypsy race in Spain which reminded me of what George Borrow says on that subject in *The Zincali*.[1]

" Not one of those women you see in this camp," said Don Pedro, " would look at a man who did not belong to the tribe. From the earliest age they have been brought up to consider *lacha ye trupos* as their most

[1] G. Borrow, *The Zincali*, London, 1841, p. 267.

precious possession. Why, every young girl dreams of the day when she is led in the marriage procession, and her white *dicló*, the proof of her maidenhood, floats in the air."

"Yes, *plaloró*," murmured I softly. "I remember how the Gypsy *copla* says :

> "' En un praíto berde
> Tendí mi pañuelo ;
> Como salieron, mare, tres rositas
> Como tres luseros.' "

"That is true," continued the chief. "The whole tribe must be sure that the bride is a virgin, for that is the most precious patrimony she can bring her husband. And after the marriage, do not imagine that he will relax his vigilance. A Gypsy husband knows the thoughts of his wife and woe betide her if she plays any tricks upon him."

"What happens, Don Pedro," said I, "if a wife is unfaithful to her husband ? Is there any secret tribunal of Gypsies which will try her and condemn her ? Is there no divorce ceremony among the Gypsies of Spain ? "

"Divorce indeed, brother ! What would we be doing with divorce ? We do not need any secret tribunal to try our wives when they are unfaithful. We ourselves act as judge and executioner. But the occasion rarely arises, brother, for every *romí* knows that her *rom's* eye is swifter and sterner than the wolf's."

Don Pedro's account of *lacha ye trupos* fascinated me because it tallied with all that Agustina Escudero had told me.

In Hungary, Transylvania and old Roumania I had been struck by the frankly promiscuous character of the Gypsy women I had met. Owing to my experience in the East of Europe I felt disposed to agree with Mérimée when he poked fun at George Borrow, the "English missionary," for his naïve belief in Gypsy chastity. But now to my delight Don Jorge el Inglés was vindicated.

Pedro de Castellón, who had been ruminating over what I had said about secret tribunals, then said : " What sort of Gypsies are those who have secret tribunals to try their wives ? "

" They call it the *manlaslo*," I replied, " and it existed among the Romany chals in the East of Europe. Nobody knew where it met, for its deliberations were secret, but there were many eyes watching the guilty woman, without her even suspecting. Then all of a sudden one night on entering her tent she would find a piece of red wood lying in a corner. That was the summons from the dread *manlaslo*. Immediately she would have to leave the tent and walk in an easterly direction. After going some distance she would meet a man wearing a mask of beast-skin over his face. Without saying a word he would lead her through the forest to a spot where a group of men were sitting around a fire. They are the chiefs of the tribe before whom the woman has to defend her case. If she is guilty they pronounce banishment against her. She must leave her husband and the tribe immediately without ever the hope of returning. Sometimes it was customary to brand unfaithful wives so that other tribes might avoid such women. Such, brother, is the secret tribunal of the Gypsies."

Don Pedro then said : " What happened to those women after their expulsion ? "

" They generally wandered farther east and became prostitutes in the streets of Constantinople."

" That punishment is all moonshine, brother. What about the husband ? Has his honour been restored by driving that unfaithful woman out of the tribe ? Won't she dishonour him still more as she wanders through life as a *lumiasca* (prostitute)? No, brother, in such cases the best medicine is the steel : it cools the fever quickest."

Don Pedro had a positive horror of mixed marriages between Gypsy and *Busnó*. " No true-born Romany *chai* could ever be happy married to a *Busnó* : she would have too much contempt for him, and she would wither away far from her own folk. I remember, *eray*, how a great lady from Madrid adopted one of my sister's daughters and brought her up like a princess. She was dressed in silk and velvet : her face was rubbed with creams and oils to whiten her skin and her hair was curled by barbers, but they couldn't rub away dusky Romany skin, no Señor, not if they rubbed for a score of years. There she was, living in her palace like a *gachí* born with a gold spoon in her mouth, and not a thought had she of her father and mother in their tents, until one day the tribe camped near the house and the girl had her *bahí* told by her own sister, though she didn't know it. To cut the story short, though the girl was all dressed up in her finery she began to fret her heart. She sat in her room high up in that castle and she kept on thinking of the Romany chals over in the pine-wood, until at last she took to her heels and fled from the castle to the camp. She came back to her own, and now she's married to a fine, strapping *chalán* with four *chabós* to her credit. The tent is palace enough for her, she says."

My conversation with Don Pedro convinced me that people err in thinking that Gypsies in the modern world have lost their old nomadic characteristics. In spite of policemen, lawyers, missionaries and social workers there are Gypsies who continue to live as nomads and to prefer tents to houses. In Spain the nomads and sedentary Gypsies are curiously intermingled with one

another.   Pedro de Castellón's family lived in tents, but
some of their relatives were dancers and guitar-players,
living in comfortable, modern houses as though they
had never belonged to the wandering race.   He admitted
to me, however, that in the cold winters the tent-dwellers
had to seek the refuge of the house, but it was very
difficult to find lodgings because people did not wish
to let their houses to Gypsies.   "For that reason," said
he, "when one of our folk does secure a house we all
rush to it and camp in it as best we can."   I can imagine
that Gypsy house outside the arched gateway leading
into the town—a huge, battered caravanserai thronged
from top to bottom with a struggling, floating population
of ragged vagabonds.   The courtyard would be full of
lean mules and uptilted carts of every size and dimension
piled with furled tents.  There would be no tables or
beds in that house, only *ucharcarisas* (blankets) strewn
about the floor and an occasional *pondoné* or cushion.
With the fires burning in every room according to
Gypsy ritual, what else is necessary for the camping
tribes ?  They may even call their Gypsy house the
" tent of stone."

As the chief's fire had burnt very low and the night
was chilly I rose to take my leave, but the chief would
not let me go.   " You are our guest and you must sleep
in the camp with us."   He went over to one of the
tents and kicked one of the sleeping boys until he awoke.
He then told him to bring up a few blankets and lay
them for me in the tent.  I preferred, however, to lie
under the open sky in preference to the stuffy tent which
reeked of garlic and stale stew.

The first night's rest in a Gypsy camp always possesses
an element of strangeness.   In a hiker's camp sleep, to
use Sancho Panza's phrase, " covers one over like a
cloak," for there is a sense of complete security.   After

the day's pleasant exertions we may float away into dreamland without a care in the world. But in the Gypsy camp the stranger on his first night there feels a prey to petty anxieties. Having a fertile imagination he runs over in his mind as he lies awake the possible dangers. First of all, what about the tribe? Will they obey the chief and respect the stranger? When the chief snores beatifically the wakeful youths may rise silently from their couches and descend upon me while I sleep. Where is my fiddle? I must put it under my head as a pillow in case it might tempt their covetous eye. I have a little money—about twenty-five pesetas : I think I'll put it in my right trouser's pocket and lie on it. Yes, they might rob me, either by subtle, snakelike guile or else by smothered violence. Where is my stick which the Spanish peasant always calls " companion " ? A fine stick it is and capable of cracking a few skulls with the inch of iron at the tip, forged by Gypsy smiths at Toledo. That stick was given me for my protection by a shepherd at Lagartera in the province of Talavera, and it has been smoked into a strange pattern. The shepherd when he gave it to me, cut with his knife upon it the magic words—

" Si esta víbora te pica
No necesitas botica."
(If this viper stings you
You won't need a chemist.)

Yes, that stick is a doughty companion, but could I use it in the way the shepherd intended, and after cracking my assailant's skull could I get away unscathed? For the hundredth time in my life I regretted that I had not been toughened in my youth. " When my son reaches twelve years of age I'll have him trained in French boxing, ju-jitsu and knife-slinging, so that he may be ready for any emergency in life."

Such were the thoughts in my mind as I lay awake listening to the countless noises in the camp. A donkey brayed; two dogs at intervals bayed disconsolately at the moon; cats miawed in concert. Never have I slept in such a restless camp. To add to my discomfort I began to feel a slight tickling sensation, followed by irritation. It was a company of earwigs advancing in extended order over my chest. Earwigs are homely creatures and they do not give me a moment's qualm, but fleas try my patience. Such is their restless agility and ingenuity that they should be called the Gypsy insect. Gypsy fleas vary according to the different countries. Those of Roumania are more sinister and vampirish and wound more cruelly; those of England are more refined and delicate in their attentions, for their function is to irritate national complacency and conceit in cleanliness; those of Spain are the merriest fleas in the world and deserve the epithet *Flamenco* which is applied to Gypsy liveliness. Only a philosopher like Socrates could measure their leaps, said I to myself, as I scratched and scratched in vain. O for a tin of Flit, and a pump to spray it over those pests! I had not taken Flit with me since the day in Transylvania when the Gypsies filched the pump, thinking it was a new form of lethal weapon. The Spanish peasant, if one may believe his proverbs, is fatalistic about his fleas. " *Cada uno tiene su modo de matar pulgas* " (" Everyone has his own way of killing fleas "), he says tolerantly, alluding to the many vagaries of human nature. A thin-skinned man is one who has bad fleas upon him (*tiene malas pulgas*): give him a wide berth, he exaggerates and he would make an elephant out of a flea (*hacer un elefante de una pulga*). After several prolonged attacks on my flesh the hopping insects departed and let me sleep in peace.

Next day the tribe was on its feet early. The men dispersed through the countryside. Some of the women sat outside their tents basket-making; others set off to sell their products in the town. As for Pedro de Castellón, he shouted himself hoarse giving directions. When everyone had received his orders he lay down under a tree and snored contentedly. One duty he entrusted to me : to buy tobacco for him and especially a *puro* (cigar) as well as the wine ration for the day. I set out with the two youths who had led me to the camp the day before. After buying the wine and tobacco we went into the fields. The two youths had their catapults with them and as a result of their efforts we brought back five rabbits to the camp. In the middle of the day the Gypsy camp was deserted. Not a soul was about except the old man, his wife and various tiny children.

I asked Don Pedro where everyone had gone and he replied that they were selling baskets. I often wondered how much of their time the men and women spent selling baskets. In my wanderings with them through villages I noticed that some of the women would leave their basket-selling comrades and prowl in the outskirts of some farmyard. Soon afterwards they would appear amongst us and draw from beneath their voluminous petticoats the limp body of a hen. For this reason I was afraid to visit the fairs in Burgos or in the villages with those women, for I had a shrewd suspicion that many a petty larceny was practised by them.

If a hue and cry had broken out I should have been detected immediately by the irate peasants, for a *Busnó* has not the calm impassive face of the *Gitana* nor the disarming suavity of manner. The Gypsies, too, with their swift limbs would outdistance even the civil guard, but what could I do with my portly form, my puffiness and my short legs ? I should be captured and arrested.

The papers might then publish headings and embroider the tale thus :

## "ECCENTRIC PROFESSOR ROBS FARMYARD

"British Professor caught with clucking hen in his pocket. Denies that his intention was stealing. States that Gypsying is his hobby. His passport may be a forgery. Police state that he is suspected of being a Russian agent."

Hence I avoided the Gypsy women when we approached the stalls of a fair.

I amused myself, however, by analysing the talents of the various women of the tribes as if I had been Monipodio, Fagin, or any other captain of a robber band. First of all we had Gildí—a bright, vivacious girl, but as restless as if she had Saint Vitus' dance. I wondered why she made so many gestures with her hands until I discovered that she was a champion at the game of *tomar de dos* otherwise *ustilar pastesas* (stealing with two fingers). No typist or piano-player had lighter fingers than Gildí : they were long, lean, sinuous, and Don Pedro called her *gujerú* or quicksilver, perhaps in allusion to her talent. On my first evening in the camp Gildí managed to abstract a red silk handkerchief out of my pocket while I was talking to Don Pedro. Don Pedro, when he heard of my loss, rebuked her for robbing a guest and made her give it back to me. Ever afterwards, I called her *safista* (robber of handkerchiefs).

Gildí's sister Pura was the opposite in character : she was older, more wrinkled and more methodical. Whenever the women visited a fair she would loiter about aimlessly with a bored expression on her face. But at the end of the day Pura returned with even more loot than her sister. I wondered what technique Pura employed, for she looked the essence of dull-witted laziness. Then one evening, when the women were laughing and cracking jokes round the fire, she lifted her heavy dress and petticoats, and I saw to my amazement various hooks and safety pins attached to the lining. From those she unfastened various pieces of cloth which she had stolen from the stalls of a fair. Pura was what is technically called in *Germania* (thieves' jargon) a *mechera*. She did not use her hands in stealing but her legs. If you watched her at a fair you would see her go up to the stall and lean over the counter. As she bargains with the seller, she makes a piece of cloth drop on the ground and then by skilful footwork she draws it up between her legs and fastens it to hooks concealed inside her petticoat.

The biggest trickster of all of them was the wife of Don Pedro, but she would have scorned to steal a hen or a piece of cloth at a fair, for she had her dignity. She preferred to extract money in other ways, either by acting as a *curandera* (quack) or by fortune-telling (*penar bahí*). Every herb or flower possessed for her a hidden secret only known to the initiated. Most of her day she spent wandering about the country collecting samples, which she would boil down into noxious brews. In a moment of weakness I allowed her to tell my fortune. It was night-time and we were alone in her tent. By the light of the solitary candle her furrowed brown face and piercing eyes looked more sinister than in the day-time and her whining, sing-song incantation mesmerized me into complete submissiveness. The heat of her hand communicated a fire to my body and my head became dizzy. Each hard metallic word of explanation cut into me as though she was using a surgeon's scalpel. She foretold misfortunes, illness, death : I wanted to spring to my feet and dash away, but I had lost my will-power under her spell. At the end I departed, filled with agonizing thoughts of woes that might descend upon my family far away.

Among the Gypsies the women take a greater part in petty thieving than the men because they are more easily able to conceal objects upon their persons owing to their voluminous petticoats. Men of Don Pedro's stamp despised such petty tricks : they wanted bigger enterprise—for instance, if a chance should arise in a village to use the famous *timo de la guitarra* or money-coining trick, Don Pedro might give the scheme his blessing, but he would not give it easily, for he knows that the police in Spain have keener noses to-day than they had in the good old days of Alonso of the Many Masters.

There was, however, one Gypsy in the tribe, who, I was informed, had been arrested some years before for complicity in a *Jonjanó Baró* or Great Trick. His name was Toñito el tuerto, and a more villainous, cross-eyed ruffian I have never seen. Ugly and coarse-featured he was and pock-marked, but none the less he swaggered about as insolently as if he had been the biggest dandy in the camp. In the old days of Picaresque Spain the *Jonjanó Baró* was an imposing piece of swindling if we believe the graphic description given by the author of *Alonso of the Many Masters*. The Gypsies weaved a compli-cated web of fantasy around that trick : they called in the invisible powers such as the greater devil, the god-dess of the Black Mountain, and they laid their scene in some dark cellar or cavern. To-day the " Great Trick " has been shorn of all its romantic trappings, for people are less impressed by the fantastic. No need for Toñito to rack his brains inventing magic formulæ when he could achieve his purpose by playing on the cupidity of the ignorant.

When I asked Don Pedro what kind of *Jonjanó*

*Baró* Toñito had contrived, he replied, grinning sardonically :

" It was all over a returned emigrant : a fellow with more money than brains. Squint-eyes acted as true *caballero* to him—took him up and down the Rambla in Barcelona, brought him into bars, introduced him to whores, held the candle for him when he undressed— yes, Plaloró, he did all that a friend could do. Then to his surprise next day, the old *Busnó*—may fleas eat his eyes—accused him to the *Tricornios* (Civil Guards), saying that Toñito had mesmerized and robbed him of a sack of *parné* (money.) Poor Toñito tried to defend himself, but the accursed old skinflint kept on saying to the judge : ' When the scoundrel got me alone, he kept talking to me in a rough lingo I did not understand, until I lost my will-power and handed him over all I had in my pocket.' And so the mangy judge sent him to the *estaribel* (gaol)."

Toñito the cross-eyed became my enemy though we had been on friendly terms before. At first he thought I would be a soft *Busnó*, and easy to impose upon. He and two of his companions led me through the arch of San Esteban to a tavern and Toñito called for drinks in a swaggering tone. After we had drunk several glasses of wine each, he got up and said to us : " Let us be going." The proprietor from behind the counter then shouted out : " What about paying for the drinks ? " " The señor will pay," replied Toñito, pointing to me. I paid without saying a word and followed my three companions. Toñito then led us to a low-class dancing-hall frequented by the soldiery of Burgos and street-women. When we were installed there, he called over four women and introduced them to me, telling me to dance with them in turn. Meanwhile he ordered drinks all round. I was in a difficult predicament, for I had

not the money to throw away in standing drinks to
Toñito the cross-eyed and his confederate whores. I
determined to steal a march upon him, so while he and
his companions were dancing with their women I left
my partner on a pretext and hurried away from the hall.
I reflected with glee that Cross-eyed and his companions
would have to pay for the drinks we all had consumed,
and for once the *Busnó* had turned the tables on a Romany
chal.

Later on, however, I regretted that I had played the
trick upon Toñito, for he came back to the camp in a
fury, vowing vengeance against me. If it had not been
for the moderating influence of Don Pedro I felt sure
he would have attacked me then and there. Don Pedro
fired a volley of oaths at him for annoying the *eray*, so
he departed, squinting malevolently at me as he went.

In spite of the chief of the tribe's protection I feared
Toñito's vengeance and I determined to shorten my stay
with the Gypsies.

Before I left, however, I had the good fortune to
witness a *Fiesta* to celebrate the birth of a Gypsy child
in the camp. The child was born in the early dawn after
a night made hideous for me by the woman's moaning.
No midwives were called in, for Gypsy women bring
their children into the world without assistance.

As soon as the child was born the matrons poured
water into a hole in the ground and washed the child
in it. According to Pedro de Castellón, it was lucky to
hold the child to the fire after its first bath, and so this
was done. The custom recalled to my mind the old
Greek legend of Demeter the Goddess of the Earth,
who took the child from its cradle and held it over the
fire in order to confer upon it immortality. In Spain
among the Gypsies there is a widespread belief in the
dangers of the evil-eye and consequently many charms

must be provided, for the evil-eye may wither up the fairest child. It is strange that Gypsy women who possess such sinister powers of casting the evil-eye (*querelar nasula*) upon others should feel such dread of its visitation upon themselves. Charms made of jet and horn were hung upon a string around the mother's neck so that if the evil eye should strike her it would pierce the amulets and leave her unscathed. I did not forget my tags of Romany lore : I insisted that sprigs of garlic should be put beneath the child to drive away evil spirits and I told Pedro de Castellón to mark the child's forehead with a semi-circular sign representing the moon. In later years that Gypsy child will thank me for having launched her in life as a true Minion of the Moon. The next business was to arrange the baptism which is usually performed as soon as possible after birth, for the Gypsy parents, with their superstitious, Pagan nature, look upon baptism as superior magic. As soon as the priest had baptized the infant it was time to think of the feast.

With the exception of the wedding, no Gypsy feast is more uproarious than a baptismal party. Wine flows plentifully, for it is paid for by some rich, anonymous *padrino* or godfather, whom the Gypsies have selected for that purpose, and there is inexhaustible singing and dancing. Our *Fiesta* was not held in the camp, but in a decrepit house inhabited by Antonio Heredia (Pipindorio), the guitarist, and his wife Grañita, the dancer. The rooms were devoid of any furniture whatever and thick with dust. There were mats and cushions on the floor, and upon these the Gypsies squatted in oriental style. The scene was illuminated by five or six candles stuck into bottles. Pipindorio and another minstrel played their guitars incessantly, creating a strange thrumming background to the excited discordant voices.

In a small adjacent room there were casks of wine ready to be broached. The tent-dwelling Gypsies looked strange and ill at ease in the house, and I wished that the *Fiesta* could have been held out of doors under the moon. In the middle of the room sat the mother of the child with her infant, and beside her Don Pedro. Around them surged an excited band of revellers. The husband of the woman distributed wine to everybody : toasts were drunk : shouts were raised in honour of the new child : there was laughter and singing, and at the back of it all were the frenzied guitars thrumming away. Pipindorio, the master of ceremonies, was valiantly supported by his henchman guitarist, a small leather-faced, black-haired man dressed picturesquely in a shabby black velvet coat with a dark *faja* around his waist. His cuffs, which he displayed prominently when he played, were ornamented with pictures of girls in coloured mantillas and high combs.

The two guitarists were rivals, and each one tried to vanquish the other. As soon as Pipindorio had played the last note of his selection his companion would dash in with a cascade of notes and start another exciting, chasing rhythm. When the guitar-playing had roused the audience to a pitch of excitement, the Gypsies began to clap hands loudly and stamp their feet. Men and women formed a circle, with the two guitarists in one corner. Then Grañita began to dance. She was a handsome woman, dignified and Junoesque in stature, but no one at first sight would take her for a dancer : she was too fat and deep-breasted. She was dressed in black with a brown shawl over her shoulders, but her red slippers gave a dash of colour. In the midst of that gesticulating and shouting audience she was the arrogant queen, scorning and yet dominating them by her magic power of the dance.

Her two arms, alternately raised above her head and descending in spirals, described an undulating rhythm which communicated itself to her body, causing it to vibrate like a long note sustained upon a violin. At times in contrast, the undulating rhythm would descend from her waist to her feet, which tapped sharply upon the ground in imitation of the castanets.

As soon as Grañita ended her dance, a bronze-faced youth took her place and began a series of wild acrobatic capers. So solemn was his face as he danced that I mentally compared him to a dancing dervish. Gradually, under the excitement of the applause and the shouts of the audience, he became hypnotized by his own dancing. His body, too, began a shimmering undulating movement, but more uncontrolled than in the case of Grañita : perspiration beaded on his brow : his eyes were shut and he moved faster and faster like an automaton. At last out of sheer exhaustion he sank to the ground. There was a moment of complete silence as though the whole audience of Gypsies needed to recover its breath after its exertions, and then the guitars began their thrumming afresh.

The whole party now became more bacchanalian : the men jumped up and down with surprising agility, some of them banging their iron-tipped sticks on the floor : through the maze of shouting and stamping I heard fragments of *coplas* and occasionally a cascade of notes from the two guitarists, whose music never ceased.

Some of the men had seized wine-skins and were rushing up and down the room, squirting the wine over the faces of the people. I had just time to put away my fiddle in its case when one of them made a dash at me and deluged me : the red Riojan liquor blinded my eyes and poured down my face on to my clothes.

A wave of madness surged over the assembly : I still heard lines of *coplas* and occasionally the very faint twang of guitars.

The *juerga* was becoming more sinister : I saw "Toñito el tuerto" at the other side of the room, with tousled hair and a fierce, sardonic grin on his face. Though I was far away from him I felt that he was always watching me. Where was Pedro de Castellón ? I looked around for him—not a sign. Now that he has disappeared I feel helpless, for I am the only *Busnó* in this assembly, and Don Pedro is my only friend. There were now big pools of red wine upon the floor like pools of blood, and some of the men as they careered and jumped, slipped and fell in them. There was a sound of breaking glass, punctuated by hysterical laughter of the women.

Suddenly there was a hush and I heard sharp voices of altercation. A quarrel had broken out between José el bulero and another Gypsy called Juanillo. In a moment the quarrel had spread to everybody in the room. The two men faced one another and from threats they came to blows. José el bulero's wife fought her way like a demon through the opposing mass of women and struck Juanillo in the face. Then the struggling began between two factions supporting either adversary. José el bulero, however, and his adversary were determined to fight their duel in their own way without interference. I saw José pull out a knife out of his *faja* and raise it to strike the other. A shriek from the women—the knife buried itself in the shoulder of Juanillo. There was a groan, and I saw the crimson blood gush out like the wine from a *bota*.

Just then I caught sight of Toñito the cross-eyed. As soon as he saw the wounding of Juanillo he rushed over to the guttering candles in the bottles and threw them on the ground. In an instant we were in total darkness, groping our way in a shouting, jostling mass. Hugging my fiddle, I tried to follow the people who were carrying out the wounded man. With difficulty I reached the door into the street and I began to congratulate myself on my good fortune, when a voice in the dark hissed the word *chivato* (informer).

My heart stopped beating, for I recognized Toñito's voice. He had waited for this chance of wreaking his vengeance upon me. "I'll get even with you yet, you dog of a *Busnó*," he snapped; "you're a spy for the Guardia Civil, but I'll make you remember this evening all your life."

In the dark I could hardly see him, but I determined to stand at bay and trust to the power of my big stick. Feigning a lion-hearted courage, I replied to his challenge saying: "You come near me and I'll break your head with this stick."

Who knows what the issue would have been if the duel had taken place? Just at that moment four Gypsies surrounded Toñito: I saw my chance; without a second's hesitation I took to my heels and away through the silent streets.

It was two o'clock in the morning and I could not return to the camp, for Toñito would find me. It was best to make my way as swiftly and as unobtrusively as possible to the opposite side of the town, far away from the Gypsies. In the deserted Espolón I rested on a seat under the trees until morning, when I set out towards the Carthusian monastery, a few miles from the city.

# CHAPTER XXV

# IN QUEST OF A MONASTERY

THE gentle tolling of the Angelus at noon from the Cartuja de Miraflores scattered all the evil phantoms that had been preying upon me. The bells swung their hymn of exorcism :

> " Laudo Deum verum,
> Plebem voco,
> Congrego clerum.
> Funera plango
> Fulgura frango,
> Sabbata pango,"

and at the end came the prolonged toll—" est mea cunctorum terror vox daemoniorum."

For the past week I had lived in the Witches' Sabbath and I longed for rest. The sound of the convent bell in the noonday sun made me dream of peaceful cloisters full of scented flowers, silent save for the buzzing of bees. I had left Burgos with the sensation of being a fugitive. I wanted to escape far away from the basket-making Gypsies to a safe retreat, for I felt sure that the sinister cross-eyed one would follow on my track. The tolling of the convent bell soothed me and made me long to live for some days, at any rate, in one of those ancient Spanish monasteries which have always been the refuge for the sinner and saint, rich and poor.

295

The white-robed Carthusian at the gate gave me food and drink in plenty as he did to the other beggars, but I drew him aside and mentioned in a low voice, " Saint Bruno." Before continuing on my way I wanted to salute Saint Bruno, the founder of the order. In a little chapel of the church his statue stands—so life-like that once King Philip IV, when he beheld it, cried : " He does not speak, but only because he is a Carthusian monk."

With Saint Bruno's blessing I set out on my journey. It was my intention to walk to Saint Domingo de Silos and rest for some days in the monastery there. But first of all I turned aside from the road to visit the ruins of San Pedro de Cardeña, sacred to the memory of the Cid, his wife and the war-horse Babieca.

When the Cid was exiled from Castile by his King, after saying farewell to Burgos he rode through the night accompanied by his retainers to the monastery of San Pedro de Cardeña, for there he had left his wife Doña Jimena and his children. The epic poem tells us that when the Campeador reached the gate of the monastery the cocks were crowing amain and the day was beginning to break. The abbot was saying matins and the church was a blaze of light. Then Doña Jimena and her ladies, with tapers in their hands, met the hero at the gate, and the Cid said farewell to his wife and children, while the bells of the monastery tolled through the cold morning air the message that the Campeador was departing for exile and needed the loyal help of his friends. The Cid never forgot San Pedro de Cardeña through those years when he fought for the Moorish King of Zaragoza, or later when he conquered Valencia. At the point of death he commanded that his body be carried, so one of the old ballads tell us, " in full armour upon his horse Babieca to the church of San Pedro de Cardeña." We can imagine that sad procession of knights and retainers, tearing their hair, beating their breasts, throwing ashes on their brow, as they followed the corpse of the Cid, clad in full armour, mounted upon the loyal Babieca. Another ballad tells us " that the horse himself understood his sad mission and looked as crestfallen as the mourners."

From far-off Valencia on the Mediterranean Sea through the vast plain of Castile the procession advanced, growing ever greater as one band after another joined to give homage to Spain's national hero.

There is little about the grim structure of San Pedro de Cardeña to inspire the imaginative dreamer, for with the exception of part of the cloisters the monastery has nothing to show of its ancient greatness. The church dates mostly from the eighteenth century as does the smug, over-ornamented tomb of the Cid and his wife, erected in 1736 by King Philip V.

The old man who acted as my guide was the epitome of dishevelled melancholy. He tried to make my flesh creep with tales of monks butchered by Moors, disembowelled soldiers, sacked churches, and he informed me that the general policy of the Spanish Government with regard to disused monasteries was to turn them into asylums. " And Spain needs plenty of madhouses to-day," he added with a wheezy laugh.

My main object in visiting San Pedro de Cardeña was not to see the tomb of the Cid, but to find out if there was any memorial to the warrior's steed, Babieca. No horse that ever lived has such a proud history as the Cid's loyal companion of whom he wrote in his last will—" when ye bury Babieca, dig deep, for shameful thing were it, that he should be eat by curs, who hath trampled down so much currish flesh of Moors."

" What ! " said I to the guide ; " have you not heard of the famous Babieca ? You ought to be ashamed of yourself."

" Well, Señor," replied the sardonic, dyspeptic old man, " the only famous horse in Spain is Rozinante, and I don't suppose they have erected a tombstone to him."

" Shame on you, O Castilian, for not knowing the ancient ballads of My Cid, hardly one of which omits to mention Babieca."

The horse Babieca was the emblem of chivalry, for he prolonged the legs of the Cid Campeador. So precious was such a horse to the mediæval knight that when he retired for the night he would keep it tethered in the same room in which he slept with his wife.

Montaigne tells us that the Parthians of old used to do all public and private business on horseback, such as trading, conversing, disputing, taking the air, and that with them the most noteworthy difference between the free and the slaves was that the former rode and the latter went on foot. Such was the tradition among the Spanish knights, and it would be as impossible to imagine the Cid without Babieca as it would be to imagine the Knight of the sorrowful figure without Rozinante.

" It is an unregenerate age that has forgotten you, O Babieca, noblest of horses. When they buried the ashes of the Cid and Doña Jimena beneath the marble slab in Burgos Cathedral in 1921, they might have reserved a niche for your remains. If the spirit of the Cid should ever return from the misty realms of Walhalla, we should hear first of all the sound of Babieca's hoofs and then in a flash see the horse gallop by over the hard-baked Castilian plain, carrying the knight in coat of mail. Therefore let me, the humble wayfarer,

*" This new classic of travel."—Sunday Times.*

# THE VALLEYS OF THE ASSASSINS

## By FREYA STARK

With 6 Maps and 34 Illustrations

12s. 6d. net.

The publication of "The Valleys of the Assassins" has met with an outburst of enthusiasm from the critics, a few of whose reviews are quoted below.

MISS V. SACKVILLE WEST *in the Observer*.

> " This truly enthralling record ought to take its place among the classics of travel. She has found out one of the most beautiful countries in the world and done it justice."

THE SUNDAY TIMES.

> " Not quite like any other book on Persia. She writes in a style altogether her own, and she has a merry wit which pops out at the most unexpected moments and the whole provides rich entertainment for the general reader as a document of intensely human interest."

THE TIMES.

> " The book's most entertaining quality is wit, sparkling dryly, ironical, gentle, expressed with the neatest and thriftiest economy."

THE TIMES LITERARY SUPPLEMENT.

> " Those who read it will set it in a place apart from all but a very small number of ' travel books.' "

THE ILLUSTRATED LONDON NEWS.

> " Pungency, vividness, wit, and a human interest which transcends the mere description of unfamiliar lands. Not a page lacks entertainment."

**MR. HOWARD SPRING** *in the Evening Standard.*

" Belongs to something bigger than geography. This adventure that she has so magnificently recounted may be read with joy. A rare and delightful book."

**THE MORNING POST.**

" One can only say ' read this book.' It will be an experience and a delight."

**THE DAILY TELEGRAPH.**

" This most fascinating book : an absorbing tale of intrepid adventure."

**THE FIELD.**

" Extremely interesting and extremely entertaining. Without doubt the best travel book that has appeared this year. Her adventures are adventures indeed."

**COUNTRY LIFE.**

" Has every quality that the most pernickety of readers can desire—modesty, reflective power, enchanting humour and a quietly fastidious yet vivid style."

**ADMIRAL SIR WILLIAM GOODENOUGH.**

" Miss Stark has given us a gem. Brilliant, full of colour. She displays a vivid power of description of the country which is at once valuable and charming."

**SIR E. DENISON ROSS.**

" Lively and unaffected ; she is one of those travellers who carry the reader with them on their travels."

**MR. R. B. CUNNINGHAME GRAHAM.**

" Certainly this is a book to be read, marked and inwardly digested, both as a record of an adventurous journey and for its descriptions of a people hardly known even to-day."

**SUNDAY DISPATCH.**

" One of the best travel books I have come across."

---

JOHN MURRAY, ALBEMARLE STREET, LONDON, W. 1.

moisten with a tear the unnamed grave wherein you lie."

After leaving San Pedro de Cardeña I plodded along the road in the heat of the afternoon.   To keep my spirits up I sang every song I could think of at the top of my voice, much to the astonishment of sleepy farmers who were dosing away their siesta on their carts, letting the mules crawl along at their own sweet will.

"Vd. tiene el demonio en el cuerpo," said one as he halted his cart and peered with an amused expression into my red, sweating face.   "This is no day to go tramping the roads—come on, jump up.   If you're thirsty take a pull at my *bota*."

I then settled myself full length in the bottom of the cart with my head resting on my *capa* and rocked by the jolting I soon fell fast asleep.   At the village of Cuevas de San Clemente, eighteen kilometres farther on, I awoke and it was time to take leave of the carter, for our ways parted : he was continuing straight on towards Barbadillo del Mercado, while I had to turn off by the road towards Covarrubias and Santo Domingo de Silos.

It was now time to take a little nourishment and my rucksack was well stored with bread, sausage and tasty cheese from Burgos.   As I was tucking into my meal with every now and then a long pull at my wineskin, a tall, dark, big-shouldered man with a black moustache and tanned complexion, passed along the road. When he saw me eating he shouted out : "Que se lo aproveche," or "good appetite "—to which I answered : "Ya lo creo : aquí hay la sopa de San Bernardo " —a proverbial phrase referring to my good appetite. In Spain the expression *hacer migas*, to break bread, is the symbol of friendship, and when I asked the man to share my meal we were soon intimate.   His name was Moreno and he was on his way back to his home town of Covarrubias.

Noticing that he carried a thick stick in his hand with hieroglyphics on it, I asked him what they meant.

" Ah ! Señor, that is my uncle's stick. He is a shepherd and it is the custom here for a shepherd to write the history of his family on his stick."

" How does he do that, pray ? "

" First of all, he carves his name upon it, then the name of his father and mother. When he marries he carves the name of his wife and her parents, and as soon as children are born he carves their names too. When they reach the age of six or seven he carves the alphabet and teaches them their letters round the winter fire. Then, look here, Señor, do you see near the handle the carving of the sun, the moon and the stars, and on the opposite side the chalice containing the sacred host, with a star over it ? That figure with wings represents María, a little child of seven years of my uncle who died—may God rest her soul. She is now an *angelito*, that is why you see the wings. Thus a stick contains the whole history of a family. And remember, Señor, in this part of Castile young men go courting the girls with a stick."

" What do you mean ? Surely they don't beat the girls."

" Not at all, Señor, not unless they find a shrew like Juanica la pelotera. But when a youth falls in love, he writes the name of his *novia* on his stick. Then at sundown he goes to her father's house and throws it in through the *gatera* or cathole in the door. Next day before sunrise he returns to the house and looks for the stick. If it is lying outside the door, then he may pick it up and take the way of Villadiego—that is to say, make himself scarce, for she will not have him for husband. If he finds no stick outside the door, then it means that the girl's father has kept it in the house, and the youth may come back later in the day with his own father to fix the date of the wedding. But he must remember to bring as a present to the girl a cow's horn carved and ornamented, with the words ' para mi nobia y yo ' engraved upon it."

" What a strange present to give a girl," I could not help saying.

" You couldn't give her anything she'd value more, Señor," said Moreno. " The horn is full of luck and will counteract the *mal de ojo* or evil eye that might wither up the marriage. For believe me, Señor, the Devil always sleeps with one eye open and that eye would shrivel up the finest pair of *novios* in the world."

" Ah! Moreno, I am surprised to hear all these superstitions from one of the republican sons of the revolution."

" Revolution indeed. The revolution has been all words and foam. When the Devil has nought to do he frightens the flies away with his tail. The *Señoritos* from Madrid tell us there has been a revolution and that we are as free as the birds in the air. But I ask you, Señor, is anybody in this world free? Must we not lead our sheep and goats to pasture and till our piece of land and sweat like the Devil himself until we give up the ghost? What's all that revolution but words, and words won't till the land or rear my goats and sheep here in Castilla la Vieja."

" Come now, Moreno, what about the agrarian reform?"

" Who cares a curse about the agrarian reform except the politicians? Why, here in Castile we all have our piece of land and what we want is to be left alone to work it."

It was useless to urge Moreno to consider the benefits of modern methods, new inventions and mechanical contrivances that would increase his output. "No tengo nada que ver con eso," was his constant refrain. "My father, my grandfather and my great-grandfather reaped and threshed in old traditional way and they were able to live *una vida honrada*. Why should I worry my head over those newfangled notions?"

As we walked along through the golden afternoon I began to understand what Unamuno had meant when he had said that the men of the *Poema del Cid* and the *Romancero* and their stock were like oak trees and rocks belonging to the Castilian landscape. All around us in the fields men and women were gathering in the harvest in the primeval way. The method of threshing had not changed in the slightest since the days of Fernán González and the Cid.

To-day the women work in the fields as well as the men; in fact in most cases it seemed to me that the woman was the moving spirit, for it was she who sat upon the wooden board, studded underneath with sharp stones, and drove the mule round and round, crushing the ears of corn that lay scattered on the *era* or threshing floor. The sight of those innumerable workers in the golden fields was a majestic one: the men dressed in brown, some of them with black, broad-brimmed hats; the women wore handkerchiefs tied round their heads, or else huge-brimmed straw hats, and all had face and arms as copper-coloured as the men's. The fields under the sun were brown and red with patches of yellow where the corn lay on the threshing-floors, and then above all was the huge blue dome of the sky, with here and there white moving clouds like wisps of cotton-wool, and in the distance burnished copper-coloured mountains.

The harvesters sang as they worked. Over the plain one group would sing in a monotonous voice and then in the distance another would answer as though it was echoing the preceding *copla*. The songs of the *trilla- dores* were free and untrammelled improvisations ; the leaders would generally start with a free vocalization before they introduced the *copla* and then they would conclude with a descending, florid passage, punctuated every now and then by an exclamation to excite the mules in their ceaseless gyrating movement. There was one of the melodies which was a traditional Burgos harvester's song according to the folklorist Olmeda.[1]

In such songs the words did not seem to matter, for they repeated the same over and over again with many variations of rhythm and vocalization adapted to their work with the mules. When the singing died down I was again conscious of the solemn immensity of the Castilian plain, and all those human beings after their moment of life became again petrified into the landscape. It is strange that there is not a greater wealth of folksong and dance in such a plain, for only song would relieve the human soul of the sense of loneli- ness which it feels in this desert. Before leaving the harvesters I pulled out my fiddle and played a tune of a Castilian *Baile Redondilla* to make them dance.

[1] F. Olmeda, *Folk-Lore de Burgos*, Burgos, 1902, p. 51.

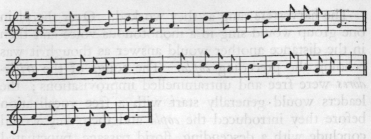

The young girls made a ring around me and began to dance holding hands, and I shouted out as I played the tune:

"Con un polvo y otro polvo, se levanta polvareda:
Con un vaso y otro vaso se coge una filosera.
Tra la ra la la lá: tra la la la la la ré:
Tra la la la la rá: la la la la la ré."

It was the girls who danced: the men clustered round and drew out wine-skins and held them out to me to drink when I finished playing.

By the time we reached Covarrubias the sun had nearly sunk behind the horizon, leaving in its wake a fiery trail across the sky, and in the uncertain glow the fields became red and purple. From the hilly, winding road we could see the town of Covarrubias below in the valley by the River Arlanza. The compact mass of red roofs and tower enclosed by the walls looked like a huge helmet left lying on the river bank. In this tiny stronghold there lived in the tenth century Count Fernán González, who after many struggles freed Castile from allegiance to the King of Leon and thus prepared the way for the Kingdom of Castile. Many legends are told of the Count, and in Spanish chivalry he joins hands with Bernardo del Carpio and the Cid. But Count Fernán González had a wife, Doña Sancha, who was as heroic as her husband, for she twice rescued him from imprisonment at the risk of her life. On

one occasion she entered the gaol where he was im-
mured and, changing clothes with him, enabled him to
pass through the enemy guards while she remained in
his place—a heroic deed that recalls the action of the
Countess of Nithsdale who effected the escape of her
lord from the Tower of London in 1715.[1]

Many ballads have sung the praises of the noble
Count and Countess, and some of that poetry still echoes
through the minds of the peasants of Covarrubias, in
whose veins runs the blood of old Castile.   An old
man in Moreno's house recited for me the story of the
Count's rescue, and brought back to my mind all the
emotion I had felt as a boy when I read Lockhart's
magic translation :

" The Infanta trembled in the wood, but forth the Count did go,
  And gazing wide, a troop descried upon the bridge below,
  ' Gramercy,' quoth González—' or else my sight is gone,
  Methinks I know the pennon yon sun is shining on.'
  Come forth, come forth, Infanta, mine own true men they be,
  Come forth and see my banner, and cry Castile ! with me :
  My merry men draw near, I see my pennon shine,
  Their swords shine bright, Infanta, and every blade is thine."

As the old man told me the stories, I could catch
here and there isolated words and phrases that had descended through the ages in this hidden corner of Castile from the ancient ballads.   A decrepit old man he
was, white-haired, trembling, but when he spoke of
Fernán González his eye brightened and his face flushed
with emotion.   I felt sure that we may say to-day as
Lockhart did a hundred years ago, that in the erect
and high-spirited peasantry of Castile we still see the
genuine and uncorrupted descendants of their manly
forefathers.   Castile in its original constitution was as
free as any nation needs to be, for the purposes of social

[1] J. G. Lockhart, *Spanish Ballads*, London, p. 38.

security and individual happiness. Her kings were her captains and her judges—the chiefs and the models of a gallant nobility, and the protectors of a manly and independent peasantry ; but the authority with which they were invested was guarded by most accurate limitations, so that every Castilian of whatever degree was penetrated with a sense of his own dignity as a freeman and his own nobility as a descendant of the Visigoths.[1]

All around me in the kitchen of Moreno's house I saw rugged types of Castilian peasantry. They sat in silence in the dark corners listening to the old man as he declaimed. From time to time the *porrón* of wine passed from one to the other, and the air was thick with the smoke of cigarettes which each man rolled mechanically. Most of the men were young, but the hard life in the fields scorched by the sun in the three-months' summer and frost-bound in the nine-months' winter had carved their figures in oak or stone. Their manners were courtly, their gestures dignified, but most of the time they sat enveloped in melancholy ; then all of a sudden one man would break out into an impetuous torrent of speech and continue until exhaustion. In this way occasionally terrible crimes break out in those small hamlets with the suddenness of a thunderstorm. For a moment the flash of lightning reveals to the world the hidden lives of those peasants who seem part and parcel of their rocky landscape. Fierce passions are aroused and there is a blood feud. But then the storm abates and there is peace in the little hamlet hidden away in the Castilian tableland. One of the village singers, generally the blind beggar or else a wandering vagabond of evil reputation, weaves a ballad about the crime and hands it on to posterity. It is thus that the folk of Covarrubias remember Doña

[1] J. G. Lockhart, *op. cit.*, Introduction, p. 8.

Urraca, the daughter of the Count Fernán González. They are never weary of inventing stories about her imprisonment by her father in the gaunt tower that rises near the walls of the town, and one man who brought me there assured me that her ghost leaves the tomb in the church near by and visits a certain vaulted cell where she was chained by her cruel father. " Come on, *amigo*," cried I, " this instrument of mine will drive away her ghost." The sound of the violin echoing and re-echoing through the dark vaulted cell sounded so macabre and dismal that the guide nearly dropped the candle he was carrying.

From Covarrubias I wended my way to Retuerta, a small village about five kilometres along the river, and here I found the profession of a minstrel far more profitable than in the former town. Covarrubias was a man's town, full of solemnity and dignity as befits the fief of the rugged Count of Castile. Retuerta's chief claim to fame is that it possesses the prettiest inn-keeper's daughter in Castile. I learnt more about Castile from her in ten minutes' gracious conversation than I had done in a whole evening's association with the heroes of Covarrubias. The women of Spain, unlike the men, do not fade into the landscape. They are too fresh and apple-cheeked to be compared to oaks and rocks. Whereas the men look weary, the women are brimful of the sap of life. Rosario, for so the heroine of Retuerta was called, had an adorable pink-and-white complexion, jet-black hair and the profile of a Madonna, but in strength she would be the equal of any young swain of twenty, whether in boxing or wrestling. When I met her she was wearing a white apron, with her sleeves tucked up showing chubby milk-white arms, and she was feeding the hens. Rosario became my ally and she brought all the girls of Retuerta within the orbit of my fiddle. In the streets I played every imaginable dance—*boleros, seguidillas, tonadas, malagueñas, jotas*—in the intervals of telling the audiences of travels in other countries. Then as a grand finale three girls in the crowd shouted out to me to play the Marseillaise. Oh! The irony of it! To travel into the farthest corner of Castile and have to play the national anthem of Republican France! When I had finished the young men applauded vociferously. I suppose " La Marseillaise " will be the symbol of all revolutionary movements.

After an hour's combative performance, I asked Rosario how it was the boys and girls of Retuerta were such dancing demons.

" It must be the influence of Saint Esteban," she replied.

" Who is Saint Esteban ? "

" He is our patron Saint and some call him the Saint of the nimble feet."

" Why did they give him such a nickname ? "

" Here in Retuerta we celebrate his *fiesta* in September, and we do him honour with our feet. The men of the village carry the statue of the Saint on their shoulders through the street, with a band of pipe-players to lead the way. A mighty procession it is, Señor, for not a man, woman or child but dances as hard as he or she can in honour of the sainted martyr."

" And what is the reason of all this dancing ? "

" Well, you see, Señor, any wish the dancer asks the Saint on that day will surely be granted."

" Bravo, Rosario : and I'll bet a peseta you begged the Saint for a handsome *novio*, but he hasn't turned up yet."

" Fie upon you, Señor : I never asked for a *novio*, because I don't want to marry one of the men from

Retuerta.  I want someone from far away—a *forastero*
with fair hair and blue eyes who will take me away
across the sea to America."

Before I left Retuerta I gave Rosario a little necklace of red and black beads and fastened it around her
soft white neck.  It added a touch of smartness to her
simple rustic dress.  From my experience of wandering through villages I found that it is always useful
for a *juglar* to have a few little cheap trinkets at the
bottom of his rucksack.  You never know when you
may meet a charming little damsel and wish to pay
tribute to her beauty.  In Spanish villages it is dangerous to pay court or even to utter verbal compliments, as I had found among the Gypsies at Burgos,
but no husband or *dueña* will grudge the wandering
minstrel his little gift shoved through the bars of the
*reja* before he hastens away in the night.  The little
necklace or trinket is the token of sentiment, and a reminder that the wanderer departs carrying in his heart
for ever a little fragrance of that beauty which capti-
vated him.  "The remembrance of that sweet smile of
yours, Rosario, will give me strength as I tramp the
dusty roads."

As I approached nearer to Santo Domingo de Silos
the land became richer and more luxuriant.  The monastery is situated in a valley surrounded by a mountain
range, called La Cervera.  On the slopes, I saw flocks
of sheep and goats pasturing : in the fields there was
a smell of hay and the delicate aromatic scent of rosemary and thyme.  After walking through the village
I came to the monastery which is surrounded by a high
wall.  At this point I began to debate with myself as
to what method I should adopt in order to be admitted
into the monastery.  Before I rang the bell I determined to play the *juglar* and I took out my fiddle and

began to play the venerable minstrel tune of Our Lady
of Covadonga :

After a few moments an old man, evidently the *con-
cierge,* threw out a copper coin, motioning me to go
away, but I paid no attention and went on with my
playing.   He came up to me and asked what I wanted.
I then addressed him in the traditional minstrel fashion :
"I am a wandering player, or *tocaor,* and I am walking
through Castilla la Vieja.   All over Spain have I heard
of the famous hospitality of the monks of Silos.   I
know they will not refuse to help a musician, for
music is the language of God and His Saints—was
Saint Cecilia not the patron Saint of music ?   Therefore go quickly and say that a humble *juglar* waits at
the convent  gate to pay his respects to the *Señor
Abad.*"

I had prepared all that speech with care so that my
Castilian might be *castizo* or pure, but the old man
shook his head incredulously and hobbled away.   After
a few minutes, however, he came back followed by a
monk dressed in a brown habit, to whom I repeated
my speech, but this time I added that I was from *Irlanda
país católico.*   The monk shook hands with me warmly
and led me straightway into the monastery.   After passing through long corridors and up stairs we came to
a whitewashed door with a number on it.   The monk
took a big key out of his habit and opened the door
—" está Vd. en su casa," said he, as he bowed me into
the room.

I expected to find a tiny, ill-ventilated cell with a
pallet in the corner, but here was a fine room with

large windows wide open, looking on to the valley.
At one side was a deep alcove containing a big old-
fashioned bed with curtains. Fray Antonio, for that
was the name of the monk, left me for a moment and
came back with a vase full of fragrant rosemary boughs
which he placed on the writing-table in the centre of
the room—a gentle attention which made me feel that
I was being welcomed as a prince, whereas I had knocked
at the monastery gate as a humble vagabond.

As a result of my sojourn in the Gypsy tents near
Burgos I was dirty and unkempt. I had not shaved
for ten days and my face was covered with a bristly,
brown beard; my khaki-coloured shirt and trousers
were grimy. "I wonder have they locked up their
spoons and forks," said I to myself; "how does this
monk know that I am not a Gypsy whose sole reason
for existence, as Cervantes said, was for robbing?"
He was, perhaps, a good physiognomist, and beneath
my dishevelled appearance he had caught a glimpse of
the professor on holiday. Hence the delicate attentions. There was a roguish glint in his eye as he questioned me closely about my vagabondage, and I felt
like the prodigal son confessing his sins to the indulgent
family chaplain, the day after his return.

Fray Antonio was portly, with generous double chin
and reposeful dignity of manner. He wore his spectacles so far forward on his curved nose that they looked
as if they were in perpetual danger of falling off, and
this gave a peering expression to his eyes. The upper
part of his face was that of a contemplative man, but
his big mouth and slightly protruding lower lip gave
a touch of malice. I was sure that the lower lip was
ever ready to snap up dainty morsels of gossip that
fell from the mouth of strangers. Poor Fray Antonio,
you are a hero of abnegation—hidden in your monas-

tery, toiling for the love of God, when base Nature intended you to live in society as a man about town.

" Yes, father, I accuse myself of being a *pícaro*. I can't help it. All my life I have lived under a tinker's curse and I must have my periods of roaming. But you were right in calling me a night-wandering scholar, for my one sadness, father, is not to have lived in the great old days of goliards and *cazurros*, when King Alfonso the Wise came with his regal suite to Silos and the cloisters resounded with the rebecks and lutes of his minstrels."

" Come, now, señor *juglar*," replied the monk gently ; " you must not talk too much here of picaresque knaves and goliards or else we shall have to pour holy water over you to exorcize you. Here at any rate you will not have to fiddle for your supper," he added with a smile as he led me downstairs into the refectory.

One by one the brown-habited monks with hands crossed filed into the hall, and after bowing to the Abbot, who sat enthroned at the head, took their places at the various tables. A monk then entered with a basin and white cloth and proceeded to wash the hands of everyone before the meal. After the long chanted grace, we sat down. I was beginning to launch a series of questions on my neighbour, a tall monk with an emaciated, furrowed face, but he nudged me to keep silent. No speech is allowed during the dinner, but in compensation a young French Benedictine mounted into the pulpit at the side of the hall and began to read aloud to us in a monotonous sing-song from a book describing the primitive life of the mountain region of Las Hurdes in the days of Lope de Vega. In the intervals of eating I had leisure to note the pictures on the walls of the refectory. There was a copy of the Santo Cristo of Velázquez, a picture of Santo Domingo and a most appropriate one of Saint Benedict, the founder of the Order, seated at dinner with his monks. The food tasted to me like a Lucullian banquet after days of raw ham, sausage, and sprigs of garlic. First of all, good, rich Spanish vegetable soup, then French beans in oil and tunny fish and salad, followed by the *plato fuerte*, a joint of mutton. For *postre* or dessert we were given apples served with delicious honey from the thyme-loving bees of Silos. Wine there was in plenty—rich and red, from the vineyards of Logroño.

After grace was said by the Abbot we filed out of the refectory and made our way to a garden at the back of the monastery called the *Jardín honradito*. Up and down the green sward we walked in groups or else sat on little rustic seats under the trees.

The Abbot Don Luciano Serrano—a small thick-set man with strong jaw and spacious forehead—welcomed me as guest to the monastery. His appearance is that of an iron disciplinarian, but he has devoted his life to writing books on the history and folk-lore of Castile. He told me that the Community of Santo Domingo de Silos is above all a centre of learning and every monk is an authority on some branch or other. " Our ideal," he said, " follows that of a Spanish mediæval bishop who in the morning sowed the seed of the Gospel in the hearts of men and in the afternoon sowed the wheat in the fields. Everyone of us must be a pioneer and colonizer, as well as scholar, able to use the spade and shovel as well as the pen. Our motto should be: ' To live as if we were to die this very night ; to work as if we were to live eternally.' Who knows what will happen in these troubled times ? It is not the first time that the monks of Silos have left the cloisters with their bundles on their shoulders and scattered to their homes to await the passing of the storm."

Don Luciano then introduced me to a youngish monk called Fray Justo Pérez de Urbel, who became my closest friend and mentor during my stay at Silos. " Ah ! Father Justo, how I bless the chance that brought me within your orbit ; how many memories crowd before my inner eye when I remember your pale, eager face and that occasional unprotected look of distress that made me long to question you on your secret sorrows." Up and down the Convent lawn I walked with Fray Justo, and he questioned me so much about my adventures that I felt like Alonso of the Many Masters when he gratifies the curiosity of the Vicar of the convent.

FR. JUSTO. " Speak on, my friend ; there is yet half an hour before Complin. Tell me one thing : were you not afraid to walk the roads of Castile alone ? "

MYSELF. " Not at all, father : you remember the adage, ' Cantabit vacuus coram latrone viator.' As I had no money upon me I could sing like a nightingale."

FR. JUSTO. " How did you make your way here without money ? "

MYSELF. " As the proverb says, I trusted to the charity of Old Castile. It is not hard to join the brotherhood of the road when one has a honied tongue and a soft manner. Whenever I am in a scrape, father, whether it is a skirmish on the road or one with the landlady or the mule-driver, I always answer in the words of Alonso of the Many Masters—Leave me alone, gentlemen ; I'm not a needle that'll get lost in a bundle of hay. I tell you I'm only a poor fellow whom God never moistens with His heavenly dew. Being disinclined to work I prefer to take my ease, rough as it is. When I throw my cloak across my shoulder I can say that the whole world's mine, for no vineyard and no home have I."

In such pleasant discourse did we pass the time until the church bell rang. It was now dark and the trees in the garden were whispering in the slight breeze. At the entrance to the church Father Justo left me to find my way alone and went off to take his place with the rest of the monks in the choir. As the monks filed in, their footsteps clanked through the huge, gaunt building.

All was pitch darkness save for faint candle lights in the distance, opposite side altars, and the light in front of the Blessed Sacrament. The faint, twinkling candles cast out huge shadows across the central empty nave. I knelt in a corner and watched the monks in the distance take their seats inside the bronze railed-off choir, and then the music began. The solemn chanting started with a low-murmuring sound and then rose and fell in unceasing melody like the ebb and flow of the calm ocean. The sound echoed and re-echoed through the lofty church, and certain notes would prolong themselves more than others and construct a strange, sympathetic counterpoint, just as if mighty strings were vibrating through all their harmonics. The ideal music for one praying in the Cathedral is Gregorian chant; it wings my thoughts away to lose themselves in the dark spaces of the Gothic nave, and the words of prayer become submerged in the unending melody. I heard the distant tinkle of the bells of the sheep and goats pasturing on the thyme-scented slopes just outside the monastery. Not another sound could be heard, and at times the silence became terrifying, for it brought home to me the sensation of my loneliness, as though I were gazing at all those monks from a lower world of darkness. Behind the bronze gates they were throned up on high in the realms of light, choiring together in praise of God. Then my emotions became associated through music with the Grail scene in *Parsifal*, where the Knights of Monsalvat in darkness bow their heads and wait for Amfortas to uncover the divine chalice. I expected to see the Grail raised and the unearthly radiance illuminate the church and transfigure us. The Gregorian chant led me from one dream to another without break, for it seemed to underline faintly each thought floating through the mind. It was then that I understood the true significance of such a monastery as Santo Domingo de Silos in the Middle Ages, when life in the world was a medley of bloody battles between feudal barons and their vassals. Within the walls of the monastery peace could always be found for those whose minds had a religious hue and wished to worship God in silence and meditation. Within the high walls there was a paradise of serenity for the artist and scholar, wherein he could express his love and longing for beauty by sculptured figures and illuminated parchments. Even warriors like Fernán González and the Cid would not disdain to halt their horses at its shrine and rest within the cloisters after the labour of the chase or after battle, and when they set out for war they would entrust wife and children to the care of the Abbot. To-day in our complex, mechanical civilization it is more difficult to enter into the life of those monks at Silos, for our souls move inexorably by clockwork and we find it hard to rest and meditate. But to-day we need such a monastery more than ever our ancestors did in the hardy days of the Middle Ages.

At last the praying ceased and the voices of the monks faded away in the distance. I found myself groping my way through the dim cloister with the sound of the singing still in my ears. Through the arches I could see the monks pass by like phantoms towards their cells.

# CHAPTER XXVI

## ADVENTURE IN A CLOISTER

### NOON

#### I

THE cloisters of Santo Domingo de Silos at noon. The sun beats down on the garden and scorches into coma the flowers and green foliage. At such an hour it is pleasant to walk up and down the cloisters gazing at the sunlit garden through the arches. At one end is a very tall cypress-tree that rises like a gigantic finger, pointing silently to the blue sky above. Fray Justo the poet has taught me to love that mystic tree which he calls the gentle, faithful companion of the monk in the cloister, pointing the narrow ascending way to the distant cloud-capped pinnacles of the golden city. Motionless it stands beneath sun or moon, casting its long, slender shade across the garden, but at times it shivers gently as though pulsating in sympathy with the echoing voices.

Here in this cloistered garden surrounded by the double row of sculptured arches the calm tranquillity of noontide is only an outer mask. Even the sun's rays that beat unchanging on the garden, as soon as they penetrate through the arches, dissolve into restless, quivering shafts of light, dancing in and out of the columns.

Such is your life, my dear friend, Fray Justo, in this

317

wonderful cloister. You have renounced the world and all its pomp, for the peace of this hermitage, but every wish and aspiration uttered in whispered prayer resounds through those arches as through a magic lute, and ascends into the sky along the silent cypress-tree. The Moors held that a note of music when once it has been played does not fade away, but is stored in the air ready to return one day. In my violin are stored all the melodies and rhythms that have been played upon it since the day when the bow first touched its strings. So, too, in these cloisters there lurk countless invocations of those who prayed here, since the days of Santo Domingo in 1073, when the artists sculptured in stone the melodies and rhythms floating through their minds.

The life described in this, the most beautiful Romanesque cloister in the world, is a reflection of the life of the simple soul Juan the Spaniard, when he set out to wander through the mediæval world. On all sides stretched the mysterious forest; at each step he saw strange faces leering at him; in the branches were gryphons and birds with human faces and snakes' tails; he saw in the distance heroes mounted on winged horses, brandishing axes, and the green grass was sprinkled with strange flowers that grew in no mortal garden. Through the forest he wended his way amidst branches with pine-cones upon them or else clustering grapes, and here and there he stopped in terror, for the gnarled trees all of a sudden transformed themselves into wild animals, the roots coiled themselves around his limbs and the forked tongues of serpents hissed at him. Through a confused maze of sight and sound he wandered until he came to trees whose branches formed the shape of a cross, and then he knew that he had reached the tree of Paradise, and the hour of his deliverance was at hand.

All that forest of strange monsters, birds and flowers is just the setting to the artist's vision of the mysteries of religion.

At the four angles of the cloister, there are eight reliefs, describing scenes from the death and resurrection of Our Lord. First of all we come to an arch over which is written : " Nil Formidetis ; Venit Deus," and beneath it we see the body of Jesus Christ laid in the sepulchre by Joseph of Arimathea and Nicodemus ; beside it is the Coming of the Holy Ghost or Finger of God, as it was called in the Middle Ages. Farther on we see the Tree springing from the side of Jesse, father of David : above the Blessed Virgin is God the Father, seated in the branches, with the Infant Jesus on his knee, and at the top is the Sacred Dove. In another corner we see doubting Thomas putting his finger into the wounds of Our Lord, and again Jesus after the Resurrection, dressed as a pilgrim, with wallet and stick and shells like a wanderer on the road of Saint James.

The eight scenes, together with their fantastic setting, form a gigantic panorama of the eleventh century, created by artists who had combined harmoniously the ornamental devices of Byzantium and the East with those of Visigothic Spain.

At first in my mind the series of scenes sculptured on the capitals produced the effect of a chaotic vision ; the artists in chiselling the stone into marvellous shapes had obeyed the impulses of their inspiration of the moment, and I remembered Vasari in his introduction to the art of painting, describing how the ancients used to produce such grotesque pictures for the decoration of vacant spaces. They would fashion monsters deformed by a freak of nature or by the whim and fancy of the workers, who in these grotesque pictures made things outside any rule. He whose imagination ran the most oddly was held to be most able. But to Fray Justo, who had lived for years in the cloister, all those sculptured capitals appeared as part of a lofty symbolism.

" They all depend," said he, " on their position with regard to the different parts of the monastery. The figures on the North of the cloister are related to the Devil and sinners, and they describe the vices of the world and the fruits thereof. Those of the South, on the contrary, signify the qualities and attributes of Our Lord and his angels, as do those on the Eastern side ; but those on the West symbolize human frailty and evil, for on the western side was the door of the monastery communicating with the outer world. Remember that many of those grotesque birds and animals appear in oriental art as symbols, and the artists of Silos incorporated them for this reason in their work. Perhaps, indeed, they took them from ancient codices that came from the Byzantine Empire."

Before we mounted the stairs to the upper cloisters, which are of the twelfth century, Fray Justo pointed out to me the paintings on the ceilings of the lower cloisters dating from the end of the fourteenth and beginning of the fifteenth century ; scenes of bull-fights and hunts of strange animals and birds. The most striking scene of all represents the funeral procession of a rat, which is celebrated with full pomp and ceremony by other animals. Some help to carry the body, others lift up a cross and silver *bénitier*, while one of them says the Mass for the dead. The scene might well be an illustration of one of the *enxemplos* or fables from Juan Ruiz, the arch-priest of Hita, who lived in the fourteenth century.

" Come now, my friend," said I to Fray Justo, " tell me truly—do you not regret those far-off days of freedom and joy of life ? Surely there was more charity and religious feeling, in those days of Juan Ruiz, when the Devil was represented with torn and bleeding feet and a heap of battered shoes in front of him, which he had worn out in toiling after sinning humanity. In those days many of the clerics would cry out—' Juvenes non possumus legem duram sequi,' and send the old hag Trotaconventos with a message for Lady Endrina, but others like Jacopone da Todi would cast their wealth away in the gutter and cry out to God to send them madness, fever, death, for all the world was nought but falsehood and illusion."

Fray Justo for sole answer gave me holy water as we entered the cell of Santo Domingo—the cell of paradise as it used to be called by the monks. It was here that the Saint, when lying at the point of death, saw the vision of Jesus and the Virgin Mary. For centuries afterwards, sick people from all over Spain came to the Saint's tomb to be cured in such numbers that the shrine rivalized with that of Saint James at Compostela. Here in this cell the Cid Campeador prayed. Here came Saint Ferdinand on repeated occasions. King Alfonso, the Wise, came here to consult the Visigothic manuscripts of the monastery for his scientific works. It was in this cell that he watched all night on the eve of the battle against rebellious Biscay and the Saint appeared to him, telling him to break his enemies with an iron rod, as though they were made of potter's clay.

For many hours I dreamed away in the cell of Santo Domingo, and when I came out into the cloisters again the shades of evening had fallen upon the silent garden. Only the tall, slender cypress-tree seemed to watch over the monastery. My hours pass slowly in this monastery, for I have no task to absorb my restless mind. Every day there are the same silent meals in the refectory, the regular church services, but between those routine duties time hangs heavy on my hands. I feel like the picaresque knave, who has entered a monastery for the purpose of lining his belly. Then when he has eaten his fill he will change the contemplative for the active life, and set out on the roads once more. I am becoming lazy and, like the lazy man, spending my days in three occupations: sleeping overmuch, eating overmuch, and vegetating overmuch. As Marcos de Obregón, the picaresque knave, said—" Eating at somebody else's cost makes you too fat, because you eat without fear or anxiety." I began to feel the virus of Gypsy wandering again in my bones, and a tingling desire to dash away out of the cloister into the open world once more.

### MIDNIGHT

### II

### THE DREAM

" There's no doubt about it; the tinker's curse is upon me to-night," said I to myself as I tossed about in bed in my cell. It must be the effect of the full moon— " The sun set and uprose the yellow moon: the devil's in the moon for mischief."

As long as the sun shines I am tranquil and contented, but as soon as the moonbeams begin to steal into my cell I feel the restless desire to escape over the monastery wall. I am becoming a Moonman again and, as Dekker said in the sixteenth century, "Moonman means madman, because the moon has greatest domination over the bodies of frantic persons; and just as she never is in one shape two nights together, but wanders up and down Heaven like an antic, so the Moonman never tarries one day in a place but is the only base runagate upon earth."

The moon awakens every Pagan idea in my mind—

thoughts of Diana, her daughter Aradia goddess of vagabonds, and the gospel of witches chanted in the silvery light.

" Why are you not here, Fray Justo ? You would exorcize the influence of Diana and the witches and bring me back again to my normal self."

The temptation was too strong, so I got out of bed and dressed. Then taking my violin out of its case I crept noiselessly downstairs and passed through the lower cloister out into the garden.

Not a soul was there. The garden looked white under the light of the moon and the pool of water in the middle gleamed silver. Across the garden stretched the slanting shadow of the cypress-tree like an ominous presence.

For a long time I sat on the marble rim of the pool, bewitched by the dangerous silence of the midnight hour. The only whispering sounds seemed to come from the twinkling stars above. The moon's rays cut the arches into white lacework pattern here and there only to deepen the gloomy shadows within.

I started to play with soft, muted tone, repeating over and over the same tune in order to hypnotize myself—

It was a tune of the fifteenth century, which was sung by the Christians, when they drove the Jews over the sea, and it became so well known that Masses were composed on its theme.

As I played I murmured to myself in time to the music an Italian witchcraft jingle song.

" Queen of the Fireflies ! Hurry apace,
   Come to me now as if running a race,
   Bridle the horse as you hear me now sing !
   Bridle, O bridle the son of the King."

In an incantation the words of the song and the melody do not matter so much as the rhythm imparted by the bow and the stamping of the feet to work the spell. The fiddle echoed through the cloister with melancholy sound and the notes died away in a distant whisper. The only effect of the fiddling in the deathly stillness was to make me drowsy and I laid aside my fiddle to rest.

All of a sudden I seemed to hear a slight murmuring in the distance—so low as to be hardly perceptible. Gradually the murmuring grew in intensity until all the cloister around began to hum in one constant note that set all my nerves on edge.

I gazed up at the moon, but it resembled a pale round face, gazing sardonically upon me. Looking down at my fiddle that was lying on my knees, I found that it had become longer and thinner, and the bow was warped like the ancient bow of a *rebeck*.

To my horror when I looked into the waters of the pool I could hardly recognize my face, for it, too, had lengthened itself out like the exaggeration of an El Greco picture, and become a hideous, pallid likeness.

The murmuring on the same note became still more insistent, and then the peaceful moonlit scene began to ruffle itself like the surface of a calm lake under a squall. I was acutely conscious that many figures hidden in corners of the cloisters were watching me. Soon I began to distinguish myriads of eyes staring fixedly. A hoarse croak from the rim of the pool made me shiver with an attack of ague : it was a large bronze-coloured frog. I was going to kick it back into the pool, but I just remembered in time the old proverb—" He who loves a frog regards it as Diana." " Be off, bronze frog, symbol of Diana, Goddess of the Moon. What have you to do with a cloister of the Church of Rome ? "

As the murmuring grew in volume, a strange transformation was taking place in the monastery garden : the green shrubs were stretching out their branches as though beckoning, and when they touched one another there was a slight snapping sound and then other trailing branches would coil and uncoil in all directions.

To my horror I found that at the end of each branch were bloodless, skeleton fingers.

In a trice, the whole garden had become so impenetrable a jungle that I could with difficulty make out the arches of the cloister. In addition to the murmuring sound there was another noise of rustling twigs and a flurry of wings. The countless eyes had come nearer and nearer to me : they shone like hosts of stars that had fallen to earth as glow-worms. In terror I tried to escape from those peering eyes, but every step I advanced through the jungle was a fierce struggle against the rank, encircling undergrowth.

I had one thought of escape—to find my way to the tall cypress-tree, the faithful friend of the monks, but I could not find it.

Battles were going on around me : a few steps away I saw two lions writhing in the coils of those terrible branches : on the other side birds with women's faces had seized wild animals in their talons and were devouring them. I then came to a space that had been cleared by the axes of two warriors mounted on winged steeds who were hacking at one another. A little farther on two gryphons flapped their wings in my face as they snapped avidly with their beaks at clusters of grapes that were hanging from branches just above my head.

I heard the barking of dogs, the neighing of horses, the croaking of frogs and the cawing of birds, and I hoped that those sounds were the magic answer to my prayer that all this chaos and confusion might cease.

Then I heard the sound of chanting; through the branches, I saw torches with very white flame flickering in the distance, and I heard the tramp of feet on the ground:

The soldiers who advanced at the head of the procession bore axes in their hands and hacked their way through the jungle in rhythm with their marching. It was a royal procession, and I saw the King Alfonso the Wise, wearing his crown, followed by two little pages who held up his train.

When they came near me they halted, and the *juglares* with lutes and viols in their hands stood around the King and played. But he looked up into the sky and pointed out something to his courtiers. I then saw looming above me the cypress-tree, and, to my amazement, on the top stood Saint Domingo himself in his robes, carrying his crook in one hand, and with the other blessing the multitude.

I thought that the hour of my deliverance was at hand, because the influence of the Saint would dispel all the phantoms, but alas! His Majesty turned aside from the Saint and beckoned to one of his courtiers who led out a brazened-face hussy of a woman.

While she stood in front of the King, arrogant and insolently beautiful, one of the pages brought up a dice board and set it down at one side, and an aged monk stood at the other and held her by the hand. Then she began to sing.  She sang in a whisper and I could not make out the words, but from the crowd I heard the faintly murmured name of La Balteira, the wandering singer who had been on a crusade to the Holy Land. The King twisted himself up with merriment as she sang her song, which must have contained many an obscene word, if one could judge from her gestures.  In fear I looked above at Santo Domingo on the summit of the cypress-tree, but he had turned his back on the scene.

At the end of the song La Balteira sank slowly to the earth and died.  Immediately a group of penitents in black hoods and habits covered her body with a crimson cloth and bore her off on a bier to the same slow tune as I had heard at the beginning, followed by the royal retinue.

Hardly had the procession departed when I heard a strange sound of neighing horses, braying asses, cackling geese and crowing cocks.  This time it was a procession of animals slowly marching up towards me with pomp and ceremony.  The strangest feature of the procession was that all the bigger animals such as the horse, the ass, and the geese were reduced to the size of the tiny animals such as the mouse.  In the middle of the *cortège* was a bier, and on the bier was a dead rat. Around the corpse marched the members of the rat and mouse tribe, carrying little tapers, and behind came other animals carrying a large cross and silver *bénitier*. Then started the Mass for the dead.

" Praesta, quaesumus, omnipotens Deus : ut anima famuli tui quae hodie de hoc saeculo migravit, his sacrificiis purgata, et a peccatis expedita, indulgentiam pariter et requiem capiat sempiternam."

It was the cat, wearing a long stole over its shoulders, who said the Latin words in a miawing tone, but forthwith the rest of the animals drowned the voice of the cat with a chorus of grunts, squeals, barks and braying. The service became a discordant din, and it was the ass who became the *juglar*. He brayed and brayed until he drowned the sounds of his companions, and he stamped with his hoofs upon the ground a deafening rhythm. At last when the multitude of mice had finished digging a grave, and the corpse of the rat was deposited therein, the procession straggled away with the minstrel donkey bringing up the rear.

I was now feeling desperate, for try as I might I could not escape from the strange forest, where every moment some fresh transformation was taking place. Obscurely in my mind I remembered what Fray Justo had told me about the orientation of the different parts of the monastery. " There is no doubt," said I to myself, " that I am bewitched, and I must be on the North or the West side of the cloister; if only I could find my way to the South or East side I should be able to slough off the evil influences as a snake does its skin. But how can I discover the way through this dense forest ? "

All the mediæval terrors stalked me as I struggled on : in one place I saw a dark cell where a woman was shrieking piteously, for a serpent was torturing her; in another I saw banquets of monks, served by horned devils with wings. I could hear from time to time the rattle of chains of captives who had been freed from Moorish prisons by the miraculous intervention of Saint Domingo : each vision passed before my eyes with the rapid variety of a kaleidoscope.

Suddenly my attention was attracted by two men walking arm in arm around the cypress-tree, talking with excited gestures. One of them was dressed in coat of mail with hood covering head and face, and carrying a spear and leather buckler; the other was clad in Moorish costume, with coloured turban flowing down his back.

The Christian Knight was saying: " Ah! My friend Aboadil—where is my grave—I cannot find it. Some terrible influence has entered into this cloister—some spirit of Beelzebub has disturbed my resting-place of peace."

To which Aboadil replied: " Allah is kind: we shall find the way once I have hacked a path with my scimitar towards the lake yonder. I remember that your little mausoleum is near by."

When they both saw me they came up with their arms outstretched, begging me to show them the way.

" Alas, Sir Knight," I replied, " I, too, have lost my way in this maze, for I am trying to reach the church side of this cloister away from all these evil spirits."

" Aye, evil spirits they are," answered the Christian Knight, " for they have disturbed my rest. Some Pagans have entered here and poisoned the air."

As he said these words both looked at me with a piercing glance and for some unaccountable reason I began to feel a sense of guilt. I could not, however, refrain from saying: " How comes it, my lords, that you wander here arm in arm as friends? Well do I remember the fierce struggles that divided your two races for centuries when the cry was ' *Santiago y cierra España.*' Just a moment ago I heard the clanking chains of Christian captives, tortured by your king, O Sir Aboadil."

But the Knights looked at one another with surprise, saying, " He must be a stranger in this cloister who knows not the story of Muño Sanchez and the Moor Aboadil. Let me, O Aboadil, tell the first part of the story.

"My name is Muño Sanchez de Hinojosa, and I sprang from one of the noblest families of Castile in the eleventh century. Many were the hand-to-hand battles I fought, many were the skirmishes I engaged in with my knights against the Moorish cavalry in this land of Castile the noble. One day when I was riding at the head of my troops towards the town of Soria I saw in the distance a company of richly dressed Moors riding across the plain. At the head was a young man called Aboadil with a beautiful young bride, whom many guests were escorting to the marriage ceremony. When we had captured the whole band, Aboadil knelt before me and with tears in his eyes begged me not to slay two lovers on their wedding day, and he ended his supplication with the words, 'If you spare our lives you will not repent.' Ah, my friend Aboadil, how I remember that day—as I gazed at you kneeling before me dressed in your wedding-garment and at your side the weeping maiden. I felt pity in my heart and I lifted you up from the ground and bade you partake of hospitality in my castle. For days there was merriment within the walls, with roast venison in plenty and sweet wine and bull-fights. I dressed you, Aboadil, and your bride in rich garments woven in Castile; I loaded you with gifts of gold and precious stones, and after the marriage ceremony I escorted you to the gates of my castle and took leave of you.

"Years afterwards I fought in a great battle at Almenar against the Moors. In the midst of the conflict I engaged a huge Moorish warrior in hand-to-hand fight. Long did we struggle together and before I killed him he had cut my arm off with a slash of his sword. But still I fought on, crying out, 'This must not be: up to this day men have called me Muño Sancho—never must they call me Muño Manco or Muño the maimed.'

My knights and I fought on through the heat of the day, but as the sun sank behind the horizon I knew that we were doomed. All the blood of my body had flowed away through my wound, and as I closed my eyes in death I saw around me lying in the golden light of the setting sun seventy of the flower of Castilian chivalry. Now, Aboadil, I have told my part of the story: it is for you to tell the rest."

Aboadil then spake: "Well do I remember that day of Almenar, when we conquered the Castilian knights. After the fierce battle I wandered over the field amidst the dead bodies of knights and horses. Suddenly I came upon a mailed figure lying on the ground, bathed in gore. The helmet and hood had fallen back and I recognized the pale lifeless face. It was Muño Sancho de Hinojosa. I called my followers together and bade them form a guard of honour around the body of the great Castilian knight. I embalmed the body in frankincense and myrrh and placed it in a coffin, covered with *guadalmecí* or gilded leather, studded with nails of silver. Then at the head of my knights I bore the body of Muño Sancho to the castle where lived the hero's wife, Doña María Palazin, and his two sons, Fernando and Domingo. From there I led the funeral procession to this monastery of Santo Domingo de Silos, where they buried you in the year 1098."

"Ah! Aboadil," said Muño Sancho, "you have omitted the one miraculous part of the story. I had made years before my death a vow that one day, accompanied by my knights, I would go on a pilgrimage to the Holy Land to the sepulchre of Jesus Christ, and as I lay dying on the field of Almenar I thought sadly of my unfulfilled vow. But it came to pass that on the day following my death, by God's grace, I appeared at the head of my seventy knights at the gates of Jerusalem. In the city there happened to be a Castilian priest who recognized me and he told the Patriarch that a most honoured Spaniard was at the gates. And the Patriarch came at the head of a great procession to meet the pilgrims and lead us to the Holy Sepulchre. The Castilian priest then wrote a faithful account of all those happenings to the King of Castile and it brought such renown to my tomb here at Silos, that ever since it has been an object of devotion."

After the two knights had finished I began to tell them my story ; that I was a minstrel wandering through the world collecting songs and stories—" and now I shall have your deeds to sing as a *chanson de geste*," I added. Then I took up my fiddle and began to play for them as softly and sweetly as I was able, but the accursed instrument must have had the Devil in it, for it would not respond to me. The tone was shrill and squeaky and my fingers played notes I never intended. Instead of a dignified song of chivalry the tune I played resembled the dance that witches perform by the light of the moon on a fairy ring in the forest.

As I played I saw lights in the distance and figures approaching. To my horror they were a band of naked witches—I knew they were witches because they all had straight black hair that curled at the end. Stark-naked they were, and what was worse they were dancing the devilish *volta* back to back, with buttock knocking against buttock. Around them were other witches, grovelling on all fours, with lighted candles stuck in their mouths to light up the macabre assembly.

The two knights at the beginning of my music had begun to fidget uneasily and gaze at me with alarm : when the witches appeared, they both took to their heels with a cry : " The curse, the curse ! "

As soon as I stopped playing, the witches began to

fade away, but I heard an ominous buzz of voices near, repeating over and over again the two words, "Digitus Dei—Digitus Dei—Digitus Dei." I heard a deep voice call out : "Where is the heretic ? He must be seized and delivered to judgment. Search on all sides for the heretic."

At those words I fell into a cold sweat and my heart trembled with fear, for I felt sure that they referred to me.

It was my turn now to take to my heels, but where was I to go ?

Luckily there happened to be a niche in the wall near by, in which stood a statue of Saint Francis.

"Dearest *poverello* of Assisi, assist me in this hour of terror. Lend me your habit to disguise myself."

Hardly had I uttered the words when I found myself clothed as a Franciscan.

I then lifted the Saint's statue down, concealed it behind a column and took my place in the niche. Just in time, for a big procession of monks approached with banners flying, accompanied by soldiers carrying spears. The words "Digitus Dei" were repeated in deafening sequence and so thick were the clouds of incense that I could hardly distinguish the members of the procession.

As my evil lot would have it, the procession halted just below my niche and everyone with the same accord turned their eyes on me. With the greatest difficulty I remained motionless, for my whole body was quaking with fear. My eyes smarted, my nose tickled, the clouds of incense made me want to cough, but fear froze my heart. I felt as if all those gazing eyes were stings piercing every inch of my flesh.

Suddenly a monk in the front of the procession cried out in an exuberant voice, "A miracle—the statue lives —it is the Saint himself." "A miracle, a miracle"—

the word caused a murmuring ripple in the crowd, swelling up into a shout. All then fell on their knees in prayer. I felt my cheeks bulge out with uncontrolled mirth in spite of my fear. But then a tall monk in black habit strode up to the front of the procession saying, " We shall soon see if it is a miracle." He pulled out of his habit a big pin and, advancing to my niche, he viciously drove the pin into my leg.

The pain was so sudden that I had no chance of summoning to my aid all my reserves of endurance. I shrieked in agony and with a bound I leapt from the niche and dashed away through the long passage of the cloisters. I might have escaped pursuit had it not been for the habit of Saint Francis which caught in my legs and caused me to fall.

In a moment I was seized, bound with ropes and carried struggling back to the concourse of monks. Then my habit was torn off, and two brawny lay-brothers in white habits swished my bare back with hazel switches until I shrieked for mercy. Bleeding and blubbering, I was then dressed up in a yellow sanbenito with black dragons on the back and front; a white cardboard *coroza* or mitre was set upon my head; an unlighted green candle was put in my hand—and I was led as a penitent for judgment by the assembly of monks.

To my surprise the assembly was composed of the Abbot Don Luciano Serrano and other monks, among whom I recognized Padre Antonio and my friend Fray Justo. By all the means in my power I tried to catch their eye and make them pity me, but alas, the baneful influence of Diana and the witches must have changed my appearance, for they did not recognize me. Before the trial started one of the monks plucked some boughs from one of the trees near by, and fashioned out of

them a green cross which was then draped in black
crape.   Suddenly I heard the sound of marching and
the words, " left right, left right," repeated incessantly.
A band of young men appeared.   They were dressed
in black with black kid gloves on their hands, black
bowler hats on their heads, and they marched erectly
and stiffly as if they were marionettes.   The leader was
a tall lanky man dressed in a long frock-coat with a
big prayer-book in his hand.   His face was a medley
of contradictions.   His eyes behind his spectacles were
raised to heaven as though habit had set them in a
permanent mould of pharisaical prayerfulness, but his
furrowed cheeks and his coarse sensual mouth with
slightly protruding canine teeth contradicted the prayerfulness and made me think of an executioner.

In a loud voice he cried : " We are the Band of
Religious Youth and we come to demand that the
culprit, commonly called ' Don Gualtero de muchos
caminos,' be condemned as heretic, pagan and idolator.
These gentlemen have volunteered of their own free
will to give testimony against the said Don Gualtero."
He then shouted : " Attention !  Will you bear witness ! "

I heard the sharp click of heels and each puppet raised
a black right hand, crying out : " We bear witness."

In normal life I should have burst out into a fit of
uncontrollable laughter at this assembly, for in the band
of solemn, black-dressed youths, I recognized men of
my city with whom I had lingered in taverns, carous-
ing until heavy-lidded dawn, but dressed in my yellow
sanbenito, barefooted, aching after my drubbing, I
longed to beg each one in turn on my knees for mercy.
Not one of them, however, would look my way and
they all kept their eyes fixed on the leader who mar-
shalled their minds and bodies with the precision of a
puppet master.

The leader then opened the book he carried under his arm and read out the accusations :

" Reverend fathers : We, the members of this Band of Religious Youth, have come here to bear testimony against this prisoner, and we demand that the maximum penalty be inflicted upon him. The reasons which are set forth in the memorandum presented to your reverence, are as follows :

" (I) That the said Don Gualtero, proclaiming himself a beggar, did gain admittance to this holy place by false pretences, for the purpose of practising witchcraft and holding commerce with the Evil One.

" (II) That the said Don Gualtero polluted with vile stories the sanctity of this cloister which like a fortress has withstood for centuries all pagan heresies. We declare that ever since the aforesaid Don Gualtero has dwelt in the monastery the cloisters have been the prey of Satan : it has even been said that throngs of little devils, like black dwarfs, were seen, running through the columns, back and forth in the choir, spurting sparks, frolicking in front of the altar, blowing out tapers, overturning lamps.

" (III) That the aforesaid Don Gualtero was heard to utter an invocation to the Goddess of the Moon, Diana, and other pagan deities.

" (IV) That he did play devilish music upon his accursed instrument for the purpose of summoning a host of witches from hell's kitchen, and not content with such a sin did actually gaze with lustful eye upon the naked abandoned women.

" (V) That he did come to this monastery after consorting with that accursed race of Gypsies which is hateful in the sight of God and man owing to its atheism, thieving and debauchery.

" Wherefore in consideration of these five accusations

we, the members of Religious Youth, whose duty it is to safeguard and protect in the world the dignity and solidarity of our religion, demand that you and your monks deliver over to us the culprit for punishment."

The Abbot then placed a large black biretta upon his head and spoke solemnly, like a judge pronouncing sentence :

" You have heard the dread accusations. I pity you who are so deluded in your credulity and whose soul is being lost ; you are at fault, but there is greater guilt in him who taught you these sins. Come, do not make yourself out a master when you have been no more than a pupil. Tell us who has led you into this foul sin. Confess all before we hand you over to the tor-turer who will soon make you speak with *bostezo, potro* or *garrucha.*"

Hearing the list of tortures uttered by the Abbot in his soft voice, I leapt to my feet and in a rage I shouted out to the whole assembly :

" Take me away and torture me : hand me over to that prince of hypocrites over there, and his mechani-cal boobs. Tear open my mouth with the *bostezo* and give me the water torture ; rack my limbs out of their sockets by the *garrucha* or the *potro*. I'll not bow my head to any Inquisition. I have come here to live the life of Spain as it was before the Inquisition. Where is your tolerance and charity to-day, without which you are no more than sounding brass and tinkling cymbals ? Where are the doctrines of Christ's pity and love that you profess to follow ? I wanted to live here the life of the Middle Ages when you had those virtues to a greater degree than to-day. In the days of the Cid and Muño Sancho there was more tolerance and charity shown by warriors to their enemy captives than there is to-day by these bigots to their neighbours.

" In the Middle Ages the Church was ready to acknowledge the temptations of its Saints. Saint Antony, Saint Simion of Trêves, even Saint Benedict himself were tortured by spirits and witches, and their courage in resisting temptation made them the glories of all ages. But nowadays in the era of peeping Toms and spies anybody who is tempted is considered already judged and condemned. The Church of to-day wants too much power and pomp for itself. It should remember Saint Martin. One day the Devil appeared to him robed in purple, a crown upon his head, and wearing gilded shoes, and said to him : ' Dost thou not know me ? I am Christ.' The Saint, however, answered : ' Thou, Christ ? Christ had neither purple robe nor crown, and I know him only naked, as He was upon the Cross. Thou art the Devil ! ' Ponder that story well, all you smug young hypocrites with your trade union of religion. There's more religion in my companion Pedro de Castellón roaming with his tent on his back over Castile than there is in the whole pack of you. ' The Lord will provide,' is the Gypsies' motto, and God feeds them as he does the birds without demanding his toll of paternosters and aves."

As I finished my impassioned speech I heard a low chanting prayer and a forest of candles advanced out of the gloom towards me. I heard the words : " Respice in auxilium Christianorum ; ut gentes paganorum, quae sua feritate confidunt, dexterae tuae potentia conterantur. . . . Alleluia. Alleluia. Excita, Domine, potentiam tuam et veni."

I heard church bells faintly ; then a murmuring breeze blew me along in a crowd of withered leaves ; the candles began to grow longer and longer and branch out into stars ; my head began to reel and there was a great buzzing in my ears—then all blackness. . . .

When I awoke the moon had disappeared behind the clouds and the sky was grey. A slight breeze blew some leaves along the path with rustling sound. Right in front, on the rim of the pool, a little frog was perched gaping at me.

Taking up my fiddle, I crept upstairs to bed.

## CHAPTER XXVII

## GYPSY VENGEANCE

IN the afternoon of the following day I gave, at the request of Fray Justo, a lecture on Gypsy life to the community.

It was a strange experience to celebrate the free, undisciplined life of the Romany chals to cloistered monks who have voluntarily renounced the world. "Yes, reverend fathers, inside your walled paradise a Gypsy would droop and languish, no matter how kindly you treated him, and, as soon as he could, he would fly out of the nearest window like the bird out of its golden cage. The Gypsies, as a famous Romany rye once said, are a living parody and satanic burlesque of all that human faith, hope or wisdom have ever accomplished in their highest forms. All over the world their black God-wanting shadow dances behind the solid religion of the ' People.' [1] But society cannot suppress them, for they slip through the net of finest meshes and disappear with a laugh down the wind. The Gypsy does what all of us dream; he is beloved of poets, artists, musicians and all those who seek for romance and mystery in this humdrum world. The world has no power over him because he lives by traditions that are a closed book to its rulers. Do not look upon him as an outcast of society because he busies himself in

[1] C. G. Leland, *The Gypsies*, 1882.

the present without care for the future, and prefers his tents, which he calls moving houses, to the stateliest palaces in cities. Do not look upon him as a lawless scoundrel because his tribal laws are not our own. Remember that he has his observance and penalties, which he enforces without fear or favour. A word given to a Gypsy chief must not be broken, and many a gorgio who transgressed the law of the sons of Egypt found to his cost that Gypsy vengeance reached to the ends of the earth."

Never had I lectured to a more eager and attentive audience. As I spoke I felt that each monk in his mind was adding as a commentary to my words little phrases, proverbs, anecdotes, culled from his experiences out in the world. Instead of lecturing to them as I should to a University class or a social club, I was merely vibrating a string which awakened all kinds of hidden harmonies in their soul. The raggle-taggle Gypsies were like fire-birds leading them out of the cloister over hill over dale.

After they had left the hall Fray Justo brought up one of the monks who wished to speak with me most urgently. "This is Padre Saturio González," said he, introducing him. "He wants to tell you the strangest story you have ever heard—one whose truth he can vouch for, as it concerned a near relation of his."

Padre Saturio González, a tall grey-haired monk with a face like a hawk and bright, beady eyes, was so excited that he could hardly stand still. He seized my arm and dragged me along with him through the corridor, saying in an eager voice : " Come, come with me, Señor : I'll tell you a story of the Gypsies that actually happened to my cousin.

" Come on, come on, Fray Justo, take the caballero's other arm and let us be off. We must get away from the monastery : I won't speak of the accursed *Gitanos* within the sanctified precincts of the cloister."

The worthy monk, with his habit billowing in the breeze behind him and his beads jingling, walked rapidly out of the monastery pulling Fray Justo and myself after him like two refractory children. Not a word would he say as he strode on, puffing and blowing like a porpoise. At last after about two kilometres' walk we came to a rocky, deserted place studded with caves, where the monk halted.

"Here," said he, "is where the Gypsies bivouacked on many an occasion. The whole district gets its name from these caves, for the word Silos is of Basque etymology and means a cave. In the earliest days wheat was stored in those subterranean caverns, and in the War of Independence at the beginning of the nineteenth century they were thronged with bandits or else monks hiding away the treasures of the monastery from the French invading army. Sometimes when I used to wander here I found a band of Gypsies encamped by the stream, so I always call this place the Gypsies' cave, and I have brought you here to tell you the story of my cousin Fernando Izquierdo or Fernandito, as all the country people in Castile called him.

"Fernando was a lawyer in Salas de los Infantes—the town of the Seven Heads, as many call it, twelve kilometres from Silos. Now in the country towns of Castile the lawyer is a personality of eminence. Go into the principal café or casino of any town and you will find the *abogado* laying down the law to a group of the principal citizens. Everyone looks on him with respect, for he knows the secrets of the home, and for that reason you'll always find a touch of arrogance about him and a portentous gravity.

" My cousin Fernando was one of those lawyers, but
without the arrogance and gravity. He was as fond of
tossing dice with the muleteers and farm hands as he
was of listening to the prolix meanderings of the apothe-
cary or the saddle-maker in the *tertulia*. He was one of
the most popular men in the town and he had as dainty
a wife as you would find in a week's search through
Castilla la Vieja : fair-haired she was, and as for eyes,
Cervantes would have voted them as choice emeralds
as Luscinda's. Two young daughters there were also,
no less beautiful than the mother. Fernando had everything any man could desire and his life was as merry as
a bagpipe.

" Then all of a sudden came the disaster.

" On that day, as the proverb goes, the Devil was in
Cantillana.

" Fernando was settling some business at Barbadillo
del Mercado, a village not more than four kilometres
from Salas, and in the evening he was riding home on
his mule. Just outside the village, he saw a band of
Gypsies encamped by the River Arlanza. Now Fernando always had a nomadic streak in his character :
nothing used to please him more than to listen to the
talk of tramps and vagabonds who had lived a roving
life, rubbing shoulders with many conditions of men.

" On that day, the Devil, not his Guardian Angel,
was at his elbow, so he halted his mule and got down to
see the Gypsy camp. It was sunset and the sight of the
tents and the dusky sons of Egypt with their children,
mules and dogs made him think of the Israelites
wandering through the desert, for Fernando, though
a notary, had a poet's soul, and that was like throwing
oil on the fire.

" In the middle of a group of Gypsies he saw a girl
dancing the *romalis*.

" Have you ever seen the *romalis* danced by a *gachí* of fifteen ?  If you did then I hope you made the sign of the Cross and said *mea culpa* to your father confessor. When I was a rollicking *mozo* in Sevilla I saw it danced in Triana and it cost me a great deal of penance.

" Poor Fernando did not cross himself—nay, he feasted his eyes on the beauty of that daughter of perdition.  Her eye had more baneful magic in it than the eyes of all the Circes, Calypsos, and Helens who ever harassed mortal frailty.  A large, dark, lustrous evil eye it was and it fairly scorched Fernando.  He saw that her skin shone like copper in the setting sun and he forgot the milk-white skin of his wife at home.  He saw ebony locks like raven's plumage instead of fleecy, golden hair.  He might have paused to reason with himself had it not been for that accursed dance, with the fatal, irrevocable guitar thrumming and the haughty arrogance of that dusky girl rolling her hips and snapping her castanets.

" Heaven preserve me, Señor, I am forgetting my sacred habit when I give you all those details.  Ah ! Many times I thank my stars that I am hidden away in my cloister far away from the temptations of the world.

" Well, to continue my story, Fernando went home a changed man.  He was like one in a dream, for his eyes were always set in the direction of the Romany *chai*.  He began to keep late hours, then to sleep out, then finally, *sin decir oxte ni moxte*, he stayed away altogether.  And there were his poor wife and his two little angels of daughters weeping their hearts out for him and lighting candles in front of the Madonna, saying —'If only father would come back.'  It was heartbreaking, I tell you.  But he did not come back. Instead, they heard that he had been adopted into the Gypsy tribe with full ceremony—though I'm inclined to doubt these ceremonies in spite of the illustrious

Cervantes.  Robbers don't waste their time in ceremonies when they are out on a robbery expedition.  Of
one thing I am certain—he did marry the Gypsy girl,
aye, and had a couple of bastards by her too—as black
as coal.

"She gave him the hell of a life as soon as he was
pledged to her by Gypsy law.  No day passed that she
would not call him *jindó Busnó* or filthy gorgio, and
pour contempt upon him.  He was for ever afraid that
in a fit of rage she would put some *drao* or poison in his
food, for she would utter curses against him that made
him, bad christian as he was, shiver as if he was already
cold and stiff in his grave.

"As the proverb says—'It isn't the cowl that makes
a monk.'  Fernando may have danced as hard as he
could to the Gypsy tune, and dressed and behaved like
a son of Egypt, but from time to time he remembered
his old life at home with his fair wife and two lawful
children, but he knew that as soon as he tried to escape,
the Gypsies would dash down on him like a thunder-
bolt, for so the chief of the Gypsies had warned him on
the day when he had been married by Romany rites.  So
he bided his time and made himself the biggest expert
of the tribe at robbing.

"Soon his exploits were the theme of the whole
*sierra* and he was as much feared as 'Long Steps' or
any other brigand of Andalucía.  Many who saw him
in those years—about 1909 and 1910—said that he was
completely transformed from the county notary they
had known.  He had let his hair grow, and his long,
matted locks fell over his shoulders ; he had a thick,
shaggy beard and his skin was tanned like leather after
his hard life in the open.  To the Gypsies he was a
godsend because he knew every nook and cranny of the
country, and what was more important, he knew how

to talk softly to the Civil Guards and make them turn their blind eye when he was about.

"To such a pitch of insolence did he reach that he even began to rob convents and monasteries. By this he showed that he was not a *Gitano castizo*, for a *Gitano* would say to himself—'Better not to touch the monastery—*quién sabe?* It might bring us *mala suerte*.' But Fernando was not abashed by any thoughts of sacrilege or evil luck. Here in Silos I used to dread hearing of his exploits, for I felt that some of the shame would fall on me for being related to him.

"One night he climbed into the monastery when we were all asleep and stole two pictures by old masters. Yes, Señor, he cut the pictures out of their frames and escaped with them over the wall without anyone catching sight of him. Not very long after, however, the Civil Guard caught him in a church about to steal vestments and silver and he was left to cool his heels in gaol for a while.

"When he was set free the Gypsies met him at the prison gates and brought him back to his old haunts. But he was a changed man. You know, Señor, there is nothing like a taste of gaol for softening and refining a man's spirit. It is in a dismal prison where, as Cervantes says, 'wretchedness keeps its residence and every dismal sound its habitation,' that a man learns to know his true self.

"The scales began to fall from Fernando's eyes and he saw the wreck he had made of his life.

"But what was he to do?

"How could he escape from the Gypsy tribe and hope to reach his home unscathed? According to Gypsy law, he was married to a daughter of the tribe and he was bound to be loyal to the law of the *Calés*.

"At last, after many weary months of wandering

through Spain, suffering the icy cold of winter blasts
or else the scorching heat of the summer, he decided to
risk the escape.  He wrote a long letter to his wife at
Salas de los Infantes, telling her of all his sufferings and
misfortunes and begging her forgiveness.  If she would
forgive him, why should they not start a new life far
away from Spain in a country where nobody would ask
questions about the past?  He then said that he would
escape from the Gypsy camp and make his way through
the country to Barcelona and from there take a boat to
the United States.  When he would have a position he
would send her the money to go out to join him with the
children.

"Soon afterwards, Fernando escaped in the night
from the Gypsies, who were then encamped near Burgos.
In order to avoid pursuit he shaved off his beard and
disguised himself as a woman.  But even in his woman's
clothes he felt uneasy.  He remembered the solemn
words of the chief of the tribe to him when he had
plighted his troth to the Romany *chai*—'Never break
your word to the *Calés*, for their vengeance reaches to
the end of the earth.'

"When he had reached Barcelona and booked his
passage on a small vessel bound for New York, his
spirits rose.  Out on the ocean he would be free from
the tentacles of the accursed Gypsies.  In New York
he tarried some time trying to find employment, but
there was little chance for a Spaniard who knew no
English.  Gradually he wandered through the States
living mostly as hobo or odd-job man until he reached
Mexico.  Here he found a country that seemed to be the
prolongation of his own Castile.  He wandered over
hard-baked tableland and mesetas such as he had known
at Salas de los Infantes.

"In Mexico city he ended his wandering and obtained

employment in a big store. Now that he was settled, it was time to call his wife and children to his side. He wrote home to Salas sending her the money for her passage out to Mexico. The letter ended with the words—' Come as soon as you can, dear wife of mine, that we may start a new life together, and may God grant me years of life to make up for all the evil I have done to you.'

" That letter was sent in 1923 and the good woman when she received it hastily made her preparations to set out in a ship called the *Vabranera*.

" Not long afterwards Fernando was walking alone down a narrow street in Mexico city when he was suddenly set upon and ambushed.

" It was night-time and nobody was about.

" When they found his body next morning it was a mass of dagger wounds.

" The shirt had been ripped open at the chest and on the skin a strange sign had been cut with the knife and also the single word ' Venganza.'

" Immediately a telegram was sent back to me at Silos asking me to inform the poor woman of her husband's fate, but she had already set out with her two children on the *Vabranera*. Alas! they never reached Mexico. Just beyond Cuba a storm caught the ship and wrecked her.

" Among the passengers lost were Fernando Izquierdo's widow and two daughters."

After Padre Saturio González had finished speaking there was a deep silence and all that could be heard was the murmuring stream flowing over the rocks beside the cave. Without a word the three of us walked slowly back to the monastery and in the dusk we heard the gentle tolling of the church bells of Silos.

# CHAPTER XXVIII

## THE BALLAD OF FERNANDO

NEXT day Padre Saturio González said to me:
"The curse of the Gypsies still pursues Fernandito's ghost in spite of all my efforts. My
uncle and I spent untold sums of money buying up
letters and documents and burning these in the hope
that the whole story might be consigned to oblivion,
but in vain. When you go to Barbadillo del Mercado
and Salas de los Infantes you will hear the accursed
*coplas* in which the folk of the *sierra* used to celebrate
the escapades of my cousin when he roamed with the
Gypsies, plundering the homesteads and churches.
They used to sing the song as far back as 1909, and they
have not forgotten it."

With the help of Fray Justo and an old man from
Barbadillo del Mercado I obtained some stanzas of the
song and some days later at Salas de los Infantes I heard
a group of women sing it as a semi-humorous ballad.
It is a characteristic piece of improvisation with a long
*estribillo* or refrain which was shouted by the singers as
if it was a comic nursery rhyme.

> " Fernandito, Fernandito,
> con titulo de abogado,
> que por tu mala cabeza
> te has ido con los Gitanos.

349

" Por la mañanita
cuando me levanto
miro la petaca,
no tiene tabaco.
no tengo tabaco
no tengo dinero
ni quien me lo dé.
A mi Gitana
yo se lo digo
y ella me dice:
vente conmigo;
vente conmigo,
que yo te quiero,
porque tu vales
más que el dinero.

" Yo tenía una mujer
que era más blanca que el sol,
y ahora tengo una Gitana
que es más negra que el carbón.

" Por la mañanita
cuando me levanto
miro la petaca,
no tiene tabaco.
no tengo tabaco
no tengo papel.
No tengo dinero,
ni quien me lo dé.
A mi Gitana
yo se lo digo
y ella me dice:
vente conmigo;
vente conmigo,
que yo te quiero
porque tu vales
más que el dinero.

" El que antes fué respetado
de las gentes de la Sierra
ahora yace en una carcel
por robar a las iglesias."

After hearing it in Spanish I recited to myself a doggerel English paraphrase which I pounded out in my head as I tramped along the dusty road from Barbadillo to Salas de los Infantes.   The first ten lines of the refrain or *estribillo* should be shouted by the boys and the seven remaining lines be shouted by the girls in order to bring out the dramatic element of the song.

"Fernando, Fernando the lawyer has flown,
Out of his house and out of the town,
Fled like a thief at the midnight hour
To join the Gypsies out on the moor.

"Early in the day
Before I wend my way,
I look in my purse,
I utter a curse,
There isn't a cent,
It has all been spent,
I am stony broke,
I haven't a smoke,
Come tell me true,
What shall I do?

"Then out speaks my Romany *chai*:
For you I'd willingly die:
You're my Romany churl,
I'm your Romany girl:
I care not for gold
While your body I hold,
You darling, rollicking Gypsy bold.

"In the town of the Infants all forlorn
Waits my wife with hair like the golden morn;
But now I have wedded a Romany queen
With hair like the raven and dusky skin.

"Early in the day
Before I wend my way,
I look in my purse,
I utter a curse,

There isn't a cent,
All has been spent,
I am stony broke,
I haven't a smoke,
Come tell me true,
What shall I do?

"Then out speaks my Romany *chai*:
For you I'd willingly die:
You're my Romany churl,
I'm your Romany girl:
I care not for gold
While your body I hold,
You darling, rollicking Gypsy bold.

"Take heed all ye shepherds and men of the plain,
Be warned by the fate of Fernando again,
Fam'd as a lawyer he sank to perdition,
A sacker of chapels he lies now in prison."

It is fascinating to study the whole process of artistic elaboration from such a folk story. Lope de Vega once said—"Ballads spring to life when men sow the wheat." Some anonymous poet recalls a striking local happening familiar to all his fellow shepherds or farmers, and as he works he improvises a rhythmic song in doggerel verse. His companions, men, women and children take up the refrain and sing it with gusto. Gradually in the course of time the poem refines itself and assumes a definite shape through the unconscious artistic efforts of all those who sing it. At first a folk poem is like a stranger who arrives at a village: everyone looks him up and down, and judgment is passed upon him. If the villagers do not like him, they tell him to make himself scarce: if they accept him, he is welcomed by all in turn. Who knows what a wealth of ballads based upon local events lies hidden in the minds of all those Castilian villagers ? In talking to the old men I was struck by their resemblance to the Scots, who have always preserved the tradition of the ballad. As I heard the *coplas* of Fernandito I recalled such a ballad as " The Gypsy Laddie " :

> " The Gypsies came to our good lord's gate,
> And wow but they sang sweetly.
> They sang sae sweet and sae very compleat
> That down came the fair lady."

In the Spanish ballads there is always a strong sense of drama and the singers when they sing them use to the full their powers of acting. They vary their voice in accordance with the various characters and the refrain becomes a chorus commenting upon the action.

After hearing the *coplas* I determined to make use of them as a minstrel might have done, and I organized for myself a kind of monodrama in several voices, relieved from time to time by music. I devised it in five short acts based on the following scheme :

ACT I. Fernando the lawyer lives happily at Salas with his wife and family. Happy music such as a *baile redondilla* and a cradle song.

ACT II. Fernando meets the Gypsies. Copious details of the dusky girl's devilish beauty. Music must have a *Flamenco* tinge with *ay ! olé !* and other hoarse cries of *Cante Jondo*.

ACT III. A sad picture of the forlorn wife and weeping daughters praying to Our Lady. Then, as a contrast, the fierce passion of Fernando and the wicked lure of the Gypsy girl. The music ranges from tender elegy to *polos*, *martinetes* and such Gypsy dances.

ACT IV. Fernando's decline and fall. His life in gaol and repentance. Music very sad ; mostly *alegrías*, those so-called songs of joy that tell of jealousy and crime, and *carceleras* or prison songs.

Act V. Retribution. Fernando's escape to U.S.A. A touch of jazz, but no more, for fear of spoiling the play. Then a Mexican tango, followed by a death song. The end should be a homily in order to send the people away in an optimistic frame of mind.

As I improvised the monodrama I thought of Ruth Draper and wished devoutly I had a spark of her genius. It was difficult to suggest the voices of my various characters. I had to use a sing-song voice for the actual story-telling, a strong, virile voice for Fernando (especially when he became a Gypsy brigand), a languid, sugary voice for his wife, and a husky, metallic voice for the Carmen of the play. In theory these ideas were brilliant, but they lost a great deal of their power in the actual performance, for in the excitement and perspiration of talking, singing, playing, whistling, gesticulating I sometimes forgot the various voices and found myself giving Fernando's rough voice to his wife and vice versa. My stage was a limited one, for I was performing in a café of Salas de los Infantes before an audience composed of men in smocks or shirt-sleeves, in an atmosphere of wine and smoke. I wished a thousand times that I had a deeper knowledge of Spanish idiom, for I was painfully conscious that my phrases lacked what the French call *le gout du terroir*. Sometimes I felt myself poised in mid-air for want of a telling phrase, whereas if the language had been English I could have scored with nippy slang.

Then there was the necessity of catching the attention of the audience by stunts, such as apposite jokes and especially digressions. It is certainly true to say that digressions are the soul of monologues. An audience becomes fatigued listening to a long story without frequent breaks. The mediæval minstrels of Spain understood this, and they would vary their performances with acrobatic stunts. One would say—"Now, lords and ladies, I shall give a hop, skip and a jump like the best chestnut horse, or else turn a somersault for you like a clown in the circus." After his little piece of buffoonery he would take up again the thread of his story.

The gods, however, were kind to me at Salas de los Infantes and I found that the audience in the café became more and more interested as my dramatized story of Fernando advanced. At first they looked upon me as a strange, grotesque character, not to be taken quite seriously, but when I arrived at Act III where Fernando pays court to the Romany *gachí*, I felt like the old rhapsodist in the shadowy halls, holding the people in subjection by his magic. I led them all by a string and I could play upon their emotions as I willed. The music, too, of my violin excited them, for it stressed the emotions of the story. From feeling like Master Peter with his puppet show I began to live the story myself as though I was Fernando. There was a murmur of indignation when I described how Fernando robbed the churches, and so immersed was I in the story that I thought the indignant exclamations were uttered against me personally. But then at the end of the story I felt a sense of satisfaction in drawing the moral of the play and bringing all that audience back to normal again. A folk-drama should always end with a chorus in which the author makes the citizens comment upon the action of the play. After the exciting incidents there is calm serenity and the audience departs after having lived through an experience.

After my performance I should have felt very lonely if it had not been for my faithful henchman Lazarillo. Lazarillo was a youth of nineteen, a tanner's apprentice, whom I called by that name because by his sharp, ready tongue and unlimited appetite he reminded me of the hero of Spain's first picaresque novel, *Lazarillo de Tormes.* Ah, Lazarillo, I blessed you more than once in Salas, for you gilded my horizon for me. I was suffering from intense loneliness until you came and cheered me up with your anecdotes and songs.

Lazarillo was a tall, bony youth with pale face, sandy-coloured hair, and eyebrows like an albino. I met Lazarillo in the *parador* or primitive inn of the town, when I was tucking in to a meal. Like a stray dog he came up to me, sniffed at me, and, finding me good-natured and liberal, he attached himself to me as a faithful companion. I never went anywhere without Lazarillo. When I played he stood and passed the hat around. He had no talents for music, singing or recitation, but he was an ideal collector. He would pass the hat round unobtrusively and yet firmly in order to spare my feelings. I never failed to share the spoils with him, and in addition keep him well supplied with tobacco, for that was his one vice. At first when I had met him he stood near me, and when I threw cigarette butts on the floor he would pick them up and smoke them with a look of triumph on his face. Lazarillo called himself a tanner's apprentice, but I never saw him at work at his trade during my stay at Salas. Instead, he seemed to be at the beck and call of everybody in the town, running for messages hither and thither, or else loitering in the main street where the buses from Burgos halted. But whenever I needed him I had only to whistle, and he would run up like a faithful dog—one of those affectionate, tousled and rather bedraggled-looking mongrels who slink along after their master. When tramping the country I would walk majestically in front, waving my stick, and, ten yards behind, Lazarillo would jog along in his tattered shoes, carrying my fiddle-

case like the squire of a knight-errant fiddler. When I
used to perform, Lazarillo would deposit the case upon
a table, open it and draw out the instrument and bow.
Then with a majestic gesture he would hand them to
me with the words—" Ahora toque Vd una cosita nada
más." I always responded to his invitation, for he had
an unerring eye for the possibilities of gain. As he said
himself, " He could scent money in the air." When I
used to tell stories or else perform my little musical play
about Fernandito, Lazarillo would station himself in a
corner and act as a *claque* for me by stimulating the
applause and initiating the bursts of laughter at any of
my modest sallies of wit. His absurd laugh, a mixture
of the neighing of a horse, and the braying of an ass,
worked miracles upon the most refractory audience.
At the end when dividing up our meagre spoils I used
to give him a special bonus for his impromptu laughter.

# CHAPTER XXIX

# THE SEVEN HEADS OF SALAS

## A STORY OF THE MIDDLE AGES

IN all my wanderings in Spain I had never seen a sadder landscape than at Salas de los Infantes. The lonely undulating plain stretches to the great rocky mesa which rises abruptly, casting a sinister shadow over the fields. Though the sun shone in Salas on the fields in harvest I felt the demon of melancholy. Even the faint sound of the church bell which I heard from the mound where I was sitting made tears come into my eyes. Who can explain the strange influences that emanate from certain places and create phantoms in the mind? The very monotony of this landscape casts a spell upon me. As I wander farther and farther into Castile my vision grows in intensity and I have the sensation of living a timeless existence. The peasants and shepherds remind me by their fatalism of the Indian rock-dwellers in New-Mexico who live in fear of awakening the spirits of earth and air and water. In this timeless land a grim tragedy of vengeance that took place over nine hundred years ago may still make its baneful influence felt as though it had been only committed yesterday. The ghost of the ferocious Doña Lambra, the Lady Macbeth of the Spanish ballads, still haunts the plain and the sierra. On stormy nights she rises from the dark lake in the mountains where she threw herself after the bastard son Mudarra had avenged the murder of the Seven Infantes. The parish priest of Salas—a bright-eyed enthusiast—acted as my cicerone. He led me into the parish church and showed me the coffin which contains the seven heads. It is set in a niche beside the *evangelio*. In 1579 and 1846 the coffin was solemnly opened in the presence of the mayor of the town who verified the presence within of the skulls of the Seven Infantes and their tutor Nuño Salido. In Salas too there was a great ancient palace with seven halls, one for each of the noble sons, but alas, to-day not a vestige of that glory remains. However, to a visionary people, bricks and stone do not count, for the human mind can create them in a flash.

The story of the Seven Infantes was a local incident that took place in the storm-tossed tenth century when Almanzor the famous Moorish King of Cordoba was ravaging Castile. The incident would have faded from men's memories just like the story of Muño Sanchez de Hinojosa and Aboadil at Silos, had it not been for the anonymous minstrel—the blind rhapsodist who strung the events together and sang them as a long narrative. Once the story was launched on the wings of poetry it began to fly far and wide. It became a symbol of Spain in the sense that the dramas of the Oresteia are a symbol of Greece. In studying the story from its origin through the centuries down to modern times as Professor Menéndez Pidal has done, we can watch the evolution of the art of literature. Let us therefore imagine the story as told by a mediæval *juglar* in the period when the minstrel was looked upon as a collaborator of the nation's history.

## The Minstrel Tells the Story

The *juglar* was blind and feeble : all day he had trudged the countryside singing to the people in taverns and in the squares. And now at dusk the old man, leaning on the arm of his faithful henchman, climbed his way up towards the castle on the hill above the town. The Count, he knew, would welcome him because he ever took delight in listening to tales and songs in the banqueting-hall after the cloths had been taken away.

We find the old minstrel seated at the table in the lofty hall. The wine-bearer pours wine into his goblet and the board is laden with bread and flesh. The people make merry and it is time for the old man to begin his song. As the blind poet Homer says of such a man : " The muse loved him dearly, and she gave him both good and evil; of his sight she reft him, but granted him sweet song." A chair adorned with gilded leather was set for him in the midst of the guests, and his henchman showed him how to lay his hands upon his lute and bow, and close by him he placed a goblet of wine, to drink when his spirit bade him. And the old man after preluding on the lute began to sing his song of famous men, and all held their peace and were spellbound throughout the shadowy halls.

For such was his song :

" I shall tell you of the days when Garci Fernández was count of Castile. Many were the brave knights who rode into battle against the Moorish King Almanzor, but none so doughty as the Seven Infantes of Salas whose sad fate I shall relate. I shall tell you also of that *alto ome* called Ruy Velázquez who married the great lady from Bureba, Doña Lambra, sister of Garci Fernández. Their marriage was celebrated at Burgos and fain would I describe its magnificence. O that I had

eyes to see such jousting, bull-fighting and dancing!
There were throngs of *juglares*, there was dice-throwing
in the taverns; such crowds filled the city that many
found no resting-place. From Castile they came and
from Navarra.

"Now to the festival came Ruy Velázquez's sister,
Doña Sancha, wife of Gonzalo Gustios, and by her side
rode her seven sons the Infantes of Salas. See them
ride into the lists: how arrogantly they sit their palfreys
with lances couched. May God soften the heart of
Doña Lambra for methinks she frowns upon the Infantes.
See how her brow is furrowed as she witnesses their
valiant jousting. Then out spake she to her ladies,
pointing to her bridegroom Ruy Velázquez—'Look on,
look on, ladies; my husband is worth four of those
Infantes from Salas.'

"But Doña Sancha, the mother of the youths,
answered forthwith: 'Hold thy peace, Doña Lambra
—say not such words: the Infantes would kill thee if
they heard.'

"'Be silent, Doña Sancha,' cries Doña Lambra,
'for silent thou shouldst be, for thou hast given birth
to seven sons—like any dunghill sow.'

"The quarrel waxes strong, and passes from the
women to the men, for González, the youngest of the
Infantes, being pressed by Doña Lambra's cousin Alvar
Sánchez, with a blow stretches him on the ground dead.
Then Doña Lambra breaks into grievous lamentation
crying out that never had *dueña* been so dishonoured on
her wedding-day. A fierce fight takes place between
the factions of Ruy Velázquez and those of the Infantes,
and woe betide the Seven Infantes were it not for Count
Garci Fernández and Gonzalo Gustios who make
peace among the warring men. But look at Doña
Lambra: her face bodes evil. Bitterly will the Seven

Infantes rue this day. By night she broods in her
palace at Barbadillo, nursing her vengeance to keep it
warm. She calls to her side one of her servants and
orders him to cast at González, the youngest of the
Infantes, a wild cucumber soaked in blood. Look how
the caitiff hurls the foul insult at González. Fain would
the servant escape the wrath of the noble-born youth, and
so he runs for refuge beneath Doña Lambra's cloak.
But the Infantes pay no heed to such a sanctuary. They
seize the wretch and plunge their swords into his body
as he lies there, and his blood flows over Doña Lambra's
dress.

"Then did she break out into despairing lament,
calling upon her handmaidens. And straightway she
set a bier in the midst of her hall and upon it the body
of her slave enshrouded, and for three days she wept and
tore her hair, crying out—' Alas, I am a widow, for no
true husband have I.'

"Ruy Velázquez, when he saw her weeping, vowed
vengeance against the Seven Infantes, but with smiling
face and honied words he plots his villainy. 'Come,'
he says to the youths, 'let us be friends. Am I not of
your blood?' So spake he and he bethought him that
he would send Gonzalo Gustios as an emissary to King
Almanzor with a letter. In this letter, which was written
in Arabic, he begged Almanzor to behead Don Gonzalo
and to advance straightway with an army to the Castilian
frontier where the seven sons of Gonzalo Gustios
would be delivered over to him. Let all hearken to the
vile treachery of Ruy Velázquez. But the Moorish
King Almanzor had more generosity in his heart than a
vile Christian traitor. He spared Gonzalo Gustios and
kept him in confinement. Then to the forlorn Christian
captive he sends a Moorish maiden as fair as the sun
to console him in his cell. Arise, fair Moorish maiden

—full honour shalt thou have, for thou shalt bear within thy womb Mudarra the Avenger. Take heed, Ruy Velázquez: in vain shalt thou slay the Seven Infantes of Salas: there's yet an heir in the halls of Gonzalo Gustios—the bastard Mudarra. But the fierce spirit of Ruy Velázquez is not yet sated. As he sits brooding in his palace he plots still fouler villainy against the Seven Infantes. With soft words he flatters the chivalry of the youths saying: ' Out on it, Sons of Gonzalo the brave, why do ye tarry here ? Go call your squires and bid them saddle your palfreys and lead out your war-horses, for it is time to joust in earnest against the currish rabble of Mahomet.' The Seven Infantes are no laggards. Watch them ride out from Salas in full panoply, with two hundred of the bravest knights and at their head Nuño Salido the ancient guardian. Fain would they have left the old man by the hearth, but he besought them to take him, for Gonzalo Gustios and Doña Sancha wished him to be ever by the side of the Infantes. Now when they had come to the pinewoods of Cañicosa, Nuño Salido saw that the omens were unfavourable, for he was a soothsayer and accustomed to read the flight of the birds. ' My sons,' cries he, ' I beseech you to turn back to Salas ;  it were rash to ride on farther with such contrary omens.' But Gonzalo González, the youngest of the Infantes, rebuked him angrily saying : ' Speak not thus Don Nuño Salido, for well thou knowst that yon omens point not to us but to Ruy Velázquez who is the leader of our band. Go thou back to Salas, for thou art old and weary, but we shall follow our lord Ruy Velázquez.'

"Then answered Nuño Salido : ' My sons, in truth I like not this journey, for the omens say that we shall never more return to our homes. Wherefore I say that if ye break those omens ye must send a herald to your mother, telling her to cover with black cloths seven biers and set them in the courtyard of the palace and weep over you all as dead.'

"Listen how the Seven Infantes mock the *ayo* Nuño Salido for his gloomy prophecy : would that they had followed the counsel of such a man wise in years. He turned his horse away to ride back to Salas, but he reasoned with himself saying : ' A coward's part forsooth I play, leaving those youths whom I have reared. Should I, being old in years, not seek death more eagerly than those who are youths and have their lives to live ? And if they should die would not all men say of me— " There goes one who was honoured in youth but in old age dishonoured." ' And so taking counsel with himself he turned back and followed his charges. Meanwhile the Infantes with their shields around their necks and lances with streamers in their hands, pricked forward their goodly horses until they reached the plain of Febros where their uncle Ruy Velázquez was awaiting them. Listen, Lords, to my story of devilish treachery ! Ruy Velázquez leads the Infantes and Nuño Salido with their two hundred knights to the plain of Almenar and orders them to make forays and skirmishes into the Moorish land. But he and his band retire swiftly into a concealed spot, having sent a secret message to the Moors to attack the Infantes with full force of arms. ' Go surround them,' saith the traitor, ' there are not no more than two hundred of them—not one will escape, for I will not give help to them.' And so the Seven Infantes ride on to their doom. All of a sudden in the distance there is a faint sound of drums which every instant grows greater. From all sides gallop the Moors armed for the fray. The Infantes then know that Ruy Velázquez has betrayed them. What can two hundred knights do against ten thousand Moors ? Nevertheless,

with the cry of Saint James the Apostle on their lips they
join in the battle, and at their head rides Nuño Salido
the *ayo*—eager to be the first to die; for better is it to
die than see the death of those you have reared with
love. 'Fight on, my sons,' he cries. 'Fear not the
omens: nay, they were fair and fortunate, for they
foretold that we should win the day and slay our enemies.'
Gallantly the Infantes fought all through that sad day:
more than a thousand Moors they slew, but alas, their
two hundred knights lie dead upon the plain. Then did
the Infantes ask for truce from the Moors, and one of
them went to their uncle Ruy Velázquez, begging him
to come to their assistance. But grim Velázquez answers:
'Go in good hour, friend; think you that I had forgotten the wrong you did me in Burgos when you killed
Alvar Sánchez? Think you I had forgotten how you
dishonoured my wife Doña Lambra when you pulled
out the man from beneath her cloak and killed him
before her eyes, sprinkling her with gore? By my
troth, you are good knights! Defend yourselves and
place no trust in me, for no help shall you receive.'
Then the fight begins again: the Moors beat their
drums and fall upon the Infantes thick as drops of rain.
They are surrounded: their horses are slain, their
lances and swords broken, and they are sorely wounded.
When they are captured the Moors behead them one by
one and the seven heads together with that of Nuño
Salido are carried to Cordoba as trophy.

"But King Almanzor when he saw the eight heads
ordered his slaves to wash them right well with wine so
that no blood or dust should remain upon them. Then
on a table in the palace hall he laid a white sheet and upon
it he placed the seven heads—all in order of birth, and
at the top he set the head of the *ayo* Nuño Salido.

"Then did Almanzor call forth Gonzalo Gustios the

father of the Seven Infantes from his prison cell and lead
him into the hall where lay the seven heads of his sons.
' Look well, old man,' quoth he, ' and tell me whether
they are known to thee, for my leaders say they are from
Lara's region.'

" But Gonzalo Gustios, when he saw the seven heads,
forthwith recognized them, and so great was his sorrow
that he fell swooning to the ground. And when he
revived he raised such lamentations, that there was not
one present who did not weep with him. One by one
he takes up the heads in his hands and talks to them as if
they had been alive. First of all he lifts up that of Nuño
Salido and he addresses it thus : ' God save thee, Nuño
Salido, my compeer and friend—what of those sons of
mine I left in thy charge, for thou wast friend and well
trusted in Castile and Leon ? May God pardon thee,
compeer: thou hadst no share in Ruy Velázquez's
treachery. Thou didst interpret the augury, but my
sons did not heed thee, for they fretted at the thought
of my captivity. So pardon me, compeer, for all this I
say in grievous sorrow.'

" He then places the head of the *ayo* upon the sheet
and takes up that of Diego González the eldest son,
and tearing his hair and beard and weeping bitter tears
he addresses it thus : ' My son, Diego González : I
loved thee more than all the rest because thou wast
born first. Proud thoughts of thee had Castile's count,
for thou wast his *Alcalde mayor*. Thou wast his standard-
bearer at the Ford of Cascajar. On that day three times
the standard was lowered but three times thou didst
raise it and with it kill three kings and an *alcalde*.' So
saying he kissed the head and laid it down.

" One after another he raised the heads of his seven
sons and kissed them, recalling amidst his tears the
qualities that each possessed in life. One was peerless

in jousting, another was unequalled in the chase. A third excelled as swordsman, a fourth was renowned for his justice. Not one but possessed some great quality of the perfect knight. And when he came to Gonzalo González, the youngest of his sons, he said as he gazed at the head: 'My son Gonzalo González, thy mother loved thee more than all the rest. Who could tell thy great virtues? How loyal a friend thou wert, how generous with thy wealth; no jouster was there in the world like thee; fair spoken wert thou with damsel and maid and many a gift thou gavest, for thou didst surpass all noble knights. Lion-hearted by my troth was he who challenged thee to fight, aye and fortunate, my son, if he was not vanquished. Alas, those who feared me of old because of thee no more will hold me of account and I shall henceforth live uncared and friendless. Verily it were better to die than see such woe.'

"Saying these words he sank unconscious to the ground still clasping the head of his youngest son. But Almanzor out of pity determined to send him back to his land and to his wife. And as Gonzalo Gustios was about to depart, the Moorish maiden, who had been his mate, draws him aside, saying: 'Don Gonzalo, I find myself in child by thee: tell me what thou wouldst have me do.' And he says to her: 'If thou bearest a manchild give two nurses to suckle him and when he be of an age to discern good from evil, tell him he is my son and send him to Castile to me at Salas.' With these parting words he takes a gold ring, breaks it in two and gives one half to her to keep as token. And the Moorish woman, when her days were accomplished, was delivered of a son to whom was given the name Mudarra González whom they call the Avenger.

"Now eighteen years have run their course and many

a dark day has dawned for Castile since the death of the
Seven Infantes. Behold the poor old man Gonzalo
Gustios : no eyes hath he to see his wretched land, for
his tears have blinded him. No treasures in the world
has he, nought but the coffin containing the heads of his
seven sons. Poor and wretched is he, poor and wretched
the land of Castile groaning under the foul tyranny
of the traitor, Ruy Velázquez. Time was it that the
Avenger should appear. Then one Sunday morning at
dawn Doña Sancha dreamed of a gigantic goshawk that
would swoop down on its prey. God be praised!
This is the sign that Mudarra the Avenger has set foot
in Castile. The flames shoot up into the sky from
Vilviestre's castle and Barbadillo lies in ruins. Who is
this proud warrior ? Castile has not seen his peer since
the Seven Infantes rode out from Salas. By the token
of the ring Gonzalo Gustios recognizes him, and there
is rejoicing in the palace of Salas. Saith the youth :
' Don Gonzalo, I have come here to avenge thy dishonour
and the death of the Seven Infantes, thy sons and my
brothers. This is no time for tarrying, so let us prick
on our horses.' And now the hour of retribution is
at hand. No truce will save Ruy Velázquez now, for
Mudarra the Avenger has tracked him to his lair. ' Thou
shalt die, false traitor,' cries Mudarra as he cleaves
Velázquez's body in twain with one sword-stroke and
stretches him dead upon the ground. Not yet is
Mudarra's vengeance complete, for Doña Lambra is still
living. But Mudarra nurses his vengeance until the
Count Garci Fernández her brother dies. Then he
seizes her and casts her into the flames to die.

" And so, my lords, the story ends, bringing just
punishment on that guilty pair who were betrayers of
their own flesh and blood.

" Now, my lords, the dusk of evening draweth nigh,

and I am weary; fain would I drink another goblet of red wine, for my needs are great. Before me lies my plate ready for gold and silver: stint not your bounty and throw in as well a Pater noster: thus you will bring gain to me and lose nought yourselves."

## WHAT BECAME OF THE STORY

The story of the Seven Infantes was originally a local one concentrated in the small region between Barbadillo, Salas and the River Hebros within a radius of six or eight leagues. But the *juglar* who recited the story was a man who knew many lands, and as he recited the narrative he included references to his own travels in order to dazzle the simple minds of his audience. Thus the scope of the poem gradually widened as the minstrel described many towns between Salas and Cordoba. The people who waited impatiently for the arrival of one of those wandering minstrels expected him to tell them of his adventures in lands outside their ken. Then, when he had departed, they preserved in their minds the salient points of the rhapsodic poem he had recited, and, recalling a turn of phrase here and a dramatic touch there, they recited them to one another around the fire in the long winter evenings.

Such was the origin of the old Spanish ballads which were the multiple offspring of the epic poems. The ballads consisted of striking passages from the old epic songs remembered by the people and handed down orally from one generation to another but with many changes due to the method of transmission. Only the boldest outline was left of the long epic poem recited by the rhapsodist. In one of the ballads dealing with the story we have a lengthy description of the marriage feasts at Burgos and the complaints of Doña Lambra to her husband. Another one tells of the grim banquet in Almanzor's palace when Gonzalo Gustios addressed the seven heads. But of all the old folk-ballads none is more justly famous than the one which describes the meeting between the traitor Ruy Velázquez and Mudarra the Avenger. The old man is going to the chase with hound and hawk, but the day is hot and he rests in the shade of a hedge. He is troubled in mind at the thoughts of Mudarra the bastard son of the renegade Moorish woman. "In vain have I slaughtered the Infantes of Salas," says he. "There's an heir in his halls—the son of the renegade spawn of Mahoun. If I meet with Mudarra, my spear will bring him down." Lo and behold a stripling, armed cap-à-pie, crosses his path. In response to the old man's welcome the youth asks him his name. "My name is Ruy Velázquez and I am waiting for Mudarra the bastard son of the renegade : if I can I'll send him to his doom." But the youth replies : "I am Mudarra the son of the renegade and brother of the Seven Infantes. With God's help I shall take thy life away." The ballad closes with following famous lines :

"'I am armed for the forest-chase not for the fight.
Let me go for my shield and my sword,' cries the knight—
'Now the mercy you dealt to my brothers of old,
Be the hope of that mercy the comfort you hold;
Die, foeman to Sancha—die, traitor to Lara!'
As he spake, there was blood on the spear of Mudarra."[1]

Such a ballad shows the method of the folk poet. Instead of describing in detail the arrival of the avenger with his knights he gives just the essential incidents that would exist in the memories of the people who had once heard the *juglar* sing the *cantar*. All the details of the killing of the traitor had faded from his mind except

[1] J. G. Lockhart, *The Spanish Ballads*, London, p. 48.

one striking incident—the meeting between the two
men. To make the scene more dramatic he describes
it in the form of a sharp dialogue.

Thus the old epic poems, after being prosified in the
chronicles and split up into the small ballads, progress a
step further and become the themes for drama. The
dramatic ballads such as I have described were the
seeds from which sprang great dramas of the Spanish
Golden Age.

The first dramatist to found his plays on the old
ballads was Juan de la Cueva, who in 1579 dramatized
the story of the Seven Infantes of Salas and thus drew
the attention of playwrights to so rich a theme. But
Cueva's play, which only dramatizes the last part of the
story, is a dull imitation of classical drama, with mytho-
logical allusions, and lacks all local colour and tradition.
It was left for Lope de Vega, the " monster of nature,"
as he was called, to dramatize the whole story in all its
grandeur, utilizing both the chronicles and the ballads.
Passage by passage he follows faithfully the " Crónica
General " in the scenes between Ruy Velázquez and
Doña Lambra, but with the genius of a great dramatist
he interprets the two characters. Ruy Velázquez is
violently in love with Doña Lambra and she uses her
ascendency over his weaker nature to excite him to
thoughts of vengeance. In the second act Don Gonzalo
is invited by Almanzor to a banquet and at the end the
King tells his sister to draw a curtain and behind it
stands a table with the seven heads upon it. In the
third act Lope de Vega casts aside the chronicles which
he had followed so meticulously and describes the life
of Gonzalo Gustios at Salas. He is blind, and Doña
Lambra reminds him every day of the loss of his seven
sons by firing seven stones at the windows of his palace.
In the final scene between Mudarra and Ruy Velázquez

the author embroiders dramatically the theme of the original ballad. The end of Lope de Vega's play, however, is inferior dramatically to *La Grande Tragedia de Los Siete Infantes de Salas* of Alfonso Hurtado de Velarde which was written some years after the former. Hurtado de Velarde, in describing the meeting between Mudarra and Ruy Velázquez, heightens the drama by a magnificent scene. Ruy Velázquez as he is about to draw his sword, sees the ghosts of the seven brothers standing beside Mudarra. Their faces are pale and blood-stained and they raise their arms as if to attack him. But Mudarra begs them by all that is sacred to allow him to accomplish his vengeance unaided.

Many authors in the seventeenth and eighteenth centuries wrote plays on the theme of the Seven Infantes, but in most cases they were mere parodies. One play, however, entitled *El Traidor contra su Sangre* (The Traitor against his own Blood), by Matos Fragoso, achieved such a lasting popularity that it has been performed even in modern days before enthusiastic audiences in the smaller towns of Castile. Abel Hugo, who lived in Spain in the years 1809-13 when his father served in the French invading army, described his impression of a performance of *El Traidor* at the *Teatro de La Cruz* at Madrid. The audience applauded vigorously the scene of the blood-stained heads on the table. To increase the effect of horror the seven actors who played the parts of the Infantes hid their bodies beneath the cloth and passed their heads, which had been painted to look as blood-stained as possible, through holes in the table.

At the opposition *teatro del Principe* in Madrid the famous actor Maiquez, who disdained the Spanish national taste in plays, once played a prank in order to turn the tragedy into a farce for the spectators. In the scene of the banquet the seven heads began to sneeze violently and disappear from the table just as their father was uttering his tearful lamentation. The mischievous Maiquez had prepared this comic effect by sprinkling on the table a big dose of sneezing powders which was more than the actors playing the heads could endure.

With the Romantic movement the story of the Seven Infantes came into favour again owing to the poetical gifts of Angel de Saavedra who in 1834 produced his verse romance, " El Moro Expósito " (The Foundling Moor). Angel de Saavedra did not base his work upon the chronicles or the ancient ballads but upon the play of Hurtado de Velarde which John Hookham Frere had brought to his notice in Malta in 1829. Frere, the translator of the " Poema del Cid," was a greater authority on the Spanish Middle Ages than any Spaniards of those days and he inspired Angel de Saavedra with a love for the epic poems of Castile. " El Moro Expósito " was the war-cry of the Spaniards who had lived too long fettered by French classicism, and for this reason it is of great significance in the literary history of the nineteenth century. In that work the great figures of the ancient story, Ruy Velázquez and Doña Lambra, fade into the background in order to leave the stage free for Mudarra, who is no longer a fierce rugged warrior of the Middle Ages but an imaginative youth full of melancholy and *mal de siècle*.

In 1853 Fernández y González wrote a novel in six books on the story of the Seven Infantes which treats the whole story from beginning to end but piles adventure upon adventure, and horror upon horror. Nevertheless, as Menéndez Pidal discovered when he investigated the traces of the legend in Castile, the villagers and townspeople read the book with the utmost eagerness, and its influence has penetrated into popular tradition.

In the towns of Lara, Covarrubias, Salas and Barbadillo where the ancient tradition should have remained purest he found that the popular notions sprang from the play of Matos Fragoso and the novel of Fernández y González. The play of Matos Fragoso was well known in the villages of the region, because every seven years it used to be performed at Salas under the auspices of the town council.

\*    \*    \*    \*    \*

In recent years attempts have been made to search the countryside for traces of the legend. The inhabitants of Barbadillo still call themselves " Alambraos " in allusion to Doña Lambra who possessed estates there. Although there are very few traces left of the Seven Infantes themselves, the ghost of Doña Lambra still haunts the popular mind. Menéndez Pidal relates how the superstitious proprietor of the stable at Barbadillo which is supposed by tradition to be the place where the insult of the wild cucumber took place, would on no account admit that Doña Lambra once lived on his land.

She haunts the mind of every man, woman and child. " She hides up in the Sierra over there," said my friend Lazarillo, " but some nights you would see her riding through the sky on her horse. She rises from the black lake up at Barbadillo de Herreros where they say she threw herself. When the winter is coming the waters seethe and you can hear a sound of lowing oxen." Lazarillo in common with most of the people at Salas did not call her Doña Lambra but Doña Urraca, perhaps confusing her with another fierce Castilian amazon of the Middle Ages—the Infanta Doña Urraca, sister of Alfonso VI, who was supposed to have plotted the murder of her brother Sancho.

To-day there is confusion in the minds of the people concerning Doña Lambra due to the fact that they have amalgamated her sinister personality with that of Doña Sancha the mother of the Seven Sons. In modern days when a woman gives birth to triplets or quadruplets she is fêted and given the King's bounty, but in olden days it was different. Even a woman who bore twins was frowned upon, because it was a sign that she had committed adultery, for how was it possible to give birth to two children at the same time unless there had been two fathers? Popular tradition supposes the mother of the Seven Infantes to have borne them at one birth and the people tell the story thus : " A poor woman was begging for alms one day at the gates of the palace for her five children, and Doña Sancha rebuked her for having so many children. The latter then cursed her saying : ' May God grant that you may bear seven babes at one birth.' When her time came Doña Sancha was delivered of her monstrous brood, and in shame she ordered her servant to put six of the seven children in pails and drown them in the river. But Gonzalo Gustios, the father, arrived just in time to save his six sons and he reared them in secret. When they were seven years old he dressed them all in the same coloured costume and invited them to the palace to a banquet with Doña Sancha and the other son. When she saw them she exclaimed : ' May God grant that a black lake will open in the ground and engulf me.' " According to Menéndez Pidal, the tradition of the woman who was delivered of seven children at one birth is associated in the Castilian mind with the famous Count Diego de Porcelos of Burgos. His name, which was derived from the Latin *porcelli*, or little pigs, according to ancient tradition, commemorated his own birth, for his mother bore him and his six brothers in her womb just as pigs

bear a litter of seven.    Hence in the modern ballads that
are recited by the villagers around Salas and Barbadillo
we find the words :

"Doña Urraca, Doña Urraca, well mayest thou praise thyself:
Thou hast given birth to seven sons like any dunghill sow," [1]

which are actually the same as those used by Doña
Lambra in the epic poem.

[1] A. Espinosa, "Sobre la leyenda de los Infantes de Lara,"
*Romanic Review*, xii, 1921, pp. 135–48.

# CHAPTER XXX

## ARMED WITH PROVERBS

### I

A WANDERER through the Spanish countryside needs to be well armed with proverbs. They are as necessary to him in the fields as they are in the tavern or market-place. Watch two Castilian peasants conducting a wordy warfare: they are armed to the teeth with proverbs, and they fire them off incessantly at one another. When one of the warriors wins, he not only stuns his opponent, but crushes him with a series of weighty sentences like a duellist, who is not content to lodge the mortal bullet in his rival's body, but also knocks him on the head with the butt.

At first the stranger finds this use of proverbs disconcerting, and he mutters to himself that a proverb is the death-blow to conversation. When it has been fired there is nothing for him to do but to bury the theme, and search his brain for another topic. Many a time I have entered the conversation full of enthusiasm, only to find myself gagged, bound and delivered over to the executioner for lack of an apposite proverb. A proverb, it has once been said, is the wisdom of many and the wit of one. A Spaniard draws his proverb from the great fund of popular lore with as much reverent care as a host does a bottle of dry, perfumed Amontillado, which

377

for many a year he has cherished in his cellar. There is no class distinction among proverbs : the ragged tramp or lean *pícaro* uses them to ornament his speech no less than king or baron. Their use is not confined between the pages of a book, but is current among all classes, being handed like a coin from one person to another. From father to son they pass through countless generations, embodying legendary stories of heroes, oriental tales of magic and witchcraft, superstitions, formulas for combating the evil-eye.

First of all they must have shortness, sense and salt. Thomas Fuller once defined them as " much matter decocted into few words." The Castilian peasant resembles the lowland Scotsman in the severe, concise significance of his sayings. Many consist of but three or four words, as for example, " ancha es Castilla "— (" Castile is broad ") ; " Jarro malo nunca quebrado " —(" A poor jar is never broken ") ; " Hoy casado, mañana cansado "—(" To-day married, to-morrow wearied "). Many proverbs are in verse and rhyme, as for instance, " No desprecies los consejos de los sabios y los viejos." There is also a tendency to employ alliteration as in the well-known " Sobre sol no hay señor, ni sobre sal sabor." The proverbs are frequently divided into two clauses, the second of which balances the first, as in the following : " No hay nadie tan perfecto, que no tenga algun defecto."

Many proverbs commemorate some tradition of ancient times, as for instance the much-used phrase, " Tomar las de Villadiego," which is used in the sense, " To take to one's heels." The phrase which literally means to " Take the breeches of Villadiego " puzzled me, for I had been to the town of that name near Burgos and I had questioned the inhabitants in vain as to its origin. Then a schoolmaster at Lerma de los Caballeros enlightened me. The phrase goes back to the Middle Ages when King Ferdinand III, father of Alfonso the Wise, published edicts to protect the Jews of Castile. He gave them the town of Villadiego as a place of retreat, but he insisted that they should wear breeches of special colour as a uniform to distinguish them from the Christians. And so, whenever a pogrom was in sight in Burgos the Jews would slip on their Villadiego breeches and away. Ever since, the phrase has been used for running away.

Sometimes out of pure spite the people of one region create a proverb against their neighbours and for ever fetter them to a phrase as in " Con los de Cuenca, ni trato ni cuenta "—(" Have no dealings with the people of Cuenca "). The town of Villalba, especially, has suffered in its reputation owing to the sarcastic proverb : " Montes sin leña, rios sin agua, mujeres sin vergüenza y hombres sin alma "—(" Villalba has four good points : mountains without timber, rivers without water, women without shame and men without heart ").

Other proverbs commemorate some great exploit of the heroic period of Spanish history. In English we say, " Rome was not built in a day," but the Spaniards say, " No se ganó Zamora en una hora "—(" Zamora was not won in an hour "), referring to the long series of battles in front of the town, between the Christians and Moors. In the saying, " Murió el conde mas no su nombre "— (" The count is dead but not his name "), the people celebrate Fernán González, the national hero of Castile. Sometimes a tiny local incident may give rise to a famous proverb, as in the expression, " Como los de Fuente Ovejuna todos a una," which expresses the unanimous solidarity of the people. The origin of the phrase is contained in a ballad—

> " Al val de Fuente Ovejuna
> La niña en cabellos baja,
> El caballero la sigue
> De la cruz de Calatrava,"

referring to the noble Hernán Pérez de Guzmán, the
Commander of the Order of Calatrava, who in 1476
dishonoured the wife of one of his vassals. The whole
village turned out as one man and stoned the Commander to death, and afterwards, when some of the
culprits were tried and tortured by the legal authorities,
the people cried out: " We all killed him." On this
little story Lope de Vega based one of his most beautiful
plays. Another proverb derived from a folk story is
" A Zaragoza o al charco "—(" To Saragossa or into the
puddle "), which is based upon the following tradition :
an Aragonese peasant was asked where he was going and
he replied that he was going to Saragossa. Instead of
adding the pious remark " if God wills it " he said :
" I am going to Saragossa even though God may not
will it." God then changed him into a frog and put
him in a puddle beside the road as a punishment. Later
on, God forgave him and returned him to his former
state. Then believing that he had learnt his lesson, God
said : " Where are you going ? " To which the incor-
rigibly obstinate Aragonese replied : " To Saragossa
or into the puddle."

Salvador de Madariaga called the Spanish proverbs
lightning *comedias*. Each one flashes a little story across
our mind complete with verse and moral. The little
scene springs up readily in the minds of people whose
imaginations are not burdened by what they have read
in books. Spanish proverbs spring directly from the
soil and are independent of the written word. It is the
possession of this wealth of popular lore that makes the
Castilian so grave and sententious, so full of dry humour,

so sturdily independent. It is for this reason that we
find a great scholar like Rodríguez Marín expressing
himself about them in the following lyrical terms :
" Oh, inexhaustible storehouse . . . in thee the man
who knows how to search for it, finds the remedy or at
least the alleviation of every ill. In thee, the sad find
consolation ; the irresolute, decision ; the despairing,
patience ; the vicious, correction ; the wasteful, wise
economy ; and all, pleasant and helpful teaching, for
thou art a book open to every glance and a wise solution
for every problem."

## II.  THE MINSTREL'S VADE-MECUM

During my wandering through Old Castile I made
valiant attempts to collect a rich store of proverbs and
although I was only able to " nibble on the dry bark
and rugged rind of those wise sayings," I became suffi-
ciently proficient to put them to good use in my minstrelsy.  A *juglar* needs to have a ready tongue if he
wishes to win sympathy in the villages, for at first every
man, woman, child and dog is against him.  When I
arrived at the town of Salas de los Infantes something
in my appearance must have struck the children as
strange, for they followed me in crowds, pointing at me
and making remarks.  Their fathers and mothers stood
at their doors to see me pass ; even the dogs sniffed at
me and barked.  As for me, I was hardened to such
demonstrations, and I sauntered along in the middle of
the road, carrying my fiddle-case in one hand and swinging my big stick in the other.  At first I was the stranger
whom all distrusted, but after a few hours' conversation
with some of the older men in the town you would
scarcely find one of them to say me nay.  And the
quickest way to reach the heart of those old men was

to draw upon my store of quaint phrases. Thus when
I stood before them in the local casino and took my fiddle
out of its case I would say : " Donde hay musica no
puede haber cosa mala "—(" Where there is music
there's no evil "), for he who sings frightens away his
sorrows.

Then, as I tuned the instrument I said : ' El violín y
el caballo ; nadie como su dueño para templallo "—
(" When it's a fiddle or a horse, there's no one like the
owner to tune it up "). At the end of a bout of fiddling,
if my audience was a trifle parsimonious I could always
tell them the story of the miserly Bachelor Cabra of
Segovia who used to put a spell on the rats in his
house to prevent them eating the crumbs that fell from
his table. Then if some of the villagers showed me
hospitality I would not for the world overstay my welcome and I would quote for them the Castilian proverb—
" El huésped y el pez, a dos días huelen "—(" Guests
like fishes smell after two days ").

After a time I worked out for my own personal use a
short vade-mecum to guide me in my various relations
with the people in the towns and villages, and I grouped
the proverbs under the following headings—Wine,
Women, and Gypsies.

## WINE

What better guide to follow than Celestina the Spanish
Bawd when she says of wine : " With Wine I fur all
my clothes at Christmas : it warms my blood ; it keeps
me still in one estate ; it makes me merry, where'er I
go ; it makes me look fresh and ruddy as a rose." Is it
any wonder that Spanish of all languages possesses the
biggest number of words for describing intoxication ?
Writers who do not suffer from " flaggonal hypocrisy "
give twenty-three different terms for describing the blissful

state, but for my frugal wants I found one or two sufficient, such as "Beber los kiries"—("To drink one's three times three"), "Estar entre dos luces"—("To be half seas over").

## WOMEN

When women come into their own in modern Spain they will revenge themselves on the nation's proverbs, for there is hardly one of them which gives women any good qualities. The anonymous authors of the *refranero* agree in calling them brittle as glass, and changeable as the wind. One proverb says : "Guárdate de la mala mujer y de la buena no fíes nada"—("Protect yourself from a bad woman and don't trust a good one"), and this cynical opinion runs through all of them. Sometimes she is a bad housewife and her husband hurls the following at her : "Magdalena, el gato te come la cena y el perro la merienda"—("Magdalena, the cat is eating the dinner and the dog the supper"), or else he accuses her of being "más puerca que María la Cazuela"—("dirtier than stewpan Mary"). If she turns up her nose at his coarse habits he'll sneer, calling her "Mariquita María"—("Dainty Mary"). When a woman is going to have a baby, people say to her, "Tienes el mal de Doña Jacinta : poco mal y mucha cinta"—("You have Doña Jacinta's illness : little illness but a large waist-line"), or else they will say that she has been bitten by a spider and has tied a sheet around herself. Even when a woman reaches old age, she is not left in peace, for she becomes the butt of the picaresque wit of Spain with its tradition stretching back to Trotaconventos, Celestina, Cañizares and Gerarda. She is then as the Spanish Bawd would say, "A trot-up-and-down, a maidenhead-monger, a box filled with nothing but the very dregs of malice." Her name will become such a

byword that men will call her by the name of her town as
if she were a heroine, like La Maratona of Segovia or La
Paregita of Avila. Then you would see her gadding
about the streets at night like " Juan of the White
Breeches " (ghost), or else she will turn up at dances,
much to the disgust of men who say of her, " Vieja que
baila, mucho polvo levanta "—(" An old woman dancing lifts a heap of dust "). But if they are courting a
maid or if their wife is pregnant they will ask her advice
for they remember the *refrán*, " El consejo de la mujer
es poco y el que no lo toma es loco "—(" A woman's
advice is of little worth but he who does not take it is
mad "). The only one who is respected by the anonymous proverb-maker is the modest girl who stays at
home. Of her he says, " La doncella honrada, la pierna
quebrada y en casa "—(" The modest maid has a broken
leg and stays at home ")—surely one of the cruellest
proverbs of all.

## GYPSIES

The wandering minstrel needs to possess a big store
of proverbs if he would compete with a Romany chal,
for the Gypsy race has a talent for the aphoristic phrase.
Most of those *rejelendres* or proverbs spring from the
*Gitano's* nomadic life and generally centre in his horse
or his mule. If I ask Old Faraón, the Gypsy wise man,
a stupid question he replies by the proverb, " Buter
sarmuñé quesa aor grel puchar, sos aor chandé rudelar "
—(" It's easier for the ass to ask than the wise man to
answer "). If you protest that Manfariel the Gypsy has
sold you a spavined mule at a fair, he will answer gravely :
" Coin camele bi visaba choré, pírese a pindré "—
(" Whoever expects to find a faultless mule should go on
foot "). A Gypsy speaks even of his women-folk in
terms of mules or horses, as for instance in the proverb :

" Ne olaceres an goró, ne tiri romí darabes a jetró "—
(" Don't ride a colt or praise your wife to another man "),
or in the following—" Ne chorí sar dojí, ne gachí bi
ratí "—(" Have nothing to do with a faulty mule, or a
woman that is not pure-blooded "). And whenever a
Gypsy wants to ask a favour, he will scratch his head
and say : " Menda y mangue grasté, os dui terablamos
manguelo yequé "—(" Both my horse and I have a
petition to make ").

&ast; &ast; &ast; &ast; &ast;

Life was easier for me once I had compiled my vade-
mecum of proverbs, and I had always a phrase on the tip
of my tongue for any eventuality, but there was grave
danger that I would become like Sancho Panza and drag
them into my discourse without rhyme or reason.
Proverbs, as Mal Lara said in his *Filosofía vulgar*, should
adorn one's speech just as precious stones do rich robes,
but they should not be used in excess. Don Quixote
rebuked Sancho, saying : " Proverbs are concise and
pithy sentences, but thou dost so often drag them in by
the head and shoulders, that they seem rather the maxims
of folly than of wisdom." [1]

[1] Cervantes, *Don Quixote*, Part II, Ch. 43.

## CHAPTER XXXI

# THE MULE OF SAINT FRANCIS [1]

IT was a weary two-days' tramp from Salas de los Infantes to Sepúlveda.

The curse of Doña Lambra must have blighted the big toe of my left foot, for soon after leaving Barbadillo it began to swell and I became the limping minstrel. A wandering fiddler needs to bestow more tenderness upon his toes than upon his fingers. A blistered finger will still allow him to scrape out a tune, but a swollen toe may paralyse his active life. In addition to inflicting suffering, it tinges a man's mind with the sickly green of prejudice. I had no eyes for the majestic relics of the town of Lerma de los Caballeros, but I added my humble curse to swell the chorus of execration against the memory of the Duke of Lerma who was responsible for the expulsion of the Moriscos in 1609. Above the town in the Church of La Colegiata his statue stands as a perpetual reminder. Yes, Francisco de Sandoval, you deserve to be sculpted in bronze in your favourite attitude of sanctimonious prayerfulness, for you will remain for ever famous as the originator of what Richelieu called the most rash and barbarous measure in Europe. You will kneel for ever in that Church of La Colegiata gazing with your well-bred face upon the open prayer-book.

[1] To ride the mule of Saint Francis means in proverbial Spanish to travel on foot (*Lazarillo de Tormes*, Part II, Ch. 12).

Aranda de Duero, where I halted next, has faded from my mind in spite of the beautiful Church of Santa María with its florid Gothic, ornamented façade, but I still remember the well outside the town where dozens of Rebeccas fill their pitchers at sunrise and sunset. Most of the day those girls spend their time in silent household tasks, but when they meet one another by the fountain the bubbling water inspires them to babble excitedly. In the distance their voices sound like the chirruping of an aviary at dawn. They have no reticence with strangers, especially when they are so dusty, begrimed and woebegone as I was. When I hobbled up on my stick to the fountain's edge, I became at once the object of their sympathy.

" What ails you, *caballero* ? " said a bright-eyed, black-haired girl with a pitcher on her head.

" I've a sore foot, Señorita, and no wife or *novia* to cure it for me."

" I'll cure it for you, *caballero*," said the girl, laughing shyly. All her companions clustered around me as I undid the rough, expanding shoe I had made out of rags. When the red, swollen limb was exposed to their gaze there was a chorus of shocked comment, and the black-haired girl insisted on leading me back to her home, where she washed and bandaged my foot. Her father, a gruff-looking old peasant, fetched a big *porrón* of red wine and insisted that I should drink half of it with him. " With your head full of wine," said he, " you won't feel your feet upon the ground." When I pulled out my purse to pay the hospitable old man he slapped me on the back saying, " *Hombre* ! Don't insult me, I am *Castellano a las derechas* and I wouldn't deny any poor devil that passes by my door."

" Que Dios se lo pague a Vd," answered I with the full consciousness of being a true *pordiosero*.

Twelve kilometres out of Aranda de Duero I met with another piece of good fortune. I was plodding along the road, when a fat man rode past me on a mule and seeing that I was limping painfully he stopped and asked me where I was going. When I told him that I was making for Sepúlveda he said : " Jump up behind me —there is room for two ; I often carry my wife this way."

With great difficulty I managed to clamber up behind the worthy man and clasp him around the waist.

" Your wife must be as thin as a wraith," said I as I endeavoured to squeeze myself on to the remaining portion of the saddle.

" People will think we are fat twins riding the same mule," replied the peasant, laughing. The mule, too, turned and lashed her tail, as much as to say, " Master, I'll be revenged on you for loading another tun-belly on my back. May I be blowed if I carry this vagrant who has ridden nought but Saint Francis's mule all his life." Each step she took jolted me perilously from one side to the other, but still I managed to cling on to my good Samaritan. In this way we advanced slowly and uneasily along the winding road towards Sepúlveda. In spite of my precarious position, I blessed my lucky stars for sparing me many a mile of limping, and I expressed my deepest gratitude to my companion. Hardly had I uttered the words when I saw a big herd of sheep approaching towards us rapidly in a cloud of dust. In a few seconds we were so blinded by the dust that we could not see anything. The mule finding herself hemmed in by the sheep began to curvet and prance like a frisky circus horse. " Hold on tight," cried the fat peasant as he threw his arms round the neck of the mule. Choking with dust I was unable to answer a word, but I tried to dig my knees into the mule's flanks —in vain, for I began to slip off on one side, and in desperation I caught hold of the end of the peasant's coat to steady myself.  Another lurch from the mule shot us both off on to the hard ground, where we lay locked in one another's arms while various sheep trod over us.  The mule, now that she had wreaked her vengeance, stood stock-still.  From my recumbent position on the road I looked up at her through the dusty cloud and I noticed a twinkle in her bulging eye.

When the sheep and their shouting shepherd had disappeared I scrambled to my feet.

I was a sorry sight to see : I was covered from head to foot in dust ; the contents of my rucksack were scattered about the road ; my fiddle-case, which I had providenti-ally thrown clear when I fell, was lying in the ditch ; and my sore foot throbbed as if someone was probing it with a surgeon's scalpel.

I expected to hear a volley of curses, but to my surprise the peasant merely sighed and shook his head sadly, gathered up my belongings, helped me to get up on the mule again and led her by the bridle.  In spite of my remonstrances he would not mount.  " There is not room for two," said he, " and you are wounded, so the hale and hearty must walk."

Seated on the mule in solitary state, I rode solemnly up the steep road towards Sepúlveda.  I was feeling like a knight returning wounded from the crusades.  My squire, preceding me on foot, led my palfrey by the bridle through the gates of the town.

## CHAPTER XXXII

## THE TOWN OF THE SEVEN KEYS

THE town of Sepúlveda, proudly perched on a mountain spur, keeps guard like a fierce watchdog over the Castilian plain. It is still called the town of the seven gates and seven keys—a memory of the fierce battles of the Middle Ages when the people used to live in feudal isolation. The clock in the tower above the *Plaza Mayor* still reminds the inhabitants of those ancient wars. Every night at ten o'clock it strikes thirty-three times in commemoration of the years of Christ's life. Formerly the people had to shut the gates and retire for the night before it finished striking.

The town itself, being built on a slope, is full of steep, narrow passages and laneways through which one may catch glimpses of enchanting panoramas. Here and there, dotted about the town, are old churches of Romanesque style, with the characteristic cloister-like corridor running along the external walls. At one moment the wanderer finds himself, as it were, at the bottom of a pit, at another he stands on a promontory gazing down on church steeples that seem to shoot out of the roofs of houses.

In the sun-baked hours Sepúlveda resembles a city of the dead, and the only life comes from the church bells that echo softly through the valley. In the torrid

390

noon those chimes seem to yawn at heaven with tongues
hanging out, eagerly thirsting for a cool wind. In
the upper part of the town many of the doors of the
houses are sculpted with coats of arms, and occasionally
a scimitar or a turban in the escutcheon reminds us of
the Moors. All the passages and lanes converge on
the *plaza*, which resembles a magnificent open-air
theatre carved out of the mountain. As it is the only
level spot in the whole town, it is crowded at every
hour of the day, whether a bull-fight, folk-dance
festival, political meeting or fair is taking place.

The inhabitants of Sepúlveda may be divided into
two rough categories : those that dwell in the upper
and those that dwell in the lower part of the town.
The behaviour of the upper towards the lower reminded
me of the Italian town of Bergamo, the birthplace of
Arlecchino, and Brighella—the stupid and the clever
clowns of the *Commedia dell' Arte*. The people in the
lower region breathe a thicker air and are in consequence more doltish than the bright-eyed citizens of
the upper town where the mountain air is like champagne. One of the upper-town citizens said to me :
" The lower town is good enough for mules and oxen
and brutish *arrieros*, but up here you'll find the brightest
folk in all Castile."

My first friend in Sepúlveda was the chemist who
dressed my foot. Through his kind offices I met the
owner of the *posada* and with the aid of a few tunes I
secured a room where I could rest my foot in peace.
All the afternoon I would sit on a balcony at the back
of the house, gazing down at the straggling town with
its houses perched on the slopes like scattered toys.
As evening advances, the setting sun illuminates those
tiny toys with fire, and the lonely plain becomes for a
brief instant flaming red, while here and there a window

catching a ray of the sun glitters like a jewel. At night I would go to the neighbouring tavern where I was always certain of an audience. One evening after I had played for the company and passed around my *boina*, my friend the chemist introduced a young man of the town to me, with the words : " Here is Mariano the communist of Sepúlveda." Mariano was a good-looking young man dressed in a smart brown suit with white shoes and a flaming red tie. At first he tried to air his French, saying that it was the best language for international relations, but he soon found himself at a loss for words, and he relapsed into Spanish. Mariano, like most revolutionaries, was a suspicious fellow. As soon as we were alone he questioned me in detail. Had I come to Spain as an emissary of any revolutionary organization ? Was I in touch with Moscow ? Was I an acknowledged communist ? When I told him I was only a poor wandering minstrel he showed frank, incredulous astonishment. " You are not the type of the *vagamundo*," said he ; " your disguise is too thin : I can see by your face that you are a communist agent. Believe me, the disguise of a fiddler is as good as any other for spreading the doctrines of communism in the villages." Mariano then proceeded to inform me that he was responsible for spreading the light of communism in Sepúlveda. He had spent some years in France where he had become initiated into the doctrines of Lenin. When the Revolution had broken out in Spain he had returned to his native village to devote himself to the new gospel. " It is an uphill task, comrade," said he, " for the folk in this part of Castile are slow-thinking and slow-moving. They have been kept in subjection so long that we should need a volcanic eruption to blow their world sky-high."

Mariano's most violent hatred was reserved for the priests. He openly scoffed at the Church and hurled insults at the parish priest. "Religion is the opium of the masses," said he, quoting the well-worn Marxian tag : "We are too tolerant with the black soutanes in this modern Spain of ours. The government has not gone far enough in its pronouncements. Why should any priests exist in the modern state ? What are they but drones and parasites who prey on the workers ? Spain is a country steeped in superstition because of their influence. Whenever I see one of those *curas* pass by I point him out to some of the youths saying : ' Look well at that soutane, comrades : it is the badge of those who have denied the rights and privileges of manhood. Shout your mockery and deride that soutane just as those priests in their Inquisition used to deride the sanbenito worn by the heretics on their way to the stake.' " I soon saw that it was useless to defend the Spanish Church against Mariano, but I mildly suggested that the Revolution had given the people of Spain freedom. Mariano replied scornfully : "You are ignorant of our country because you are a *forastero*. The Revolution of April did next to nothing : it was just a ripple on the water. ' *Ha sido una verbena sin vino* ' (' It was a feast without wine '). The people were told that the millennium would come : they were led up to a beautiful palace. Through the glittering gates they saw the tables beneath the trees laid with golden dishes. They were told that all the banquet was for them if they would only have the patience to wait a moment at the gates. And so they waited and waited day and night outside in the cold. Then, to their dismay, they watched the drones and parasites of the country invade that palace and gorge themselves upon the banquet laid for workers. What have the workers derived from this much-vaunted revolution except tantalizing promises? All that has happened is that the bourgeois parasite has gobbled up the spoils. Spain has exchanged one set of capitalists for another, and, as for me, I would even prefer the old-fashioned aristocrat, who believes in his blood and race, to the pestiferous, place-hunting bourgeois, who shouts himself hoarse in the name of Socialism, and loosens his belt as his belly swells with loot. No, comrade, the true Revolution has yet to come in Spain. Watch events to-day and you will see the disillusion of the people. They will become disgusted with those wretched profiteer leaders, who have desecrated the name of Socialism and by their betrayals prepared the way for a reaction which will postpone the true revolution. But one day that revolution will come, and the workers will be merciless towards those who have betrayed them. Already there is a band of young men in Spain ready to devote their lives to the ideals of communism. It is not enough for us who are communists to give devoted personal service : we must also spread the doctrine. A young communist must be educated in the new theories and he must marry and have children. Then he must be prepared to live his life out in the wilds, wherever he is sent by his leaders, and spread his influence among the ignorant masses. Spain needs men who will believe in communism, the religion of the present century, with the same passionate sincerity as the ascetics and mystics of the past believed in the dogmas of Rome."

"But, Señor Mariano," said I timidly when I was able to find an opening, "what about the women of Spain ? It always seems to me that you communist idealists forget that women are by nature conservative. New Spain has given Spanish women freedom at the polls, but none of you yet know how they will vote."

" Men must educate women," replied Mariano.
" Spanish woman has been enslaved by man, because
Church and State said that her place was in the home.
She was deliberately condemned to be the drudge with
no personality of her own.   We Spaniards acted worse
than the Moors towards our women.   In new communist Spain, woman will be on equal terms with man.
She will have complete independence at home and
abroad.   No longer shall the Spanish man tyrannize
over his wife and daughters, ruling them according to
the ridiculous code of honour which made us the
laughing-stock of Europe.   When divorce is as easy
and as cheap as it is in Russia, the barbarous, intolerant
egoism of man towards woman will disappear, and
we shall be able to call her comrade.   To-night, Señor,
you shall meet my *novia*.   She, too, is a communist and
we shall be married in front of the statue of Lenin
instead of in the Church.   Instead of a bouquet of
white lilies she will carry the gilded sickle and hammer
of the communist."

Mariano's words concerning women gave me food
for meditation.   Was it possible that such a change
had come over Spanish men since April 1931 ?   Was it
possible so soon to bury the old-fashioned, jealous
Spaniard ?   Surely this would be a miracle.   The
evening following my conversation with Mariano happened to be a *fiesta* and there was great merry-making
in the town.   The square was thronged with people
listening to a local band.   Many of the peasants from
the neighbouring villages came with their wives and
families.   Mariano introduced me to his *novia*, a very
pretty, black-haired girl wearing a white blouse and a
red skirt.   Immediately I felt that a bond of sympathy
was possible between us.   Remembering Mariano's
violent tirade against jealous husbands, I felt no scruples

about flirting with his *novia*. My opportunity came
when he had to go away on an errand. The band
was playing a slow waltz, so I asked the girl to dance
with me. Away we started in the midst of the serried
throng of dancers. While I clasped her slender body
in my arms, I whispered compliments in her ear, which
she accepted with blushes of pleasure. As we danced,
some people gazed at us and nudged one another, as
much as to say : " There goes a fine pair of *novios*."

" So you are a communist, Señorita ? " said I at length
after exhausting all my stock of bright *persiflage*.

" I don't know that I am, Señor : I have never
thought about it. Mariano my *novio* is communist
enough for both of us."

" Ah ! Señorita, you are not behaving as a true
comrade. You should demand your rights fiercely and
you should go to political meetings arm in arm with
Mariano and make speeches, too, on platforms, dressed
in red."

" Señor, you are totally wrong there. I am in love
with Mariano. That is enough for me. I leave all
those theories and ideas to him and I say every day :
' You, Mariano, must have eyes, brain and speech for
both of us : my part is to mind the home.' "

While we were dancing blissfully around the square,
I saw Mariano on the outskirts of the crowd. As soon
as he saw us, he elbowed his way through the crowd
to the front and shouted imperiously to us to stop
dancing. When he came up, he was so livid with rage
that he could hardly blurt out his words.

" What do you mean, Señor ? "

" What have I done, Señor Mariano ? " said I guiltily.

" Who gave you leave to dance with my *novia* ? "

" I meant no harm. I thought that I might dance
with a comrade's *novia*," said I, preparing myself for a

long and bitter argument. Mariano, however, seized the girl roughly by the arm and walked away rapidly into the crowd.

Later on that evening the band played a *jota* and the whole square became alive with frenzied dancing. In one group I saw Mariano dancing opposite to his *novia*. He was flushed and perspiring at every pore as he valiantly tried to execute every intricate step of the ancient traditional dance. As I walked away from Sepúlveda I wondered what the future would have in store for Spaniards of Mariano's type. How long would it take for the theories of Lenin to conquer the *jota* and all the traditions it symbolized? I then remembered the words of the Knight of the Sorrowful Figure which described the only great communism in the world. "O happy age," he cried, "which our first parents called the age of gold! Not because gold, so much adored in this iron age, was then easily purchased, but because those two fatal words ' mine ' and ' thine ' were distinctions unknown to the people of those fortunate times; for all things were in common in that holy age . . . all there was union, all peace, all love and friendship in the world."

## CHAPTER XXXIII

## THE CITY OF PICAROONS

SEGOVIA resembles a huge ship with sails set towards the West, manned by picaresque rogues. No city in Spain is richer in anecdotes about robbers, Gypsies, dwarfs, witches and devils. As I stand on the ramparts of the Alcazar gazing on the majestic panorama I remember the words uttered by Alonso of the many Masters. " I entered," he said, " the ancient, loyal, noble and wealthy city of Segovia ; ancient because Hercules was its founder ; loyal because it was the first to hand its keys to the Catholic queen Doña Isabel ; noble because of the great number of its illustrious knights ; wealthy because it possesses the most honourable industry of cloth-making." By a strange irony of fate Alonso, Pablos the Sharper, the Bachelor Trapaza and their crew begat in their old age a sturdy brood, for there are still many descendants to carry on their impish ways. Even to-day Segovia is the most picaresque city in Spain with the exception of Sevilla. Anyone who strolls into the *Plaza de Azoquejo* at the foot of the Devil's Bridge, as they call the Roman aqueduct, will find himself surrounded by as picturesque a group of ragged idlers as ever was etched by Cervantes or Quevedo.

" Why do you call the Roman aqueduct the Devil's Bridge ? " said I to one of the loungers.

" It is an old story," said he, " that old women tell their grandchildren. They say that the Devil built it in a night for the love of a slip of a girl from Segovia. One morning he met her on the way from a well in the hills, and he saw that she was toiling along the dusty road with her pitcher on her head.

" ' You are too pretty a girl,' said he with a leer, ' to weary yourself thus. If you promise to marry me I'll build in a night a bridge which will carry the pure waters of the Guadarrama's stream to Segovia.'

" The girl gave a nod and a smile, and the Devil bustled off, chuckling, for she was a merry morsel.

" Next morning when the Segovians awoke, they rubbed their eyes in wonder, for they found in their midst a mighty aqueduct, and straightway a chorus of gratitude arose from the girls with their pitchers. Meanwhile the Devil stood at the door, hat in hand, waiting for his bride. But she tossed her head with a scornful air, saying : ' Men are fools if they think that a girl's word is as good as her bond. The wind may change from night to morning, and so may a maiden change her mind. I have seen your bridge and I found a stone loose under the seventh arch. So fare you well, good sir : the bargain is null and void.' The Devil slunk away with his tail between his legs, grunting to himself : ' I renounce my power : the only devils in the world are women. Henceforth they should call it the bridge of the she-devil.' "

When I fiddled in the *Plaza de Azoquejo* I found to my dismay that I was performing before an audience of beggars. At the first note of the fiddle they crowded round me, eyeing me from head to toe and murmuring among themselves. There were blind men with dogs, pin- and boot-lace sellers, ballad-mongers, jugglers—a whole picaresque society in miniature. When I stopped playing there was no applause, for I was an interloper, and it was necessary for me to be admitted to the brotherhood. Whenever I find myself in the midst of a crowd of *pícaros* I remember the precepts given to Estebanillo González the good-humoured rogue. " Carry with you," says his mentor, " needle and thread : you'll need them on three occasions in life. When you feel tempted to speak foolishly, sew up your mouth : when you are in generous mood and want to play ducks and drakes with your hard-earned cash, sew up your pocket : I leave you to guess what is the third thing you must sew up."

I needed all those precepts during my first day as a fiddler in Segovia. It was so easy to say to the cynical old pin-seller who was my first mentor : " Come up, *compañero*, let us take our ease in yonder tavern : do you hear my pocket jingling ? I'll stand a few rounds to you and your blind friend." If I had done so I should have had a herd of hungry beggars on my track from morn to eve. As a member of the picaresque society in Segovia I must forget to be a knight-errant. When I was at Salas de los Infantes I behaved as a minstrel, and a minstrel needs to possess a good dose of knight-errantry, for he serves humanity in his humble way and believes in heroes. But the *pícaro* in the rough and humble existence among other rogues must be egotistical : his experience of life is bitter and the world is wicked. He has lost his faith in humanity, but he remains a stoic, even though his smile at times is corrosive.

As a *pícaro* at Segovia I needed to evolve for myself a technique of the picaresque, and I remembered the counsels of Guzmán de Alfarache, arch-mentor of rogues. The surprising point about Guzmán's ordinances is that they apply to the twentieth nearly as well as they did to the sixteenth and seventeenth centuries.

I wrote down on a piece of paper the following five of Guzmán's rules to aid me in my peregrinations :

I. "*Beggars must carry substantial staves.*" A most important rule as I found at Segovia, for my iron-tipped companion imposed respect by its uncompromising thickness.

II. "*Alms must be received only in the hat, though hidden purses and pockets are permissible.*" I should like to add a gloss to that rule. A fiddler who passes round his *boina* would do well to put in beforehand a silver coin of his own, for one piece of silver encourages another and it is a subtle reminder of the Gypsy belief that copper brings misfortune.

III. "*Maimed beggars must not frequent the haunt of the healthy.*" From experience I can testify to the excellence of this provision. A maimed beggar is as different to a good-humoured, picaresque *juglar* as chalk is to cheese. The cripple makes appeal to charity by woeful face, cringing manner and whining voice. A *juglar* must be a merry-faced, honey-tongued individual and he must have a little touch of arrogant pride in his own skill, for he comes of ancient and noble tradition. When playing my fiddle I need bow to no man and I can accept a goblet of wine from the hands of the Duke of Alba as naturally as a skin of wine from Antón the Shepherd of Pedraza. A beggar who follows the profession of a cripple must learn the knack of raising swellings, false leprosies and ulcers, and he must drink vinegar to give himself a pale face—all tricks which are distasteful to the honest, hearty minstrel.

IV. "*The beggar must look pretty women in the eyes and, on kissing their hands fervently, his pleasure in the caress will be mistaken for the overflow of gratitude.*" A most important ordinance is this, and one which I have always taken to heart. A fiddler should always

DD

keep his eyes fixed on the damsel, for often his eye has more power than his bow, and it carries the tune deeper into her heart. As to kissing hands, I found that Spanish girls spend many hours powdering and perfuming their hands in the hope of having them kissed by cavaliers. In Spain a kiss on the hand is worth two on the lips, for it costs nothing, it renders homage, and leaves you a free man.

V. *"No beggar should think of the morrow."* A *juglar* who has earned by his fiddling enough to pay for his dinner, wine, glass of *aguardiente* and bed for the night, should put his fiddle back in its case and enjoy the rest of the day at his ease. Those who become covetous of money and try to lay up wealth for the morrow, are false to the creed of *pícaro* which insisted on the doctrine of liberty. The moment a *pícaro* becomes obsessed by ideas of money or work he is lost, for money, as Guzmán says, " is a ferocious beast ; it vanquishes and besmirches everything above and below the earth." A man who hugs a sack full of gold cannot enjoy the sound, dreamless sleep of the *pícaro* who sleeps on both ears. And as for work : what *pícaro* ever thinks of the adage—" Thou shalt work by the sweat of thy brow " ? The humblest *pícaro* and the most blue-blooded noble have this in common : both firmly believe that to work for the sake of work is to be unworthy of the dignity of man. The only rub is that the *pícaro* needs nowadays to slave by the sweat of his brow to win the few pesetas necessary to keep the wolf from the door.

During my stay in Segovia I often reflected upon the causes that determine the vagabond life of the *pícaro*. Segovia became the rendezvous of the picaresque heroes as a result of the unification of the country by Ferdinand and Isabella, when the city lost its important status.

Later on, poverty increased, due to the disastrous wars in the sixteenth and seventeenth centuries and the vast unemployment caused as a result of the Moorish expulsions. Perhaps even the word *pícaro* may be derived from the Arabic. A *pícaro*, we are told, was a youth who had to train himself to carry as heavy bundles as his shoulders would stand. When all Moors of fourteen years and upwards were ordered to leave Castile and Leon, the boys, being deprived of all occupations, took up the profession of carrying baskets (*esportilleros*) and made it into the picaresque job *par excellence*.

My initiation into the secrets of Segovian *pícaros* was actually due to a basket-carrying messenger whom I met in the *Plaza de Azoquejo*. His name was Tomasito and he was about twenty-two years of age, tall, bony, lanky, snub-nosed, and he wore a patch over one eye. His clothes were ragged, but to make up for his slatternly appearance he wore a battered chauffeur cap at a rakish angle, and he puffed a cheap cigar as he sauntered about the *plaza* with his basket on his arm. It was Tomasito's walk that stamped him in my mind as a true *pícaro*. There is no mistaking the jaunty step of the picaresque *guapo* or fancy-man, with the languid roll of the hips and slight touch of swaggering insolence. His actions, gestures and walk explained more of his intimate psychology than dozens of speeches. At first I was under a debt of gratitude, for he rescued me from the old pin-seller's clutches and took me under his wing after delivering his basket at its destination. Tomasito was a fund of knowledge : there was nobody in Segovia he did not know. Together we wandered high and low through the city, visiting churches, squares, court-yards and laneways. At the outset we made a pact that I was to play, and Tomasito, owing to his knowledge of the bright spots in the city, was to organize my efforts. In the early part of the day all went well and I congratulated myself that Tomasito, though in appearance a picaresque rogue, did not possess the cloven hoof. His behaviour was in fact most disinterested. While I played in a café he would lounge negligently against a colonnade or sit straddle-legged across a chair, resting his arms on the back and gaze meditatively at the company, with his chauffeur cap pulled down over his patched eye. He did not claim any money, for it was I who passed the hat round, and his interest in calculating my earnings was most touching. Towards the evening some of his strange, grotesque friends began to gather as if by magic and follow us from place to place without saying a word. One of them who was blind had an urchin to guide his uncertain footsteps ; another was a tall, brutal-looking individual in a dirty smock, carrying a big stick in his hand ; the third was a swarthy dwarf who hobbled after us leaning on a stick. If I had met that dwarf alone in a dark alley I should have crossed myself and taken to my heels. His presence made me feel that some plot or other was being hatched. For the moment, however, there was no sign of trouble. Tomasito and I kept together and the others stood in the background watching us. As it was dusk I wanted to cease work, for I remembered the fifth rule laid down by Guzmán de Alfarache.

"Enough is as good as a feast, *compañero*," said I to Tomasito as I laid my fiddle in its case.

"Don't give up when the luck is good," he replied. "You'll need a *duro* or so more for the needs of the evening."

I yielded to Tomasito's superior judgment and we moved on to another field of operations.

When we ceased work Tomasito suggested that we should retire to an eating-house in a side-street off the *Plaza de Azoquejo.* When we entered I found that our retinue was already ensconced awaiting our arrival.

" Welcome, friends, welcome ! " shouted the dwarf in his hoarse voice, giving me a malignant side-glance. " Beer is our drink," chorused the other two rapscallions ; " we'll elect the stranger king of the feast."

" Am I supposed to stand the whole round ? " said I in a low voice to Tomasito.

" Ah well, *amigo,* you have had all the luck to-day. It would be ungracious to refuse a drink to those honest fellows, whose palates haven't been moistened for many a day."

Inwardly cursing my luck I ordered drinks all round. Tomasito, meanwhile, asked for the bill of fare and ordered soup and meat for the whole party, saying in a low voice : " You are generous, friend, and you deserve all your luck."

" Why the hell should I feed all this rabble ? " said I, incensed.

" Don't get angry, *compañero,*" replied the *picaro* calmly ; " I haven't yet asked you for my share ; come now, I am willing to forgo part of it just to entertain those friends of mine."

There was nothing for it but to acquiesce gracefully. It was a noisy party, though not one word was said until all the food was gobbled up.

The blind man's toothless chaps clapped, the muscular man's jaws rattled, the dwarf's teeth gritted, and as for Tomasito he gormandized with grunts and snorts. Truly the philosophy of the *picaro* is one of hunger, and the heaven he sees in his dreams is a gigantic *posada* with twelve furnaces, in front of which are spitted a dozen bloated, juicy, sizzling turkeys.

After everybody had finished the meal, I thought it was time to shed my companions and win my freedom, so I stood up and called for the bill. After paying over a half of my day's earnings I thought that I could escape with a " good night " and " *hasta luego*," but I had not counted on the picaresque tenacity of Tomasito. Hardly had I walked a few steps down the streets when he was at my side.

" You walk too fast, *compañero* : one would think you were trying to shun your friends."

" No wonder, Tomasito : I can't afford to be a friend of yours. I am not a commissioner of charities."

" You should not leave me : am I not your companion and guide ? The night is young and we are vigorous : follow me, and I'll introduce you to some of the friskiest molls in all Castile. And as for *brujas*, I know one who will make every hair on your head stand on end. She's the best *curandera* in Segovia and every pregnant woman goes to her : husbands avoid her, for they say she has the evil-eye and might put a spell on them."

I heard a clock strike midnight as we walked through the *Plaza de Azoquejo*. After a few minutes groping in dark alleys we came to a dilapidated house in what Tomasito called the " Street of Love." After knocking for a long time an ugly old hag came to the door.

" Are the girls there ? " shouted Tomasito.

The old woman grunted in reply : " Have you any money on you ?—that is my first question, young man. The last time you came here you brought me no good. You won't come in here unless there's the price of a couple of bottles on you."

" Shut your mouth, *maldita vieja*," snapped Tomasito, nudging me. " Here's the *amigo* who'll pour two bottles of your filthy wine down his gullet just to see Luz and Lola."

Luz and Lola were the two attractions of the establishment. Luz was a fat, baby-faced girl whom I labelled *Boule de suif*, though she had none of the vivacious charm of Maupassant's heroine. Lola was thin, nervy, brown-skinned, with eyes like a ferret. The old woman led us into a low-roofed room illuminated by several smoky lamps. In a corner a little, old man sat huddled up in a chair fast asleep, with his head bent over a guitar that lay across his knees. At our entry he awoke with a start and began precipitately to tune his instrument.

No sooner had I ordered wine than the old woman lit another lamp, the guitarist roused himself and began to play tangos, the two girls shed their shawls and stood up to dance and two men entered the room as if by magic. To my surprise they were the muscular bruiser and the dwarf whom I had entertained earlier in the evening. I am destined for ever to be the *barbalote* or victim in this brotherhood, said I to myself. What can I do ? The muscular, hairy-chested man will act as the " bouncer " and lay me out if I utter a cross word ; the dwarf will put a spell on me with that evil eye of his ; as for Tomasito, he will use guile to fool me out of every cent I have made since I came to Segovia. However, I kept a brave face and danced with the two girls in turn.

After the company had consumed two bottles of wine (paid for by me) Tomasito said : " Come now, *amigo*, you have not done your duty by those damsels."

" Have I not stood the whole company wine ? What else is there for me to do ? "

" After wine comes love, my friend : look at Luz— where would you find a more rollicking girl in all

Segovia; that is if your taste is for a plump *paloma*?
If you want something brown and devilish like a
Morisca, there you have Lola."

"But I want neither, Tomasito. I am sleepy and
out of sorts: I want to go back to my *posada*."

"Listen to him, ladies and gentlemen," shouted
Tomasito to the whole company: "he will have nothing
to do with our beauties—poor Luz, poor Lola—never
have you received such an insult. I think the *caballero*
should pay a tribute of two pesetas. Come, friend,
don't be a miser: open your purse and give a little of
your wealth. Hand it to Angelito; he is Luz's protector and he'll know how to make the poor girl forget
the insult to her beauty."

Angelito, who was the bouncer, pocketed the two
pesetas and took the fat girl's arm: everyone then
stood up and toasted them as if they had been bride
and bridegroom. The old woman opened a door and
ushered Angelito and Luz into a small room, which
was mainly occupied by a huge four-poster, covered
with a purple bed-spread. To my surprise I noticed
in a corner above the chest of drawers a picture of
Saint Antony with a little red lamp burning before it.

"Why does Luz light a lamp to Saint Antony?"
said I to the old woman.

"He is the luckiest saint in the calendar," she replied.
"Luz talks to him like a father; you should hear her
curse him when she has had a bad day. Some mornings
I have found the picture under the bed with the glass
smashed to smithereens. I am sure the saint is afraid
to say her nay in anything."

Truly Saint Antony you appear in strange places, but
since I have found you, I too have a prayer for you.
Find me a way out of this den and I'll light seven candles
to you, one for every day of the week.

It was now nearly two o'clock and I thought with longing of my bed in the *posada*, but Tomasito was adamant. "We must," said he, "see 'La Higuera' the old witch I spoke to you about. Come let us be off : she lives just round the corner."

"Surely, Tomasito, she won't be awake at this hour."

"She's awake at all hours when there's work to be done. Besides, women like 'La Higuera' sleep in the daytime and only awaken when the moon rises. Have you any enemies you wish to injure? Do you need cures against evil-eye, fevers, impotence or pox? If you do, 'La Higuera' is the witch for you."

When we reached "La Higuera's" ramshackle dwelling Tomasito knocked repeatedly on the door, but there was no answer. We then stood under the windows and shouted her name. Our voices echoed in the yard, then dead silence. The city of Segovia was fast asleep. As I listened intently I heard a distant rumbling. Tomasito cocked his ear saying : "I recognize the sound : that is 'La Higuera' snoring." He went over the house and banged with my big stick upon the door, making enough noise to awaken the dead. At length we heard the clattering sound of falling chairs and a white face appeared at the window.

"Who wants 'La Higuera'?" said the face.

"Open at once : it is Tomasito speaking."

"The door's open : you've only to lift the latch. Come in and be damned to you for troubling the rest of an honest woman."

Groping our way with difficulty through the dark doorway we entered "La Higuera's" room. At first I had to hold my hand to my nose, for the stench was overpowering. The only light came from one tiny candle which cast flickering shadows upon the wall. In a bed at one side of the room lay an enormously

fat woman. Her round, puffy, white face glistened
in the candlelight as if it was made of tallow. So fat
were her cheeks that they dwarfed her nose, and her
dark eyes shone like pin-points from within the enveloping layers of fat. The front part of her head was
as bald as the palm of my hand, but at the back hung
wisps of matted grey hair. Not a tooth in her mouth
had she and when she spoke in her rasping voice she
would wheeze and whistle, and her bosom would heave
like worn-out bellows.

" Young man," said she to Tomasito, " what brings
you here at this hour ? "

" I have a companion who wants to consult you, so
I brought him along."

There was an ominous creaking of the bed as " La
Higuera " rolled her huge bulk over on one side and
scrutinized my face intently. She then spoke in a
drawling, dreamy voice, as if she was reciting an
incantation. Tomasito tried several times to interrupt
her, but she paid no heed and continued in the same
droning monotone, gazing at me all the time.

" You are young, it seems, but not as young as
Tomasito : you're as plump as a capon but tougher in
the wing and leg I'll bet. You've a belly on you like
a curate in days gone by when the parish fed the priest
but prayed to San Silvestre to be delivered from him.
You've blue eyes, red lips, hairy chest and a ring on
your finger. Your wife must be young and saucy or
the ring would be at the bottom of the Eresma river.
What is it, my boy ? What is it ? If she's pregnant
mind her eye : she might give you a stye in yours.
Put some pig-dung and coal in a tiny purse and hang
it around her neck. But perhaps it's your child who
is ill and you've come to the witch for a pill. Throw
the child's foul napkins up on the roof for the moon

to see : better still, take the child out in its pelt one
night and show its bare bum to the moon before you
show its face. If the moon's cure is of no avail, then
bring me a lock of the child's hair to hold between
finger and thumb. If the hairs give a jump, then it's
the evil eye is withering that child of yours, and I'll
give you a cure in return for a thick silver coin with
the sound of the Resurrection about it. But I see you
are still frowning : you're not thinking of wives or
infants this moment : you've a blasting hatred in your
heart this night against someone who has bested you
and so you come to old ' Higuera ' the witch, with your
heart in your mouth and a couple of solid *duros* in your
hand. Bring me a hair off his head or a nail off his
toe and I'll put a curse on him that'll last a year of
Saturdays. Now you've had your answer mum's the
word after you've put your *duros* at the end of the
bed."

After this long, rambling monologue the old witch's
wheezing voice stopped, and she was seized with a
violent attack of coughing. I then heard a queer
purring sound and a big black cat suddenly uncurled
itself from its hiding-place at the end of the bed and
walked gingerly over "La Higuera's" body towards
us, miawing and waving its tail.

" Put a *duro*, at any rate, on the plate at the end of the
bed," whispered Tomasito to me ; " you can give her
the rest when she has told you more. If you don't
pay her she will let fly a volley of curses at you."

" But I haven't got a *duro*," said I rapidly. " I have
only a peseta."

I gently deposited the coin upon the plate and tried
to slip swiftly from the room, but "La Higuera,"
when she saw the amount, rose up in her bed like an
ogress ready to devour her prey. She raised her naked

arms and gesticulated with her hands, uttering foul-mouthed curses at my retreating figure. As a result of her excited gestures, her smock slipped off her shoulders and I had a monstrous vision. Unluckily, in my hasty retreat I slipped near the door and fell to the ground. " La Higuera," quick to perceive her opportunity, picked up the nearest object to hand—a jar, which she hurled at me. It whizzed through the air, just grazed my ear and fell to the floor with a crash. I scrambled to my feet and dashed through the door and out into the street. As I sped away through the lane I heard the old witch coughing her heart out.

" You were lucky to get away safe and sound," said Tomasito when he rejoined me. " The women round here believe that ' La Higuera ' with her black cat rides a broomstick at night. They say that when she has cursed a man she can by her magic make him walk in his sleep, and draw him out into the street in his underclothes so that all the people may make a mockery of him. When you go home, *amigo*, I'd advise you leave the light full on in your room for the next few nights, for one never knows what kind of devilment a witch can do."

When I was leaving Tomasito the grey dawn was breaking, and all the cocks in Segovia were straining their necks and throats crowing in concert.

" Now that the cocks have crowed," said I to Tomasito, as I stanched the blood from my ear with my hand-kerchief, " I don't care a rap for ' La Higuera ' and her cat and her black magic."

I returned to my *posada* whistling a gay tune. My pockets were empty, two days' earnings had vanished. What odds ? The sun is shining, there's a long day before me and I still have in my rucksack the five silver coins of the wandering Jew.

That evening I slept in the mountain town of Venta de San Rafael.   Next morning as I was threading my way through the majestic Sierra de Guadarrama, I awakened the pity of a passing lorry-driver.   He invited me to jump beside him, and in less than two hours I found myself in Madrid.

# CHAPTER XXXIV

## MADRID

### I. THE GATE OF THE SUN

THE inhabitants of Madrid may proudly boast that their Gate of the Sun is the navel of the Spanish world. No matter how fiercely regionalist a Spaniard may be, he will always admit that all Spanish roads lead to the hallowed square called *Puerta del Sol*. I have even heard Peruvians and Venezuelans declare that, before they loved Spain, they lost their hearts to the *Puerta del Sol*.

Originally the Gate of the Sun was a broad, sunny field on the Eastern side of the *pueblo* of Madrid. During the war of the *Comuneros* in 1520 a castle was built on the field and over its gate a sun was sculpted. This gate became the main entrance to the city. Many transformations have taken place since the days of Philip II, when Madrid was made the capital of all Spains, but the *Puerta del Sol* has never lost its unique character. It was the paradise of the fop and lounger, even in the days of Cervantes, Quevedo, Lope de Vega and Moreto, when young nobles of cloak and sword used to foregather at the *Mentidero* or Liar's Walk beside the church of San Felipe el Real. Through the *Puerta del Sol* the Town Crier would go, proclaiming to the people that the faggots were piled up ready for the *auto de Fé* in the neighbouring *plaza Mayor*. Sometimes the *Puerta del Sol*

414

witnessed tragic scenes of murder and assassination ; at other times scenes of carnival. It was also the scene of glorious patriotic impulse, as on the second day in May, 1808, when the populace of Madrid rose up, unarmed as they were, against the French invaders. To-day the *Puerta del Sol* is a theme of disillusion to the superficial foreign globe-trotters. " Is this the famous Gate of the Sun ? " they cry. " Why, we were told that it was the finest square in the world—finer than the Place de L'Opéra, or Piccadilly Circus, with the *calle de Alcalá* a mixture of Fifth Avenue and Unter den Linden. This is just a tram-centre like Nelson's Pillar in Dublin." To which we should reply—" Ladies and gentlemen, you have taken the wrong ticket. You should take your holidays in some obvious beauty-spot like Mallorca or Capri. The Gate of the Sun is a spiritual junction : all Spanish roads branch from here. The square is a gigantic caravanserai, open day and night to rich and poor alike, a free sun-parlour where the ragged cripple hobbling on his stick and the wealthy lounger may bask contentedly."

It takes some time to become initiated into the secrets of the *Puerta del Sol*. When I visited Madrid first I used to take up my position on the pavement outside the Home Office, between the *calle Mayor* and the *calle de Carretas*, but I felt that I was outside the pale. After meeting several *Madrileños legítimos*, as Benavente picturesquely calls the men about town, and reading the works of Ramón Gómez de la Serna, the peerless cicerone of Madrid ancient and modern, I discovered that the true observation-post of the *Puertasolinos* or *habitués* was the section between the ancient book-shop of Fernando Fé and the *calle de Arenal*, which runs parallel to the *calle Mayor*. In that small space of not more than eighty yards the wanderer may see the panorama of Spanish life pass before his eyes. The best time to see the *tertulia* is, I was told, from six to eight o'clock in the evening, for then the streets are crowded with the people who have just left their offices and shops, but I found that every hour of the day had its own special types. In the morning I met the flower-sellers, who are so characteristic of Madrid. Any susceptible man finds it hard to refuse to buy from those charming damsels. Their dress may be ragged, but they wear silk stockings, wave their hair, and have a smartness that many ladies might envy. I also saw women in black lace mantillas hurrying to Mass ; nurse-maids and children on their way up the *calle de Alcalá* to the gardens of the *Retiro*; blind musicians setting out to take up their positions for the day. There was one old blind fiddler I used to meet every morning outside the café del Correo in the *Puerta del Sol* : his daily beat lay between the *Puerta del Sol* and the Fountain of Cibeles.

After one o'clock in the day comes the first crowded hour of the *Puerta del Sol*, for two o'clock is the dinner-time in Spain, and no self-respecting Spaniard would retire for his meal and siesta without having a saunter in the *Plaza*. The pedestrians move at a slower pace than in any city in the world, and they prefer to walk in the roadway, at the risk of being run over by a motor, than keep to the footpaths. On one occasion I heard an irate pedestrian, who was walking in the middle of the road, rebuke a taxi-driver, who had nearly run into him, in the following terms—" to hell with you ! This is the King's highway and it belongs to all." In the afternoon the *Puerta del Sol* sleeps peacefully and the empty trams glide slowly past. A few pathetic beggars, toy-sellers and women hawking lottery tickets lounge languidly in the shade. At six o'clock life begins to hum again. The waiters, who have been snoozing in the cafés, spring into action ; there is a buzz of excited voices :

the streets are already black with people—the trams clank, bells and motor horns sound ; I can even smell the coffee grains out in the street, and every few seconds I catch the whiff of a strong cigar or else the powder of some passing damsel.

The *Puertasolinos* stand in groups, gossiping mainly about politics, for governments rise or fall at the whim of the *Puerta del Sol.* This is the reason that so many politicians are to be found among those groups of *habitués.* Many years of experience have taught them to call upon the spirit of the Gate of the Sun to aid them as Egeria did King Numa.

It is in the *Puerta del Sol* that the newsvendors start to distribute their papers. In England the cries of newsvendors do not attract much attention, for the Briton takes his news calmly. He knows how to balance his *Evening News* against his *Standard* or against his *Star.* In Spain it is different, for the Spaniard expects news to be presented to him in the most dramatic way possible. There is a touch of ritual in the Madrid method of distributing the evening's news. The proprietors of the various papers seem to have agreed among themselves to issue them one after another at special hours. First of all we have *Informaciones.* Then when the band of newsboys selling that paper have exhausted their lungs and the *Puertasolinos* have started acrimonious discussions, there is suddenly fresh commotion. Another band of boys rush through the streets shouting *Heraldo del Madrid* as if their whole life depended upon it. The headlines in large print shout at the people as loudly as the boys, and so every paper is eagerly snapped up. Half an hour later I hear in the distance the word " *Voz* " shouted by countless hoarse throats and in a moment all previous papers are forgotten in the flurry and excitement of buying *La Voz.*

It is often said abroad, that the Spaniards are a people lacking in political wisdom. One critic informed me that Spain was the land of bulls, castanets and *hasta mañana*; hence it was absurd to expect such a people to take any interest in the problems of state and government. If that critic spent one evening in the *Puerta del Sol* he would have a different tale to tell. I have never seen such passionate interest in politics displayed by any people as by post-revolutionary Madrid. The difficulty of governing such a people does not lie in their apathetic but in their passionate attitude towards politics. Every Spaniard is a Satanic rebel and only rarely is it possible to persuade him to combine with others towards a common policy. In my conversations with *Puerta-solinos* I was impressed by their keen interest in European politics—an interest which was all the more striking because it was disinterested. Madrid to-day is one of the few cities where the traveller finds a balanced and unprejudiced point of view towards European affairs. This is due mainly to the tremendous influx of new ideas from other countries. As I wandered around the *Puerta del Sol* examining the numerous bookstalls, I found cheap editions of translations from English, French, German and even Russian authors. If one believed the Madrid bookstalls, the man in the street must have ceased to read yellow-backed fiction and given himself up to economics, sociology and religion. Later on in the night, however, from midnight on to half-past one, I noticed that the serious books on the sciences disappeared from the stalls, to be replaced by strange booklets of various series called " passionate novels," " novels of the night," " collection Frufru," " picaresque novels." Each booklet had on its cover provocative pictures and titles such as —*The Little Countess finds a Husband, A Venus of Fifteen, The Perversities of Pura, The Vicious Vixen, Clarita's*

*Tickles*, and so on. I bought one with the title *At a village in La Mancha*, thinking it would contain some variation on the story of Don Quixote, but to my surprise it consisted of a lustful Englishman's amatory adventures in La Mancha, described with a wealth of picaresque detail that would give theme for a week's discussion to a board of censors of evil literature. Pornography must be a special art in Spain, requiring wide reading, for in most of the booklets I examined, the writers paraded their knowledge of the classics, with as much assurance as if they had been pupils of Guillaume Apollinaire. But the quotations were introduced with a note of malicious irony into improper contexts. Thus the beautiful lines of the great Augustinian monk Fray Luis de León on a life of peace (" Qué descansada vida ") were applied as an admonition to an old rake, who was chasing a flashy *demi-mondaine*. Another recipe of those pornographic *pícaros* consisted in taking the plot of a well-known novel of the golden age that everyone had thumbed at school, and in transporting it to modern days with modern characters and modern vices. " I take the old stuff," the writers say—" I dish it up hot, with a new-fashioned, exotic sauce and trimmings, and the people gobble it up."

When at last the crowd of night revellers has departed to bed, the *Puerta del Sol* settles down to silent meditation. The cafés are all shuttered, the newsvendors and lottery ticket-sellers have slunk away, and the only people left are the toughened vagabonds who sleep under the stars. The *plaza* is dark except for the luminous, full-moon face of the clock in the little tower above the Home Office, which gazes sardonically upon the scene. As I stand alone, I hear the sound of tapping, and an old man creeps up to me. It is my friend the blind fiddler tapping his way along the curb with his stick. He was now on his way down the *calle Mayor* and on to his home in the district near the *Rastro*.

" It's all right to cool your heels on a night like this," said he, " but wait until November comes around. Then the North wind blows from the Guadarrama and it would pierce you through and through like a Toledo rapier. Then you may pity poor devils like myself who haven't enough money to buy a *capa* to wrap around us. You're a *forastero* and I'll give you a word of advice —don't trust Madrid. It has the most treacherous climate in Spain, for it is always changing. Remember the proverb which says—*El viento de Madrid mata a un hombre y no apaga un candil*—(' Madrid wind kills a man and doesn't put out a candle ')."

The air was beginning to be chilly, so I followed the old fiddler down the *calle Mayor* until I came to the street where my lodgings were situated. As I said farewell, he murmured again in his hoarse voice—" Remember the *refrán—El viento de Madrid mata a un hombre y no apaga un candil.*"

# CHAPTER XXXV

# MADRID

## II

*" Esta noche mi guitarra
ronda por los barrios bajos."*

### VERBENA DE LA PALOMA

MY first necessity on arriving in Madrid was to earn some money, so I devoted my attentions to the lower part of the city below the *Puerta del Sol*. If I had taken the *calle de Alcalá* or the *carrera de San Jerónimo* as my beat, I should have felt as self-conscious as a ragged urchin who had strayed by mistake into a fashion parade. Besides, there was always the danger of being recognized by friends, when it would be necessary to explain myself by a long-winded story. No, it was better to start off on my minstrel's vagabondage from the *plaza Mayor*. Fortunately my arrival in Madrid coincided with the famous Madrid festival called *La Verbena de la Paloma*.

" Why do they call the festival a *verbena* ? " said I to a friend some days later.

" The word," said he, " originated with the fragrant plant. In the time of the ancient Romans the priests used to carry a branch of verbena as a symbol of their power. They used to gather it on the second night of the Summer solstice, the twenty-third of June. Later

on, the Christians converted the *fiesta* into a *romería* or
religious festival, and as you know, my friend, a *romería*
is not all prayers and psalms : in fact the proverb says :
' *Romería de cerca : mucho vino y poca cera* '—(' When
there's a *romería* : plenty of wine but scarce a candle ').
There are *verbenas* for all the sunny months of the year.
The first belongs to Saint Antony and is the most lively,
because it ushers in the summer ; then there is the
*Verbena* of Saint John and after some minor *fiestas* we
have the *Verbena de la Paloma* which is the grand farewell
to summer."

I set out on my adventures in the poorer, picaresque
quarters of Madrid late at night, when the *plaza Mayor*
was silent and peaceful. In this *plaza* most of the
pageantry of Spain's golden age was enacted. It was
here that the knights rode in their tournaments before
the King ; here too bull-fights and carnivals were held
and from time to time the crowded square witnessed
the tragic burning of heretics by the Inquisition. Here
too the beatification of San Isidro the patron saint of the
city took place in 1620. San Isidro was a humble work-
man, and his spirit lives on in this square after all the pomp
and pageantry of kings and nobles has passed away.
San Isidro shall be my patron on my minstrel journey.

The square is dark and deserted, but through the lofty
arch leading to the *calle de Toledo* I see a mass of coloured
lights, which for a moment give me the impression that
the saint has illuminated a fantastic proscenium in answer
to my prayer and the walls of the houses in the *plaza
Mayor* echo to the sound of distant voices.

As soon as I passed through the archway I found
myself in another world. The long winding street was
thronged with people : the balconies were full to overflowing with excited women and children. There were
paper garlands suspended from wires and the arc lamps

cast a brilliant, flaming light upon the scene. Here and there, in corners, Japanese lanterns swayed in the gentle night breeze and cast discreet light upon the groups of people seated in taverns and bars. Out in the middle of the street were ice-cream carts, barrows full of buns, cakes and the classical *churros* (strips of paste fried in olive oil and sugar).

At this hour the streets belong to the merrymakers and we may dance or dawdle to our heart's content without fear of coachman or taxi-driver. Occasionally a horse-driven car drives by slowly and the great mass of people opens out to allow it to pass unmolested. A *verbena* I found by experience is the humble minstrel's forlorn hope. When I walked slowly down the *calle de Toledo* towards the *plaza de la Cebada* it seemed to me as if every dusty old guitar, fiddle, mandoline, flute or fife had been pulled out of the lumber-room. The difficulty was to find a camping-ground devoid of music. The wandering minstrels at this hour generally performed in the middle of the street surrounded by groups of people. They did not take up their position on the footpath, for the majority of the tiny shops or booths had their gramophones with disks revolving round and round, scratching and screaming. At first I was deafened by the discordant din, then I began to thread my way through the maze of sound. Here and there I could distinguish popular themes and I noted them in my mind by a kind of rapid shorthand : Jota aragonesa—jumpy music that—must stamp it with my feet as well as sing it—dúm dădă dúm dúm dădă dă dă dúm dă dúm ! Bother ! It has disappeared, overwhelmed by a flood of sound from a gramophone record of Fleta's singing of " ay ay ay ! " Fleta's ghost strains its voice in agonized struggle, the gramophone needle scrapes and scrapes in vain : the voice sinks back into the ocean like a shipwrecked mariner clinging to a plank—and I am only conscious of the " Habanera " from Carmen grinding away on a penny-in-the-slot organ in a bar. It was as if I turned the wireless pointer round and round the dial rapidly from one station to another, at the hour when all the jazz bands of Europe are simultaneously blaring forth their machine-made music.

For the first time in my wandering I felt deeply depressed and disillusioned with the minstrel's calling. Why did I leave the countryside where I was a welcome guest, to enter this inferno ? In the villages of Old Castile the wanderer with a fiddle could hold his head high and say to himself : " I perform a necessary duty in the state : I prevent the people from becoming starved musically : I can play folk tunes and dances and tell them stories about my wanderings." Here in the city the machine has made music the cheapest and least-valued commodity in the world. Poor Saint Cecilia, patroness of musicians—your cloak has trailed in the mud and your lute has been defiled by mankind. Now is the time for you to perform a miracle ! Strike the whole of mankind with deafness for ten years, so that no one will be able to hear anything softer than the sound of ten saxophones played together in unison. Then, at the end of the ten years, give the power of sensitive hearing to fifty chosen spirits and let them delve in the dust-heaps for the relics of Bach and Beethoven, and feed their minds upon such pabulum. When educated, let the fifty live together in the convent of Thélème and beget ear-conscious children, who will, in their turn, create a new musical universe.

## THE MADRID CABBY

I made one friend during my peregrinations along the descending road—Don Eleuterio, the cabman, one of the

aristocratic inhabitants of the famous Lavapiés quarter
sacred to the memory of Goya and Ramón de la Cruz.
When I first met Don Eleuterio he was throned on the
box of his cab,[1] gazing silently on the excited throng of
revellers beneath him. Since early childhood I have
always looked upon cab-drivers with reverence, for in
my native city of Dublin the jarvey is looked upon as a
Philosopher, who rises above the transient miseries of life.
An old jarvey has taken part in the whole pageant of
life : he drives the mother with her new-born to the
baptism : he drives the bride and groom to the wedding.
He drives behind the glass hearse, carrying Everyman
on his last journey. A cab with its coarse and shabby
exterior may yet be a magic, movable palace like those
created by the genii of the *Arabian Nights*. At one
moment it may house the family of the cabby himself :
at another it may, like the famous cab in *Madame Bovary*,
become the couch of lovers. When I watch a cab circle
slowly round the squares of the city at night with its
black curtains half-drawn, I think of the eighteenth century—the age of Casanova—when Cupid was discreet
and induced his victims to seek out gondolas and sedan
chairs as the scene for their amorous toying. In time
of national revolution and political upheaval, too, the
cabby plays a leading part, for his cab is a safe hiding-
place. I know a friendly cabby, who in the Irish civil
war stored in his vehicle a monk's habit as disguise for
political leaders " on the run." Don Eleuterio belongs
to the ever-diminishing brotherhood of cabby philosophers. He knows that the modern inhabitants of Madrid
have doomed him and his horse in favour of the
motor-car, but he gazes from his eminence upon them

[1] The word for a cab in Spanish is *simón*, derived from a certain
Simón González who introduced the vehicle into Madrid at the
end of the eighteenth century.

with pity in his heart. With his gruff, red face, white bushy moustache and side-whiskers, he is a relic of a past age when men were content to amble gently through life.

" I wish," said he, " you could have seen the streets of Madrid thirty years ago ! Then one could inhale the pure air straight from the Guadarrama. Nowadays I can hardly breathe with the foul fumes of petrol which the Devil dug up from the bowels of the earth for the destruction of men. How I long to see the *calle de Alcalá* as it was in the old days, with piles of good, honest horse-dung on the pavement."

" Come now, Don Eleuterio ; surely you will agree that the people in Madrid are happier to-day with all the comforts that modern civilization has introduced ? "

" Don't you believe it, Señor. All that has happened is that the new inventions have made the people discontented. I was born and bred in the Lavapiés quarter and I don't want to leave it. For me it is a long journey to drive a fare to the *Hipódromo*. But look at the youths and girls of to-day. They want to be always rushing off here and there. They read in a paper of other countries, and straightway they can't sleep at night for thinking of foreign fancies. I tell you Señor, it's not natural. None of these youths will reach old age : they'll wear out before they're forty."

" Ah well, Don Eleuterio, you still have your *Verbena de la Paloma*."

" You surely wouldn't call what you have seen to-night a *Verbena*. Why, even my horse has a face of misery on him with looking at it. You should have been here thirty or forty years ago when there were real *Verbenas* : you could not have heard yourself speak with the shouting, laughing, singing. No cars could drive through the street then, for it was railed off by wooden posts wreathed in flowers. The men wore big hats and shirts of silk : every girl came dressed in her white or red mantón de Manila. At five in the morning when the people had gone home, the streets were covered with red carnations, hairpins and brooches. After one *verbena* I myself picked up three gold rings with emeralds and sapphires in them."

" I am sure, Don Eleuterio, that lovers still prefer your cab to any motor-car."

" You're wrong there, Señor. Nowadays there's no more mystery in love, because nothing is forbidden. A girl to-day sees so much of her *novio* that she's tired of him before the priest unites them. In my day it was different. Look at this old cab of mine : it has had its romances, I tell you. I remember the night when a woman was murdered in my cab—nice-looking girl she was too. She came up to me one night, leaning on the arm of a tall, handsome *caballero*. I drove them out into the country, and on five successive nights. I used to halt the cab in a dark, quiet place and go off for a smoke, leaving the lovers to themselves. On the sixth night when I returned to the cab I looked in through the window and I was surprised to see her all alone. The moon was shining on her face : she looked so pale that at first I thought she had fainted : I called out to her, but she did not move. She was wearing a white dress, and when I went up close I saw a great stain in front. She was dead—dead as a slab of white marble. I shall never forget the sound of the blood dripping, dripping on to the floor. What had happened ? Why had they quarrelled ? I don't know to this day—she lies in the cemetery yonder. May God rest her soul."

Don Eleuterio talked so long to me of his reminiscences that the old horse turned his head and gazed at us with so pathetic an expression that I felt that it was time to say farewell. Madrid cab-horses always seem to me to be more afflicted by melancholy than the cab-horses of any other country. Perhaps this is due to the bull-fight, for I had the sad presentiment that they would all end their days in the ring. There is only one consolation for the disappearance of the *simón* from the streets of Madrid. When it has gone no one will be able to send worn-out cab-horses to the *corrida* to become the victims of the bull's pitiless horns.

## LAVAPIÉS QUARTER

After continuing my wandering down the long, winding street I found myself all of a sudden in the *plaza de Lavapiés*, and I began to dream of the Madrid of Goya. I remembered 1928, the centenary of the great painter's death, when for one week we lived in retrospect the life of the *majo* and *maja* with their picturesque trappings. The *majo* was the street gallant of the eighteenth century and dressed himself in a costume resembling that of a bull-fighter. The *maja* was the incarnation of Goya's ideal of feminine beauty. In character she resembled the sparkling " Colombina " of Goldoni's Venetian plays— a playful, mischievous chatterbox who flirted her way through life. Goya immortalized her in his two pictures " The Maja Clothed " and " The Maja Naked," which hang in the Prado, but the type appears again and again through his pictures of Madrid life. It was popularly believed that the beautiful Duchess of Alba sat as model for the picture, and malicious tongues gossiped indiscreetly.

Although Beruete, the great authority on Goya, refuted the idle tittle-tattle, it will not die, for what beautiful woman in history has not inspired *croniques scandaleuses* about her private life? Probably if the ghost of the fair Duchess arose from the Elysian fields she would rebuke the learned Beruete for depriving her of her supremacy as Madrid's ideal heroine.

When we consider the *maja* as the heroine of Spain it is unfair to give all the credit to Goya, for Ramón de la Cruz in his one-act plays described her on the stage as brilliantly as the painter did on canvas. Ramón de la Cruz fought the battle for Spanish nationality no less than Goya did. He lived in the eighteenth century when Spain alternately bowed the knee to France and Italy. He lived through the era of Farinelli and Voltaire, when Spanish serious drama was a weak imitation of foreign models, producing hundreds of those one-act *sainetes* which are a treasure-house of wit and fantasy. In writing those plays he was obeying an ancient tradition of the Spanish stage, for in the Golden Age it was customary to insert between the acts of a long three-act play, little comedies which took twenty or twenty-five minutes to perform.[1] Ramón de la Cruz founded the majority of his *sainetes* on the life of the poor people living in the neighbourhood of the *plaza de Lavapiés*.

As soon as I think of his plays, I hear a sound of guitars and *bandurrias* in the distance and I see a host of girls approaching. They are dressed in short skirts, transparent stockings : a mantilla floats round their neck and they hold fans in their hands. Instead of *majas* the author called them *manolas*. By their side swagger youths in white frilly shirt, tight-fitting trousers and red sash. The air resounds with little folk-poems called *seguidillas* and everyone dances. There is gaiety and joy in Lavapiés square, in spite of occasional bickering. If a grumbler puts his nose out of a café and tells them all to stop laughing and shouting, he is hounded away to his solitary garret without mercy by the company.

The tradition of Ramón de la Cruz and Goya has

[1] These one-act plays were called *entremeses* or *sainetes*: *entremés* was the play performed between the first and second acts ; *sainete* was the play performed between the second and third acts.

lasted on even into our modern, mechanical age. In the Spanish theatre to-day the most flourishing type of play is the *sainete*. During the week of the *Verbena de la Paloma* the *sainete* of that name by Ricardo de la Viga written in the traditional style was performed in honour of the festival. The brothers Quintero and Arniches more than anyone have continued the tradition of Ramón de la Cruz in their sparkling scenes. Arniches himself told me that when he is in the mood for writing a *sainete* he puts on old clothes, pulls a cap down over one eye and slouches off down to the Lavapiés quarter to seek inspiration.

At first sight the quarter reminded me of slums in Naples, or else the ancient streets of Georgian Dublin where numerous families squat in drawing-rooms formerly inhabited by the lords and ladies of the eighteenth century. There was an air of squalid poverty everywhere : the women were ragged, dishevelled and worried : the children rachitic and under-nourished. But after living a few days with these people, a minstrel begins to see them in brighter colours, for he is able to talk to them as an equal, and if they do not want to talk to him they will always listen to a tune. Hunger, poverty and unemployment have not been able to stifle that spontaneous vivacity which is so characteristic of the Madrid populace. The Castilian is a solemn and dignified fellow, but the air of the Guadarrama sharpens his wits and turns him into a *chispero* (sparkler), which is the name applied to the witty loungers of the Lavapiés quarter. Madrid is the highest capital in Europe and the inhabitants may boast like the Athenians of old that they walk through the clear air. After days spent in the Lavapiés quarter I came to the conclusion that Madrid should be called the " City of Good Humour." Under the blue sky and golden sunshine poverty refuses to remain squalid. "As our houses are devoid of comforts," the people of Lavapiés cry, "let us camp in the street like *Gitanos*, under God's sky which belongs to all."

## THE RASTRO

The humming centre of activity is the *plaza* opening on to the celebrated *Rastro*. At sunset every imaginable type of picaresque rogue gathers in this square near the statue of the hero of Cascorro—an unknown private soldier—the only one to be immortalized in stone. I see Lazarillo de Tormes leading his blind man over to a barrow where sizzling hot *churros* are for sale : not two steps away from me is *pícara Justina*, a bouncing, black-haired, red-faced wench, dressed in a faded purple skirt and pink blouse. She is bare-footed, but she wears gold ear-rings. She would be strong enough to drub a herd of boisterous, night-denying students and send them off like Samson's foxes with their tails afire.

From the *plaza* I can see below me in the distance the broad panorama of parched, yellow plain. The main street of the *Rastro* called the *Ribera de Curtidores*, which descends steeply towards the plain, is full of booths covered with awnings and reminds me of a huge Gypsy camp. Each tent is crammed with junk of every description : worn-out bedsteads, presses, chairs, clocks, braziers, candlesticks—all are thrown together in monstrous confusion. If Adam and Eve were again cast out of Paradise and dropped into the *plaza del Rastro* they could descend the *Ribera de Curtidores* hand in hand and arrive at the bottom of the hill fully clothed, and they could set up house in the plain with the objects they had collected. The majority of the booths cater for the utilitarian householder of tiny means, but the gaunt unwieldy shanties lining the street, and the enclosed

squares called the "Two Americas," are the most
fantastic curiosity shops in Europe. So closely stacked
are the goods that there is only a tiny passage by which
the buyer can squeeze his way into the dark recesses of
the shop. Every object has a history which I feel
tempted to reconstruct. The most melancholy of all
are the costumes of faded silk and brocade. Here is a
torn and tattered bull-fighter's costume with the front all
stained. What visions that costume calls up in my
mind of the *matador* gored in the ring—the torn, blood-
stained *traje de luces* ripped off the corpse in the infirmary
and cast on the dust-heap. He died and was forgotten
years ago, but the memory of the fatal wound lives on
in that torn and crumpled piece of faded brocade and
tinsel. Quantities of family heirlooms are stacked from
floor to ceiling: snuff-boxes, perfume-bottles, ancient
medals, engraved watches, ivory crucifixes—all of them
seemed to whisper from their hiding-places some melancholy story of the vanity of earthly possessions.

As I wander slowly down this slope to the plain I
recall the words of an English Romany chal: "We
Gypsies, *rai*, are happier than you folks, for we've nought
in the world but our rawnie and our van: and when we
die they burn the van, so we leave nothing behind us."
It is an ironical commentary on human society that the
*Rastro* with its bric-à-brac gathered from the dust-heap
of former grandeur should be situated in the poorest
quarter of the city, where the people have no possessions.
Strange, too, that the sellers of the *Rastro* should be so
Gypsy-like in appearance and manner. There is not one
of them but looks as if he was a Morisco. They are
a mysterious race, completely apart from the ordinary
*Madrileños*. They live like Gypsies, encamped in the
dark corners of the rough wooden contraptions they
have erected over their heaps of junk. Originally their

shanties were run up as a temporary make-shift, but they
have lasted for countless years, and they have become
hoary, worm-eaten and dilapidated. To the casual
observer it looks as if a puff of North Wind from the
Guadarrama would topple them over like a house of
cards, but their phlegmatic owners never think of such
an eventuality, for they trust to their good star. One
of them solemnly informed me that he would as soon
build a new royal palace as put up a new shop. " It
would bring me *mala suerte*," said he ; " luck goes by
tradition and my father was lucky in this place before I
was born."

The day I descended the hill of the *Rastro* was a Thursday and I was on my way to the Gypsy fair beyond the
*matadero*, for I had promised Agustina Escudero that I
would visit her brother the *chalán* Ramón el Andaluz.
When I reached the bottom of the hill I had to tramp over
a long stretch of road on the outskirts of the city before
I arrived at the entrance of the fair.

## The Gypsy Fair

When I arrived at the fair it was about ten o'clock in
the morning. The sun's rays had wellnigh scorched me
into coma : I sweated at every pore, and the thick white
dust of the road made me cough and sputter every
moment. Business had started early in the morning
and I saw Gypsies here and there resting in the shade
beside their tethered mules and donkeys. The actual
buying and selling took place under a huge shed. Here
there was an animated scene. Horses, mules, donkeys
led by Gypsies of every sex, age and condition : the
horses neighed, the donkeys brayed, the men swore, the
children squealed : I could hardly breathe, so powerful
was the combined smell of dust, dung and sweat. Here
and there groups of men gathered around one particular

mule. The owner, holding the animal by a rope, would with his stick point out the good points to the others, explaining his meaning with a wealth of excited gestures. They would shake their heads, scratch their chins, yawn, shrug their shoulders and grunt their disapproval. A Gypsy fair is a most dramatic business, for the Romany chals are past masters of the art of creating illusion in the *Busnó*, to be followed later by disillusion. A Gypsy could make a " white face " believe that pine-apples grow off fig-trees : he is expert in the art of embellishment. The old mule is a pathetic, woebegone wreck, but he describes it in terms of Pegasus, Bucephalus and Babieca and dazzles the simple man by his flow of rhetoric. Besides, according to George Borrow and other Romany ryes the *chalán* has other more sinister arts at his disposal. He can dose a spavined mule with arsenic to give it temporary vivacity : he can make it lively by the " trick of the eel," which consists in shoving a live eel into the hindquarters of the beast ; he can paint the sores and weals so that you would hardly think the skin had been broken. All those knavish tricks will do for the mere *Busnó*, but when Gypsy meets Gypsy it is a case of " Greek meets Greek." The sale of a horse, mule or donkey becomes in that case a long-drawn-out tussle of wits with the chorus of Gypsies to arbitrate.

Many such struggles were taking place in that large shed at the Gypsy fair. Nobody paid any attention to me. I shouted myself hoarse, but no one answered : I spoke to various brown-faced urchins, but they rushed away to join the excited groups.

At last I came across a youth who was disconsolately leading up and down his mule—evidently one of the forlorn beasts whose luck had not been in the ascendant. For the fifth time I repeated mechanically the words Agustina had taught me : " Lead me to ' Ramón el

Andaluz ' and ' El Pelao.' I've no evil in my mind : I've come with a message from sister Agustina."

As soon as I mentioned the two names, the youth started and said : " Hold the mule and I'll run and fetch them." Off he went like a flash of lightning. A few moments later he returned followed by a tall, bearded man.

" Who are you ? " said the tall man in a stern voice, gazing at me from head to foot. When I repeated my message, I added in a few words of Romany to strengthen my position, and I pulled out of my pocket a photograph of Agustina which I had taken at San Sebastian.

" I am Ramón el Andaluz," said he more softly ; " no need to show pictures when you know the passwords, friend. Come with me and meet 'El Pelao.' " So saying he led me into a corner of the shed, where a man dressed in a long, grey smock was arguing fiercely with a group of young Gypsies. Again I repeated my message from Agustina, and " El Pelao," after spitting on the ground, welcomed me with open arms. I was soon surrounded by a whole tribe of Gypsies—all of whom seemed to be related to " Ramón el Andaluz " and " El Pelao."

Ramón himself was the finest-looking Gypsy I had met in Spain. He was tall, slender and as bronzed in complexion as his sister, but there was very little of Agustina's aristocratic elegance about him. His bare arms were long, lanky and knotted with muscles. In his hand he held a stick which was thinner than my " companion," but shod at the end with a murderous iron tip. He was dressed in a faded red shirt, grey tight-fitting trousers and on his head he wore a broad-brimmed felt hat. In manner he was courteous, but he had none of Agustina's vivacity. When all the rest would crack jokes, laugh, whistle, play pranks, he would sit by himself with a melancholy expression on his face.

" El Pelao " was a gruff, coarse-grained Gypsy, Andalusian in type, always cursing and swearing with the
good-humoured verve of a *chaval* from Triana. The
younger members of the family were of more puny build.
There were several youths, whose slim, waisted figures
and languid poses would have genuinely fitted them for
a gigolo parade, if they had belonged to a higher stratum
of society. One youth in particular fascinated me by
his incongruous appearance at a horse fair. He was
dressed in a cream-coloured suit with brown stripes and
his feet were shod in the daintiest grey suède shoes with
thin, pointed toes. His black hair was greased and
curled into ringlets, his face powdered and his lips
rouged. His twin brother (for so he seemed to be) was
attired in grey, with waisted coat cut *a lo torero*.

" What have those two dainty dawdlers to do with
this horse fair? " said I to " El Pelao " in a whisper.

" Both of them are *quelararós* (dancers). They start
their day's work when we are sleeping on both ears.
They never fail to come to the *matadero* on Thursdays to
meet the family. Don't imagine that because they are
dressed like *señoritos* they are any the less Romany chals.
Whenever they can escape from the *bayunca* (tavern),
where they have been dancing and singing, they go
straight to the *matadero* to meet the folk of their own
*rati*."

## Juerga Gitana

A few evenings later I found myself in the *barrio de
Tetuan*, the guest of my Gypsy friends. We sat in a cool
courtyard at the back of a tavern and the party was
becoming a *juerga*. I had been at a festival of Gypsy
song in the popular resort, *La Bombilla*, the night before,
and I described my disillusion to " El Pelao " in the
intervals of consuming big glasses of golden Manzanilla.

" I tell you, *amigo*," said I ; " Gypsy *Cante Jondo* is dead
and buried. There's not a *Gitano* can sing a *caña* or a
*siguiriya* to-day. I heard twenty Romany chals last night,
but I would as soon listen to cats love-duetting under
the moon. None of those *chavales* have the throat for
*polos* or *martinetes* nor the red blood either."

" Say that again, *plaloró*."

" I say that none of the Gypsy singers to-day have any
red blood in their veins."

" What do you say to that, Currito ? " said " El Pelao "
excitedly to a mournful-looking youth with pock-marked
face who was seated beside him.

" Where did you say you heard the singing ? " said
Currito.

" In *La Bombilla*."

" What would you call *La Bombilla*, brother ? "

" Oh, well, I suppose it is a fashionable lounger's
paradise."

" You've said it, brother : a hunting-ground for white-
faced *paillos*, but not for self-respecting Romany chals."

" How could you," interrupted " El Pelao," " expect
a Gypsy to sing in such a place and before such an
audience ? Why, the notes would freeze in his throat
at the sight of them."

Then Ramón el Andaluz's cavernous voice boomed
from a dark corner where he sat scowling : " Fill up the
stranger's glass and call for Paco."

Paco was a wizened-faced Gypsy of diminutive stature,
bright-eyed as a ferret and as agile as a monkey. With
him came " Pepe el gordo," a fat, lumbering, grey-haired
rom with a guitar. First of all there were glasses of
Manzanilla all round and then the *zambra* started.
" Pepe el gordo " sat in the middle of the courtyard and
began to thrum his guitar, while the rest of the company
clapped their hands. Paco sat beside the guitarist, and

after the preluding had continued for some time and the
shouts and clapping of hands had worked everyone up
to a state of rhythmic excitement, he suddenly leant
forward with his face contracted into what looked like
a spasm of agonizing pain and raised his right hand to
his forehead, as if to keep his head from splitting.  I
thought he was going to drop to the floor writhing in
a fit, but suddenly he uttered a long cry—" Ay—ay ! "
repeated again and again against the frenzied accompaniment of the guitar.   Then with upturned eyes the singer
started off his song as if he meant to defy the world with
his despairing grief.

> " Los celos me ajogan.
> Mardito er queré !
> que pone en mi mano la navaja abierta
> y a ná se atrevé."

The first two lines of the song were the defiance : the
long third line started at the same high-pitched note,
but the singer then prolonged the notes in breathless,
descending vocalization, and at the end it seemed as if
they would never die, for the shouts of " olé " and
claps of the audience revived the dying voice into
yet another turn and trill.   Hardly had Paco recovered
from the exhaustion of one *siguiriya gitana* when he
started off on another.   They were all passionately
sad songs describing jealous love, hunger, gaol, death,
and there was hardly one that did not bring in the
*maresita vieja* (old mother), or the *punalá* (dagger-thrust).
Most of them were sung in Spanish of the Triana kind,
but some were in strongly accentuated *Caló*.

As Paco continued singing, the company began to
increase in numbers and I noticed signs of impatience in
some of the women.   Suddenly an oldish woman edged
her way into the middle of the courtyard, pushed aside
Paco and stood over " Pepe el gordo " the guitarist,

forcing him to cease the *siguiriya* and play a *polo* for her. The old woman's singing was more bacchanalian than Paco's, for she seemed to dance her song as well as sing it. The *polo* meanders along like a long stream of molten lava, but then comes the *macho* or refrain which is a sudden, flaming outburst. As the old woman sings she sways about the courtyard with her arms on her hips : her grey hair has come loose and falls in dishevelled mass over her shoulders. Then come the shouts of " olé," the clinking of glasses, and when I look round I find that the courtyard is full to overflowing.

From now on the *juerga* became more lively and interruptions became more frequent. It was all like an *eranos* or contribution feast of music, in which every man, woman or child added their share.

" Where do the majority of those *cantaores* come from ? " said I to " El Pelao " when I could make myself heard.

" Mostly from Jérez and Cádiz," he replied.

The *Cante Jondo* or " Deep Song " of the Gypsies in its purest form springs from the small region in Andalucía comprising Jérez de la Frontera and Cádiz. In these two cities and their suburbs the streets at dusk resound with " ay " and " leli " and the twang of countless guitars.

The oldest of the *Cante Jondo* songs is the *caña*, which is derived from the slender glass in which Manzanilla is drunk. The *caña* is a full-blooded song in which the guitar fades into the background as an accompaniment, or else limits itself to embroidering the singer's phrase. The Gypsy singers of Spain, like those of Hungary, sing their songs in a special order. They start with sad, meandering songs in order to awaken melancholy associations in the minds of their audience. The *siguiriya gitana*, like the Hungarian *lassu*, must draw tears to the eyes and call up visions of hunger,

humiliation, death. Sometimes the singers divert the
sad song into religious emotion and create a *saeta* or
arrow of song in honour of Our Lady. Later on they
quicken the rhythm in *polos* just as the *cigany* of the
Puszta raps out his *friss*, leading it on to the bacchanalian
*csárdás*. But in Spain the Gypsies also sing narrative
songs describing their own particular Gypsy occupation.
Thus " El Chato," a Gypsy from Cádiz who was a
metal-worker, sang *martinetes* or songs of the forge. He
would allow no guitar to accompany him, but he rapped
out the accompanying rhythm with his iron-tipped stick
upon the stone floor. The *martinete* is a savage song
describing tribal struggles and blood feuds of the Gypsies.
In some of them the song became drama with dancing
and dialogue, for when the singer came to the *tercio* or
chorus other voices would alternate with him.

After the fierce, dramatic *martinetes* Paco brought us
back to normal once more by singing *soleares* on gay,
frisky themes that roused the audience to Gargantuan
laughter. One after another I heard, amidst the roars
of mirth, verses in *Caló* that would have made the arch-
priest of Hita blush.

As I walked away, with the songs still ringing in my
ears, I reflected that the Gypsies are always the same wild,
unspoilt children of Nature, whether they are camped in
Spain or Hungary, Russia or America. They possess
in themselves a primitive quality which enables them to
adapt themselves to the different peoples and take from
them what is really national. The Gypsy did not create
the picaresque life in Spain, but he found in it something
agreeable to his nomadic life.

# CHAPTER XXXVI

# MADRID

## III.  *TERTULIA* [1]

I SLEPT for two days and two nights after the *Juerga Gitana* and awoke a new man.  Strange, quoth I, what a difference a bath and a shave make to a traveller.  I am no longer *Gualtero de muchos caminos*, the footsore vagabond : I've shed my rakish, picaresque air with my beard.  Yes, my friends, when you see me dressed in my black suit you will take me for a city man by birth and breeding.  " Waiter, bring me a vermuth, olives and to-day's *Sol* and A B C."  The sun is shining brightly and the *calle de Alcalá* lies before me.  But I must possess my soul in patience until sunset, for at that hour my Madrid friends will be at their *tertulias*.

No institution is more characteristically Spanish than the *tertulias*, which give Madrid the reputation among foreigners of being the " City of conversation."  The *tertulia* should correspond to the London club, but there is a world of difference between the Castilian and the Anglo-Saxon temperament.  A club in London is a majestic edifice hallowed by classic tradition.  Over its portals should be inscribed the motto : " Abandon

[1] A *tertulia* is a customary reunion of people for the purpose of discussion on subjects of common interest.

441

speech all ye who enter here." The words have never
been inscribed because it would be superfluous to do so
as the well-bred Briton has learnt the adage while at
school. Conversation and hilarity are strongly discour-
aged in a London club and for a good reason. The
Englishman belongs to a suburban civilization, whose
strength lies in its hearty friendliness. He needs for
his soul's sake to escape for a few hours from the society
of those whom Americans aptly call " good mixers "
and retire into splendid isolation. England was supreme
so long as she adopted the policy of splendid isolation,
and the gaunt, grim London clubs that stand like for-
tresses in Pall Mall are pathetic reminders of that
ideal.

The Castilian could never be called a " good mixer,"
for his life lacks all suburbia's attributes. I found by
experience that the Spaniard, though one of the most
hospitable men in Europe, rarely asks a foreign guest to
dine at his house. He will invite him to an hotel, where
a sumptuous banquet is prepared, and later on, if the
evening is to be *castizo*, he will engage Gypsy singers
and dancers from Villa Rosa. The Spanish home is preserved from prying eyes—it is a paradise, in the original
meaning of the word—a place with a high wall around
it. Since the Spaniard lives his family life apart from the
world, he needs his hours of club life in common with
other men. Hence he chooses the noisiest place in the
world—the café. When I was at Madrid in 1924 I was
made a member of several *tertulias* of men of letters.
When I announced this fact to an English friend he
congratulated me with as much warmth as if I had been
elected to an exclusive London club.

" What are they like, those Madrid clubs ? " said he.

" There are no silence rooms," I answered. " No,
not even a ' snug.' They meet in the noisiest room in

the café and the members stand the new-comer his drink
the first evening he comes amongst them."

The *tertulia* possesses immense advantages over the
British club system.   If a foreigner comes to London,
eager to study the manners and the customs of the
British people, he finds to his dismay that his temporary
membership of a great club does not bring him any
exciting information concerning England's social, political or literary life.   Nearly every subject he broaches in
the hallowed precincts is tabu : he must not talk shop :
he must not talk politics because there may be Cabinet
ministers present, who would think he was a journalist
spy : he must not talk about women, for that is bad
form.   In sheer desperation he makes a friend of the
aristocratic, omniscient porter of the club and learns
about cricket scores from him.

When entering a *tertulia* the Spaniard murmurs to
himself the adage—" Abandon discreet words all ye who
enter here."   The man who sets a curb upon his tongue
would soon be shunned by the innumerable *tertulias*
that blossom gaily in the *calle de Alcalá*.   From seven to
nine o'clock every night the *Madrileños* resemble the Irish
of whom Dr. Johnson tersely remarked—" They are a
fair people : they never speak well of one another."
With the exception of Dublin, no city in Europe blasts
so many reputations in an evening by witty conversation
as Madrid does.   But, whereas the Dublin wits live in
Celtic twilight and take refuge from their adversaries'
arrows in the fog, the Madrid sharpshooters in the limpid
atmosphere never miss an aim, and gloat over their
writhing victims.   I am more grateful than I can say
to the *tertulias* for schooling me in my ignorance.   From
one side of Madrid to another I ranged—from the
*café del Correo*, where I used to sit with my horse-dealing
Gypsy friends, to the *café Colonial*, where the *tertulia*

became spiced by the presence of *cocottes* ; from thence
on to the *Regina,* where the subtle poet and dramatic
critic Díez Canedo and his friends held court, and later
in the evening I would double up the narrow *calle del
Clavel* to a café in the *Gran Vía* where I would find a band
of Portuguese exiles arguing about the wrongs of their
country.

Every *tertulia* has its own great leader who sets the
tone of the meetings. If he is a poet such as Antonio
Machado, then the conversation would generally turn
upon the poets of modern Spain, and the author of
*Campos de Castilla* would speak in his slow, measured
tone, and we would all marvel at the talent of this
Andalusian who made himself the most Castilian of
contemporary bards. If on the other hand the leader of
the *tertulia* happens to be an oracle of the theatre, then
the stranger would find himself assailed, the moment he
tried to say a word in favour of modern Spanish drama.
" What a misguided man you are to think that Spanish
drama has anything to offer. We have nothing to show
you : nothing but melodrama, the eternal melodrama
with its threadbare jests and ridiculous plot."

" What about Benavente ? " says the stranger timidly.

" Benavente is written out," answers the critic. " Blot
out everything except the early satiric plays and *The Bonds
of Interest.* Besides, Benavente does not understand the
psychology of women : his heroines are all boys disguised
as girls, like the page model of Leonardo da Vinci in his
play *The Smile of la Gioconda."*

It is useless for the stranger to contradict such august
opinion, though he knows in his heart that such severity
is due to the sharp atmosphere of the *tertulia.* Another
member of the *tertulia* then whispers to him that the critic
has already subscribed to the public homage that is to
be given to Benavente in the Madrid bull-ring.

The days of the true theatrical *tertulia*, alas, seem to have departed since the death of María Guerrero, Spain's queen of the stage. When she and her husband, the Marquis Díaz de Mendoza, directed the *Teatro Español*, which performed in Madrid analogous functions to the *Comédie Française* in Paris, I used to take part regularly in the *tertulia* in the spacious green-room of the theatre. That green-room, with its ancient portraits of actors on the walls, was the rendezvous of playwrights. There Benavente would dart his latest epigram, Marquina would read his latest play and María herself would preside over the meeting.

One of the most intellectual *tertulias* in Spain takes place under the auspices of *La Revista de Occidente* and is presided over by the editor, José Ortega y Gasset. Originally it used to meet in the noisy café, *Granja el henar*, but Ortega y Gasset, being the most European mind in Spain, must have felt that the garrulous atmosphere of a Madrid café was unsuited to calm deliberations, and so the *tertulia* migrated to the editorial offices of the review, and now meets in a round room hung with grey curtains and illuminated by discreet lamps. The migration has changed the meeting from a *tertulia* into a *cénacle*, or, to be more precise, a symposium in which Ortega y Gasset plays the part of Socrates. I was intensely interested in the *tertulia* of this Spanish Socrates, because he has succeeded in doing for modern Spain what George Russell (AE) valiantly tried to do for modern Ireland with the *Irish Statesman*. Ortega y Gasset like the bearded philosopher AE has the great range of mind and the wide sympathy that attracts the young idealists as well as the old. Such men should be given palaces to dwell in by new-fledged governments, and they should be freed from all taxes, for they are the greatest benefactors of the State. Not only are they the interpreters of affairs in their own country but they are magnetic forces attracting the ideas of other countries. The *Revista de Occidente* has made the voices of thinkers such as Einstein, Spengler, Keyserling heard in Spain. It has welcomed Paul Valéry, Marcel Proust, James Joyce. The room with the grey curtains is perched in a watch-tower high above the dust and conflict of Madrid, where not a whiff of Grub Street poisons the clear air. Around the squat, thickset little man with the leonine head I see historians and philosophers as well as men of letters. The conversation may pass from the Decline of the West to Belmonte the *Torero* ; from *Los Borrachos* of Velázquez to Picasso's latest manner ; from a violent speech in the *Cortes* by Largo Caballero, the Spanish Lenin, to the question whether *serenos* or night-watchmen are a relic of feudalism ; but always the Master will draw together the scattered threads of the discourse and try to consider it *sub specie aeternitatis*.

As I descended the *Gran Vía* from Ortega y Gasset's *tertulia* I met Fernández Arbos walking slowly along the pavement as if he had the cares of the world upon his shoulders. Fernández Arbos, the celebrated conductor of the Madrid Symphony Orchestra, in addition to being a musical genius, is one of the best *raconteurs* in the city. He belongs to no *tertulia* because he is one in himself. " Why do you drawl with your feet so languidly, *maestro* ? " said I, shaking him by the hand.

" I have just returned," he replied, " from a musical tour in the United States, and I shall need some weeks of Guadarrama air before I recover from the flurry and bustle of modern musical life."

Arbos might be called the conductor of the vagabond band, for in the summer he wanders around Spain with his symphony orchestra after him like the Gypsy Duke Panuel with his tribe. Concerts are given in the small as well as the big towns and the spirit of classical music reaches the masses.

When I had left the worthy Arbos I wondered in my mind why I had met so few musicians at *tertulias*.   Music is the social art and yet musicians as a rule shun *tertulias*. Perhaps it is their revenge against conversation which so often disturbs their performances.   I could imagine the sensitive personality of Manuel de Falla, Spain's greatest composer, shuddering with torture at the coarse, grating sounds of the noisy café meeting.   While the others shout, gesticulate, cough, grunt, expectorate, he lies back in his chair with an abstracted air, waiting for silence when he could begin a long, passionate harangue about music.   But silence is not to be found in modern Madrid. He must go back to the moonlit Gardens of the Musician at Granada.   One musician, however, I did meet, and it was at Ortega y Gasset's *tertulia*—Adolfo Salazar, the critic of *El Sol*, but then Salazar is poet and man of letters as well as musician.

The most picturesque *tertulia* in Madrid was certainly that of Ramón María del Valle Inclán, prince of literary dandies and Galician troubadour of the twentieth century.   At his literary birth the spirits of D'Annunzio, Eça de Queiroz and Barbey D'Aurévilly joined hands and saluted him with songs and clashing of cymbals. Upon his cradle they left an embroidered suit of Beau Brummell and the red waistcoat of Théophile Gautier. If this literary dandy had lived in England he would have shunned the rough and tumble of mankind and enclosed himself in a Pre-Raphaelite room with curtains drawn. Two slender candles would burn before a picture of Fra Angelico, and the poet would appear like a ghost through clouds of incense.   But Don Ramón lives in Spain and he has inherited a strong dose of the picaresque from Quevedo, aye, and from the arch-priest of Hita.   In appearance he is tall and slender, with pale, cadaverous face and huge, tortoiseshell-rimmed spectacles which give him the look of a bird of prey. The bird-of-prey aspect is increased by his long, fluffy, grey beard, which falls half-way to his waist, and his funereal black cape, which loosely envelops his emaciated body.

"How did he lose his left arm?" said I in a whisper to one of the satellites who sat beside me in the café.

"Many," he replied, "have said that it was lost in a glorious battle worthy of the days of Cervantes the one-armed hero of Lepanto. In point of fact it was the result of a duel which the poet had with the critic, Manuel Bueno."

Don Ramón speaks in a lisping voice that hypnotizes his listeners, for in it they hear echoes of long-lost refrains. Every word drops into the void like a crystalline note of music. The rise and fall of his veiled tones made me think of shanachies and magicians who could charm away sickness and death by their silver speech. Every sentence was a melody, and the poet would pause every now and then to listen to the echoing cadence.

"He has the most vitriolic tongue in all Spain," said the satellite to me in a low voice, "but so witty is he that people prefer to be abused than praised by him. Over the most trivial subject he can erect a flaming palace of fantasy. His own early life, they say, must have been prosaic and uneventful for him to have created such a fantastic autobiography. He says that he is sprung from oriental princesses and has lived a life worthy of Benvenuto Cellini—first as lay brother in a Carthusian monastery, then as a soldier of fortune in Spanish America."

In the life of Madrid Don Ramón proudly affirms his independence. On one occasion I saw him in a theatre

create a big disturbance leading to his arrest and imprisonment, because the principal actress murdered her lines.
Before 1931 he was arrested for his revolutionary utter-
ances and cast again into gaol, but the authorities soon
let him out, for he made the prison into a huge *tertulia*.
He sat behind the bars, dressed in a gorgeous silk robe
with a brocaded, tasselled cap upon his head, and received
his countless admirers as if he had been Lorenzo the
Magnificent.

Meanwhile the poet's dreamy voice flowed on like a
purling stream through a wooded glen in Galicia. The
tables near by were crowded with devotees. Every few
minutes journalists would slip in quietly from the *Cortes*
near by, and hand the poet slips of paper containing the
latest political gossip. He was like an emperor receiving
the homage of his subjects.

\*       \*       \*       \*       \*

The day after my visit to the *tertulias* I ascended to the
pinnacles of Madrid, where stands the *Residencia de Estu-
diantes*. The *Residencia* rises from a plateau, with clear,
uninterrupted view of the Sierra. When I had mounted
the hill I halted on the terrace in front of the buildings.
Down in the city the heat was suffocating, but up here
the air was cool and bracing. No place in all Madrid
is so sun-bathed as this terrace of the *Residencia*, and I
mentally labelled it the " Upper Gate of the Sun." Up
here the Spanish idealists have created a small, select
centre of learning. Here are library, laboratories and
lecture-halls. Students who live in this delightful spot
possess all the advantages of the residential university
life as we understand it in British countries. The rooms
are severe in their simplicity like a monastic cell, but they
look on to gardens. There is a spirit of happy fellow-
ship, for students and professors dine together in hall
and gather together in open-air *tertulias* under the trees,

for all the world as if they had been living in the Renaissance with Castiglione.

The Director of this modern Urbino is Alberto Jiménez
Fraud, follower of the ideals of Francisco Giner de los
Ríos, and one who fights for the spirit of true humanism
in modern Spanish University education. Whenever I
think of Alberto Jiménez and his charming, cultured wife,
Doña Natalia, I remember many happy days spent in that
house in *calle Pinar*. What a joy it was to hear Doña
Natalia's father, the scholar Manuel Cossío—author of
the epoch-making life of El Greco—converse about
Spain's popular art. Whether the theme of discussion
was a piece of embroidery of the *Charros* from Salamanca's region, a *tonada* from Murcia or a green and blue
pottery vase from Paterna, Don Manuel would always
make us see it as a significant symbol of Spain's greatness.
The house is a rendezvous of intellectuals from other
countries, for Don Alberto has been tireless in his efforts
to bring the humanists of Europe to the *Residencia*.

It is, however, as a meeting-place of Spanish humanists
that the *Residencia* is supremely important in Spain.
Spanish scholars stand high to-day, because they possess
European minds. In addition to being proudly conscious of their nationality, they absorb what is best in
the humanism of other countries. From France they
welcome clear, logical exposition and concision of style;
from Germany methodical thoroughness; from Italy
imaginative criticism. The *Centro de Estudios Históricos*
which grew out of the same movement as the *Residencia*
is a veritable clearing-house for European ideas of
scholarship, owing to such men as Ramón Menéndez
Pidal, king of Spanish scholars and successor to the
throne occupied in a former age by Menéndez y Pelayo,
and Américo Castro the great interpreter of Cervantes
and Lope de Vega.

Through the efforts of the indefatigable enthusiast, José Castillejo, the ideals of the humanists have penetrated into the schools of the country as well as the universities, but the fight has been an uphill one in a country that still needs the missionary to spread the gospel of education. Credit therefore must be given to the Government of the Republic for its attempts to cope with the problem of education in the backward rural parts of the country. In 1931 a *Patronato de Misiones Pedagójicas* was founded to undertake this task of general culture. The methods employed by the educational missionaries are a reminder that Spain has always welcomed the nomad. The teachers, in order to educate the country folk, have to become wandering scholars and goliards like their ancestors in the Middle Ages. In addition to wandering schools there are wandering theatres, museums and cinemas. One day at the entrance to a village I saw a lumbering waggon arrive full of players dressed in bright costumes. I rubbed my eyes, thinking that I had been transported back to the sixteenth century, for there upon the miniature stage were the characters of Cervantes' play, *The Mayors of Daganzo*. In this way the humanists of Spain are gradually spreading the light of civilization among the people. In spite of fierce political upheavals this calm, unselfish work will not go unrewarded. In time it will produce in the whole country a broader spirit of tolerance and mutual co-operation, which will combine the warring regions into one unified country.

In recent years I have been struck by the influx of English customs into cultivated Spain, due to the harmonious relations that exist between intellectual London and Madrid. For many years this spirit of mutual comprehension was nobly fostered by the Marquis Merry del Val. To-day the spirit of humanistic Spain enriches

English life mainly through the efforts of three outstanding Spanish personalities—Antonio Pastor, Ramón Pérez de Ayala and the Duke of Alba. Dr. Antonio Pastor, Cervantes professor in the University of London, has not only interpreted for England the humanism of Spain, which combines the chivalrous spirit of a Garcilaso de la Vega with the measure and taste of a Gracián, but he has balanced it with English humanism. Ramón Pérez de Ayala, one of modern Spain's greatest writers, becomes at the Court of Saint James far more than mere ambassador : he is a spiritual envoy sent by the countless literary artists who have created a Spanish tradition in the realms of the imagination. Finally we come to the Duke of Berwick and Alba, whose very name symbolizes the closest connection between Spain and Great Britain. No name personifies more completely the doctrine of *Nobleza* which runs through all Spanish history from the earliest times. In the Duke of Alba's palace at Madrid there is one room sacred to the memory of the iron duke his ancestor, whose name was the theme of sixteenth-century chivalry. In one corner of the room stands the coat of mail belonging to the great warrior. Beside it from an easel hangs the famous portrait by Titian, showing the hero in the vigour of his age, dressed in black armour damascened with gold. His pale face, long, thin beard and prominent nose are grim reminders of his power, and his eyes pierce right through me. Such was the great Duke of Alba, but divine Providence refused to transmit to posterity so severe and relentless an image. She preferred to let mankind remember the hero of Garcilaso's eclogue, who was Spain's Maecenas —friend and companion of poets. To-day the bearer of this famous name is academician, historian as well as lover of the arts. For many years he has devoted himself to the task of making the culture of Spain known to other countries.　He might describe himself in the words of Prince Albert, the hero of Benavente's play, *The School for Princesses* : " My philosophy in life is very simple —to accept my position in life with all its obligations, to realize, that only by fulfilling them completely, of my own free will, can I be happy, for in this way, and in this way only, can we in our unreal station become the equals of other men who have not been born princes."

# EPILOGUE

## PAGES FROM THE END OF A DIARY

"Mi venga la morte di Spagna."

THE dark shadow of the Escorial fell across my path and put an end to my Spanish journey. If I had followed my original intention and set out for the plains of La Mancha I should have avoided disaster. But it was my destiny to turn aside from my journey from North to South in order to visit Spain's grey, sombre palace of Death. "I see it in the tarots," said Dojiá the fortune-teller. "You're lying stiff on a slab, as pale as a ghost and there's blood flowing from your mouth. You'll fall in a fit near a tomb, so they won't have to carry you far."

I arrived at the Escorial in the early morning after a jolty journey on a cart from the village of Las Rozas. In the grey dawn the country looked as harsh and barren as one of El Greco's later vision pictures : the fields were so parched and stony that I murmured to myself the proverb of Avila—*cantos y santos* ("stones and saints "). In the distance the massive palace began to rise out of its enveloping grey mountains like a giant from slumber. Here and there on each side of the road were boulders twisted into every imaginable shape, like writhing monsters. In one place I came across a tribe of nomad Gypsies resting in the recesses of the rocks, with their ragged children creeping in and out of the cracks like lizards. I had intended to accomplish the journey from Madrid to the Escorial on foot, but I fell ill at Las Rozas and had to " hitch hike " the rest of the way.

At first I suffered from violent dyspepsia and I thought that my symptoms were the natural result of a rough meal the previous day with my Gypsy friends in the *barrio de Tetuan*.

" I'm poisoned by *mulo mas* (meat killed by the hand of God)," said I to my inner self.

" No," replied my inner self sharply ; " it is not mere dyspepsia, for you're chilly and there's an icy current down your back."

" Then," said I, " it must be the wind of Madrid which may kill a man though its blast is not strong enough to put out a candle. Alas, I remember the warning of my friend the blind fiddler."

" It's an ill wind that blows nobody any good," said my inner self ; " you've a throbbing fever, there are fiery circles before your eyes and your head is buzzing like a hive of bees."

" Surely," cried I, " it is the result of the curse which La Higuera put upon me."

At last the carter deposited me in the town of the Escorial, which with its shady avenues and green trees forms a delightful oasis in the midst of the harsh, Castilian landscape—a resting-place where the weary wanderer may lull himself to sleep to the sound of birds and murmuring fountains. I was feeling so ill that I had no eyes for any beauty. I hardly remember how I ever reached the monastery, for my legs were tottering so that I could only drag myself along by the aid of my stick : my eyes refused to stay open, and yet when I closed them, the circles of fire expanded and contracted, giving me a sickening sensation of vertigo. I passed through the main entrance of the monastery under the statue of Saint Laurence and his gridiron, through the courtyard of the kings and the cloisters into the church. Whether it was the sinister influence of the Escorial I know not, but my suffering increased tenfold the moment that I entered its grim portals. "It is not the curse of La Higuera," said I to myself, "nor the wind of Madrid which has withered me, but the sinister influence of this gloomy palace. I was as fit as a fiddle until I started on my journey to this abode of death." I followed my guide down the marble staircase to the little vault beneath the high altar. In this Pantheon are niches in which were placed the coffins of the kings and queens. The ghost of the mournful King Philip has haunted this vault to welcome each reigning monarch to the empty sarcophagus which would be his eternal resting-place. Above the vault is the high altar where the priest will say for ever Masses for the souls of the kings below, and near by is the suite of gloomy rooms, where the greatest of Spanish kings while lying on his death-bed could gaze at the lamp burning before the Blessed Sacrament in the church. The guide rambled on in a droning voice, telling me of Philip's agony in that cell: how his body became a mass of suppurating sores and liquefied into decay, but his spirit to the end soared triumphant over agonizing suffering. He told us of the crucifix of the Emperor his father which Philip kept for ever before his eyes and the blood-stained discipline with which he used to flog himself in penance. Gradually the droning voice became fainter in my ears and the light faded: I could only smell in my nostrils the damp, musty smell of the vault and the buzzing in my ears became louder and louder. I tried to rush away from my guide, but my feet seemed to be nailed to the ground.

Just outside the church I was seized with a sudden
swift spasm of giddiness—the earth swam around me
and I sank to the ground. . . .

(Ten days later.)

I have been lying in bed in my cell in the Residencia
ever since the day when I collapsed outside the church
in the Escorial. Years seem to have passed since I
wandered through Old Castile. Raging fever and
racking cough have so wasted away my strength that
I despair of ever continuing my journey. From my
bed I can see my fiddle-case on a shelf in the corner
and my rucksack and stick hang from the three-pronged
hat-rack on the wall. When shall I ever use them
again ? Magdalena the black-haired, rosy-faced house-
maid, whose radiant smile is my one solace, handed
me the fiddle this morning, telling me to sit up in bed
and play a tune. When I took the instrument in my
hands I found two strings broken. Surely they must
have snapped out of sympathy for the minstrel who has
been stricken down. I was so weak that I could hardly
draw the bow across the two remaining strings. Though
my body feels as if it was encased in a lead coffin, my
head is like a transparent balloon, bobbing, straining
and tugging at the end of a stout rope. My body lies
inert, but my mind refuses to be imprisoned and dashes
recklessly here and there.

During the ten days I have been lying in this lonely
cell, I have wandered backwards and forwards over
my Spanish journey scores of times. I start from the
beginning and call up in turn the personalities I have
met, setting each one into relationship with the other.
It is a fascinating mental exercise to attempt to discover
a semblance of unity in all the various types of Spaniard.
In wandering through Castile I found to my surprise

that the study of the mediæval heroes as reflected
through epic poems and ballads helped me more than
any modern guide-books, for there is the element of
indestructibility in the Spanish character. In many
villages I met aged patriarchs, whose characters might
be described in terms of the Cid campeador—proud,
chivalrous, loyal, a loving father and faithful husband.
To possess these qualities the hero need not have sprung
from dukedom or marquisate : even my friend Pedro
de Castellón, the Gypsy chief, had a proud dignity which
many an earl might envy. There is a hard, ascetic
element in this Castilian *nobleza* which shows itself all
through the life of those men. None but a race of
ascetics would remain satisfied with existence in those
tiny villages, where *posada*, tavern and threshing-floor
have not changed in the slightest degree since the days
of Cervantes.

The prototype of Spanish *nobleza* is the patriarchal
Castilian living in his village the same isolated life as
the Cid's father did in his castle on the River Ubierna
in the eleventh century. He is the progenitor of four
different, contrasting types, who to a greater or lesser
degree possess the sterling qualities of their ancient
sire.

First of all we have the knight who rides out into
battle against the Moors, like the Cid campeador, or
against foe in foreign lands, like the great Duke of Alba.
The knight may fight for his king in Spain itself or else
he may become a *conquistador* and set out to conquer
lands for the king in the New World.

The second type is the spiritual knight, whose life
is spent in the cloister in God's service. Such is my
friend Fray Justo Pérez de Urbel, praying in his cell at
Santo Domingo de Silos. Call such a knight a mystic
if you will, but remember that in Spain the mystic

follows Saint Teresa, one of the most practical idealists who ever lived.

The third type is Don Juan the gallant. Like his brothers he was born a knight, but in him there is no humility to balance his arrogance. I remember how the patriarchal marquis Don Gonzalo rebuked me for my conception of Don Juan, saying : " You are wrong to consider Don Juan Tenorio as the mere gallant, who wanders through the world collecting the scalps of all the maidens who cross his path. Remember the original Don Juan legend. An arrogant youth finds a skull in his path and kicks it aside, mocking it and asking it to dine with him. The skull, to the amazement of all, accepts the invitation and the youth's overweening pride is punished with death." Don Juan at his birth inherited some of the *nobleza* of his ancient sire, but he grew up wilful, and he thought that the flesh was greater than the spirit. Whenever his elder brothers rebuked him and pointed to the evil consequences of his sinful life he would reply haughtily : " *qué largo me fiáis !* the day of doom is a long way off, brothers : I am young and there are still many worldly joys I have not tasted. When I am old and long in the tooth it will be time for me to call for my prayer book and my rosary beads."

The fourth type is Lázaro Guzmán Alonso Esteban, the *pícaro*. He was given four names, because he was the youngest of the family and his old father believed that he would transmit the noblest names of Spain to a numerous progeny. He was the white-headed boy of the family, hence he was always called by the diminutives Lazarillo or Estebanillo. But Lazarillo was an old man's son : he grew up untended and uncared for, like a weed in a deserted path. His brothers were far away, so he sought the company of rogues and vagabonds. The mother was dead, the old father was sinking into dotage, the castle was falling into rack and ruin. Lazarillo then began to roam through the country, for he had in his blood the craze for roving no less than his brothers. I met him often on my journey under various names. He was always the same hungry, ragged rascal with bright eyes, jaunty manner and that remnant of dignity and *nobleza* which he had inherited at birth.

In imagination I played the bountiful Maecenas and I gave a great banquet in the *plaza* of Sepúlveda in honour of the hero, the mystic, the gallant and the rogue of Spain. At the head of the long, oaken table I placed the two patriarchs, the marquis Don Gonzalo and Miguel de Unamuno. On each side of them I seated the Duke of Alba and the Abbot of Silos. A little farther down the table I placed Mariano the communist, Pedro de Castellón the Gypsy, Juanito the *picador* and Tomasito the *pícaro* from Segovia. The health of Spain was pledged in silver goblets, and Lucas the guitarist acted as the *juglar* for the company. As a concession to Gypsy custom I allowed the Romany chals present to depart with the silver drinking vessels at the end of the banquet.

Such were my meditations in the early part of the day when my brain was unclouded, but at the hour of dusk a strange transformation would take place. The familiar objects around my room would gradually change into queer shapes as though by magic. The hat-rack on the opposite wall with its three prongs became three greyhounds rampant; the solitary electric light hanging by a wire from the ceiling began to oscillate to and fro and the bulb became a tiny, screwed-up face gazing at me with two pin-prick eyes. In the dim light the room expanded into a huge, shadowy hall, illuminated by pink-shaded lights. Around this hall there were many niches covered over with curtains of transparent gauze. To my amazement this strange, pink room contracted and expanded in the most disconcerting manner. At one moment it was a vast, illuminated auditorium and I would wander around, examining the niches. In one I saw Agustina and her brother, Ramón el Andaluz; in another I saw Dolores Nuñez lying dead at the foot of a statue of the Blessed Virgin; in a third Tomasito and the dwarf were holding up the witch, La Higuera, who had her black cat perched on her shoulder. Through the transparent gauze curtains I could just see the outline of those familiar figures, but when I tried to talk to them, the pink lights would go out and the room would suddenly contract and change back to my own tiny cell.

Gradually in my hallucination I began to distinguish voices far away. I heard my name called. The voices approached nearer and nearer and I recognized them as belonging to my family. First of all I heard my mother's voice, then the voices of my sisters and various friends. In the next room I heard someone play Chopin's Study in A flat—a piece which possesses many ancient memories for me. All of a sudden there was a sound of weeping, and I heard a woman say, " His fair-haired wife has gone away—away." The word " away " was taken up by countless voices and repeated in a buzzing monotone. The voices incessantly whispering in my ear drove me to distraction. I rushed around the room trying to find a way out, but in vain. I must get away—I must get away and save my home from disaster. My flurry and excitement brought on a spasm of asthma, which awoke me temporarily from my hallucination to reality, but whenever my wheezing would die down and a slight drowsiness creep over me, I would find myself back again in the sinister, pink-lit room with its whispering voices.

Such was my experience night after night, but one morning, to my horror, the visions did not fade away with the rising sun. "It is not a dream," I cried; "I hear the voices in the next room—why, I can even shout to them." I rushed to the window and called out the name of the friend whose voice I heard, but nobody answered. Two students of the *Residencia* walking in the gardens below my room looked up at me with amazement.

When the doctor came, he found me sitting on the bed fully dressed and ready to depart. He ordered me back to bed, but as soon as his back was turned I rushed downstairs and over to Don Alberto's office.

Don Alberto was closeted with the Conde de Palomares and some other members of the Board of the *Residencia*. I burst into the sanctum and shouted out : " My relations are here, Don Alberto : I must leave at once with them. I have bad news from home." To my surprise and indignation Don Alberto paid no heed to my story but led me into another room and told me to rest there a while.

" Now that he has gone," said I to myself, " I shall escape." When I opened the door I saw a man standing on guard in the passage to prevent me escaping. At last a doctor came with a hypodermic needle in his hand. . . .

When I awoke to sanity ten days later I vowed that my recovery was solely due to the magic ministrations of " the white sisters " as I affectionately called my two nurses.

" We were afraid at first to take you into the nursing-home," said Sister Lewis, "for some said that you were a mental case."

"What nonsense!" interrupted Sister Hart in her breezy Irish way; "anyone could see that you were simply delirious owing to double pneumonia."

"I was mad, sisters," said I, "but your bewitching influence has driven away all the demons. Sister Lewis, I want to go mad again if only to have the opportunity of telling all my sorrows to you in the silent watches of the night and feel your cool white hands soothing my feverish forehead. Then in the daytime Sister Hart will continue your magic spell and talk to me of Ireland which seems so far away."

One day as I was telling her about my wife at home and my two fair-haired children, Sister Lewis entered the room saying, "There is a telephone message for you."

"Who wants to telephone to me?" said I.

"It is a trunk call from Dublin."

With the aid of the two sisters I staggered to the telephone, and in the midst of a confused babel of English, French and Spanish, I heard the clear voice of my dear wife speaking from our home. Thus does the modern world abolish the long-drawn-out and agonizing return home of Ulysses the wanderer. Once I had heard my wife's voice, I knew that I was already at home. The day I left Madrid was grey and cloudy; the wind swept down the *paseo de la Castellana*, blowing the withered leaves in all directions. Before I left the nursing-home I put the two missing strings on my fiddle and played for the "white sisters" the minstrel's farewell to wandering.

As I entered the garden gate of my home I murmured to myself the words of Homer: "Even as when the sight of land is welcome to swimmers, whose well-wrought ship Poseidon hath smitten on the deep, all driven with the wind and swelling waves, and gladly have they set foot on land and fled an evil end; so welcome to me was the sight of my lady, and her white arms would never quite leave hold of my neck. . . ."

# A WANDERER'S LIBRARY
## SHORT BIBLIOGRAPHY

IN the following list of books I have limited myself to those which helped me to write the account of my journey through the North of Spain. During my months of wandering I had no opportunities of reading or study, for a poor minstrel has few thoughts beyond his bread-earning tune and the *porrón* of red Riojan wine. On my return from Spain it was a joy to take down from my bookshelves the volumes that had given me in the past many hours of pleasure and profit. It was like meeting old friends of mature experience, who would correct my impressions and enable me to balance my mind. Late in the evening after my return home, when I had divested myself of my rough vagabond clothes, I put on a purple silk dressing-gown and sat in an arm-chair in my library. My son and daughter took down the books from the shelves and piled them around me. I felt like Machiavelli, who, after playing chuck-halfpenny with the village clodhoppers, used to return pensively to his house at dusk. At the door of his library he would take off his muddy, rustic garments and put on regal raiment before entering, as he said, the society of the ancients.

To all the books that are piled around me, I owe a debt of gratitude for the help they have given me.

### THE SPIRIT OF SPAIN

Before I set out on my Spanish journey I read the books of that *chevalier sans peur et sans reproche*—R. B. Cunninghame Graham— one of the greatest interpreters of the Spanish spirit in the world. His biographies of the *conquistadores* are thrilling reminders of Spain's adventurous knights, and they are indispensable to the wanderer to-day, who needs to remember that Don Quixote's horizon was not bounded by La Mancha. After reading of Jiménez de Quesada, the conqueror of New Granada, and Pedro de Valdivia, the conqueror of Chile, I understood the strong racial spirit of Spain in the world.

*The Idea of Robinson Crusoe*, by A. Pastor, London, 1930. A profound study of the theme of adventure as a symbol of Spain. It should be read in conjunction with the same author's essay on the chivalry of Spain in *Chivalry*, ed. by E. Prestage, London, 1928.

*The Soul of Spain*, by Havelock Ellis, London, 1908. One of the most valuable interpretations of Spain, especially in its chapters on "the Spanish people," "women" and "art of Spain."

*The Tragic Sense of Life*, by M. de Unamuno, London, 1921. This is the translation by J. E. Crawford Flitch, of *El Sentimiento Trágico de la Vida*, Unamuno's greatest book. Some of Unamuno's most important work is contained in the seven volumes of essays (1916–19) and in the *Life of Don Quixote and Sancho* (1905). The wanderer should set as a pendant to Unamuno's essays and soliloquies the *Idearium Español*, by Angel Ganivet, Madrid, 1896.

*Psicología del Pueblo Español*, by R. Altamira, Barcelona, 1917. Account of Spanish personality as reflected in the history of the country.

*Meditaciones del Quijote*, by José Ortega y Gasset, Madrid, 1914. Taking Cervantes and Don Quixote as symbols, the author explores the problems of the Spanish spirit and draws comparisons with other nations.

*España Invertebrada*, by José Ortega y Gasset, Madrid, 1925. A prophetic book foreshadowing the events of 1931. Invaluable as a clear exposition of the problems of regionalism versus centralized government.

*Fray Luis de León*, by Aubrey Bell, Oxford, 1925. A magnificent study of the noblest figure of the Renaissance in Spain, who was poet, mystic and scholar.

*Studies of the Spanish Mystics*, Vol. I, by E. Allison Peers, London, 1927. Valuable essays on St. Ignatius de Loyola, St. Teresa, St. John of the Cross, and other mystics.

*The Genius of Spain*, by Salvador de Madariaga, Oxford, 1923. Excellent essay on Spain and studies of modern writers such as Unamuno, Baroja, Ramón del Valle Inclán.

*Englishmen, Frenchmen, Spaniards*, by Salvador de Madariaga, Oxford, 1928.

*A Picture of Modern Spain*, by J. B. Trend, London, 1921. Attractive account of modern writers, theatre and music.

*The Origins of Modern Spain*, by J. B. Trend, Cambridge, 1934. Study of Francisco Giner, Sanz del Río and other thinkers, who have profoundly influenced modern Spain.

*Romanesque Sculpture of the Pilgrimage Roads*, 10 vols., by Kingsley Porter, Boston, 1923. A monumental work by the greatest authority on Romanesque art in Europe. As a monk said to me, his spirit will haunt the cloister at Santo Domingo de Silos for ever.

*El Greco*, by Manuel B. Cossío, Madrid, 1908.

## BASQUE

*A Book of the Basques*, by Rodney Gallop, London, 1930. This is the best book ever written on the Basques and invaluable for the wanderer among the Spanish as well as the French divisions of that mysterious race. The author studies the history, language, customs, and devotes fascinating chapters to folk music, dance and witchcraft.

*Ramuntcho*, by Pierre Loti, gives a beautiful description of Basque scenery, but I prefer to read of the Spanish Basques in the novels of Pío Baroja, especially in *Zalacaín el aventurero* (1909), a book that every wanderer through Guipúzcoa should put in his knapsack.

*La Casa de Aizgorri* (1900), and *El Mayorazgo de Labraz* (1903) describe the life of a Basque town with its struggle between industrial and agricultural life; in *La Leyenda de Jaun de Alzate* (1922), the author returns again to the scenes of *Zalacaín el aventurero*.

## CASTILIAN

*Poesiá Juglaresca y Juglares*, by Ramón Menéndez Pidal, Madrid, 1924. A most interesting account of the *Juglares* and their methods of performance. It was the only book I carried with me in my rucksack. To-day in Castile a minstrel may learn with profit many of the tricks practised by Marcabrú, La Balteira, Villasandino and their merry crew in the Middle Ages in order to secure bed, food, wine and welcome.

*La España del Cid*, 2 vols., by Ramón Menéndez Pidal, Madrid, 1929. This book, which has been translated by Harold Sunderland under the title, *The Cid and his Spain* (London, 1934), is a monumental account of the life of Spain's national hero and the Spain of his time. It is Menéndez Pidal's greatest book.

*La Leyenda de los Infantes de Lara*, by Ramón Menéndez Pidal, Madrid, 1934. This is the revised and augmented edition of the author's first work (1896). In accordance with his literary and scientific method, he has studied the story from the beginning, following it through the centuries in its various transformations from epic poem into chronicle, ballads, dramas down to modern days. By studying the story in such a way, the author has succeeded in explaining the process of evolution of literature.

*The Way of Saint James*, 3 vols., by Georgiana G. King, New York and London, 1920. A most imaginative and scholarly work, written by an enthusiastic wanderer. Not only has the author studied the historical records and artistic monuments but she has incorporated in her book much of the popular lore of the North of Spain.

*Ramón de la Cruz*, by E. Cotarelo y Mori, Madrid, 1899. The wanderer in Madrid would do well to read this book written by the foremost authority on the Spanish Drama. Ramón de la Cruz was the social historian of eighteenth-century Madrid in his *sainetes* and in this book the author describes the background to the dramatist's plays. It should be set as a pendant to Ramón Gómez de la Serna's modern books on the *Puerta del Sol* and *Rastro*.

### TRAVEL BOOKS

*The Bible in Spain*, by George Borrow, London, 1843.
*Gatherings from Spain*, by Richard Ford, London, 1846.
*Voyage en Espagne*, by Théophile Gautier, Paris, 1843.

Those three books do not grow old, for age mellows them, and they linger in the traveller's mind as a fragrant memory. *The Bible in Spain* still makes the greatest appeal to the true wanderer, who longs for hardship, provided that he can meet with adventure at every turn of the road. Anybody with pretensions to be a Romany rye will cast away all other books and pack George Borrow in his rucksack.

In my travels through Castile, however, I found Richard Ford a more profitable companion than Don Jorge. The information he gives concerning *posadas*, mules and muleteers is still of service to the inquisitive traveller in the small Castilian *pueblos*.

Gautier inherited a good share of the fantasy that makes the

*Voyage D'Espagne* of La Comtesse D'Aulnoy (1679) such attractive reading. He preached the gospel of picturesque Spain, but with his tongue in his cheek. And yet all his imitators ever since have taken him seriously and created an exaggerated, romantic Spain.

Pierre Louÿs wrote *La Femme et le Pantin* ; Maurice Barrès wrote *Du Sang, de la Volupté, de la Mort* ; René Schwob wrote *Profondeurs de l'Espagne* ; all of them eager to describe scenes of ecstasy, blood, sacrifice. Henri de Montherlant in *Les Bestiaires* even formulated a religion of pan-taurism, linking up the bull-fight with the worship of Mithras. Truly a reaction was needed and this came with the publication of *Unromantic Spain*, by Mario Praz, London, 1929. Mario Praz is an Italian and feels a slight sense of arrogant superiority in dealing with Spain, but some of his criticisms against the false Spain which has become " the Davos of the sexually obsessed intellectuals " deserve consideration.

The truest and most sympathetic guide for the modern wanderer through Castile is José Martínez Ruiz, whose pseudonym is Azorín. Azorín has the keen eyes of the east-coast Spaniard born upon the shores of the Mediterranean, but he has been absorbed by Castile. He is an ideal companion for the wanderer, because he is the most silent individual in Spain's literary Walhalla : he does not shout his opinions, but he suggests and outlines, so that I may fill in the picture. In *Castilla* and *los Pueblos* he sketches in fragments the towns, villages, *posadas* of the country. He enables me to remember the landscape, the lonely cypress trees, even the moving clouds in the sunset. In *Don Juan* he paints for me an unforgettable picture of life in a tiny cathedral town. Azorín is the ideal companion for the slow-moving, philosophical traveller.

## The Picaresque and Gypsy Journey

To enjoy the picaresque life in Spain the wanderer must first have absorbed the maxims of the Archpriest of Hita Juan Ruiz—the greatest writer before Cervantes. *El Libro de Buen Amor* (1343) is the Golden Treasury of the vagabonds. With the refrains of the Archpriest ringing in his ears and a few golden sentences from *La Celestina* (1499) as well, the wanderer should turn his attention to some of the picaresque novels. He would, however, do well to consider them in the following order :

*Lazarillo de Tormes* (1554) : the father of all *pícaros*. A hungry, cynical, bitter rogue.

*Guzmán de Alfarache*, by Mateo Aleman (1599) : the archmentor and law-giver of rogues.

*La Pícara Justina*, by Francisco de Ubeda (1605) : the queen of all Spanish rogues and coiner of proverbs.

*Marcos de Obregón*, by Vicente Espinel (1618) : a rogue more sinned against than sinning. The most respectable of the *pícaros*.

*El Buscón*, by Quevedo (1626). Don Pablos the sharper—anti-hero of Segovia—the greatest rogue of all, with the exception of Lazarillo.

*Alonso Mozo de Muchos Amos*, by Jerónimo de Alcalá (1624–6). The most instructive novel for the Romany rye, because it gives the completest account of Gypsy life and customs. Famous among Gypsy enthusiasts for its description of the *Jonjanó Baró* (Great Trick).

*Estebanillo González* (1646). The only Falstaffian *pícaro*. A good-humoured, cowardly glutton.

*Romances do Germanía*, by Juan Hidalgo, Madrid, 1779. The volume includes some of the most characteristic thieves' ballads by Juan Hidalgo and Quevedo, with a discourse by Dr. Sancho Moncada of Toledo on the expulsion of the Gypsies. There is also a most useful vocabulary of *Germanía* at the end.


*Romances of Roguery*, by F. W. Chandler, New York, 1899. The best guide to the picaresque novels ever written. It is a treasure-house of quaint knowledge which should be visited by the vagabond to-day.

*The Zincali ; or an Account of the Gypsies of Spain*, by George Borrow, London, 1841. Still the classical work on the *Gitanos*.

*Hampa* (Antropología Picaresca), 2 vols., by R. Salillas, Madrid, 1898. Gives the best account of the Gypsy mentality in Spain. Indispensable to the Romany rye, who mixes with nomadic Gypsies. Also studies deeply the question of *Germanía*.

*La Fascinación en España*, by R. Salillas, Madrid, 1905. Accounts of evil-eye, black magic, cures by quacks in the various regions of Spain.

*Historia y Costumbres de los Gitanos*, by F. M. Pabanó, Barcelona, 1915. Most useful to the Romany rye on account of its Gypsy anecdotes and proverbs.

*Cantos Populares Españoles*, by Rodríguez Marín, 5 vols., Sevilla, 1882. Indispensable to the wanderer, who should always have a *copla* on the tip of his tongue. He includes *coplas* from every region of Spain. Rodríguez Marín also wrote a study on the *refrán* to which I referred in Chapter XXX.

*Personajes, Personas y Personillas que corren por las tierras de Ambas Castillas*, 2 vols., by Luis Montoto y Rautenstrauch, Sevilla, 1921. A museum of proverbs, idioms and popular lore.

## CALÓ

Caló is one of the most corrupt of the Gypsy dialects, and there are very few to-day of the *Cales* who would satisfy Don Jorge el Inglés. The *Gitano* often uses *Caló* words, but mixed up with Spanish. When he wants to introduce a telling phrase he lapses into *Caló*. Among the *Canasteros* and other nomads the language still remains in its mutilated form as a symbol of the brotherhood.

The following dictionaries of *Caló*-Spanish may be recommended in addition to the vocabularies in the works of Borrow, Salillas and Pabanó:

*Origen, usos y Costumbres de los Jitanos, y Diccionario de su Dialecto*, by R. Campuzano, Madrid, 1848.

*Los Gitanos. Con un vocabulario Caló-Castellano*, by F. Sales Mayo (Quindalé), Madrid, 1869.

*Vocabulario del Dialecto Jitano*, by Augusto Jiménez, Sevilla, 1846.

*A Chipicallí*, by J. Tineo Rebolledo, Granada, 1900.

*Diccionario de Argot Español*, by Luis Besses, Barcelona (no date). Includes words from *Caló, Germanía*, and slang.

## MUSIC

To the following works on Spanish music I express my indebtedness:

*A Book of the Basques*, by Rodney Gallop, London, 1930.

*Música Popular Española*, by Chavarri, Barcelona, 1927.

*El Canto Popular Castellano*, by Gonzalo Castrillo, Palencia, 1925.

*Folklore de Burgos*, by F. Olmeda, Burgos, 1902.

*The Music of Spanish History*, by J. B. Trend, Oxford, 1925.

*Manuel de Falla*, by J. B. Trend, New York, 1929.

*L'Essor de la Musique Espagnole au XX^e siècle*, by Henri Collet, Paris, 1929.

In a further volume I hope to discuss the Gypsy music of Spain in the South at Jérez de la Frontera, Puerto de Santa María and Cádiz, the homes of the true *Cante Jondo* or Deep Song.

# NOTES

## VILLASANDINO

*Ch. I, p.* 5.—Villasandino was a celebrated *Juglar* of circ. 1380. Some of his poems may be read in the *Cancionero de Baena*. He was one of the most characteristic minstrels of the fourteenth century : he diced and gambled ; was a fervent devotee of the red wine of Illescas ; played *laúd*, lute and rebeck ; mocked himself as well as others ; claimed gifts of money, food, wine and raiment for his songs ; was full of pride in his minstrel's calling.

## ROMANY CHAL

*Ch. VI, p.* 57.—Throughout the book I have used the term Romany chal as a general synonym for Gypsy or Gitano. If I had been a purist I should have written it Romanichal on the analogy of the French *Romanichel*. I used the term Romany chal in order to suggest the verb *chalar* (to go, move, walk, wander) which is one of the fundamental words of *Caló*. The verb *chalar*, which is derived from the root *cha* (grass), describes in essence the nomadic activity of the Gypsy. From *chalar* springs *chalán* (horse-dealer), one of the most characteristic Gypsy professions in Spain. From the same root we get such words as : *chamullar* (to talk), *chanar* (to know), *chapescar* (to run), *chanaró* (intelligent), *chachipé* (truth), *chaval* (youth).

## EZQUIOGA

*Ch. XI, p.* 112.—According to the Madrid newspaper, *El Debate*, of September 20, 1933, the bishop of Vitoria, Dr. Mateo Mugica, published an edict on the 7th of that month banning the celebrations at Ezquioga. He forbade the people of his diocese to sing the hymn " Our Lady of Ezquioga " or to say the prayers which had been composed for the functions on the hill. Furthermore, those who had seen visions at Ezquioga were to be forbidden by their parish priests to go to pray there any more.

### GALICIAN MUSIC

*Ch. XVII.*—The whole question of Galician folk rhythms is studied in the article by Julián Ribera entitled " De Música y Métrica Gallegas " in Vol. 3 of the *Homage to R. Menéndez Pidal*, Madrid, 1925. Professor Ribera is author of the *La Música de las Cantigas*, Madrid, 1922, and the informative book, *La Música Árabe y su Influencia en la Española*, Madrid, 1927. See also the chapter on " Early Galician Music " in J. B. Trend's excellent book, *The Music of Spanish History to 1600*, Oxford, 1926.

### ROMANY JOTER

*Ch. XXIV, p.* 268.—The information concerning the " Romany Joter " comes from *English Gypsies*, by C. G. Leland, London, 1893, p. 227; the words " Romany Joter," however, merely mean " Romany Whistle." The Gypsy does not shout them; he whistles the two notes.

*Ch. XXIV, p.* 272.—For the swastika as a Gypsy sign see *Gli Zingari*, by A. Colocci, Torino, 1889, p. 182. A Gypsy would call it a *patrin* or *trushul*.

*Ch. XXIV, p.* 279.—For Gypsy divorce in the East of Europe and the *Manlaslo* see " Vehmgerichte bei den Bosnichen und Bulgarischen Wanderzigeunern " in *Ethnologische Mittheilungen aus Ungarn*, by H. Wlislocki, Budapest, 1894, Vol. III.

### THE SEVEN INFANTES OF SALAS

*Ch. XXIX, p.* 358.—In the chronicles of the Middle Ages the title " Seven Infantes of Salas " is always used. From the fifteenth century onwards the story was more often entitled " The Seven Infantes of Lara." The town of Salas was in the *alfoz* or district of Lara. See *La Leyenda de los Infantes de Lara*, by R. Menéndez Pidal, Madrid, 1934, p. 179.

# GLOSSARY

C. denotes *Caló* words.   G. denotes *Germanía* (thieves' slang).

| | | | | |
|---|---|---|---|---|
| *abejorro* | . . | buzzing sound. | *averí* . . . | other (C.). |
| *abelar* | . . | to have (C.). | *ayo* . . . | guardian. |
| *abierta* | . . | open. | | |
| *abogado* | . . | lawyer. | *bacalao* . . | cod. |
| *Adalí.* | . . | Madrid (C.). | *bahí* . . . | fortune (C.). |
| *aguardiente* | . | brandy. | *baile* . . . | dance. |
| *ajo* . . . | | garlic. | *bajirina* . . | basket (C.). |
| *ajogar (abogar)* | | to throttle. | *bajirinanós* . | basket-makers |
| *alalá* . . . | | Galician folk- | | (C.). |
| | | song. | *banderillas* . | darts (bull-fight- |
| *alcalde* | . . | mayor. | | ing). |
| *alcorabisar* | . | to win (C.). | *banderillas de* | explosive darts |
| *almejas* | . . | mussels. | *fuego* | for sluggish |
| *almacén* | . . | store-house. | | bull. |
| *alpargatas* | . | cord shoes for | *barajar* . . | to shuffle cards. |
| | | labourers. | *barbalote* . . | victim (G.). |
| *alto ome* | . . | noble man | *barrancas* . . | barriers. |
| | | (mediæval). | *barrio* . . | district. |
| *ama* . . . | | mother | *bayunca* . . | tavern (C.). |
| | | (Basque). | *beatas* . . | religious |
| *ambiente* | . . | surroundings. | | women. |
| *amigo* | . . | friend. | *bedoró* . . | boy (C.). |
| *ancha* . . . | | broad. | *bertsularis* . | improvisers |
| *anguín* | . . | honey (C.). | | (Basque). |
| *apagar* . . | | to quench. | *bi* . . . | without (C.). |
| *aquí* . . . | | eye (C.). | *boda* . . . | marriage. |
| *arriero* | . . | muleteer. | *boina* . . . | béret. |
| *arroz* . . . | | rice. | *borrachera* . | drunken bout. |
| *atreverse* | . . | to have the | *bostán (or* | |
| | | courage. | *postán)* . . | soft, loose (C.). |
| *auprar* . . | | to reach (C.). | *bota* . . . | wine-skin. |

475

*breje* . . . year (C.).
*bruja* . . . witch.
*buscar* . . to search.
*Busnó* . . non-Gypsy, gorgio (C.).
*buter* . . . more (C.).

*cabellos* . . hair.
*cada cual* . . each one.
*caja* . . . box.
*Calés* . . . Gypsies of Spain (C.).
*Caló* . . . language of the Gypsies of Spain.
*Calorró* . . Gypsy (C.).
*calle* . . . street.
*calamares* . squids.
*camelar* . . to love, wish (C.).
*camarero* . . waiter.
*camarones* . prawns.
*caña* . . . glass, Gypsy song.
*canasteros* . basket-makers.
*canciones* . songs.
*cante jondo* . deep song (C.). Traditional song form of Andalucía.
*capa* . . . cloak.
*capitalista* . apprentice in bull-fighting.
*cara* . . . face.
*carajo* . . phallic oath (male member).
*caramba* . . mild exclamation.
*Castellano a las* genuine Castilian.
*derechas*
*castizo* . . pure, genuine.

*castoreño* . . picador's hat.
*Castumba* . Castile (C.).
*cayicó* . . . to-morrow (C.).
*cazurros* . . street singers (mediæval).
*celos* . . . jealousy.
*cera* . . . wax, candle.
*cerrar* . . . to close.
*cocido* . . . stew.
*cogida* . . goring.
*coin* . . . who (C.).
*comedor* . . dining-room.
*condarí* . . beam (C.).
*contrabandistas* smugglers.
*copla* . . . folk poem.
*cornichas* . . baskets (C.).
*corrida* . . bull-fight.
*Cortes* . . Parliament.
*corto* . . . short.
*crayí* . . . king (C.).
*cura* . . . priest.
*curandera* . . quack.

*chabó* (or *cha-borró*) . . boy (C.).
*chachipirá* . . pure, undefiled (C.).
*chai* . . . girl (C.).
*chalán* . . . Gypsy horse-dealer (C.).
*chalar* . . . to go, wander (C.).
*chamuyar* (or *chamullar*) . to talk (C.).
*chandé* . . wise man (C.).
*chapescar* . . to run (C.).
*charlá* . . . mad (C.).
*charó* . . . heaven (C.).
*charros* . . peasants from Salamanca.
*chaval* . . youth (C.).

chavala . . . girl (C.).

chaví . . . charm made of jet (C.).

chibé baró . . festival (C.).

chico . . . youth.

chinga . . . quarrel (C.).

chiquitos . . small glasses of wine.

chirirí . . . mote (C.).

chispero . . witty fellow.

chivato . . informer, snooper (G.).

choré . . . mule (C.).

chorizo . . sausage.

chuanjañí . . witch (C.).

chulé . . . dollar (C.).

chulos . . cloak-wavers (bull-fight).

chuquel . . dog (C.).

churí . . . knife (C.).

churumbeles . children (C.).

chuyó (or chulló) . fat man (C.).

dai . . . mother (C.).

dañé . . . year (C.).

darabar . . to praise (C.).

Debla . . Virgin Mary (C.).

despreciar . to despise.

desqueró, desquerí . . his, her (C.).

dicló . . . white cloth (C.).

diñelar . . to give (C.).

dineló . . fool, mad (C.).

diquelar . . to see (C.).

dojí . . . sin, fault (C.).

dorreak . . houses (Basque).

drao . . poison (C.).

dui . . . two (C.).

duro . . . dollar (5 pesetas).

echar . . . to throw.

echar piropos . pay compliments to lady.

embozado . . with face covered.

empersó . . on (C.).

enjayé . . memory (C.).

enxemplos . fables.

era . . . threshing-floor.

eray . . . gentleman (rye) (C.).

er queré (el querer) . love.

esportillero . basket-carrier.

estaribel . . gaol (C.).

estribillo . . refrain.

faja . . . waist-band.

feria . . fair.

fiesta . . festival.

flachá . . ashes (C.).

Flamenco . . music made by those affecting Gypsy mannerisms.

fonda . . inn.

forastero . stranger.

fueros . . charters.

gachí . . . girl (C.) (used of Gypsies and non-Gypsies).

gambara . . attic (Basque).

garrucha . . rack.

gatera . . cat hole.

gentuza . . rabble.

Germanía . . language of the brotherhood, thieves' slang.

goles . . braying (C.).

golfos . . ragamuffins.

goró . . . colt (C.).

gorrón. . . sponger (G.).

grasnó. . . tight (C.).

grastí . . mare (C.).

grel (or gel) . ass (C.).

grito . . . shout.

guadalmecí . gilded leather.

guapo . . . fancy-man.

gusto . . . pleasure.

hacer migas . to break bread.

hatch the tan . to pitch tent (E. Gypsy).

hereje . . . heretic.

hijo . . . son.

huelga. . . strike.

huésped . . guest.

jaleo . . . noise, whoopee.

jamar . . to eat (C.).

jayeré . . . money (C.).

jetró . . . other (C.).

jindó . . . filthy (C.).

jojoi . . . rabbit (C.).

jonjanó baró . Great Trick (C.).

Juan de las calzas blancas juan of the white breeches, i.e. ghost.

Juan Español . the simple Spaniard.

Juanica la pelotera shrew.

judías . . beans.

juerga . . spree.

juglar . . minstrel, performer.

lacha . . . purity, virginity (C.).

lacha ye trupos corporeal chastity (C.).

lachó . . . good (C.).

lachés chibeses good day (C.).

largo . . . long.

lilipendó . . stupid, mad (C.).

longaniza . . blood puddings.

lumiasca . . prostitute (C.).

macho. . . refrain.

majo . . . dandy of Madrid folk (18th century).

maja . . . heroine of Madrid folk (18th century).

mal de ojo . . evil eye.

mala suerte . bad luck.

maldecir . . to curse.

manguelo . . petition (C.).

manlaslo . . secret tribunal (Gypsy E. Europe).

manicomio . madhouse.

manolo . . fancy-man (18th century).

mardito (maldito) accursed.

marimorena . row.

mariquita María dainty Mary.

matadero . . slaughter-yard.

matador . . bullfighter who kills the bull.

mechera . . one who steals with her legs (G.).

meclí . . . come, come! (excl.) (C.).

menda. . . I (C.).

mendigo . . beggar.

| | | |
|---|---|---|
| *meneo* . . | swaying motion of a dancer's hips. | |
| *merienda* . . | supper, snack. | |
| *migueletes* . . | Basque police. | |
| *mistó* . . . | good (C.). | |
| *mol* . . . | wine (C.). | |
| *monjas* . . | nuns. | |
| *morapio* . . | wine. | |
| *moreno* . . | dark. | |
| *morriña* . . | home-sickness. | |
| *mi venga la morte di Spagna* | Let my death come from Spain; for then it is sure to be long in coming. (Italian proverb, 16th century). | |
| *mozo* . . . | youth. | |
| *mul* . . . | mouth (C.). | |
| *muiñeira* . . | Galician dance. | |
| *mujerona* . . | big woman. | |
| *muleta* . . | red rag attached to stick used by matador. | |
| *mulo mas* . | dead meat (Gypsy). | |
| *ná (nada)* . . | nothing. | |
| *navaja* . . | knife. | |
| *niña* . . . | maiden. | |
| *nobleza* . . | racial sense of nobility. | |
| *novio* . . . | fiancé. | |
| *odoroso* . . | jealous (C.). | |
| *hacer ojos blancos* | give the glad eye. | |
| *olacerar* . . | to ride (C.). | |

| | | |
|---|---|---|
| *olajai* . . . | curse (C.). | |
| *on* . . . | in (C.). | |
| *ortrica* . . | crupper strap (C.). | |
| *padrino* . . | godfather. | |
| *pagar* . . . | to pay. | |
| *paillo* . . | non-Gypsy (C.). | |
| *pajabar* . . | to play instrument (C.). | |
| *paloma* . . | whore, moll(G.). | |
| *pañuelo* . . | handkerchief. | |
| *parador* . . | inn. | |
| *parchandrá* . | carnival (C.). | |
| *pare* . . . | father (Sicilian). | |
| *parné* . . . | money (C.). | |
| *pasar bocatas* | be hungry (C.). | |
| *patillas* . . | side-whiskers. | |
| *pelota* . . | Basque ball game. | |
| *penar* . . . | to tell (C.). | |
| *peón caminero* . | road-mender. | |
| *pesetejas* . . | wretched pesetas. | |
| *picador* . . | bullfighter on horseback. | |
| *pícaro* . . | (derived from picar, (1) to provoke; (2) to go bad or sour). | |
| *pindrés (or pinrés)* | feet. | |
| *pintar un jabeque* | to wound in the face (G.). | |
| *pirar* . . . | to go (C.). | |
| *pirriá* . . | stew (C.). | |
| *plaloró (or planoró)* | brother (C.). | |
| *polomias* . . | hips (C.). | |
| *pondoné* . . | cushion (C.). | |

| | | | | |
|---|---|---|---|---|
| *pordiosero* . . | beggar. | *sabio* . . . | learned. |
| *porrón* . . | glass vessel for wine. | *Safácoro* . . | Seville (C.). |
| | | *saeta* . . . | arrow of song. |
| *posada* . . | inn. | *safista* . . . | one who steals handkerchiefs (G.). |
| *praíto* . . | meadow. | | |
| *propina* . . | tip. | | |
| *puchar* . . | to ask (C.). | *sainete* . . | theatrical tit-bit. |
| *puchero* . . | stew. | | |
| *pulga* . . . | flea. | *salero* . . | witty person. |
| *puro* . . . | cigar. | *salud y pesetas* | Spanish toast. |
| *puró* . . . | old (C.). | *sandía* . . | water melon. |
| *puta* . . . | whore. | *sar* (or *sat*) . | with (C.). |
| | | *saré* . . . | all (C.). |
| *quebrado* . . | broken. | *sarmuñé* . . | ready (C.). |
| *quelararós* (or *queleraló*) | dancers (C.). | *sarsalé* . . | accompaniment (C.). |
| *querelar* . . | to make (C.). | *sastí* . . . | healthy (C.). |
| *quesar* . . | to be (C.). | *sauyó* (or *saulló*) | colt (C.). |
| *quibilero* . . | companion (C.). | *señorita de pan pringado* | dainty miss. |
| *randiñar* . . | to work (C.). | *sereno* . . | night-watch-man. |
| *ratí* . . . | blood, race (C.). | | |
| | | *serrano* . . | lively. |
| *rebridaque* . | compliment (C.) | *simachí* . . | sign (C.). |
| *rechipotí* . . | nude (C.). | *sinar* . . . | to be (C.). |
| *refrán* . . . | proverb. | *sin decir oxte ni moxte* | without by your leave. |
| *reja* . . . | barred window. | | |
| *rejelendre* . . | proverb (C.). | *singa* . . . | music (C.). |
| *repañí* . . . | brandy (C.). | *soberbia* . . | arrogance. |
| *retejós* . . . | joyful (C.). | *solibar* . . | bridle (C.). |
| *rom* . . . | man, husband (Gypsy). | *somíd* . . | for (C.). |
| | | *sonacai* . . | gold (C.). |
| *romalis* . . | Gypsy dance (C.). | *sonanta* . . | guitar (G.). |
| | | *sopa de San Bernardo.* | appetite. |
| *romería* . . | pilgrimage, festival. | | |
| | | *soplar la dama* | snatch the girl (G.). |
| *romero* . . | rosemary. | | |
| *romí* . . . | woman (C.). | *sos* . . . | for (C.). |
| *rondar* . . | to serenade. | *sukaldia* . . | kitchen (Basque). |
| *rubio* . . . | fair. | | |
| *rudelar* . . | to answer (C.). | *sustirí* . . | fate (C.). |

| | | | | |
|---|---|---|---|---|
| *taberna* . . | tavern. | *trillo* . . . | harrow studded with flints for threshing. |
| *terablar* . . | to have (C.). | | |
| *ternoró* . . | ass (C.). | | |
| *tertulia* . . | reunion. | *trupos.* . . | body (C.). |
| *timo de la guitarra* | money-coining trick (G.). | *tuerto* . . | cross-eyed. |
| *tinta* . . . | ink. | *ucharcarisas* . | blankets (C.). |
| *tío.* . . . | uncle (term of familiar address). | *ustilar pastesas* | steal with hands (C.). |
| *tipo raro* . . | a strange fellow. | *vagamundo* . | wanderer. |
| *tiró, tirí* . . | thy (C.). | *vaso* . . . | glass. |
| *tocaor* . . | player, minstrel. | *verbena* . . | festival. |
| *tocino* . . . | bacon. | *verónica* . . | play with " muleta " against bull. |
| *tomar de dos* | to steal with 2 fingers (G.). | | |
| *tomar las (calzas) de Villadiego* | to take the breeches of Villa diego, i.e. to take to one's heels. | *vida* . . . | life. |
| | | *viejo* . . . | old. |
| | | *visaba.* . . | fault (C.). |
| | | *voltu* . . . | witch dance. |
| *torero* . . | bullfighter. | *ye* . . . . | of (C.). |
| *tricornios* . . | Civil Guard (G.). | *yequé* (or *yes*) | one (C.). |
| *trilladores.* . | harvesters. | *zambra* . . | spree. |